Jane's TANK

& COMBAT VEHICLE RECOGNITION GUIDE

Christopher F. Foss

HarperCollins*Publishers*

Design: Rod Teasdale

HarperCollinsPublishers
PO Box, Glasgow G4 0NB

First published 1996

Reprint   3 5 7 9 10 8 6 4 2

© Christopher F. Foss 1996

ISBN 0 00 4709950

Printed in Italy by Amadeus S.p.A.

Contents

3

CONTENTS

Introduction

The aim of this book is twofold: firstly, to act as a convenient handbook for the reader to identify quickly and accurately almost any modern armoured fighting vehicle (AFV) in service today; secondly, to provide key information on the vehicle.

Some entries are more highly illustrated because there are so many local variants; indeed for some vehicles space limitations have prevented inclusion of every possible variation. A typical example is the M48. This was built with a 90 mm gun, but many countries have refitted it with a 105 mm gun which has a distinctive bore evacuator mid-way along the barrel; some countries have also added a thermal sleeve. US M48s have never been fitted with skirts, but the South Korean vehicles have skirts, and German and Spanish vehicles have distinctive smoke grenade dischargers each side.

Recognition features can be further complicated by additional stowage bins and baskets, while the introduction of reactive armour, for example on the Israeli M48, M60 and Centurion tanks and Russian T-64, T-72 and T-80 MBTs, alters their appearance completely.

This Iraqi T-55 sports add-on armour on both turret and hull.

Complications can arise from placing a vehicle in one particular section. For example, the Alvis Scimitar is used by the British Army as a reconnaissance vehicle, other countries use it as a light tank. As it is one of the few tracked reconnaissance vehicles, we have included it under tanks. 4x4, 6x6 and 8x8 vehicles have all been grouped, as they have in the wheeled armoured personnel carriers section, but some vehicles have been developed for use in a wide range of roles. For example, the Cadillac Gage LAV-150 and the Swiss MOWAG Piranha range of 4x4, 6x6 and 8x8 vehicles can be fitted with weapons ranging from a 7.62 mm machine gun to a 105 mm gun in the case of the 8x8 version.

Although space limitations have prevented all possible versions being included, many of these are mentioned in the text. Each entry has full technical specifications, key recognition features, development notes, list of variants, current status and list of users, manufacturer and, for most entries, a side view drawing and three photographs.

The third edition of this book, which has become the standard work of its type in its class, was compiled in the Spring of 1996. This edition has over 500 new photographs and drawings and virtually every entry has been updated. In addition there are 23 new entries covering new armoured vehicles that have entered production or service or are expected to do so in the near future.

Comments and new photographs for future editions should be sent to the author as soon as

6x6 vehicles can carry many different turrets. In the APC role the Pandur has a 30mm gun turret.

possible. The author would like to thank the many companies, governments and individuals who have provided information and photographs for the book. Special thanks are due to my wife Sheila for her help and encouragement while the book was being compiled.

Christopher F Foss

TANKS

TAM Tank (Germany/Argentina)

Key recognition features

- Hull similar to Marder MICV with well sloped glacis plate. Driver front left, horizontal hull top with turret towards rear, hull back slopes to rear then inward at mid point
- Turret has flat sides that slope slightly inward, turret bustle extends almost to hull rear, commander's cupola right side of flat roof. 105mm gun mounted in external mantlet, with fume extractor
- Suspension each side has six road wheels, drive sprocket front, idler rear and three track-return rollers. Upper part sometimes covered by skirt.

Specifications

Crew: 4
Armament: 1 x 105mm, 1 x 7.62mm MG (coaxial), 1 x 7.62 MG (anti-aircraft), 2 x 4 smoke grenade dischargers
Ammunition: 50 x 105mm, 6,000 x 7.62mm
Length gun forwards: 8.23m
Length hull: 6.775m
Width: 3.29m
Height to turret top: 2.43m
Power-to-weight ratio: 24.27hp/tonne
Ground clearance: 0.45m
Weight, combat: 30,000kg
Weight, empty: 28,000kg
Ground pressure: 0.78kg/cm²
Engine: MTU MB 833 Ka 500 supercharged 6-cylinder diesel developing 720hp at 2,200 rpm
Maximum road speed: 75km/hr
Maximum road range: 550km
Maximum road range with auxiliary tanks: 940
Fuel capacity: 640 lit
Fording: 1.5m
Fording with preparation: 2.25m
Fording with snorkel: 4m
Vertical obstacle: 1.0m
Trench: 2.5m
Gradient: 60%
Side slope: 30%
Armour: Classified
Armour type: Steel
NBC system: Yes
Night vision equipment: Optional

Development

In 1974 Thyssen Henschel was awarded a contract by Argentina for design and development of a new medium tank designated TAM (*Tanque Argentino Mediano*), as well as infantry combat vehicle VCI (*Vehiculo Combate Infanteria*) subsequently redesignated VCTP. Three prototypes of each were built and shipped to Argentina. Production commenced at a new factory in Argentina with a requirement for 512 TAMs and VCTPs, but production was stopped after about 350 vehicles, for budgetary reasons. Further development by Thyssen Henschel has resulted in the TH301, which has a number of improvements including a new fire-control system and a more powerful engine.

Driver sits front left of TAM, engine to his right and turret towards rear. Commander and gunner sit right of turret, loader left. The 105mm gun power-elevates from -7° to +18° and turret traverses through 360°. A 7.62mm MG is mounted coaxial with main armament and there is a similar weapon on the roof for air defence.

To extend its operational range, long range fuel tanks can be fitted at hull rear. Optional equipment for TH301 includes additional armour protection.

Variants

VCA 155, lengthened TAM chassis fitted with turret of Italian Palmaria 155mm self-propelled howitzer, developed to meet requirements of Argentinian Army.
VCRT, ARV based on chassis of TAM for Argentinian Army, prototype only.
Rocket launchers, prototypes of 160mm and 350mm multiple launch rocket systems have been built (chassis is Argentinian with rocket launchers from Israel). In addition many trial versions in Germany.

Above: TH301

Above right: TAM

Right: TH301

Status
Production completed in Argentina. Production yet to commence in Germany. In service with Argentina.

Manufacturers
Thyssen Henschel, Kassel, Germany; TAMSE, Buenos Aires, Argentina.

11

Steyr SK 105 Light Tank (Austria)

Key recognition features

● Distinctive oscillating turret centre of vehicle, commander's cupola left, large box-shaped infra-red/white searchlight right side of turret roof, laser rangefinder below

● 105mm gun has double baffle muzzle brake and thermal sleeve, overhangs front of vehicle

● Suspension has five road wheels, idler front, drive sprocket rear, three track-return rollers

Specifications

Crew: 3
Armament: 1 x 105mm, 1.7.62mm MG (coaxial), 2 x 3 smoke grenade dischargers
Ammunition: 41 x 105mm, 2,000 x 7.62mm
Length gun forwards: 7.735m
Length hull: 5.582m
Width: 2.5m
Height: (2.88m (searchlight), 2.529m (commander's cupola)
Ground clearance: 0.4m
Weight, combat: 17,700kg
Power-to-weight ratio: 18.1hp/tonne
Ground pressure: 0.67kg/cm^2
Engine: Steyr 7FA 6-cylinder liquid-cooled 4-stroke turbocharged diesel developing 320hp at 2,300rpm
Maximum road speed: 70km/hr
Maximum range: 500km
Fuel capacity: 420 lit
Fording: 1m
Vertical obstacle: 0.8m
Trench: 2.41m
Gradient: 75%
Side slope: 40%
Armour: 40mm (maximum)
Armour type: Steel
NBC system: Yes
Night vision equipment: Yes (infra-red for driver and commander)

Development

SK 105, also known as *Kürassier*, was developed from 1965 by Saurer-Werke, taken over by Steyr-Daimler-Puch in 1970, to meet the requirements of the Austrian Army for a mobile anti-tank vehicle.

First prototype was completed in 1967 with pre-production vehicles following in 1971.

Driver sits front left, turret centre, engine and transmission rear. Oscillating turret is an improved French Fives-Cail Babcock FL-12 in which 105mm gun is fixed on upper part, commander left, gunner right. The 105mm gun is fed by two revolver-type magazines, each of which holds six rounds. Ammunition fired includes HE, HEAT and smoke, but with modifications SK 105 also fires APFSDS projectiles.

Turret traverse and elevation is powered, manual controls for emergency use, turret traverse 360°, 105mm gun in upper part of turret elevates from -8° to +12°.

Variants

Steyr SK 105/A2 is upgraded SK 105/A1 with a number of improvements including new FCS and fully automatic ammunition loading system.

Steyr SK 105/A3 is still at prototype stage and has a new oscillating turret with improved armour protection and fitted with 105mm M68 rifled tank gun which can fire standard NATO 105mm ammunition including APFSDS.

Greif armoured recovery vehicle.

Pioneer vehicle is based on ARV.

Driver training vehicle is SK 105 with turret removed and replaced by new superstructure for instructor and other trainee drivers.

SK 105

Above: SK 105 with laser range finder

Above: SK 105

Right: SK 105

Status

Production complete. In service with Argentina, Austria, Bolivia, Morocco and Tunisia.

Manufacturer

Steyr-Daimler-Puch AG, Vienna, Austria.

NORINCO Type 85-II MBT (China)

Key recognition features

● Well sloped glacis plate, turret centre and raised engine compartment at rear. 125 mm gun has fume extractor mid-way down barrel
● Turret has sloping front with vertical sides with six smoke grenade launchers mounted halfway along turret side, large stowage basket at rear, 12.7 mm MG on right side of turret roof
● Suspension either side consists of six road wheels with idler at front, drive sprocket at rear and track return rollers, upper part of suspension covered by skirt with wavy line to lower part

Specifications

Crew: 3
Armament: 1 x 125 mm gun, 1 x 7.62 mm MG (coaxial), 1 x 12.7 mm (anti-aircraft), 2 x 6 smoke grenade launchers
Ammunition: 40 x 125 mm, 2000 x 7.62 mm, 300 x 12.7 mm (estimate)
Length gun forwards: 10.28 m
Length hull: 7.3 m (estimate)
Width: 3.45 m
Height: 2.30 m (turret top)
Ground clearance: 0.48 m
Weight, combat: 41,000 kg
Power-to-weight ratio: 18.5 hp/t
Engine: V-12 supercharged diesel developing 730 hp
Maximum road speed: 57.25 km/h
Maximum road range: 500 km (estimate)
Fuel capacity: 1000 l (estimate)
Fording: 1.4 m
Vertical obstacle: 0.8 m
Trench: 2.7 m
Gradient: 60%
Side slope: 40%
Armour: classified
Armour type: steel/laminate
NBC: yes
Night vision equipment: yes

Development

The Type 85-II MBT is further development of the Type 80 MBT (qv) but has many improvements including a different hull and turret with a significant improvement in armour protection. The driver is seated in the hull at front left with ammunition to his right with turret in centre. The gunner is seated on the left of the turret and the commander on the right.

Main armament is a 125 mm smooth bore gun which is fed by an automatic loader, so enabling the crew to be reduced to three. Ammunition is of the separate loading type eg projectile and charge and is similar to that used in the Russian T-72 MBT Turret traverse is 360 degrees with weapon elevation from -6 to +16 degrees. The main armament is fully stabilised and the computerised fire control system includes a laser rangefinder.

Variants

There are a number of models of the Type 85-II including the Type 85-IIA and the Type 85-IIM. The vehicle is also co-produced in Pakistan as the Type 85-IIAP. Further development of the Type 85 has resulted in the Type 85-III which has many improvements including a 1000 hp diesel engine. The latest Chinese MBT is the Type 90-II which weighs 48 t and is at present at the prototype stage. This has been developed in association with Pakistan and is also known as the Khalid, MBT 2000 or P-90.

Status

In production. In service with China and Pakistan.

Manufacturer

Chinese state factories.

Above:
Type 85-11AP

Top right:
Type 85-11M

Left:
Type 85-11M

Right:
Type 85-11AP

NORINCO Type 80 MBT (China)

Key recognition features

● Well sloped glacis plate with splash board running across mid-way up, turret centre and engine compartment at rear. Unlike Type 59 and Type 69 there is no exhaust outlet on left side of hull above last road wheel station. Long-range fuel drum and unditching beam often carried on hull rear

● Circular turret has curved sides with loader's cupola on right side with externally mounted 12.7mm AA MG, 105mm gun barrel has thermal sleeve and fume extractor, cage type stowage basket around sides and rear of turret. Bank of four smoke grenade dischargers either side of the turret

● Suspension has six road wheels with gap between 1st/2nd and 2nd/3rd road wheels, idler front, drive sprocket rear, track return rollers, upper part of suspension covered by skirt

Specifications

Crew: 4
Armament: 1 x 105mm, 1 x 7.62mm MG (coaxial), 1 x 12.7mm MG (AA), 2 x 4 smoke grenade dischargers
Ammunition: 44 x 105mm, 2,250 x 7.62mm, 500 x 12.7mm
Length gun forwards: 9.328m
Length hull: 6.325m
Height: 2.29m (turret roof), 2.874m (with AA MG)
Ground clearance: 0.48m
Weight, combat: 38,000kg
Power-to-weight ratio: 19.2hp/tonne
Engine: V-12 diesel developing 730hp
Maximum road speed: 60km/hr
Maximum road range: 430km
Fuel capacity: 1,400 lit
Fording: 1.4m
Vertical obstacle: 0.8m
Trench: 2.7m
Grdient: 60%
Side slope: 30%
Armour: Classified
Armour type: Steel/composite
NBC system: Yes
Night vision equipment: Yes

Development

Whilst the earlier Type 69 MBT was a further development of the Type 59 MBT, the Type 80 has a number of new features including a brand new hull. The driver is seated at the front left with some ready use ammunition to his right, the three man turret is in the centre with the commander and gunner on the left and the loader on the right. The powerpack is at the rear.

The 105mm rifled tank gun fires standard NATO ammunition and can be elevated from -4˚ to +18˚ under full power control with turret trverse a full 360˚, manual controls are provided for emergency use. A 7.62mm machine gun is mounted coaxial with the main armament and a 12.7mm machine gun is mounted on the turret roof for anti-aircraft defence.

A computerised fire control system is fitted and this includes a laser rangefinder for the gunner. One version has the laser rangefinder installed in the gunner's sight while another has the laser rangefinder mounted over the 105mm gun in a similar manner to that of some versions of the older NORINCO Type 69 MBT.

For deep fording, a snorkel can be fitted to the vehicle and a fire detection/suppression system is standard. If required a layer of composite armour can be fitted to the glacis plate for improved battlefield survivability.

Variants

Type 80-II, this has a number of modifications and is offered with various types of computerised fire control system.
Type 85-II and Type 85-IIA have a similar chassis to the Type 80 MBT but are fitted with a new turret of welded rather than cast steel construction. As an option, composite armour can be fitted to the turret and hull.

Status

Production probably complete. In service with Chinese Army.

Manufacturer

Chinese state factories.

Top: *Type 80 MBT*
Above: *Type 80 MBT*
Above right: *Type 80 MBT*
Right: *Type 85-11 MBT (Model)*

NORINCO Type 69 MBT (China)

Key recognition features

● Well sloped glacis plate with splash-board across upper part, turret centre, slightly raised enginer compartment rear. Unditching beam often carried across vertical hull rear

● Circular turret has curved sides, loader's cupola right side with external 12.7mm MG, long-barrelled 100mm gun with externally mounted laser rangefinder above, large infra-red searchlight above and to right of 100mm gun

● Suspension has five road wheels, each of which has five small holes, distinct gap between first and second road wheel, idler front, drive sprocket rear, no track-return rollers, upper part often covered with five-part skin with saw tooth bottom

Specifications

Crew: 4
Armament: 1 x 100mm, 1 x 7.62mm MG (coaxial), 1 x 7.62mm MG (bow), 1 x 12.7mm MG (AA)
Length gun forwards: 8.657m
Length hull: 6.243m
Width over skirts: 3.298m
Width over hull: 3.27m
Height to axis of MG: 2.807m
Ground clearance: 0.425m
Weight, combat: 36,000 to 37,000kg
Power-to-weight ratio: 15.98hp/tonne
Ground pressure: 0.82kg/cm^2
Engine: Type 12150L-7BW V-12 diesel developing 580hp at 2,000rpm
Maximum road speed: 50km/hr
Maximum road range: 420 to 440km
Fuel capacity: Not available
Fording: 1.4m
Vertical obstacle: 0.8m
Trench: 2.7m
Gradient: 60%
Side slope: 40%
Armour: 100mm (maximum) (estimate)
Armour type: Steel
NBC system: Yes
Night vision equipment: Yes (infra-red for commander, gunner and driver)

Development

Type 69 series is a further development of the earlier Type 59 and was first seen in public during 1982. It has been exported in significant numbers to Iraq. Layout is conventional, with driver front left, some ammunition to his right, turret centre, engine and transmission rear. Commander and gunner sit left of turret, loader right. Both loader and commander have a cupola.

Type 69 I has a smooth bore gun. Type 69 II has a rifled gun. Both have powered elevation from -4˚ to +17˚ with turret traverse through 360˚. Types of ammunition for Type 69 II include HEAT, HE, APDS and APFSDS. A 7.62mm MG is mounted coaxial with main armament and a similar, driver-operated weapon is fixed in glacis plate firing forwards. The 12.7mm AA MG is manned by loader.

Type 69 lays its own smoke screen by injecting diesel fuel into its exhaust pipe on left side of hull above last road wheel station.

In addition there is also a Type 79 MBT with a 105mm gun which is similar to the Type 59/Type 69.

Variants

Type 80 self-propelled anti-aircraft gun is Chinese equivalent of Soviet ZSU-57-2 but uses Type 69 chassis.
Twin 37mm SPAAG, still at prototype stage, has Type 69 chassis fitted with new two-man turret armed with twin 37mm guns. Two versions of this system have been developed, one with a radar fire control system and the other a clear weather system.
Type 84 AVLB has Type 69 chassis and hydraulic launching mechanism similar in concept to the German Biber AVLB on Leopard 1 chassis, which launches a bridge 18m long.
Type 653 ARV has Type 69 chassis but turret replaced by superstructure, stabiliser/dozer blade front of hull and hydraulic crane right side of hull. In service with Chinese Army.
Further development has resulted in the Type 80 and Type 85 MBTs (qv).

Status

In production. In service with China, Iran, Iraq, Pakistan (with local production) and Thailand.

Manufacturer

Chinese state arsenals.

Top: Type 69-II

Right: Type 69-II

NORINCO Type 59 MBT (China)

Key recognition features

● Well sloped glacis plate with splash board across upper part, turret centre and slightly raised engine compartment rear. Unditching beam and long-range fuel tanks often carried across vertical hull rear.

● Circular turret has curved sides, loader's cupola on right side, externally mounted 12.7mm AA MG, standard 100mm gun with fume extractor to immediate rear of muzzle. Some vehicles have laser rangefinder externally above main armament

● Suspension has five road wheels, idler front, drive sprocket rear, no track-return rollers

Specifications

Crew: 4
Armament: 1 x 100mm, 1 x 7.62mm MG (coaxial), 1 x 7.62mm MG (bow), 1 x 12.7mm MG (AA)
Ammunition: 34 x 100mm, 3,500 x 7.62mm, 200 x 12.7mm
Length gun forwards: 9m
Length hull: 6.04m
Width: 3.27m
Height: 2.59m
Ground clearance: 0.425m
Weight, combat: 36,000kg
Power-to-weight ratio: 14.44hp/tonne
Ground pressure: 0.8kg/cm²
Engine: Model 12150L V-12 liquid cooled diesel developing 520hp at 2,000rpm
Maximum road speed: 40 to 50km/hr
Maximum range: 420 to 440km
Fuel capacity: 815 lit
Fording without preparation: 1.4m
Fording with preparation: 5.5m
Vertical obstacle: 0.79m
Trench: 2.7m
Gradient: 60%
Side slope: 40%
Armour: 100mm (maximum)
Armour type: Steel
NBC system: None
Night vision equipment: Yes (infra-red for commander, gunner and driver) (retrofitted)

Development

In the early 1950s the USSR provided China with a quantity of T-54s and production was subsequently undertaken in China under the designation Type 59.

First production vehicles were identical to the T-54 but had no night vision equipment and no stabiliser for the 100mm gun. Late production Type 59s had a fume extractor for the 100mm gun, weapon stabilisation system and infra-red night vision equipment. More recently, some vehicles have been fitted with a laser rangefinder box mounted externally above the 100mm gun.

Layout is almost identical to the Soviet T-54 but with some internal differences. Driver sits front left with some ammunition to his right, turret centre, loader right. Both commander and loader have a cupola.

Type 59 is armed with a 100mm rifled gun which power-elevates from -4° to +17° (early vehicles had manual elevation), turret traverses through 360°. Ammunition is similar to Soviet T-54/T-55s and includes AP, APC-T, HE, HE-FRAG, HEAT-FS and HVAPDS-T. A 7.62mm MG is mounted coaxial with main armament and a similar, driver-operated weapon is fixed in glacis plate firing forwards. The 12.7mm AA MG is manned by the loader.

Type 59 lays its own smoke screen by injecting diesel fuel into its exhaust pipe left side of hull above last road wheel. To extend its operational range to 600km long-range fuel drums are mounted on hull rear.

Late production vehicles were called Type 59-I.

Variants

Type 59 with 105mm gun has a 105mm L7/M68 type rifled gun with fume extractor and thermal sleeve and has been in service with the Chinese Army since the early 1980s. Referred to as M1984 by the US Army. This is called the Type 59-II.

Type 59 ARV, which may well be a local modification, is a Type 59 with turret removed and armed with 12.7mm AA MG. It is not believed to be fitted with a winch.

Many companies have proposed upgrade packages for the Type 59 ranging from simply replacing 100mm gun with 105mm rifled gun to more comprehensive refits including fire-control system, suspension, armour, powerpack and night vision equipment.

Above: Type 59 with 105mm gun (via G Jacobs)

Above right: Type 59

Right: Type 59 with Royal Ordnance 105mm gun

Status
Production complete. In service with Albania, Bangladesh, China, Congo, North Korea, Pakistan, Tanzania, Vietnam and Zimbabwe.

Manufacturer
Chinese state arsenals.

21

NORINCO Type 62 Light Tank (China)

Key recognition features

● Driver's compartment front, rounded turret centre, engine and transmission rear

● 85mm gun overhangs front of chassis, fume extractor rear of muzzle

● Suspension has five large road wheels, drive sprocket rear, idler front, no track-return rollers, no skirts

Specifications

Crew: 4
Armament: 1 x 85mm gun, 1 x 7.62mm MG (coaxial), 1 x 7.62mm MG (bow), 1 x 12.7mm MG (AA)
Ammunition: 47 x 85mm, 1,750 x 7.62mm, 1,250 x 12.7mm
Length gun forwards: 7.9m
Length hull: 5.55m
Width: 2.86m
Height: 2.25m
Ground clearance: 0.42m
Weight, combat: 21,000kg
Power-to-weight ratio: 20.47hp/tonne
Ground pressure: $0.71kg/cm^2$
Engine: Liquid-cooled diesel developing 430hp at 1,800rpm
Maximum road speed: 60km/hr
Maximum road range: 500km
Fuel capacity: 730 lit
Fording: 1.3m
Vertical obstacle: 0.7m
Trench: 2.55m
Gradient: 60%
Side slope: 40%
NBC system: None
Night vision equipment: None

Development

Type 62 is virtually a scaled-down Type 59 and is used in rugged terrain as found in southern China. It has seen action in both the Far East and Africa.

Layout is identical to Type 59s, with driver seated front left, three-man turret centre, commander and gunner left, loader right, engine and transmission rear.

Main armament comprises 85mm gun, probably identical to that fitted to Type 63 light amphibious tank (qv) which fires AP, APHE, HE, HEAT and smoke projectiles. It has an elevation from -4° to +20° with turret traverse 360°. A 7.62mm MG is mounted coaxial to right of main armament and a similar, driver-operated weapon fixed in glacis plate. A 12.7mm Type 54 MG is mounted on turret roof for anti-aircraft defence.

Type 62 lays its own smoke screen by injecting diesel fuel into the exhaust and, more recently, models have been observed with a laser rangefinder over main armament to improve first round hit probability.

In addition to being used by the Chinese Army it is also used by Chinese Marines.

Variants
No variants.

Status
Production as required. In service with Albania, Bangladesh, China, Congo, North Korea, Mali, Sudan, Tanzania, Vietnam and Zaire.

Manufacturer
Chinese state arsenals.

Right: Type 62 light tank

NORINCO Type 63 Light Amphibious Tank (China)

Key recognition features

● Hull has vertical sides and rear, almost horizontal glacis plate, nose sloping inwards at about 50o
● Rounded turret in centre with 85mm gun overhanging front, fume extractor slightly to rear of muzzle
● Suspension has six road wheels, drive sprocket rear, idler front, no track-return rollers or skirt

Specifications

Crew: 4
Armament: 1 x 85mm gun, 1 x 7.62mm MG (coaxial), 1 x 12.7mm MG (anti-aircraft)
Ammunition: 47 x 85mm, 1,000 x 7.62mm, 500 x 12.7mm
Length gun forwards: 8.437m
Length hull: 7.15m
Width: 3.2m
Height: 3.122m (inc AA MG), 2.522m (turret top)
Ground clearance: 0.4m
Weight, combat: 18,700kg
Power-to-weight ratio: 21.39hp/tonne
Engine: Model 12150-L 12-cylinder water-cooled diesel developing 400hp at 2,000rpm
Maximum road speed: 64km/hr
Maximum water speed: 12km/hr
Maximum range: 370km
Fuel capacity: 545 lit
Fording: Amphibious
Vertical obstacle: 0.87m
Trench: 2.9m
Gradient: 60%
Side slope: 30%
Armour: 14mm (maximum)
Armour type: Steel
NBC system: Yes
Night vision equipment: Yes (infra-red for driver only)

Development

Type 63 has a similar hull to the Soviet PT-76 light amphibious tank but is based on automotive components of the Chinese Type 77 series APC which is covered in the armoured personnel carriers section. Compared with PT-76 Type 63 has a more powerful engine providing greater road speed and improved power-to-weight ratio.

Main armament comprises an 85mm gun firing AP, APHE, HE, HEAT and smoke projectiles, with elevation of +18° and depression of -5°, and turret traverse 360°. The 7.62mm MG is mounted coaxial to right of 85mm gun and a 12.7mm Type 54 MG is mounted on turret roof for anti-aircraft defence.

The vehicle is fully amphibious, propelled in the water by two water jets mounted rear. Before entering the water bilge pumps are switched on and trim vane erected on glacis plate. To extend operational range, additional fuel tanks are installed on rear decking.

Variants

No variants.

Status

Production complete. In service with China, North Korea and Vietnam.

Manufacturer

Chinese state arsenals.

Right: Type 63

GIAT AMX-13 Light Tank (France)

Key recognition features

● Well-sloped glacis plate, normally with splash-board on lower part, driver front left, engine to his right, flat roof with turret slightly to rear

● Turret is oscillating type, gun in upper part of turret pivots on lower part with canvas cover joining them, commander's domed hatch cover on left side of turret roof, bustle turret extends to rear

● Suspension has five large road wheels, drive sprocket front, idler rear, two or three track-return rollers, no skirts

Specifications (90mm version)

Crew: 3
Armament: 1 x 90mm, 1 x 7.62mm MG (coaxial), 1 x 7.62mm (MG (anti-aircraft) (optional), 2 x 2 smoke grenade dischargers
Ammunition: 32 x 90mm, 3,600 x 7.62mm
Length gun forwards: 6.36m
Length hull: 4.88m
Width: 2.51m
Height to commander's hatch: 2.3m
Ground clearance: 0.37m
Weight, combat: 15,000kg
Weight, empty: 13,000kg
Power-to-weight ratio: 16.66bhp/tonne
Ground pressure: 0.76kg/cm²
Engine: SOFAM Model 8Gxb 8-cylinder water-cooled petrol developing 250hp at 3,200rpm
Maximum road speed: 60km/hr
Maximum road range: 350 to 400km
Fuel capacity: 480 lit
Fording: 0.6m
Vertical obstacle: 0.65m
Trench: 1.6m
Gradient: 60%
Side slope: 60%
Armour: 25mm (maximum)
Armour type: Steel
NBC system: None
Night vision equipment: Optional

Development

Shortly after the Second World War the French Army drew up requirements for three new AFVs including a new light tank. It was subsequently developed by Atelier de Construction d'Issy-les-Moulineaux under the designation AMX-13. First prototypes were completed in the late 1940s, production commencing at Atelier de Construction Roanne in 1952. When production of AMX-30 was under way, production of AMX-13 and its many variants was transferred to Creusot-Loire. Total production of AMX-13 light tank has mounted to over 3,000. (See separate entries for AMX VCI MICV and 155mm self-propelled howitzers.)

All versions of AMX-13 have similar layout, driver front left, engine to his right and turret to rear. AMX-13 Model 51 was armed with 75mm gun later replaced by 90mm gun with thermal sleeve. A 105mm armed version was built for export. Turret traverses through 360°. Upper part of turret contains main armament, elevates from -5° to +12.5°. FL-10 and FL-12 turrets both oscillating type, commander sits left, gunner right. Automatic loader mounted in turret bustle includes two revolver type magazines, each of which holds six rounds of ammunition, empty cartridge cases ejected from turret bustle. After 12 rounds, magazines have to be reloaded manually.

Wide range of optional equipment available, including passive night vision equipment, additional armour protection, improved fire-control systems and laser rangefinder. A number of companies are offering upgrade packages for AMX-13, including GLS of Germany and Singapore Automotive Engineering. AMX-13 can be fitted with other engines including Detroit Diesel, Baudouin and Poyaud.

Variants

Singapore Automotive Engineering has rebuilt most of the AMX-13 fleet of the Singapore Army to SM1 configuration that includes a new engine, new cooling system and new transmission.

Above: AMX-13 with 75mm gun (ECP Armees)

AMX-13 with 90mm gun

Rocket launcher: Venezuela has AMX-13 chassis with Israeli 160mm LAR multiple rocket launcher.
AMX-13 ARV.
AMX-13 AVLB.

Status
Production as required. In service with Argentina, Dominican Republic, Ecuador, Indonesia, Ivory Coast, Lebanon, Peru, Singapore and Venezuela.

Manufacturers
Creusot-Loire Industrie at Chalon sur Saone; Atelier de Construction Roanne, Roanne, France. (GIAT Industries has now taken over Creusot-Loire.)

Right: AMX-13 with 90mm gun

GIAT AMX-30 MBT (France)

Key recognition features

● Well sloped glacis plate with driver's hatch in upper left part, turret centre, engine rear, hull rear vertical, silencer on track guard above rear drive sprocket
● Cast turret has sides that slope inwards with turret bustle extending over engine deck, stowage basket each side of turret, two smoke grenade dischargers each side at rear, commander's cupola on right side of turret roof. 105mm gun has thermal sleeve, 20mm cannon mounted left of gun
● Suspension each side has five road wheels, drive sprocket rear, idler front, five track-return rollers, no skirts

Specifications

Crew: 4
Armament: 1 x 105mm, 1 x 20mm cannon (coaxial), 1 x 7.62 MG (AA), 2 x 2 smoke grenade dischargers
Ammunition: 47 x 105mm, 1,050 x 20mm, 2,050 x 7.62mm
Length gun forwards: 9.48m
Length hull: 6.59m
Width: 3.1m
Height including searchlight: 2.86m
Height to turret top: 2.29m
Ground clearance: 0.44m
Weight, combat: 36,000kg
Weight, empty: 34,000kg
Power-to-weight ratio: 20hp/tonne
Ground pressure: 0.77kg/cm^2
Engine: Hispano-Suiza HS 110 12-cylinder water-cooled supercharged multi-fuel developing 720hp at 2,000rpm
Maximum road speed: 65km/hr
Maximum road range: 500 to 600km
Fuel capacity: 970 lit
Fording: 1.3m
Fording with preparation: 2.2m
Fording with snorkel: 4m
Vertical obstacle: 0.93m
Trench: 2.9m
Gradient: 60%
Side slope: 30%
Armour: 80mm (max)
Armour type: Steel
NBC system: Yes
Night vision equipment: Yes (passive on AJMX-30 B2)

Development

AMX-30 was developed from the mid1950s by the Atelier de Construction d'Issy-les-Moulineaux to meet the requirements of the French Army. First prototypes were completed in 1960 with production commencing at the Atelier de Construction Roanne (ARE) in 1966, since when over 3,500 AMX-30 MBT and variants have been built for home and export markets. Production of the AMX-30 MBT has been completed and in French Army it has started to be replaced by GIAT Industries Leclerc MBT.

Driver sits front left with cast turret centre, engine and transmission rear. Commander and gunner sit right of turret, loader left. The 105mm gun power-elevates from -8° to +20°, turret traverses through 360°. Main armament fires APFSDS, HEAT, HE, smoke and illuminating rounds with a 20mm cannon or 12.7mm MG mounted coaxial to the left. The cannon has independent elevation for engaging low-flying aircraft and helicopters A 7.62mm MG is mounted right of commander's cupola.

Variants

AMX-30D was developed for desert operations with sand shields for its tracks, engine developing 620hp and reduction in gearbox ratios which limits its speed to 60km/hr.
AMX-30B2: Modifications include a new fire-control system with laser rangefinder and LLLTV as well as automotive improvements. In addition to taking delivery of new build AMX-30B2, the French Army also had many earlier vehicles upgraded to this standard.
Modernised AMX-30s: A number of countries and companies have developed modernisation packages for AMX-30 MBT, only one has entered production, in Spain.
AMX-30D ARV.

AMX-30 AVLB.
155mm GCT self-propelled howitzer uses AMX-30 chassis
(see SPAAGs).
AMX-30 driver training tank is AMX-30 with turret replaced
by observation cupola.
AMX-30 EBG Combat Engineer Tractor.
Roland anti-aircraft missile system (see SPAAMs).
Shahine anti-aircraft missile system, built for Saudi Arabia
(see SPAAMs).
AMX-30 DCA twin 30mm self-propelled anti-aircraft
system (see SPAAGs).

Top: AMX-30

Top right:
AMX-30B2

Right: AMX-
30B2
(Christopher
F Foss)

Status
Production complete. In service with Chile, Cyprus, France,
Greece, Qatar, Saudi Arabia, Spain, United Arab Emirates and
Venezuela.

Manufacturer
GIAT Industries, Roanne, France.

GIAT Leclerc MBT (France)

Key recognition features

● Vertical hull front which then slopes back under front of hull, very well sloped glacis plate, turret centre, slightly raised engine compartment at rear. Hull rear is vertical with horizontal louvres
● Turret front and sides have vertical lower part with chamfer to upper part, distinctive array of periscopes around upper part of forward part of turret roof. Large periscopic sight on left side of turret roof, externally mounted 7.62mm machine gun
● Suspension has six road wheels either side with idler front, drive sprocket rear, and track return rollers. Upper part of suspension is covered by armoured skirts with those above the front two road wheels being thicker

Specifications

Crew: 3
Armament: 1 x 120mm, 1 x 12.7mm MG (coaxial), 1 x 7.62 MG (AA), 3 x 9 smoke grenade dischargers
Ammunition: 40 x 120mm
Length gun forwards: 9.87m
Length hull: 6.88m
Width: 3.71m
Height: 2.53m (turret roof)
Ground clearance: 0.5m
Weight, combat: 54,500kg
Power-to-weight ratio: 27.52hp/tonne
Ground pressure: 0.9kg/cm²
Engine: SACM V8X 8-cylinder Hyperbar diesel developing 1,500hp
Maximum road speed: 71km/hr (forwards, 38km/hr (reverse)
Maximum road range: 550km
Fuel capacity: 1,300 lit
Fording: 1m
Vertical obstacle: 1.25m
Trench: 3m
Gradient: 60%
Side slope: 30%
Armour: Classified
Armour type: Steel/composite/laminate
NBC system: Yes
Night vision equipment: Yes (passive)

Development

The Leclerc MBT has been developed by GIAT Industries as the replacement for the French Army's existing fleet of AMX-30 B2 series of MBTs. Development started in 1983 and the first of six prototypes was completed in 1989, these were however preceded by a number of test rig vehicles. The first production Leclerc was completed in December 1991 and delivered to the French Army in 1992. In 1993 the United Arab Emirates ordered a total of 436 Leclerc MBTs, including variants.

The Leclerc turrets are assembled by GIAT's Tarbes facility while the chassis is built at Roanne, the latter also integrate the turret with the chassis and then deliver the complete vehicle to the French Army.

The hull and turret of the Leclerc are of advanced modular armour. The driver is seated at the front of the hull on the left with some ammunition stowed to his right. The two man power-operated turret is in the centre with the commander being seated on the left and the gunner on the right. No loader is required as a bustle-mounted automatic loader holds a total of 22 rounds of ready use ammunition. Turret traverse is a full 360° with weapon elevation from -8° to +15° under full power control. A 12.7mm MG is mounted externally on the turret roof and operated by remote control. In either side of the turret are 9 dischargers that can also launch a variety of grenades including smoke and decoy.

The suspension system of the Leclerc is of the hydropneumatic type and standard equipment includes a fire detection/suppression system and if required long-range fuel tanks can be fitted at the rear of the hull to increase operational range.

Variants

ARV, in production for UAE.
AEV, project.
AVLB, project.

Status

Production. In service with France and the UAE.

Manufacturer

GIAT Industries, Satory,
France (see text).

Above: GIAT Leclerc MBT

Above right: GIAT Leclerc for UAE

Right: GIAT Leclerc MBT

Krauss-Maffei Leopard 2 MBT (Germany)

Key recognition features

● Nose slopes back under hull with 45˚ glacis plate, then horizontal hull. Driver front right, turret centre and raised engine compartment rear. Vertical hull sides and rear, louvres extending full width of vehicle rear

● Turret has vertical front, sides and rear with bustle extending right over engine compartment, commander's low profile cupola on right with periscopic sight to his front, 120mm gun (with thermal sleeve and fume extractor) has large mantlet with gunner's sight in forward part of turret to immediate right of mantlet

● Suspension each side has seven road wheels, drive sprocket rear, idler front and four track-return rollers. Upper part covered by skirting, front idler and first two road wheels also covered by armoured skirts

Specifications

Crew: 4
Armament: 1 x 120mm, 1 x 7.62mm MG (coaxial), 1 x 7.62mm MG (anti-aircraft), 2 x 8 smoke grenade dischargers
Ammunition: 42 x 120mm, 4,750 x 7.62mm
Length gun forwards: 9.668m
Length hull: 7.722m
Width overall: 3.7m
Height to top of commander's periscopes: 2.787m
Height to turret top: 2.48m
Ground clearance: 0.54m (front), 0.49 (rear)
Weight, combat: 55,150kg
Power-to-weight ratio: 27.27hp/tonne
Ground pressure: 0.83kg/cm^2
Engine: MTU MB 873 Ka 501 4-stroke, 12-cylinder multi-fuel, exhaust turbocharged liquid-cooled diesel developing 1,500hp at 2,600rpm
Maximum road speed: 72km/hr
Maximum road range: 550km
Fuel capacity: 1,200 lit
Fording: 1m
Fording with preparation: 2.25m
Fording with snorkel: 4m
Vertical obstacle: 1.1m
Trench: 3m
Gradient: 60%
Side slope: 30%
Armour: Classified
Armour type: Laminate/steel
NBC system: Yes
Night vision equipment: Yes (passive for commander, gunner and driver)

Development

Following cancellation of MBT-70, full-scale development of a new German MBT commenced. First prototypes of this new MBT were completed by Krauss-Maffei between 1972 and 1974, some armed with a 105mm gun and some with a 120mm. With further improvements it became the Leopard 2, and in 1977 Krauss-Maffei was selected as prime contractor and an order for 1,800 vehicles placed, 810 of which were built by MaK and the remainder by Krauss-Maffei. First production vehicles were completed in 1979 with the last of 2,125 vehicles for the German Army delivered in 1992.

In 1979 the Dutch Army ordered 445 Leopard 2s which were all delivered by 1986, and in 1983 Switzerland selected the Leopard 2 with 35 from Germany and the remaining 345 to be built in Switzerland. More recently, Leopard 2 has been selected by Spain and Sweden.

Layout is conventional with driver front right, turret centre and engine and transmission rear. Commander sits on right of turret, gunner to his front and loader left. The 120mm smooth bore gun fires APFSDS-T and HEAT multi-purpose rounds and power-elevates at +20˚ to -9˚, with powered traverse through 360˚. Main armament is stabilised in both elevation and traverse.

Variants

Buffel armoured recovery vehicle
Leopard 2 (Improved) is an upgrade of earlier Leopard 2 with many improvements including additional armour over frontal arc. Some Leopard 2s of German and Netherlands are being upgraded to this standard. Spanish and Swedish Leopard 2s are being built brand new to this standard.
Leopard 2 driver-training vehicle, turret replaced by observation type turret (used by Germany and Netherlands).

Left: Leopard 2 of Netherlands Army (Richard Stickland)   *Above: Leopard 2*   *Below: Leopard 2 (Improved)*

Status
In production. In service with Germany, Netherlands, Spain, Sweden and Switzerland.

Manufacturers
Krauss-Maffei, Munich, Germany; MaK, Kiel, Germany; Federal Construction Works, Thun, Switzerland (licensed production).

Krauss-Maffei Leopard 1 MBT (Germany)

Key recognition features

● Well sloped glacis plate leads up to horizontal hull top extending right to rear of hull, driver's hatch in right side of roof to immediate rear of glacis plate, turret centre, engine rear, hull rear slopes slightly inwards. Hull sides above suspension slope inwards with horizontal louvres above rear drive sprocket
● Cast turret with sides sloping inwards, external mantlet and 105mm gun with thermal sleeve and fume extractor, infra-red/white light searchlight often mounted above gun mantlet, stowage basket on turret rear, smoke grenade dischargers on turret sides towards rear
● Suspension each side has seven road wheels, idler front, drive sprocket rear, four track-return rollers. Upper part often covered by skirts

Specifications

Crew: 4
Armament: 1 x 105mm, 1 x 7.62mm MG (coaxial), 1 x 7.62 MG (anti-aircraft), 2 x 4 smoke grenade dischargers
Ammunition: 60 x 105mm, 5,500 x 7.62mm
Length gun forwards: 9.543m
Length hull: 7.09m
Width without skirts: 3.25m
Height to top of commander's periscope: 2.613m
Ground clearance: 0.44m
Weight, combat: 40,000kg
Weight, empty: 38,700kg
Power-to-weight ratio: 20.75hp/tonne
Ground pressure: 0.86kg/cm²
Engine: MTU MB 838 Ca M500, 10-cylinder multi-fuel developing 830hp at 2,200rpm
Maximum road speed: 65km/hr
Maximum road range: 600km
Fuel capacity: 955 lit
Fording: 2.25m
Fording with preparation: 4m
Vertical obstacle: 1.15m
Trench: 3m
Gradient: 60%
Side slope: 30%
Armour: 70mm (maximum)
Armour type: Steel
NBC system: Yes
Night vision equipment: Yes (was infra-red, now replaced by passive in some armies)

Development

Leopard 1 was developed from the late 1950s and after trials with various prototypes, Krauss-Maffei of Munich was selected as prime contractor in 1963, with MaK responsible for the specialised versions.

First production Leopard 1 was delivered to the German Army in 1965 and production continued, with interruptions, until 1984. OTOBREDA produced Leopard 1 for the Italian Army, and MaK built a small quantity for both home and export markets.

Driver sits front right with NBC pack and some ammunition to his left, turret centre, engine and transmission rear. Commander and gunner sit on right side of turret, loader left.

The 105mm gun is fully stabilised and power-elevates from -9° to +20° with turret traverse 360°. Types of ammunition include APDS, APFSDS, HEAT and smoke. A 7.62mm MG is mounted coaxial to left of 105mm gun and a similar weapon can be mounted on commander's or loader's hatch.

A wide range of optional equipment is available including additional armour, different fire-control systems, various night vision devices and a dozer blade. Many armies, including Germany, have already upgraded their Leopard 1s to extend their lives into the 1990s.

Variants

Leopard 1A1A1 has a number of improvements including additional armour protection for the turret.
Leopard 1A2 has passive night equipment for commander and driver and improved turret.
Leopard 1A3 has new all-welded turret with improved armour, as well as all the improvements of Leopard 1A2 and 1A3.
Leopard 1A4 was the final model for the German Army and has

all-welded turret and integrated fire-control system.

Leopard 1A5 is latest upgrade for German Army and has new computerised fire control system and thermal night vision equipment.

Leopard 1 with 105mm Improved Weapon System, trials only.

Leopard 1 with 120mm gun of Leopard 2, trials only.

Leopard 1 AVLB (Biber).

Leopard 1 ARV.

Leopard 1 AEV.

Gepard twin 35mm anti-aircraft system (see SPAAGs).

Leopard 1 driver training tank has large observation type cupola in place of turret.

Leopard 1 chassis has also been proposed as carrier for the Roland surface-to-air missile system, Italian 76mm OTOMATIC anti-aircraft/anti-helicopter weapon and turret of French GCT 155mm self-propelled gun, but none has entered service.

Status

Production complete but resumed if further orders. In service with Australia, Belgium, Botswana, Brazil, Canada, Denmark, Germany, Greece, Italy, Netherlands, Norway and Turkey.

Manufacturers

Krauss-Maffei, Munich, and MaK, Kiel, Germany; OTOBREDA, La Spezia, Italy.

Right:
Leopard 1A3

Below:
Leopard 1
of the
Netherlands
army.

Left: Leopard 1 of the Netherlands army.   **Above: Leopard 1 (Krauss Maffei)**

Merkava MBT (Israel)

Key recognition features

● Almost vertical hull front, well sloped glacis plate with distinct bulge in right side for engine. Horizontal hull top extends right to rear, driver's hatch forward of turret on left side

● Turret mounted slightly to rear of vehicle with distinctive pointed front, 105mm gun with thermal sleeve and fume extractor, large turret bustle with stowage rack that extends to hull rear, entry hatch in vertical hull rear

● Suspension each side has six road wheels, drive sprocket front, idler rear and four track-return rollers. Upper part of suspension covered by skirts with wavy bottom.

Specifications (MK 1)

Crew: 4
Armament: 1 x 105mm, 1 x 7.62mm MG (coaxial), 2 x 7.62 MG (anti-aircraft), 1 x 60mm mortar
Ammunition: 62 x 105mm, 10,000 x 7.62mm
Length gun forwards: 8.63m
Length hull: 7.45m
Width: 3.7m
Height to commander's cupola: 2.75m
Height to turret roof: 2.64m
Ground clearance: 0.47m
Power-to-weight ratio: 14.28hp/tonne
Weight, combat: 61,000kg
Weight, empty: 60,000kg
Ground pressure: 0.9kg/cm²
Engine: Teledyne Continental AVDS-1790-6A V-12 diesel developing 900hp
Maximum road speed: 46km/hr
Maximum range: 400km
Fuel capacity: 900 lit
Gradient: 70%
Side slope: 38%
Armour: Classified
Fording: 1.38m, 2m (with preparation)
Vertical obstacle: 0.95m
Trench: 3m
Armour type: Steel/spaced/laminate
NBC system: Yes
Night vision equipment: Yes

Development

Merkava was developed from the late 1960s to meet Israeli Army requirements, with particular emphasis on battlefield survivability. First prototype was completed in 1974 with first production vehicles following in 1979. It was used in combat for the first time against Syrian forces in 1982.

Layout is unconventional with engine compartment front, fighting compartment rear and turret above. The commander and gunner sit right of turret, loader left. Main armament comprises a 105mm M68 series gun, which is a modified M68 and power-elevates from -8.5° to +20° with turret traverse through 360°. A 7.62mm MG is mounted coaxial to left of main armament and both commander and loader have roof-mounted 7.62mm MG for anti-aircraft or defence suppression. A 60mm mortar is mounted in the turret roof.

The 105mm gun is fully stabilised. Fire-control system includes a ballistic computer and laser rangefinder. Merkava carries a basic load of 62 rounds of 105mm which can be increased to 85 rounds.

Left: Merkava Mk 1   *Right: Merkava Mk 2*
(Israeli MoD)

Variants

Merkava Mk 2 entered production in 1983 and has several improvements, including improved armour protection and fire-control system.

Merkava Mk 3 is current production model and was first shown in 1989. Has many improvements including a 120mm smooth bore gun, more powerful 1200hp engine coupled to a new transmission, new armour, threat warning system, new suspension and improved fir control system.

The prototype of a 155mm self-propelled artillery system, called the Slammer, has been built but not placed in production.

Status

In production. In service with Israeli Army only.

Manufacturer

Israel Ordnance Corps facility at Tel a Shomer, Israel.

IVECO/OTOBREDA C1 Ariete MBT (Italy)

Key recognition features

● Turret front slopes well to rear, 120mm gun in internal mantlet, flat roof with commander's cupola on right side with large periscopic sight to front, vertical turret sides with bank of four smoke grenade dischargers either side, ammunition hatch in left side of turret, gunner's sight in forward part of turret roof on right side

● Hull sides vertical, raised engine compartment at back with louvres above each side of last road wheel station

● Suspension either side has seven road wheels, idler front, drive sprocket rear and track return rollers. Upper part of suspension is covered by skirts

Specifications

Crew: 4
Armament: 1 x 120mm, 1 x 7.62mm MG (coaxial), 1 x 7.62mm MG (anti-aircraft), 2 x 4 smoke grenade dischargers
Ammunition: 40 x 120mm, 2500 x 7.62mm
Length overall: 9.669m
Length hull: 7.59m
Width overall: 3.601m
Height to turret roof: 2.5m
Ground clearance: 0.44m
Weight, combat: 54,000kg
Power-to-weight ratio: 27.4hp/tonne
Ground pressure: 0.85kg/cm^2
Engine: IVECO V-12 MTCA 12-cylinder turbo-charged diesel developing 1300hp at 2,300rpm
Maximum road speed: 65+km/h
Maximum range: 550+km
Fuel capacity: Not available
Fording: 1.2m (without preparation); 2.1m (with preparation)
Vertical obstacle: 2.1m
Trench: 3m
Gradient: 60%
Side slope: 30%
Armour: Classified
Armour type: Steel/composite
NBC system: Yes
Night vision equipment: Yes (passive)

Development

In 1984 the now OTOBREDA and IVECO formed a consortium to develop a new family of vehicles for the Italian Army, the B1 Centauro (8x8) tank destroyer (qv), the C1 Ariete MBT and the VCC-80 infantry fighting vehicle (qv). OTOBREDA developed the C1 MBT with IVECO providing the powerpack and other automotive components. The Italian Army has placed an order for 200 C1 Ariete MBTs which are being built at the OTOBREDA facility at La Spezia with IVECO supplying automotive components.

The layout of the C1 Ariete MBT is conventional with the driver at the front right, power operated turret in the centre with commander and gunner on right and loader on left, and powerpack at the rear.

The Galileo computerised fire control fire system, which shares many components with the fire control system installed in the B1 tank destroyer (already in production and service with the Italian Army) and the VCC-80 IFV (which is still at the prototype stage) includes day/night sights and a laser rangefinder. The tank commander has a stabilised roof-mounted sight. The 120mm smooth bore gun fires the same ammunition as the Leopard 2 and M1A1/M1A2 MBTs with weapon elevation being from -9˚ to +20˚ and turret traverse a full 360˚. The main armament is fully stabilised with the ordnance being provided with a fume extractor, muzzle reference system and thermal sleeve.

The Ariete Mk 2 MBT is currently under development.

Variants
None.

Status
Production. In service with Italian Army.

Manufacturer
OTOBREDA, La Spezia, Italy (but see text).

Left: C1 Ariete MBT   **Above: C1 Ariete MBT**

Below left: C1 Ariete MBT   **Below: C1 Ariete MBT**

OTOBREDA OF40 MBT (Italy)

Key recognition features

● Well-sloped glacis plate leading up to horizontal hull roof. Driver's position front right, turret centre and slightly raised engine compartment rear

● Turret has wedge-shaped mantlet and 105mm gun with thermal sleeve and fume extractor. Almost vertical turret sides, large bustle rear with stowage basket each side. Commander's cupola right with prominent periscopic sight in front

● Hull sides vertical. Suspension has seven road wheels, idler front, drive sprocket rear and five track-return rollers. Upper part of suspension is normally covered by skirts. Exhaust outlets each side at hull rear with horizontal louvres

Specifications

Crew: 4
Armament: 1 x 105mm, 1 x 7.62mm MG (coaxial), 1 x 7.62mm MG (anti-aircraft), 2 x 4 smoke grenade dischargers
Ammunition: 57 x 105mm, 5,700 x 7.62mm
Length gun forwards: 9.222m
Length hull: 6.893m
Width with skirts: 3.51m
Height with sight: 2.68m
Height to turret top: 2.45m
Ground clearance: 0.44m
Weight, combat: 45,500kg
Weight, empty: 43,100kg
Power-to-weight ratio: 18.24hp/tonne
Ground pressure: 0.92kg/cm²
Engine: MTU MB 838 Ca M500 V10 supercharged diesel developing 830hp at 2,200rpm
Maximum road speed: 60km/hr
Maximum range: 600km
Fuel capacity: 1,000 lit
Fording: 1.2m (without preparation), 2.25m (with preparation), 4m with snorkel
Vertical obstacle: 1.1m
Trench: 3m
Gradient: 60%
Side slope: 30%
Armour: Classified
Armour type: Steel
NBC system: Yes
Night vision equipment: Optional

Development

OF-40 was designed as a private venture specifically for the export market from 1977, with OTOBREDA responsible for the overall design and production and FIAT for the powerpack. The first prototype was completed in 1980 and in 1981 the United Arab Emirates took delivery of the first of 18 Mk 1s. This was followed by a second order for 18 Mk 2s and three armoured recovery vehicles, all of which have been delivered. The original Mk 1s have now been brought up to Mk 2 standard.

Layout is similar to Leopard 1s with which it shares some components, driver front right, ammunition and NBC pack left, turret centre and engine and transmission rear. Commander and gunner sit right of turret, loader left.

Main armament comprises a 105mm rifled gun that fires standard NATO ammunition and power-elevates from -9° to +20°, with turret traverse 360°. A 7.62mm MG is mounted coaxial left of the main armament, and a 7.62mm or 12.7mm MG is mounted on turret roof for anti-aircraft defence. Fire-control system includes laser rangefinder and stabilised day/night roof sight for commander.

Variants

OF-40 Mk 2 has the Galileo OG14L2A fire-control system which includes stabilisation system for 105mm gun and a LLTV camera mounted on the turret mantlet and aligned to the 105mm gun.
OF-40 ARV.
OF-40 chassis can be used for other weapons systems, such as the twin 35mm anti-aircraft turret, and with a different engine it is used for the Palmaria 155mm self-propelled howitzer and the OTO 76/62 76mm anti-aircraft tank, which is still at prototype stage. The Palmaria has entered production and

Above: OF-40 Mk 2

details are given in the Self-propelled guns and howitzers section.

Above: OF-40 Mk 2

Status

Production complete but resumed if further orders. In service with United Arab Emirates only.

Right: OF-40 Mk 2

Manufacturer

OTOBREDA, La Spezia, Italy

Mitsubishi Heavy Industries Type 90 MBT (Japan)

Key recognition features

● Well sloped glacis plate which is almost horizontal, hull top horizontal and slightly raised at the rear, hull rear vertical with horizontal louvres
● Turret has vertical sides and rear with distinct chamfer between turret front and sides, commander's cupola on right with large gunner's sight in left side of roof, 120mm gun has thermal sleeve with fume extractor
● Suspension either side has six road wheels, idler front, drive sprocket rear, and track return rollers. Upper part of suspension covered by skirts

Specifications

Crew: 3
Armament: 1 x 120mm, 1 x 7.62mm MG (coaxial), 1 x 12.7mm MG (anti-aircraft), 2 x 3 smoke grenade dischargers
Ammunition: Not available
Length gun forwards: 9.755m
Length hull: 7.5m
Width: 3.42m
Height: 2.34m
Ground clearance: 0.45m (variable)
Weight, combat: 50,000kg
Power-to-weight ratio: 30hp/tonne
Ground pressure: 0.89kg/cm²
Engine: Mitsubishi 10ZG 10-cylinder water-cooled diesel engine developing 1,500hp at 2,400rpm
Maximum road speed: 70km/h (forwards); 42km/h (reverse)
Range: 400km (approx)
Fuel capacity: Not available
Fording: 2m
Vertical obstacle: 1m
Trench: 2.7m
Gradient: 60%
Side slope: 30%
Armour: Classified
Armour type: Steel/composite/laminate
NBC system: Yes
Night vision equipment: Yes (passive)

Development

In the mid-1970s the Japanese Self-Defence Agency started development work on a new MBT to meet the requirements of the Japanese Ground Self-Defence Force. This was known as the TK-X MBT and the first prototypes were completed in the mid-1980s. This was subsequently accepted for service as the Type 90 MBT with first production vehicles completed in 1992.

Prime contractor is Mitsubishi Heavy Industries, with Japan Steel Works being responsible for the 120mm smooth bore gun which is essentially the German Rheinmetall weapon made under licence with the computerised fire control system being developed by Mitsubishi Electric.

The driver's compartment is at the front, turret in the centre and powerpack at the rear. The commander is seated on the right of the turret with the gunner on the left, no loader is required as an automatic loading system is provided for the 120mm smooth bore gun which fires HEAT-MP and APFSDS-T rounds with a semi-combustible cartridge case.

The computerised fire control system allows either the commander or gunner to aim and fire the main armament whether the Type 90 is moving or stationary with a high probability of a first round hit. A 7.62mm machine gun is mounted co-axial with the main armament with a 12.7mm machine gun being mounted on the roof for anti-aircraft purposes. A laser detector is mounted on the forward part of the roof and a dozer blade can be mounted at the front of the hull.

Variants

Type 90 ARV is based on the chassis of the Type 90 MBT and has a new superstructure with crane mounted at front right, dozer/stabiliser blade at front of hull and hydraulically operated winch.

Type 91 AVLB is based on chassis of Type 90 MBT and has scissors type bridge.

Status

Production. In service with Japanese Ground Self-Defence Force.

Manufacturer

Mitsubishi Heavy Industries, Tokyo, Japan.

*Left: Type 90 MBT
(Kensuke Ebata)*   *Right: Type 90 MBT
(Kensuke Ebata)*

Mitsubishi Heavy Industries Type 74 MBT (Japan)

Key recognition features

● Well sloped glacis plate with driver's hatch upper left side, turret slightly forward of hull centre, engine compartment rear. Hull sides slope inwards with exhaust pipes each side at rear. Vertical hull rear

● 105mm gun has fume extractor but no thermal sleeve, prominent external mantlet, cast turret with well sloped sides, stowage basket rear, large infra-red searchlight left of main armament

● Suspension has five road wheels, drive sprocket rear, idler front, no track-return rollers. Suspension can be raised or lowered to give a ground clearance of 0.2 to 0.65m

Specifications

Crew: 4
Armament: 1 x 105mm, 1 x 7.62mm MG (coaxial), 1 x 12.7mm MG (anti-aircraft), 2 x 3 smoke grenade discharges
Ammunition: 55 x 105mm, 4,500 x 7.62mm, 660 x 12.7mm
Length gun forwards: 9.42m
Length hull: 6.7m
Width: 3.18m
Height including AA MG: 2.67m
Height to turret top: 2.48m
Ground clearance: 0.2 to 0.65m (adjustable)
Weight, combat: 38,000kg
Weight, empty: 36,300kg
Power-to-weight ratio: 18.94hp/tonne
Ground pressure: 0.86kg/cm²
Engine: Mitsubishi 10ZF Type 22 WT 10-cylinder air-cooled diesel developing 720hp at 2,200rpm
Maximum road speed: 53km/hr
Maximum range: 400km
Fuel capacity: 950 lit
Fording: 1m
Fording with preparation: 2m
Vertical obstacle: 1m
Trench: 2.7m
Gradient: 60%
Side slope: 40%
Armour: Classified
Armour type: Steel
NBC system: Yes
Night vision equipment: Yes (infra-red for commander and driver)

Development

Development of a new MBT to supplement the Type 61 commenced in the early 1960s with first prototypes completed in 1969. This was followed by a number of further prototypes and first production Type 74s were completed in 1975. Production of the Type 74 has now been completed after about 870 had been built. It was followed in production by the 120mm-armed Type 90 (qv) which was also designed and built by Mitsubishi Heavy Industries.

Layout is conventional with driver front left, turret centre, engine and transmission rear. Commander and gunner sit on turret right, loader left. Commander's cupola is raised above roof line for all-round visibility.

105mm gun is the British L7, made under licence in Japan, which power-elevates from -6˚ to +12˚ (-12˚ to 15˚ using suspension). The driver can adjust the suspension to suit the type of ground, raise or lower the front or rear, or tilt the tank from side to side.

7.62mm MG is mounted coaxial with main armament and a 12.7mm M2 HB MG is mounted on turret roof for anti-aircraft defence. Some vehicles have been fitted with a dozer blade.

Variants

Type 78 armoured recovery vehicle and Type 87 twin 35mm self-propelled anti-aircraft gun system (see SPAAGs).

Status

Production complete. In service with Japanese Ground Self Defence Force only.

Manufacturer

Mitsubishi Heavy Industries, Tokyo, Japan.

Above: Type 74 (K Nogi)

Right: Type 74

Left: Type 74 (K Nogi)

Mitsubishi Heavy Industries Type 61 MBT (Japan)

Key recognition features

● Well sloped glacis plate leading up to horizontal hull top that extends right to rear, driver to immediate front of turret on right side, vertical hull rear with exhaust pipe on each side

● Cast turret in hull centre, 90mm gun with T-shaped muzzle brake and fume extractor to rear, rounded turret front with turret bustle extending to rear and external stowage box, commander's cupola right of turret with 12.7mm M2 HB MG forward

● Suspension has six road wheels, drive sprocket front, idler rear and three track-return rollers, no skirts

Specifications

Crew: 4
Armament: 1 x 90mm, 1 x 7.62mm MG (coaxial), 1 x 12.7mm MG (anti-aircraft), 2 x 3 smoke grenade dischargers
Ammunition: Not available
Length gun forwards: 8.19m
Length hull: 6.3m
Width: 2.95m
Height including AA MG: 3.16m
Height to turret roof: 2.49m
Ground clearance: 0.4m
Weight, combat: 35,000kg
Weight, empty: 33,500kg
Power-to-weight ratio: 16.28hp/tonne
Ground pressure: 0.65kg/cm²
Engine: Mitsubishi Type 12 HM 21 WT, V-12, 4-cycle direct injection turbocharged diesel developing 600hp at 2,100rpm
Maximum road speed: 45km/hr
Maximum range: 200km
Fuel capacity: Not available
Fording: 0.99m
Vertical obstacle: 0.685m
Trench: 2.489m
Gradient: 60%
Side slope: 40%
Armour: 64mm (maximum)
Armour type: Steel
NBC system: No
Night vision equipment: Yes (infra-red on some vehicles)

Development

Design work on the first post-Second World War Japanese MBT commenced in 1954 and, following trials with prototype vehicles, was accepted for service as the Type 61 in 1961. First production tanks were completed in 1962 and production finally ended in the early 1970s, by which time about 560 had been built. In many respects the Type 61 MBT is a scaled down US M47 medium tank which was evaluated by the Japanese Ground Self Defence Forces in the 1950s. From 1984 the Type 61 started to be phased out of service.

Layout is conventional, with driver front right, some ammunition to his left, turret centre and engine rear. Commander and gunner sit right of turret, loader left.

Main armament comprises 90mm gun, 7.62mm MG mounted coaxial and 12.7mm MG on commander's cupola.

The 90mm gun has powered/manual elevation with turret traverse also being powered/manual. The main armament of the Type 61 MBT is not stabilised.

Left: Type 61
without AA MG   *Right: Type 61*

Variants

Some Type 61s have been fitted with wooden minesweeping
equipment at hull front so they resemble Russian T-54/T-55
mine-clearing tanks for training purposes.
Type 70 ARV is based on Type 61 chassis.
Type 67 AVLB is based on Type 61 chassis.
Type 67 AEV, used for engineer support on the battlefield,
has a dozer blade and light crane.

Status

Production complete. In service with Japanese Ground Self
Defence Force only but being phased out of service.

Manufacturer

Mitsubishi Heavy Industries, Tokyo, Japan

PT-91 MBT (Poland)

Key recognition features

● Well sloped glacis plate with drivers position top centre, turret centre of hull, engine compartment rear, exhaust outlet on left side of hull above last road wheel.

● Hull front, turret front and sides is covered in closely packed explosive reactive armour array. Circular turret with raised cupola on right side with externally mounted 12.7 mm MG. 125 mm main gun has thermal sleeve and fume extractor.

● Suspension each side has six road wheels, drive sprocket rear, idler front and three track return rollers. Upper part of suspension is covered by side skirt with closely packed explosive reactive armour

Specifications

Crew: 3
Armament: 1 x 125 mm, 1 x 7.62 mm MG (coaxial), 1 x 12.7 mm (anti-aircraft), 2 x 12 smoke grenade launchers
Ammunition: 42 x 125 mm, 2000 x 7.62 mm, 300 x 12.7 mm
Length gun forwards: 9.67 m
Length hull: 6.95 m
Width: 3.59 m
Height: 2.19 m (turret top)
Ground clearance: 0.395 m
Weight, combat: 45 300 kg
Power-to-weight ratio: 18.49 hp/t
Engine: Type S-12U supercharged diesel developing 848 hp at 2300 rpm
Maximum road speed: 60 km/h
Maximum road range: 650 km
Fuel capacity: 1000 l
Fording: 1.4 m
Vertical obstacle: 0.85 m
Trench: 2.8 m
Gradient: 60%
Side slope: 40%
Armour: classified
Armour type: steel/laminate/ERA
NBC: yes
Night vision equipment: yes

Development

For many years Poland manufactured the Russian T-72M1 series MBT under licence for both the home and export markets. Further development of this resulted in the PT-91 which is also referred to as the *Twardy* (Hard). First prototype was completed in 1992 and a small batch has been built for the Polish Army. The layout of the PT-91 is identical to the T-72 MBT with driver front, turret in centre and powerpack at the rear. The gunner is seated on left of turret and commander on right. Turret can be traversed through 360 degrees with weapon elevation from -6 to +13 degrees.

Main improvements over the T-72 include a new Polish-developed explosive reactive armour package to the hull and turret, laser warning system, installation of a computerised fire control system, bank of 12 electically operated smoke grenade launchers either side of the turret, increased protection against mines and more powerful engine.

Variants

Poland is now developing another MBT called the *Gorilla*. Poland also builds a number of variants on the T-72M1 MBT chassis including the T-72M1K commanders tank, WZT-3 armoured recovery vehicle, armoured engineer vehicle and a driver training tank.

Status

Production. In service with Poland.

Manufacturer

Zaklady Mechaniczne Bumar-Labedy SA, Poland.

Above:
PT-91

Top right:
PT-91

Left:
PT-91

Right.
PT-91

TM-800 Medium Tank (Romania)

Key recognition features

● Well sloped glacis plate with splash board across upper part with headlamps to right, turret centre and slightly raised engine compartment to the rear. Unditching beam and long range fuel tanks often carried at rear

● Circular turret has curved sides, loader's cupola on right side with externally mounted 12.7 mm AA MG, MG ammunition boxes on turret sides

● Suspension has six road wheels each side, idler front, drive sprocket rear, upper part of suspension covered by skirt

Specifications

Crew: 4
Armament: 1 x 100 mm, 1 x 7.62 mm MG (coaxial), 1 x 12.7 mm (anti-aircraft), 2 x 5 smoke grenade launchers
Ammunition: 40 x 100 mm, 3500 x 7.62 mm, 500 x 12.7 mm
Length gun forwards: 9.00 m
Length hull: 6.74 m
Width: 3.30 m
Height: 2.35 m (turret top)
Ground clearance: 0.425 m
Weight, combat: 45 000 kg
Power-to-weight ratio: 18.45 hp/t
Engine: diesel developing 830 hp
Maximum road speed: 64 km/h
Maximum road range: 500 km
Fuel capacity: 1100 l
Fording: 1.4 m
Vertical obstacle: 0.9 m
Trench: 2.8 m
Gradient: 60%
Side slope: 40%
Armour: classified
Armour type: steel
NBC: yes
Night vision equipment: yes

Development

The TM-800 MBT is very similar to the Russian T-54/T-55 and has almost same hull and turret, main external difference that it has six smaller road wheels whereas the T-54/T-55 has five larger road wheels. The TM-800 also has side skirts which extend the full length of the vehicle and unlike the Russian T-54/T-55/T-62/T-72 there is no exhaust outlet on the left side of the hull. The driver is seated front left with some ammunition to his right with turret in centre and powerpack at the rear. Commander and gunner are on the left with the loader on the right.

Main armament consists of a 100 mm gun which is fitted with a fume extractor near the muzzle. Turret traverse is 360 degrees with weapon elevation from -5 to +17 degrees.

Standard equipment includes infa-red night vision equipment for commander, gunner and driver and a computerised fire control system. A dozer blade and mine clearing system can be mounted at front of the hull.

Variants

TR-85, similar to T-55 but has laser rangefinder above 100 mm mantlet, chassis has six road wheels, different rear engine decks and side skirts
TR-580, this is believed to have preceeded the TR-85 and has a similar hull but the six road wheels are spoked, has side skirts fitted
TR-125 is Romanian version of Russian T-72 with seven road wheels

Status

Production probably complete. In service with Romania.

Manufacturer

Romanian state factories.

Above:
TM-800

Top Right:
TM-800

Left:
TM-800

Right:
TM-800

T-80 MBT (Russia)

Key recognition features

● Well sloped glacis plate with distinctive V splash board, turret centre and engine compartment rear. Long-range fuel tanks and unditching beam often carried on far rear of hull which also has distinctive rectangular air outlet (not on T-64 series).
● Rounded turret, machine gun ammunition boxes on left, stowage box right, snorkel carried horizontally at rear. Main gun has thermal sleeve and fume extractor, 12.7mm AA MG on roof and smoke grenade dischargers each side of main armament. Infra-red searchlight on right of main armament
● Suspension each side has six road wheels, idler front, drive sprocket rear and track-return rollers covered by skirts. Unlike T-64 and T-72 there is no exhaust outlet left side of engine compartment. Road wheels larger than T-64's with gap between 2nd/3rd and 4th/5th road wheels

Specifications (provisional)

Crew: 3
Armament: 1 x 125mm gun/missile launcher, 1 x 7.62mm MG (coaxial), 1 x 12.7mm MG (anti-aircraft), smoke grenade dischargers (number depends on model)
Ammunition: 36 x 125mm, 1,250 x 7.62mm MG (coaxial), 300 x 12.7mm (anti-aircraft) and 5 AT-8 Songster ATGW
Length gun forwards: 9.9m
Length hull: 7.4m
Width: 3.4m
Height to commander's cupola: 2.2m
Ground clearance: 0.38m
Weight, combat: 42,500kg
Power-to-weight ratio: 23.52hp/tonne
Ground pressure: 0.86kg/cm²
Engine: Gas turbine developing 1000hp
Maximum road speed: 70km/hr
Maximum road range: 450km
Fuel capacity: 1100 lit
Fording: 1.8m
Fording with preparation: 5.0m
Vertical obstacle: 1m
Trench: 2.85m
Gradient: 60%
Side slope: 40%
Armour: Classified
Armour type: Steel/composite/reactive
NBC system: Yes
Night vision equipment: Yes (commander, driver and gunner)

Development

The T-80 MBT was developed in the late 1970s and is believed

to have entered production in 1983 with first production MBTs being completed the following year. By early 1996 it is estimated that total production of the T-80 amounted to 20,000 vehicles. The most significant features of the T-80 over the earlier T-72 are its gas turbine engine and the ability to fire the Songster AT-8 ATGW from the 125mm gun.

The overall layout of the T-80 is similar to that of other recent Soviet MTBs with the driver at the front, two man turret in centre with the gunner on the left and commander, who also mans the 12.7mm anti-aircraft machine gun, on the right. The powerpack, which includes a gas turbine engine, is at the rear. With the exception of the T-64, all post Second-World War Russian MBTs had the exhaust outlet on the left side towards the rear. The more recent T-80 has a distinct oblong outlet in the centre of the hull at the rear.

The T-80 has a 125mm smooth bore gun that is fed by an automatic loader which can fire HE-FRAG (FS), HEAT-FS and APFSDS-T rounds, or an AT-8 Songster ATGW. Turret traverse is a full 360° with weapon elevation from -5° to +14°. The gun is fully stabilised.

Variants

T-80, original production model, not built in large numbers.
T-80B, first version produced in large numbers.
T-80BK, command version of T-80B with additional communications equipment.
T-80BV, T-80 with explosive reactive armour, combat weight 41.7 tonnes.
T-80BVK, command version of T-80BV with additional communications equipment.
T-80U, first seen in 1989 and sometimes referred to as M1989 by NATO, has diesel rather than gas turbine engine, different

engine decking, new commander's cupola, four smoke grenade dischargers either side of turret, different vision equipment, and new armour package that includes armoured side skirts.

T-80UD, has gas turbine replaced by 1100hp diesel engine.

T-80UK, command tank version of T-80U.

T-80UM, powered by 1250hp gas turbine, new fire control system.

T-84, further development of T-80 in the Ukraine (qv).

Status
Production. In service with China and Russia.

Manufacturers
Kirov Works (Leningrad), Khar'kov (Ukraine) and Omsk.

Above:
T-80 MBT

Above right:
T-80U MBT

Right:
**T-80U MBT
(Christopher
Foss)**

T-64 MBT (Russia)

Key recognition features

● Well sloped glacis plate with driver's position top centre, distinctive V splash plate on glacis, turret centre of hull, engine and transmission rear. Unlike T-72, no exhaust outlet on left side of hull
● Circular turret, raised cupola with external 12.7mm MG on right of roof, two stowage boxes right side of turret and one on turret rear (above which is the snorkel), three MG ammunition boxes on left side of turret. Infra-red searchlight to left of 125mm gun with thermal sleeve and fume extractor.
● Suspension each side has six road wheels (much smaller than those on T-72), idler front, drive sprocket rear and four track-return rollers. Side skirts or gill type armour panels often installed over upper part of suspension. Unditching beam and fuel drums often carried rear

Specifications (T-64B)

Crew: 3
Armament: 1 x 125mm, 1 x 7.62 MG (coaxial), 1 x 12.7mm MG (AA)
Ammunition: 36 x 125mm, 1250 x 7.62mm, 300 x 12.7mm
Length gun forwards: 9.9m
Length hull: 7.4m
Width without skirts: 3.38m
Width with skirts: 4.64m
Ground clearance: 0.377m
Weight, combat: 39,500kg
Power-to-weight ratio: 17.7hp/tonne
Ground pressure: 0.86kg/cm²
Engine: Model 5DTF 5-cylinder opposed diesel developing 700hp
Maximum road speed: 75km/hr
Maximum road range: 400km
Maximum road range with long-range fuel tanks: 550km
Fuel capacity: 1,000 lit
Fording: 1.8m
Fording with preparation: 5.0m
Vertical obstacle: 0.8m
Trench: 2.28m
Gradient: 60%
Side slope: 40%
Armour: Classified
Armour type: Laminate/steel/reactive
NBC system: Yes
Night vision equipment: Yes (infra-red for commander, gunner and driver)

Above: T-64A (Christopher F Foss)

Development

T-64 entered production in 1966 and was first seen in public in 1970. It has never been exported outside the former USSR and has not appeared in any Russian military parades.

T-64 looks similar to T-72 but has infra-red searchlight on left of 125mm gun, different powerpack, narrower track, different suspension and slightly different turret. Layout is similar to T-72 with driver front, turret centre, commander left, gunner right, engine and transmission rear.

Main armament comprises a 125mm smooth bore gun which power-elevates from -6° to 14°, turret traverses 360°. Similar to that installed in the T-72, it has an automatic loader which delivers eight rounds a minute. Three types of ammunition are fired: APFSDS, HEAT-FRAG and HE-FRAG (FS). A 7.62mm MG is mounted coaxial to right of main armament and a 12.7mm MG is mounted on gunner's cupola for use in the anti-aircraft role.

Left: T-64A   **Below: T-64A**   **Above: T-64**
(Steven Zaloga)

Variants

T-64, original model, no thermal sleeve for 115mm gun.

T-64A, first production model to be built in quantity, smoke grenade dischargers either side of gun, side skirts.

T-64AK, command vehicle.

T-64B, can fire AT-8 Songster ATGW.

T-64BK, command vehicle.

T-64BV, T-64 with explosive reactive armour.

T-64B1, Soviet designation, differences not known.

T-64B1K, command version of T-64B1.

T-64BV1K, T-64B with explosive reactive armour and communications equipment for use in command role.

T-64R, believed to be T-64 with gun of T-72/T-80 firing ATGW.

T-64 can be fitted with mineclearing equipment.

Status

Production complete. In service only with Russia.

Manufacturer

Russian state arsenals.

T-72 MBT (Russia)

Key recognition features

● Well sloped glacis plate with driver's position top centre, distinctive V splash plate on glacis, turret centre of hull, engine and transmission rear, exhaust outlet on left side of hull above last road wheel station

● Circular turret, raised cupola with external 12.7mm MG on right of roof, stowage box rear and right, snorkel left side, infra-red searchlight right of 125mm gun which has thermal sleeve and fume extractor. Undomitching beam and long-range fuel tanks sometimes fitted rear

● Suspension each side has six road wheels, drive sprocket rear, idler front and three track-return rollers. Upper part often covered by rubber skirt or fold-out armour panels over forward wheel stations

Specifications (T-72B1)

Crew: 3
Armament: 1 x 125mm, 1 x 7.62mm MG (coaxial), 1 x 12.7mm MG (AA)
Ammunition: 45 x 125mm, 2,000 x 7.62mm, 300 x 12.7mm
Length gun forwards: 9.24m
Length hull: 6.95m
Width without skirts: 3.6m
Width with skirts: 4.75m
Height without AA MG: 2.37m
Ground clearance: 0.47m
Weight, combat: 44,500kg
Power-to-weight ratio: 18.9hp/tonne
Ground pressure: 0.84kg/cm²
Engine: V-46 V-12 diesel developing 840hp at 2,000rpm
Maximum road speed: 80km/hr
Maximum road range: 480km, 550km (with long-range tanks)
Fuel capacity: 1,000 lit
Fording: 1.8m (without preparation), 5m (with preparation)
Vertical obstacle: 0.85m
Trench: 2.8m
Gradient: 60%
Side slope: 40%
Armour: Classified
Armour type: Composite/steel
NBC system: Yes
Night vision equipment: Yes (infra-red for commander, gunner and driver)

Development

T-72 entered production in 1971 and was first seen in public in 1977. As well as being produced in the former USSR it has been built under licence in Czechoslovakia, India, Poland and former Yugoslavia.

Layout is conventional, with driver front, turret centre, engine and transmission rear. Commander sits left, gunner right. There is no loader as the 125mm smooth bore gun has an automatic carousel loader with charge above and projectiles below. Types of ammunition include HEAT-FS, HE-FRAG (FS) and APFSDS, a normal mix being 12 APFSDS, 21 HE-FRAG (FS) and six HEAT-FS. A 7.62mm MG is mounted coaxial to right of 125mm gun and a 12.7mm AA MG mounted externally on gunner's hatch. Composite armour is used in forward part of hull.

A dozer blade is mounted under the nose and additional fuel tanks can be placed at the rear to extend operational range.

Variants

The Russians have the following designations for the T-72 series of MBT which differ in some areas from those used by NATO:
T-72, original production model with coincidence rangefinder.
T-72K, command version of above.
T-72A, a number of improvements including laser rangefinder, in the Warsaw Pact was called T-72M with T-72G being export version.
T-72AK, command version of T-72A.
T-72AV, T-72 with explosive reactive armour.
T-72M, export model of T-72A.
T-72M1, modernised T-72M with additional armour.
T-72B, thicker turret armour.
T-72BK, command version of above.
T72B1, T-72 without capability to launch laser guided anti-tank projectile.

Right: T-72

T-72 MBT (Russia)

**T-72M
(Steven Zaloga)**

T-72S, export version of T-72B.
T-72S1, export version of T-72B1.
T-72BM, has second generation explosive reactive armour.
T90, further development of T-72 (qv).
PT-91, Polish version of T-72 (qv).
TR-125, Romanian version of T-72.
M-84, former Yugoslav version of T-84 (qv).
T-72 with 155mm turret, for trials purposes. India has fitted
French, Slovakian, South African and UK 155mm artillery
turrets.
T-72 can be fitted with various types of mineclearing systems.
MTU-72 AVLB, similar to MTU-20 (qv) but on T-72 chassis.
BREM-1 armoured recovery and repair vehicle (qv).
BREM-2 armoured recovery and repair vehicle.
IMR-2 combat engineer vehicle based on T-72 chassis.

Status

In production. In service with Algeria, Bulgaria, Cuba, Czech
Republic, Finland, Hungary, India, Iraq, Libya, Poland, Romania,
Russia, Syria and former Yugoslavia.

Manufacturers

Russia (Chelybinsk, Kirov and Nizhnyi Tagil), has also been built
under licence, often with modifications, in following countries:
former Czechoslovakia, India (T-72M1), Iraq (T-72M1), Poland
(T-72M1), Romania (TR-125) and former Yugoslavia (M-84).

Left: T-72A MBT

Right: T-72M MBT (Richard Stickland)

T-62 MBT (Russia)

Key recognition features

● Well sloped glacis plate with splash board mid-way, horizontal hull top with driver's hatch front left, turret centre, engine and transmission rear
● Turret is circular and well sloped all round, loader's cupola on right normally mounts 12.7mm AA MG, MG ammunition boxes sometimes stowed right side of turret to rear, snorkel left side of turret rear. Main armament has fume extractor about one-third distance from muzzle, infra-red searchlight right of main armament
● Suspension each side has five road wheels, idler front, drive sprocket rear, no track-return rollers, no skirts. Exhaust port on left track guard above fourth/fifth road wheel, flat fuel/oil storage tanks right side of hull above track

Specifications

Crew: 4
Armament: 1 x 115mm, 1 x 7.62mm MG (coaxial), 1 x 12.7mm MG (anti-aircraft)
Ammunition: 40 x 115mm, 2,500 x 7.62mm, 300 x 12.7mm
Length gun forwards: 9.335m
Length hull: 6.63m
Width: 3.3m
Height: 2.395m (without AA MG)
Ground clearance: 0.43m
Weight, combat: 40,000kg
Weight, empty: 38,000kg
Power-to-weight ratio: 14.5hp/tonne
Ground pressure: 0.77kg/cm²
Engine: Model V-55-5 V-12 water-cooled diesel developing 580hp at 2,000rpm
Maximum road speed: 50km/hr
Maximum road range: 450km
Maximum road range (with auxiliary tanks): 650km
Fuel capacity: 675+285 lit
Vertical obstacle: 0.8m
Trench: 2.85m
Gradient: 60%
Side slope: 30%
Armour: 242mm (maximum)
Armour type: Steel
NBC system: Yes
Night vision equipment: Yes (infra-red for commander, gunner and driver)

Above: T-62M   *Right: T-62M MBT*

Development

T-62, a further development of T-54/T-55, entered production in 1961, continuing until 1975. A small number were also built in former Czechoslovakia.

Layout is conventional with driver front left, some ammunition stowed to his right, turret centre and engine and transmission rear. Commander and gunner sit left of turret, loader right. Loader also mans 12.7mm MG.

115mm smooth bore gun power-elevates from -6˚ to +16˚ and powered turret traverses through 360˚. The gun fires HE-FRAG(FS), HEAT-FS and APFSDS rounds and empty cartridge cases are ejected from a trap door in turret rear. A 7.62mm MG is mounted coaxial to right of main armament and a 12.7mm AA MG is mounted on roof. The gun is fully stabilised in both horizontal and vertical planes.

T-62 lays its own smoke screen by injecting diesel fuel into the exhaust, and additional fuel tanks can be fitted at hull rear to extend its operational range. An unditching beam is usually carried rear.

T-62 MBT (Russia)

Above: T-62MBT with laser rangefinder over 115mm gun

Left: T-62M used by Iraqi (Christopher F Foss)

Right: T-62M with laser rangefinder

Variants

T-62K, K in designation means command.
T-62D, has Drozd anti-tank defensive system, additional armour.
T-62D-1, as above but different engine.
T-62M, can fire laser guided projectile, passive armour and many other improvements.
T-62M-1, similar to above.
T-62M1, passive armour, different engine.
T-62M1-1, upgrade without laser guided projectile capability and passive armour.
T-62M1-2, similar to above.
T-62M1-2-1, similar to above.
T-62MV, upgrade with capability to fire laser guided projectile, also has explosive reactive armour.

T-62 flamethrower (in service), has flame gun mounted coaxial with 115mm gun.
Egyptian T-62s, some of which have two smoke rockets each side of turret.

Status

Production complete. In service with Afghanistan, Angola, Algeria, Cuba, Egypt, Ethiopia (limited numbers), Iran, Iraq, Israel, North Korea, Libya, Mongolia, Russia, Syria, Vietnam, Yemen.

Manufacturers

Former Czechoslovakian, North Korean and Russian state factories.

T-54/T-55 MBT (Russia)

Key recognition features

● Well sloped glacis plate with splash board mid-way up, horizontal hull top with driver's hatch front left, turret centre, engine compartment rear. Vertical hull rear
● Turret circular and well sloped all round, loader's cupola on right normally mounts 12.7mm AA MG. 100mm gun has no thermal sleeve but bore evacuator to immediate rear of muzzle. Infra-red night searchlight right of main armament
● Suspension each side has five road wheels, idler front, drive sprocket rear, no track-return rollers or skirts, exhaust pipe on left track guard above fourth/fifth road wheel, distinct gap between first and second road wheels. Flat fuel/oil storage tanks right side of hull above track

Specifications (T-54)

Crew: 4
Armament: 1 x 100mm, 1 x 7.62mm MG (coaxial), 1 x 7.62 mm (bow), 1 x 12.7mm MG (anti-aircraft)
Ammunition: 34 x 100mm, 3,000 x 7.62mm, 500 x 12.7mm
Length gun forwards: 9m
Length hull: 6.04m
Width: 3.27m
Height without AA MG: 2.4m
Ground clearance: 0.425m
Weight, combat: 36,000kg
Weight, empty: 34,000kg
Power-to-weight ratio: 14.44hp/tonne
Ground pressure: 0.81kg/cm²
Engine: V-12 water-cooled diesel developing 520hp at 2,000rpm
Maximum road speed: 50km/hr
Maximum road range: 510km
Maximum road range with long range fuel tanks: 720km
Fuel capacity: 812 lit
Fording: 1.4m
Fording with preparation: 5.0m
Vertical obstacle: 0.8m
Trench: 2.7m
Gradient: 60%
Side slope: 40%
Armour: 203mm (maximum)
Armour type: Steel
NBC system: None
Night vision equipment: Yes (infra-red for commander, gunner and driver)

Development

T-54 is a further development of T-44 which itself was a development of T-34. First T-54 prototype was completed in 1946 with first production vehicles following in 1947. Production continued in the former USSR as late as 1981 and was also undertaken in China (Type 59 qv), former Czechoslovakia and Poland. Further development resulted in the T-62 with its 115mm gun (qv).

Layout is conventional, with driver front left, some ammunition stowed to his right, turret centre, engine and transmission rear. Commander and gunner sit on left of turret, loader right. Loader also mans 12.7mm AA MG.

Main armament comprises 100mm rifled gun which power-elevates from -5° to +17°, and turret traverses through 360°. The gun fires AP, APC-T, HE, HE-FRAG, HEAT-FS, and HVAPDS-T rounds with average rate of fire of four rounds a minute. A 7.62mm MG is mounted coaxial right of main armament and a similar weapon, operated by the driver, is fixed in the glacis plate firing forwards. A 12.7mm AA MG is mounted on the loader's cupola. The T-54 series lays its own smoke screen by injecting diesel fuel into the exhaust outlet on left side of hull. The tank can also be fitted with a dozer blade and various types of mine-clearing system.

Variants

There are countless variants of the T-54/T-55 and listed below is a resumé of those from Soviet sources.
T-54, there are numerous differences between early production T-54 vehicles and later models with some having a wider mantlet and turret undercut at the rear. These are sometimes referred to as the T-54 (1949), T-54 (1951) and T-54 (1953).
T-54A, has fume extractor for 100mm gun, stabilisation system

and deep fording equipment.

T-54AK, command tank (Polish model is T-54AD).

T-54M, T-54 upgraded to T-55M standard.

T-54B, first model to have infra-red night vision equipment.

T-55M, 580hp engine, no loader's cupola, stabilised gun, increased ammunition stowage fitted.

T-54 command vehicles have designation of **T-54K, T-54BK** and **T-54MK.** T-55 command vehicles are **T-55K, T55AK, T-55MK** and **T-55MVK.**

T-55, T-54 with new turret and numerous other improvements,

Right: T-54B

Below: T-55 with Royal Ordanance 105mm gun.

T-54/T-55 MBT (Russia)

Above: T-55 without AA MG (Michael Green/US Army)

Right: T-55AM2B with additional armour (Terry Gander)

late production models have 12.7mm AA MG.

T-55A, radiation shielding added plus 12.7mm AA MG.

T-55K, command versions, eg T-55K1 and T-55K2.

T-55M, T-55 upgrade can fire AT-10 Stabber laser guided ATGW through 100mm gun, plus many other improvements.

T-55M-1, as above but further improvements including passive armour

T-55MV, as T-55M but with explosive reactive armour.

T-55AM-1, T-55A upgrade to fire AT-10 Stabber plus passive armour, also:

  Czechoslovakian built = T-55AM2B
  Polish built = T-55AM2P
  Russian built = T-55AM2PB

T-55AD, T-55M with *Drozd* countermeasure system.

T-55AD-1, as above but with different engine.

There are many variations between production tanks, eg Polish-built vehicles often have large stowage boxes on left side of turret. More recently many have laser rangefinder over 100mm gun.

TO-55 is flamethrower version, flamegun replacing 7.62mm coaxial MG.

T-54 ARVs, many versions.

T-54 AVLBs, many versions.

IMR combat engineer vehicle.

Many countries have carried out extensive modifications, including Egypt (105mm gun and new night vision equipment) and Israeli TI-67 (105mm gun, new fire-control system).

Romania has upgraded many T-54 vehicles with side skirts, six road wheels and improved engine cooling. Many companies are now offering upgrade packages for the T-54/T-55.

Status

Production complete. In service with Afghanistan, Albania, Algeria, Angola, Bangladesh, Bulgaria, Cambodia, Central African Republic, China, Congo, Cuba, Czech Republic, Egypt, Finland, Guinea, Hungary, India, Iran, Iraq, Israel, North Korea, Laos, Lebanon, Libya, Mongolia, Mozambique, Nicaragua, Nigeria, Pakistan, Peru, Poland, Romania, Russia, Slovakia, Sudan, Syria, Tanzania, Togo, Yemen, former Yugoslavia, Vietnam, Zambia and Zimbabwe.

Manufacturers

Former Czechoslovakia, Poland, Russia and China as Type 59 (qv).

PT-76 Light Amphibious Tank (Russia)

Key recognition features

● Hull has pointed nose with vertical sides, turret mounted well to front of chassis, rear of driver
● Round turret with sloping sides and flat roof with large oval-shaped roof hatch opening forwards
● Suspension has six ribbed road wheels, idler front, drive sprocket rear, no track-return rollers

Specifications

Crew: 3
Armament: 1 x 76.2mm (main), 1 x 7.62mm MG (coaxial)
Ammunition: 40 x 76.2mm, 1,000 x 7.62mm
Length gun forwards: 7.66m
Length hull: 7.22m
Width: 3.17m
Height: 2.255m (late model), 2.195m (early model)
Ground clearance: 0.34mm
Weight, combat: 14,600kg
Power-to-weight ratio: 16.4hp/tonne
Ground pressure: 0.50kg/cm²
Engine: Model V-6B 6-cylinder in-line water-cooled diesel developing 240hp at 1,800rpm
Maximum road speed: 44km/hr
Maximum water speed: 10km/hr
Road range: 394km
Fuel capacity: 250 lit
Fording: Amphibious
Vertical obstacle: 1.1m
Trench: 2.8m
Gradient: 70%
Side slope: 35%
Armour: 14mm (maximum)
Armour type: Steel
NBC system: No
Night vision equipment: Yes (infra-red for driver)

Top: PT-76 (insert shows early barrel)

Development

PT-76 was developed shortly after the Second World War with first production vehicles completed in 1950 and production continuing until the late 1960s. In Russian army units PT-76 has been replaced by MBTs or specialised versions of BMP-1/BMP/2.

Many automotive components of PT-76 were subsequently used in the BTR-50P amphibious APC, which has a similar chassis.

Drivers sits front, two-man turret centre, engine and transmission rear. It is fully amphibious, propelled in the water by its tracks. Before entering the water the trim vane is erected at front and bilge pumps switched on. To extend the operational range of PT-76 auxiliary fuel tanks can be installed on rear decking; these contain an additional 180 litres and extend road range to 480km.

Main armament comprises a D-56T with elevation from -4˚ to +30˚, turret traverses through 360˚. Ammunition fired includes AP-T, API-T, HE-FRAG, HEAT and HVAP-T. Some PT-76s have been fitted with a roof-mounted 12.7mm DShKM MG.

Variants

First production vehicles had D-56T gun with a multi-slotted muzzle brake, but most common version has a double baffle muzzle brake and bore evacuator towards muzzle.

PT-76B has D-56TM fully stabilised gun.

China has produced an improved version of PT-76, Type 63 (qv), which has a new turret with 85mm gun.

Status

Production complete. In service with Afghanistan, Angola, Benin, Cambodia, Congo, Cuba, Guinea, Guinea-Bissau, Indonesia, Iraq, Madagascar, Nicaragua, North Korea, Laos, Poland, Vietnam, and Zambia.

Manufacturer

Russian state arsenals.

Above: PT-76
(Richard Stickland)

Hyundai Type 88 MBT (South Korea)

Key recognition features

● Blunt nose with almost horizontal glacis plate, driver's hatch in left side, turret centre, raised engine compartment at rear

● Front of turret slopes slightly to rear, sides slope inwards with turret rear vertical. Stowage basket on either side of turret with bank of smoke grenade dischargers on either side of turret. 7.62mm MG on left side of turret roof with 12.7mm MG on right side.

● Suspension either side has six road wheels, idler front, drive sprocket at rear, return rollers with upper part of running gear covered by armoured skirt that extends to rear of vehicle

Specifications

Crew: 4
Armament: 1 x 105mm, 1 x 7.62mm MG (coaxial), 1 x 7.62mm MG (anti-aircraft), 1 x 12.7mm MG (anti-aircraft), 1 x 12.7mm MG (anti-aircraft), 2 x 6 smoke grenade dischargers
Ammunition: 47 x 105mm, 2,000 x 12.7mm, 8,800 x 7.62mm
Length gun forwards: 9.672m
Length hull: 7.477m
Width: 3.594m
Height to turret top: 2.248m
Ground clearance: 0.46m
Weight, combat: 51,000kg
Power-to-weight ratio: 23.5hp/tonne
Ground pressure: 0.86kg/cm²
Engine: MTU 871 Ka-501 diesel developing 1,200hp at 2,600rpm
Maximum road speed: 65km/h
Cruising range: 500km
Fuel capacity: Not available
Fording without kit: 1.2m
Fording with kit: 1.8m
Vertical obstacle: 1m
Trench: 2.74m
Gradient: 60%
Side slope: 30%
Armour: Classified
Armour type: Laminate
NBC system: Yes
Night vision equipment: Yes

Development

The Type 88 MBT (previously known as the XK-1) was developed by the now General Dynamic Land Systems Division (who designed and built the M1/M1A1 and M1A2 Abrams series of MBT) to meet the specific operational requirements of the South Korean Army. The first of two prototypes was completed in the United States in 1983 and production commenced by Hyundai Precision & Ind Co Ltd at Changwon in 1985/1986 and since then it is estimated that 1000 vehicles have been manufactured. Many of the key sub-systems, such as engine, transmission, fire control system and sights were developed overseas.

Layout of the Type 88 MBT is conventional with the driver at front left, turret in centre and powerpack at the rear. The commander and gunner are seated on the right of the turret with the loader on the left. Turret traverse and weapon elevation is powered with manual controls for emergency use. The 105mm rifled tank gun has an elevation of +20° and a depression of -10° with turret traverse being a full 360°. An unusual feature of the Type 88 MBT is its hybrid suspension type which has torsion bars at the centre road wheel stations with hydro-pneumatic units at the front and rear stations, this allows the driver to adjust the suspension to suit the type of terrain being crossed.

The computerised fire control system includes a stabilised sight for the tank commander, digital computer, day/night sights and a laser rangefinder. A fire detection/suppression system is fitted as is a heater.

A new version of the Type 88 is under development with a number of improvements including a 120mm smooth bore gun.

Variants

AVLB, the bridge and launching system was designed and built by Vickers Defence Systems of the UK in 1990 and integrated

on a modified Type 88 chassis in South Korea. Launches a
scissors bridge with a length of 22m when opened out.
ARV, this was developed by MaK and is similar to the Leopard 1
ARV and has a winch, dozer/stabiliser blade and hydraulic crane
for changing powerpacks in the field.

Status
In production. In service with South Korean Army.

Manufacturer
Hyundai Precision & Ind Co Ltd, Changwon, South Korea

Above left:
Prototype of
Type 88 MBT

Top right:
Type 88 MBT

Right:
Type 88 MBT

Bofors Stridsvagn 103 MBT (Sweden)

Key recognition features

● 105mm gun fixed centre of well sloped glacis plate which extends half-way along vehicle, horizontal roof, vertical hull rear, two rectangular stowage boxes rear
● Commander's cupola with external 7.62mm MG on right side of hull top, driver's hatch to his left, dozer blade mounted under nose
● Suspension each side has four road wheels, drive sprocket front, idler rear, two track-return rollers, flotation screen (collapsed around hull top)

Specifications

Crew: 3
Armament: 1 x 105mm, 2 x 7.62mm MG (coaxial), 1 x 7.62mm MG (anti-aircraft), 8 smoke grenade dischargers, 2 x Lyran launchers
Length gun forwards: 8.99m
Length hull: 7.04m
Width: 3.63m
Height overall: 2.43m
Weight, combat: 39,700kg
Weight, unloaded: 37,000kg
Power-to-weight ratio: 18.4hp/tonne
Ground pressure: 1.04kg/cm²
Engines: Rolls-Royce K60 multi-fuel developing 240bhp at 3,750rpm, Boeing 553 gas turbine developing 490shp at 38,000rpm (but see text)
Maximum road speed: 50km/hr
Maximum water speed: 6km/hr
Maximum road range: 390km
Fuel capacity: 960 lit
Fording: 1.5m, amphibious with preparation
Vertical obstacle: 0.9m
Trench: 2.3m
Gradient: 60%
Side slope: 40%
Armour: Classified
Armour type: Steel
NBC system: None
Night vision equipment: None

Development

Stridsvagn 103, commonly known as S-tank, was developed in the late 1950s by Bofors to meet requirements of the Swedish Army. First prototypes completed in 1961 and production undertaken from 1966 to 1971, by which time 300 had been built. First models were Stridsvagn 103s. Later models, with the flotation screen and dozer blade, were Stridsvagn 103Bs; all vehicles were eventually brought up to this standard.

Stridsvagn 103 is unique in that the 105mm gun is fixed in the glacis plate and is aimed in traverse by pivoting the vehicle on its tracks, and in elevation by adjusting the hydropneumatic suspension from -10˚ to +12˚, with driver acting as gunner. The 105mm gun has an automatic loader and fires APDS, APFSDS, HE and smoke rounds, empty cartridge cases being automatically ejected from the rear. Two 7.62mm MGs are mounted on left hull front, aligned to 105mm gun. Engine compartment at front of vehicle, driver front left, commander to his right, radio operator rear of driver, magazine rear.

For road use the Rolls-Royce diesel is normally used with the Boeing gas turbine engaged when in combat or moving across country. A flotation screen is carried (collapsed around top of hull) and when erected the vehicle is propelled in the water by its tracks. A dozer blade is mounted under front of vehicle.

In 1986 the Swedish Army took delivery of the first modernised vehicles known as Strv 103C, which have many improvements including replacement of Rolls-Royce diesel by a Detroit Diesel 6V-53T developing 290hp at 2,800rpm, modified transmission, laser rangefinder and fuel cans arranged alongside hull sides.

A laser rangefinder has been fitted for improved first round hit probability and Lyran launchers that launch illuminating rockets have been fitted. The S-tank is now being replaced by the Leopard 2 MBT.

Variants

No variants except for the **Strv 103C**. The Strv 103C can be fitted with mineclearing rollers at the front of the hull and components of the vehicle are used in the Swedish Bandkanon 1A 155mm self-propelled gun (qv).

Status

Production complete. In service with Swedish Army only.

Manufacturer

Bofors AB, Bofors, Sweden

***Right:
Bofors Strv
103B***

***Below:
Bofors Strv
103C with
additional
armour***

Hagglunds Vehicle Ikv-91 Tank Destroyer (Sweden)

Key recognition features

● Six large road wheels, drive sprocket rear, idler front, wavy side skirt covers upper part of track

● Long thin gun barrel with thermal sleeve and fume extractor

● Turret to rear of well sloped glacis plate

Specifications

Crew: 4
Armament: 1 x 90mm gun, 1 x 7.62mm coaxial MG, 1 x 7.62mm AA MG, 2 x 6 smoke grenade dischargers, 2 x Lyran launchers
Ammunition: 59 x 90mm, 4,250 x 7.62mm
Length gun forwards: 8.84m
Length hull: 6.41m
Width: 3m
Height: 2.32m (top of commander's cupola)
Ground clearance: 0.37m
Weight, combat: 16,300kg
Power-to-weight ratio: 20.2hp/tonne
Ground pressure: 0.49kg/cm2
Engine: Volvo-Penta TD 120 A, 4-stroke 6-cylinder turbocharged diesel developing 330hp at 2,200rpm
Maximum road speed: 65km/hr
Maximum water speed: 6.5km/hr
Maximum road range: 500km
Fuel capacity: 400 lit
Fording: Amphibious
Vertical obstacle: 0.8m
Trench: 2.8m
Gradient: 60%
Side slope: 30%
Armour: Classified but protects against 20mm over frontal arc
Armour type: Steel
NBC system: Yes
Night vision equipment: None

Development

The Ikv 91 (Infanterikanonvagn 91) tank destroyer was developed by H%ogglund and S¨ner (now H%ogglunds Vehicle) to meet requirements of Swedish Army. First prototypes completed in 1969 with production running from 1975 to 1978.

The 90mm low pressure gun has elevation of +15 degrees and depression of -10, with 360 degree turret traverse. Two Lyran flare launchers mounted on turret roof.

The Ikv 91 is fully amphibious, propelled by its tracks. Before entering the water a trim vane is erected at front of hull, screens erected round air inlets, exhaust and air outlets, and bilge pumps switched on.

Computerised fire-control system has laser rangefinder for increased first-round hit probability. Tracks can be fitted with studs or spikes for deep snow. More recently, vehicles have been modified with Bofors Lyran launchers, thermal sleeve for low pressure gun and additional external stowage.

Variants

Ikv 91 with 105mm gun is still at prototype stage and has 90mm Bofors low pressure gun replaced by 105mm weapon. Optional equipment includes passive night vision equipment, increased armour protection and propellers for increased water speed.

Status

Production complete. In service with Swedish Army only.

Manufacturer

Hagglunds Vehicle AB, Ornsk¨ldsvik, Sweden.

Above: Ikv 91 with trim vane on glacis plate

Ikv 91

Pz 68 MBT (Switzerland)

Key recognition features

● Cast hull front with rounded nose and well sloped glacis plate, trim board just above nose, driver's hatch in upper part (hinges to rear), turret centre, enginer rear in engine compartment roof sloping slightly to rear. Three stowage boxes above racks in line with turret

● Rounded cast turret in centre, loader's cupola on left side with externally mounted 7.5mm MG, stowage basket on upper rear of turret (unusual in having no bustle), 105mm gun with fume extrctor and thermal sleeve

● Suspension each side has six road wheels, drive sprocket rear, idler front and three track-return rollers

Specifications

Crew: 4
Armament: 1 x 105mm, 1 x 7.5mm MG (coaxial), 1 x 7.5mm MG (anti-aircraft), 2 x 3 smoke grenade dischargers
Ammunition: 56 x 105mm, 5,200 x 7.5mm
Length gun forwards: 9.49m
Length hull: 6.88m
Width: 3.14m
Height with AA MG: 2.88m
Height to commander's cupola: 2.75m
Ground clearance: 0.41m
Weight, combat: 39,700kg
Weight, empty: 38,700kg
Power-to-weight ratio: 16.62hp/tonne
Ground pressure: 0.86kg/cm^2
Engine: MTU MB 837 8-cylinder diesel developing 660hp at 2,200rpm
Maximum road speed: 55km/hr
Maximum road range: 350km
Fuel capacity: 710 lit
Fording: 1.1m
Vertical obstacle: 0.75m
Trench: 2.6m
Gradient: 60%
Side slope: 30%
Armour: 120mm (maximum)
Armour type: Steel
NBC system: Yes
Night vision equipment: None

Development

Further development of the Pz 61 (qv) by the Federal Construction Works at Thun resulted in the Pz 68, with first prototype completed in 1968. Major differences are stabilisation system for the 105mm gun, more powerful engine, modified transmission, wider tracks with replaceable rubber pads and greater length of track in contact with ground.

Between 1971 and 1974, 170 Pz 68s (later designated Pz 68 Mk 1) were delivered to the Swiss Army. In 1977, 50 Pz 68 Mk 2s were delivered; these have thermal sleeve for 105mm gun, system for extracting carbon monoxide, and alternator. A total of 110 Pz 68 Mk3s were delivered during 1978-79, which have all improvements of the Mk 1 and Mk 2 plus a larger turret. Last production model was the Pz 68 Mk 4, 60 of which were delivered during 1983-84 almost identical to the Mk 3.

Layout is identical to the Pz 61 with driver front, turret centre, commander and gunner right, loader left, engine and transmission rear. 105mm gun fires APDS, APFSDS, HE and smoke projectiles. Turret traverses through 360°, gun power-elevates from -10° to +21°.

In 1988 it was decided to upgrade 195 Pz 68 MBTs to the Pz 68/88 standard. This will have a new fire control system, muzzle reference system, stabilised sight for gunner with eyepiece for commander, upgraded suspension and improved NBC system. These upgraded vehicles are known as the Pz 68/88.

Variants

Entpannungspanzer Pz 65 ARV.
Brückenlegepanzer Pz 68 armoured bridgelayer.
Target tank (Pz Zielfz 68) has additional armour protection and new turret with dummy gun.
For trials purposes a Pz 68 MBT has been upgraded with a 120mm Compact Tank Gun.

Status

Production complete. In service with Swiss Army only.

Manufacturer

Federal Construction Works, Thun, Switzerland.

Above: Pz 68 Mk 3 (Swiss Army)

Top right: Pz 68 Mk 1/2 (Swiss Army)

Right: Pz Zielfz 68 target tank (Swiss Army)

Pz 61 MBT (Switzerland)

Key recognition features

● Cast hull front with rounded nose and well sloped glacis plate, driver's hatch in upper part (hinged to rear), turret centre, engine rear with engine compartment roof sloping slightly to rear. Three stowage boxes above tracks in line with turret

● Rounded cast turret centre, loader's cupola on left with externally mounted 7.5mm MG, stowage basket on upper rear of turret (unusual in having no bustle), 105mm gun with fume extractor and thermal sleeve

● Suspension each side has six road wheels, drive sprocket rear, idler front and three track-return rollers

Specifications

Crew: 4
Armament: 1 x 105mm, 1 x 7.5mm MG (coaxial), 1 x 7.5mm MG (anti-aircraft), 2 x 3 smoke grenade dischargers
Ammunition: 52 x 105mm, 5,400 x 7.5mm
Length gun forwards: 9.43m
Length hull: 6.78m
Width: 3.08m
Height with AA MG: 2.85m
Height to commander's cupola: 2.72m
Ground clearance: 0.42m
Weight, combat: 38,000kg
Weight, empty: 37,000kg
Power-to-weight ratio: 17hp/tonne
Ground pressure: 0.85kg/cm²
Engine: MTU MB 837 8-cylinder diesel developing 630bhp at 2,200rpm
Maximum road speed: 55km/hr
Maximum road range: 300km
Fuel capacity: 760 lit
Fording: 1.1m
Vertical obstacle: 0.75m
Trench: 2.6m
Gradient: 60%
Side slope: 30%
Armour: 120mm (Maximum)
Armour type: Steel
NBC system: Yes
Night vision equipment: None

Development

In the 1950s the Federal Construction Works at Thun commenced development work on an MBT to meet the requirements of the Swiss Army. First of two prototypes was completed as KW 30 in 1958, armed with a 90mm gun. They were followed by ten pre-production tanks, the Panzer 58 (or Pz 58), armed with 20 Pounder guns as installed in the Centurion. In 1961 a production order was placed for 150 Pz 61s, similar to the Pz 58 but with modifications including replacement of the 20 Pounder gun by the British 105mm L7. Pz 61s were deli9vered to the Swiss Army between January 1965 and December 1966. Further development of the Pz 61 resulted in the Pz 68 (qv).

Layout is conventional, with driver front, turret centre, engine from -10° to +21° and fires APDS, APFSDS, HE and smoke projectiles, turret traverses through 360°.

All Pz 61s have been modernised to the Pz 61 AA9 configuration, with modifications including 20mm coaxial cannon replaced by 7.5mm coaxial MG, new radio and air filter, thermal sleeve for 105mm gun and improved maintenance facilities.

Variants

No variants.

Status

Production complete. In service with Swiss Army only. The Pz 61 MBT is now being phased out of service with the Swiss Army.

Manufacturer

Federal Construction Works, Thun, Switzerland.

Above: Pz 61 AA9 (Swiss Army)

Above right: Pz 61 AA9 (Swiss Army)

Right: Pz 61 (Stephen Tunbridge)

Vickers Defence Systems Challenger 2 MBT (UK)

Key recognition features

● Front idlers project ahead of nose which slopes back under hull front, well sloped glacis plate with driver's hatch recessed in centre, slightly raised engine compartment at rear. Hull rear slopes inwards at sharp angle

● Turret has well sloped front angled to rear, turret sides and rear vertical, gunner's sight on right side of turret roof, raised periscopic sight in front of commander's cupola, 7.62mm machine gun above loader's position

● Suspension either side has six road wheels, idler front, drive sprocket rear, four track-return rollers. Upper part of suspension covered by skirts

Specifications
Crew: 4
Armament: 1 x 120mm, 1 x 7.62mm MG (coaxial), 1 x 7.62mm MG (anti-aircraft), 2 x 5 smoke grenade dischargers
Ammunition: 50 x 120mm, 4,000 x 7.62mm
Length gun forwards: 11.55m
Length hull: 8.327m
Width: 3.52m
Height: 2.49m (turret roof)
Ground clearance: 0.50m
Weight, combat: 62,500kg
Power-to-weight ratio: 19.2hp/tonne
Ground pressure: 0.9kg/cm²
Engine: Perkins Engines (Shrewsbury) Condor V-12 12-cylinder diesel developing 1,200bhp at 2,300rpm
Maximum road speed: 56km/h

Range: 450km
Fuel capacity: 1592 lit
Fording: 1.07m
Vertical obstacle: 0.9m
Trench: 2.34m
Gradient: 60%
Side slope: 30%
Armour: Classified
Armour type: Chobham/steel
NBC system: Yes
Night vision equipment: Yes (passive for commander, gunner and driver)

Development
The Challenger 2 was originally developed as a private venture by Vickers Defence Systems and was selected by the British

Right:
Challenger 2 MBT

Above:
Challenger 2
MBT

Army in 1991 to meet its requirement for a MBT to replace the Chieftain MBT. First production Challenger 2 MBTs were completed in mid-1994. As of late 1995 the British Army had ordered 386 Challenger 2 MBTs, Oman ordered 18.

Although the Challenger 2 has some external resemblance to the earlier Challenger 1 MBT it is essentially a new MBT. The new turret is armed with a Royal Ordnance 120mm L30 rifled tank gun. Turret traverse and gun elevation is all electric and gun is fully stabilised. Turret traverse is a full 360° with weapon elevation from -10° to +20°. A 7.62mm

Vickers Defence Systems Challenger 2 MBT (UK)

machine gun is mounted coaxial to the left of the main armament and a 7.62mm machine gun is mounted at the loader's station. The computerised fire control system gives a high first round hit probability with the thermal camera over the 120mm gun mantlet being coupled to the gunner's sight. The commander has a roof mounted 360° stabilised periscopic day sight that also includes a laser rangefinder.

The driver is seated at the front of the vehicle, turret in the centre and the engine and transmission at the rear. The commander and gunner are seated on the right of the turret with the loader on the left. To increase the operational range of the tank additional fuel tanks can be fitted at the rear of the hull. A dozer blade can be mounted at the front of the hull.

Variants
A Challenger 2 Driver Training Tank has been developed. This is a Challenger 2 with its turret removed and fitted with a new module with seats for the instructor and additional students.

Status
Production. In service with Oman and the UK.

Manufacturer
Vickers Defence Systems, Leeds and Newcastle-upon-Tyne, UK.

Left: Challenger 2 MBT

Right: Challenger 2 MBT

Vickers Defence Systems Challenger MBT 1 (UK)

Key recognition features

● Front idlers project ahead of nose which slopes back under hull, well sloped glacis plate with driver's hatch recessed in centre, turret centre, slightly raised engine compartment rear, hull rear slopes inwards at sharp angle

● Turret has well sloped front angled to rear, turret sides vertical. Commander's cupola on right side with external 7.62mm MG, opening in right side of turret for TOGS

● Suspension each side has six road wheels, idler front, drive sprocket rear, four track-return rollers. Upper part of road wheels and suspension covered by skirts

Specifications

Crew: 4
Armament: 1 x 120mm, 1 x 7.62mm MG (coaxial), 1 x 7.62mm MG (anti-aircraft), 2 x 5 smoke grenade dischargers
Ammunition: 64 x 120mm, 4,000 x 7.62mm
Length gun forwards: 11.56mm
Length hull: 8.327m
Height to top of commander's sight: 2.95m
Height to turret top: 2.5m
Ground clearance: 0.5m
Power-to-weight ratio: 19.35bhp/tonne
Width overall: 3.518m
Weight, combat: 62,000kg
Weight, empty: 60,000 kg]
Ground pressure: 0.97kg/cm²
Engine: Perkins Engines (Shrewsbury) Condor 12V 1,200 12-cylinder diesel developing 1,200bhp at 2,300rpm
Maximum road speed: 56km/hr

Maximum range: 450m
Fuel capacity: 1,592 lit
Fording: 1.07m
Gradient: 58%
Side slope: 40%
Armour: Classified
Armour type: Chobham/steel
Vertical obstacle: 0.9m
NBC system: Yes
Trench: 2.8m
Night vision equipment: Yes (passive for commander, gunner and driver)

Development

Challenger 1 is a development of the Shir 2 MBT originally built to meet for Iran. First production tanks were delivered by Royal Ordnance Leeds (taken over by Vickers Defence Systems in 1986) in March 1983 and production continued to 1990 by

Right: Challenger 1

which time 420 had been built. Further development resulted in the Challenger 2 MBT (qv).

Challenger has Chobham armour in its hull and turret, which gives a high degree of protection against both kinetic and chemical energy attack. Driver sits front, turret centre, engine and transmission rear.

Commander and gunner sit right of turret, loader left. 120mm L11A5 rifled gun is identical to Chieftain's and power-elevates from -10˚ to +20˚, with turret traverse 360˚. Ammunition includes APDS-T, APFSDS-T, HESH, smoke and training, all rounds of separate loading type. A 7.62mm MG is mounted coaxial to left of main armament, and a second on the commander's cupola. The Improved Fire Control System includes laser rangefinder. Challenger 1s have been fitted with the Barr and Stroud Thermal Observation and Gunnery system. It is expected that the Challenger 1 MBT will be phased out of British Army service by the year 2000, its replacement being the Challenger 2 MBT.

Challenger 1

Variants
Challenger 1 can be fitted with front mounted dozer blade or mine clearing systems.
Challenger 1s used in Middle East were fitted with additional armour protection.
Challenger Armoured Repair and Recovery Vehicle.
Challenger Driver Training Tank, Challenger 1 with turret replaced by non-rotating turret.

Status
Production complete. In service with British Army.

Manufacturer
Vickers Defence Systems, Leeds, England.

*Right:
Challenger 1*

Alvis Scorpion Reconnaissance Vehicle (UK)

Key recognition features

● Rounded nose with well sloped glacis plate, driver's hatch in upper left side and louvres to right, horizontal hull top, vertical hull rear with oblong stowage box

● Turret on hull top to rear with short-barrelled 76mm gun, no muzzle brake or fume extractor, sight to right of 76mm gun. Upper part of turret sides slope inwards to roof, lower turret sides slope inwards towards hull roof. Stowage box each side of turret

● Suspension each side has five large road wheels, drive sprocket front, idler rear, no track-return rollers. Original flotation screen round hull top has been removed from British Army vehicles. Long stowage box above rear road wheels

Right: Alvis Scimitar

Specifications
Crew: 3
Armament: 1 x 76mm, 1 x 7.62mm MG (coaxial), 2 x 4 smoke grenade dischargers
Ammunition: 40 x 76mm, 3,000 x 7.62mm
Length: 4.794m
Width: 2.235m
Height: 2.102m
Ground clearance: 0.356m
Weight combat: 8,073kg
Power-to-weight ratio: 23.54bhp/tonne

Ground pressure: 0.36kg/cm²
Engine: Jaguar J60 4.2 lit 6-cylinder petrol developing 190hp at 4,750rpm
Maximum road speed: 80.5km/hr
Maximum range: 644km
Fuel capacity: 423 lit
Fording: 1.067m, amphibious with preparation
Vertical obstacle: 0.5m
Trench: 2.057m
Gradient: 60%
Side slope: 40%

Armour: Classified
Armour type: Aluminium
NBC system: Yes
Night vision equipment: Yes

Development

Scorpion (FV101), officially named Combat Vehicle
Reconnaissance (Tracked), was developed by Alvis to replace
Saladin armoured car. First prototype completed in 1969 and
first production vehicles in 1972. By 1996 well over 3,500
had been built for home and export. Driver sits front left
with engine to right and two-man turret rear. Turret has
commander on left and gunner right. Turret traverse is
manual through 360° and 76mm gun elevates from -10° to
+35°. Main armament fires HESH, HE and smoke rounds with
7.62mm MG mounted coaxial to left. Flotation screen is
carried collapsed round top of hull which when erected
makes vehicle fully amphibious, propelled by its tracks. Wide
range of optional equipment available including various fire-
control systems, laser rangefinders, diesel engine, 90mm gun,
7.62mm anti-aircraft MG and air-conditioning system. The
standard 76mm Scorpion is no longer used by the British
Army.

Variants

Scorpion 90 has Belgian Cockerill 90mm MK III gun.
Striker (FV102) ATGW carrier.
Spartan (FV103), APC member of family (see APCs).
Stormer, based on components of CVR(T) (see APCs).
Streaker high mobility loader carrier, prototypes.
Samson (FV106), ARV member of family.
Samaritan (FV104), armoured ambulance with higher roof.

Alvis Scorpion (76mm)

*Below: Alvis
Scorpion
(90mm)*

Alvis Scorpion Reconnaissance Vehicle (UK)

Right: Alvis Sultan command post (Terry Gander)

Sultan (FV105), command post vehicle with higher roof.
Scimitar (FV107), similar to Scorpion, but has 30mm RARDEN cannon in two-man turret.
Sabre, is Scorpion chassis with Fox turret (UK only).

Status

In production. In service with Belgium, Botswana, Brunei, Chile, Honduras, Indonesia, Iran, Ireland, Malaysia, New Zealand, Nigeria, Oman, Spain, Tanzania, Thailand, Togo, Philippines, United Arab Emirates, UK and Venezuela.

Manufacturer

Alvis Limited, Coventry, West Midlands, England, UK

Left: Alvis Scimitar (Richard Stickland)

Right: Alvis Samaritan ambulance (Terry Gander)

Khalid MBT (UK)

Key recognition features

● Well sloped glacis plate with driver's circular hatch in upper part, turret centre and raised engine compartment rear. Vertical sides.

● 120mm gun mounted internally. Turret identical to Chieftain's except for external stowage, commander's cupola has tall day/night sight with 7.62mm MG left, no day/night searchlight on left side of turret

● Suspension has six road wheels, drive sprocket rear, idler front and three track-return rollers. Upper part of suspension covered by track guards

Specifications

Crew: 4
Armament: 1 x 120mm, 1 x 7.62mm MG (coaxial), 1 x 7.62mm MG (anti-aircraft), 2 x 6 smoke grenade dischargers
Ammunition: 65 x 120mm, 6,000 x 7.62mm
Length gun forwards: 10.795m
Length hull: 8.39m
Width: 3.518m
Height overall: 3.012m
Ground clearance: 0.508m
Weight, combat: 58,000kg
Weight, empty: 56,500kg
Power-to-weight ratio: 20.68bhp/tonne
Ground pressure: 0.9kg/cm²
Engine: Perkins Condor 12V 12-cylinder diesel developing 1,200bhp at 2,300 rpm
Maximum road speed: 56km/hr
Maximum range: 450km (estimate)
Fuel capacity: 1,200 lit (estimate)
Fording: 1.066m
Vertical obstacle: 0.914m
Trench: 3.149m
Gradient: 60%
Side slope: 40%
Armour: Classified
Armour type: Steel
NBC system: Yes
Night vision equipment: Yes (passive for commander, gunner and driver)

Development

In 1974 Royal Ordnance Leeds was awarded contracts by the Iranian Government for 125 Shir 1s and 1,225 Shir 2s, but in 1979 the order was cancelled by the new government although Shir 1 production was then under way. In 1979, Jordan ordered 274 slightly modified Shir 1s under the name Khalid, which were delivered from 1981. Khalid is essentially a late production Chieftain with major changes to the fire-control system and powerpack; the latter is the same as Challenger 1 MBT used by the British Army.

Driver sits front, turret is centre and engine and transmission rear. The 120mm gun has no depression over hull rear. Commander and gunner sit on turret right, loader on left. The 120mm L11A5 rifled gun is identical to that in Chieftain and Challenger 1, and power-elevates from -10˚ to +20˚ with turret traverse through 360˚. Types of ammunition include APDS-T, APFSDS-T, HESH, smoke and training, all rounds with separate loading. A 7.62mm MG is mounted coaxial to left of main armament and a second is mounted on the commander's cupola.

Khalid has a Pilkington Condor commander's day/night sight. Barr and Stroud laser rangefinder and a GEC-Marconi Improved Fire Control System and all electric gun control and stabilisation system. It is also fitted with the Kidde-Graviner Crew Bay explosion and detection system.

Variants

No variants.

Status

Production complete. In service with Jordan.

Manufacturer

Royal Ordnance Factory Leeds, England, taken over by Vickers Defence Systems in 1986.

Chieftain Mk 5 MBT (UK)

Key recognition features

● Well sloped glacis plate with driver's hatch in upper part, splash board across lower part of glacis plate, turret centre, raised engine compartment rear. Long stowage boxes each side of engine compartment

● Cast turret has well sloped front, 120mm gun mounted in internal mantlet has thermal sleeve and fume extractor. Commander's cupola right side of turret roof, NBC pack on turret rear, stowage basket each side of turret rear

● Suspension each side has six road wheels, drive sprocket rear, idler front and track-return rollers. Upper part normally covered by skirts

Right: Chieftain with Stillbrew armour and TOGS (Richard Stickland)

Far right: Cheiftain Mk 5

Specifications

Crew: 4
Armament: 1 x 120mm gun, 1 x 7.62mm MG (coaxial), 1 x 7.62mm MG (commander's cupola), 1 x 12.7mm RMG (see text), 2 x 6 smoke grenade dischargers
Ammunition: 64 x 120mm, 300 x 12.7mm (see text), 6,000 x 7.62mm
Length gun forwards: 10.795
Length hull: 7.518m
Width hull: 3.504m
Weight empty: 53,500kg
Height overall: 2.895m
Ground clearance: 0.508m
Weight combat: 55,000kg
Power-to-weight ratio: 13.63hp/tonne
Ground pressure: 0.9kg/cm²
Engine: Leyland L60, 2-stroke, compression ignition, 6 cylinder (12 opposed pistons) multi-fuel developing 750bhp at 2,100rpm
Maximum road speed: 48km/hr
Maximum range: 400 to 500km

Chieftain Mk 5 MBT (UK)

Chieftain Mk 3

Fuel capacity: 950 lit
Fording: 1.066m
Vertical obstacle: 0.914m
Trench: 3.149m
Gradient: 60%
Side slope: 40%
Armour: Classified
Armour type: Steel
NBC system: Yes
Night vision equipment: Yes (for commander, gunner and driver)

Development

Developed from late 1950s with first prototypes completed in 1959, first production vehicles completed in early 1970s, production continuing until 1978. Layout conventional with driver front, turret centre and engine and transmission rear. Commander and gunner sit right of turret with loader left. Main armament consists of 120mm L11 series rifled gun mounted in powered turret with 360° traverse. Main armament elevates from -10° to +20°. Ammunition is separate loading type (eg projectile and charge) and ammunition includes APFSDS, APDS, HESH and smoke. 7.62mm MG is mounted coaxial, with similar weapon on commander's cupola. Original version used 12.7mm ranging MG but was replaced on British Army vehicles by a Tank Laser Sight (TLS). Computerised fire-control system and main armament stabilised. All front line British Army Chieftains have had search light on left side of turret removed and are fitted with Thermal Observation and Gunnery Sight. Chieftain can be fitted with front-mounted dozer blade and mineclearing systems.

Variants

British: Mk 1, Mk 1/2, Mk 1/3, Mk 1/4, Mk 2, Mk 3, Mk 3/S, Mk 3/3, Mk 5, Mk 6, Mk 7, Mk 8, Mk 9, Mk 10, Mk 11 and Mk 12 for British Army. Mk 9 onwards have Improved Fire Control System (IFCS). Chieftain Stillbrew is British Army Chieftain MBT only with additional armour each side of turret front.
Mk 3/3P is Mk 3/3 for Iran.
Mk 5/2K is Mk 5 for Kuwait.
Mk 5/3P is Mk 5 for Iran.
Shir 1 was modified Chieftain for Iran but became Khalid (qv).
Qayis Al Ardh is modified Chieftain for Oman.
Chieftain ARV and **ARRV**.
Chieftain AVLB.
Chieftain AVRE.

Status

Production complete. In service with Iran, Iraq, Jordan (ARV only), Kuwait, Oman and UK.

Manufacturers

Royal Ordnance Leeds (taken over by Vickers in 1986); Vickers Defence Systems, Newcastle-upon-Tyne, England, UK.

Above: Chieftain Mk 3

Top right: Chieftain Mk 5

Right: Chieftain Mk 5/2K for Kuwait

Vickers Defence Systems Mk 3 MBT (UK)

Key recognition features

● Well sloped glacis plate, horizontal hull top with driver's hatch right side to immediate rear of glacis plate, turret centre, slightly raised engine compartment rear, vertical hull rear with projecting track guards
● Turret has cast rounded front and external mantlet for 105mm gun with fume extractor and thermal sleeve, stowage boxes each side to turret rear, stowage basket on turret rear, commander's cupola right side of turret roof with prominent day/night sight in forward part
● Suspension each side has six road wheels, large idler front, drive sprocket rear and three track-return rollers. Upper part of track and suspension normally covered by sheet steel skirts which are ribbed horizontally

Specifications

Crew: 4
Armament: 1 x 105mm, 1 x 7.62mm MG (coaxial), 1 x 7.62mm MG (anti-aircraft), 1 x 12.7mm MG (ranging), 2 x 6 smoke grenade dischargers
Ammunition: 50 x 105mm, 700 x 12.7mm, 2,600 x 7.62mm
Length gun forwards: 9.788mm
Length hull: 7.561m
Width: 3.168m
Height to commander's cupola: 3.099m
Height to turret roof: 2.476m
Ground clearance: 0.432m
Weight, combat: 40,000kg
Weight, empty: 37,500kg
Power-to-weight ratio: 18bhp/tonne
Ground pressure: 0.89kg/cm^2
Engine: Detroit Diesel 12V-71T turbocharged diesel developing 720bhp at 2,500rpm
Maximum road speed: 50km/hr
Maximum road range: 530km
Fuel capacity: 1,000 lit
Fording: 1.1m
Vertical obstacle: 0.83m
Trench: 3m
Gradient: 60%
Side slope: 30%
Armour: 80mm (maximum) (estimate)
Armour type: Steel
NBC system: Optional
Night vision equipment: Optional (passive)

Development

In late-1950 Vickers Defence Systems designed a new MBT specifically for export which used the standard 105mm L7 rifled tank gun and automotive components of the Chieftain MBT. It was subsequently adopted by the Indian Army with first vehicles, designated Vickers Mk 1 (Vijayanta by India), completed in the UK. Production also began at a new tank plant at Avadi, India. First production vehicles, completed in India in 1965. Production was completed in India in the mid-1980s, by which time about 2,200 had been built. The Vickers Mk 1 differed from the current Mk 3 in having a Leyland L60 engine (as in Chieftain) and a welded turret. Vickers also built 70 Mk 1s for Kuwait, delivered between 1970 and 1972.

Vickers Mk 2 was never built and further development of Mk 1 resulted in Mk 3 which has a new engine and new turret with cast front. Kenya ordered 38 Mk 3s and three ARVs in 1977, with a second order for 38 Mk 3s and four5 ARVs in 1978. In 1981 Nigeria ordered 36 Mk 3s, five ARVs and six AVLBs, with a repeat order in 1985. Final deliveries were made late in 1986. In 1990 Vickers Defence Systems received another order from Nigeria with first vehicles being completed late in 1991.

Layout of the Mk 3 is conventional, with driver front right, turret centre, commander and gunner right, loader left, engine and transmission rear. 105mm gun power-elevates from -10° to +20°, turret traverses 360°. Gun fires full range of NATO ammunition including APFSDS, APDS, HESH and smoke. A 7.62mm MG is mounted coaxial with main armament and a 12.7mm ranging MG is installed. Commander's cupola has 7.62mm MG which can be aimed from inside the vehicle.

A wide range of optional equipment is available for the Mk 3, including computerised fire-control system, day/night observation equipment, laser rangefinder, NBC system, deep

*Vickers
Mk 3*

wading or flotation system, air-conditioning system,
automatic fire detection and suppression system, and Perkins
V12 diesel.

*Right:
Vickers
Mk 3*

Variants

Vickers armoured bridgelayer.
Vickers armoured recovery vehicle.
Vickers anti-aircraft tank: Mk 3 chassis fitted with Marconi
Marksman twin 35mm turret; trials only.
Vickers SPG: Mk 3 chassis fitted with Vickers Shipbuilding
and engineering 155mm GBT 155 turret; trials only.

*Right:
Vickers
Mk 3*

Status

Production of Mk 1 completed. Production of Mk 3 as
required. In service with India (Mk 1), Kenya (Mk 3), Kuwait
(Mk 1), and Nigeria (Mk 3). Tanzania has a small number of
Vickers ARVs.

Manufacturers

Vickers Defence Systems, Newcastle-upon-Tyne, England (Mk
1 and Mk 3); Avadi Company, Madras, India (Mk 1).

Centurion Mk 13 MBT (UK)

Key recognition features

● Well sloped glacis leads up to horizontal hull top with driver's hatch in roof to immediate rear of glacis plate on right side, turret centre and raised engine compartment rear. Hull rear slopes slightly inwards. Flat stowage boxes above hull sides with exhaust pipes each side at rear
● 105mm gun has non-concentric fume extractor and is often fitted with thermal sleeve, rectangular external mantlet which is often uncovered. Commander's cupola on right side, large stowage boxes each side of turret and large stowage rack on rear. Circular ammunition resupply hatch lower left side of turret.
● Suspension each side has six road wheels, idler front, drive sprocket rear and return rollers. Upper part of suspension usually covered by skirts

Specifications

Crew: 4
Armament: 1 x 105mm, 1 x 12.7mm RMG, 1 x 7.62mm MG (coaxial), 1 x 7.62mm MG (commander's cupola), 2 x 6 smoke grenade dischargers
Ammunition: 64 x 105mm, 600 x 12.7mm, 4,750 x 7.62mm
Length gun forwards: 9.854m
Length hull: 7.823m
Width: 3.39m
Height without AA MG: 3.009m
Ground clearance: 0.51m
Weight combat: 51,820kg
Power-to-weight ratio: 12.54hp/tonne
Ground pressure: 0.95kg/cm²
Engine: Rolls-Royce Mk IVB 12-cylinder liquid-cooled petrol developing 650bhp at 2,550rpm
Maximum road speed: 34.6km/hr
Maximum road range: 190km
Fuel capacity: 1037 lit
Fording: 1.45m
Fording with preparation: 2.74m
Vertical obstacle: 0.914m
Trench: 3.352m
Gradient: 60%
Side slope: 40%
Armour: 152mm (maximum)
Armour type: Steel
NBC system: None
Night vision equipment: Yes (but not always fitted today)

Above: Centurion Mk 10 MBT (105mm gun)

Development

Centurion was developed towards the end of the Second World War with 4,423 vehicles produced between 1945/46 and 1961/62. First vehicles armed with a 17 Pounder but this was replaced by a 20 Pounder and finally the famous 105mm L7 series gun which has since been adopted by many other countries. Layout of all versions is similar, with driver front right, turret centre, engine and transmission rear. Commander and gunner sit right of turret, loader left. Main armament is stabilised and power-elevates from -10˚ to 20˚ with turret traverse 360˚. 105mm ammunition includes APFSDS, APDS, HESH and smoke. Main armament on later models is aimed using 12.7mm RMG, 7.62mm MG mounted coaxial with main armament and similar weapon mounted on commander's cupola. To extend operational range a mono-wheel fuel trailer could be towed behind. Can also be fitted with front-mounted dozer blade.

Variants

There were 13 basic versions of Centurion gun tank plus many sub-variants but most countries now use only 105mm armed versions.

*Olifant Mk 1B MBT
(Christopher F Foss)*

◣ Centurion Mk 13 MBT (UK)

Right: Olifant Mk 1A

Below: Israeli Puma PAC based on Centurion chassis (M Gelbart)

Israeli Centurions have all been rebuilt with 105mm gun and diesel engine, many fitted with explosive reactive armour. Can also have dozer blade and mine-clearing devices. Israel has Centurions with turret removed for use in APC role.

Jordan Centurions have 1055mm gun, computerised fire-control system, new diesel powerpack and new hydropneumatic suspension. These are called the Tariq.

South African Centurions are known as the Olifant (Elephant). Mk1A has many improvements including new powerpack and 105mm gun. Mk1B has upgraded powerpack, new suspension, 105mm gun and new hull and turret armour.

Swedish Centurions have 105mm gun and were upgraded with many improvements including new powerpack.
Centurion ARV
Centurion BARV

Status
Production complete. In service with Austria (turrets only in static role), Denmark, Israel, Jordan (Tariq), Singapore (based in Taiwan for training), South Africa and Sweden.

Manufacturers
Leyland Motors, Leyland; Royal Ordnance Factory Leeds; Vickers, Elswick; Royal Ordnance Factory Woolwich, England, UK.

General Dynamics, Land Systems Division, M1/M1A1/M1A2 Abrams MBT (USA)

Key recognition features

● Nose slopes back under hull, almost horizontal glacis plate, driver's hatch centre under gun mantlet, turret centre, raised engine compartment rear. Hull rear vertical with air louvres in upper part

● Large turret with almost vertical front that slopes to rear, hull sides slope inwards with bustle extending well to rear, stowage box and basket on each side of turret towards rear. Rectangular gunner's sight on right side of turret roof forward of commander's cupola, which has externally mounted 12.7mm MG. 105mm gun has fume extractor and muzzle reference system

● Suspension each side has seven road wheels, drive sprocket rear, large idler front, two return rollers. Upper part of suspension, idler and most of drive sprocket covered by armoured skirts

Specifications (M1)

Crew: 4
Armament: 1 x 105mm, 1 x 7.62mm MG (coaxial), 1 x 7.62mm MG (AA), 1 x 12.7mm MG (AA), 2 x 6 smoke grenade dischargers
Ammunition: 55 x 105mm, 1,000 x 12.7mm, 11,400 x 7.62mm
Length gun forwards: 9.766m
Length hull: 7.918m
Width: 3.653m
Height to turret roof: 2.375m
Height overall: 2.885m
Ground clearance: 0.482m
Weight, combat: 54,545kg
Power-to-weight ratio: 27hp/tonne
Engine: Textron Lycoming AGT 1500 gas turbine developing 1,500hp at 30,000rpm
Maximum road speed: 72.421km/hr
Maximum range: 498km
Fuel capacity: 1,907 lit
Fording: 1.219m, 1.98m (with preparation)
Vehicle obstacle: 1.244m
Trench: 2.743m
Gradient: 60%
Side slope: 40%
Armour: Classified
Armour type: Laminate/steel
NBC system: Yes
Night vision equipment: Yes (passive for commander, gunner and driver)

Above: M1 (US Army)

Development

After trials of XM1 prototypes built by Chrysler (now General Dynamics Land Systems Division) and General Motors, the tank was further developed and eventually accepted for service as M1 Abrams MBT. The first production M1 was completed in 1980 and production was undertaken at the Lima Army Tank Plant, Ohio and at the Detroit Arsenal Tank Plant, Sarren, Michigan, but production is now concentrated at Lima. The M1 was followed in production by the improved M1 and then the M1A1 with 120mm gun and numerous other improvements. Final production model was the M1A2 which has been built for Kuwait, Saudi Arabia and United States. Some M1s are being upgraded to M1A2 for US Army.

Layout is conventional with driver front, turret centre and engine and transmission rear. Commander and gunner sit on right of turret, loader on left. Commander mans a roof-mounted 12.7mm MG, loader mans a 7.62mm roof-mounted MG.

Main armament comprises 105mm M68 rifled gun with powered elevation from -9° to +20° and turret traverse through 360°. A 7.62mm MG is mounted coaxial to right of main armament which is stabilised in elevation and traverse. The 105mm gun fires standard ammunition as well as APFSDS-T rounds.

Variants

M1, basic vehicle with 105mm gun, built from 1980/1985. Improved M1, M1 with additional armour and built 1984/1986.

Right: M1

Below: M1 (US Army)

General Dynamics, Land Systems Division, M1/M1A1/M1A2 Abrams MBT (USA)

M1A1 many improvements, including 120mm smooth bore gun, late production vehicles include heavy armour package.

M1A2, has 120mm gun, new armour, Commanders Independent Thermal Viewer (CITV) and land navigation system.

M1AVLB, at prototype stage.

Combat Mobility Vehicle - under development by United Defense IP and based on modified M1 chassis.

Abrams Recovery Vehicle, developed as a private venture, only single prototype built.

M1/M1A1/M1A2 can be fitted with dozer or mine clearing systems at front of hull.

Below: M1A2

Status

M1, production completed. In service with US Army.

M1A1, production complete, in service with Egypt, US Army And Marines.

M1A2, production completed 1996, in service with Kuwait, Saudi Arabia and US Army (some M1 to be upgraded to M1A2 standard).

Manufacturer

General Dynamics Ltd, Land Systems Division, Lima Army Tank Plant, Lima, Ohio, also assembled in Egypt.

Above: M1A2

Right: M1A1

General Dynamics Land Systems Division
M60A3 MBT (USA)

Key recognition features

● Well sloped glacis plate with driver centre, turret centre of hull with slightly raised engine compartment rear, which is almost identical to M48 series
● Main armament has non-concentric fume extractor, usually thermal sleeve, and mounted in large external mantlet with rounded corners. Well sloped turret sides with wire basket on rear of bustle. Commander's cupola right side of roof
● Suspension each side has six road wheels, idler front, drive sprocket rear and three track-return rollers

Specifications

Crew: 4
Armament: 1 x 105mm, 1 x 7.62mm MG (coaxial), 1 x 12.7mm MG (anti-aircraft), 2 x 6 smoke grenade dischargers
Ammunition: 63 x 105mm, 900 x 12.7mm, 5,950 x 7.62mm
Length gun forwards: 9.436m
Length hull: 6.946m
Width: 3.631m
Height: 3.27m
Ground clearance: 0.45m
Weight combat: 52,617kg
Weight empty: 48,684kg
Power-to-weight ratio: 14.24bhp/tonne
Ground pressure: 0.87kg/cm²
Engine: Teledyne Continental AVDS-1790-2C 12-cylinder air-cooled diesel developing 750bhp at 2,400rpm
Maximum road speed: 48.28km/hr
Maximum road range: 480km
Fuel capacity: 1,420 lit
Fording: 1.22m
Fording with preparation: 2.4m
Vertical obstacle: 0.914m
Trench: 2.59m
Gradient: 60%
Side slope: 30%
Armour: 120mm (maximum) (estimate)
Armour type: Steel
NBC system: Yes
Night vision equipment: Yes (passive)

Above: M60A1

Development

M60 MBT series is a further development of M48 series with first prototypes completed in 1958 and first production vehicles completed by Chrysler Corporation, Delaware Defense Plant. From 1960 production was at the Detroit Tank Plant, also operated by Chrysler (later taken over by General Dynamics), and by the time production was completed in 1987 over 15,000 vehicles had been built for home and export markets.

Layout is conventional with driver front, turret centre and engine and transmission rear. Turret has slightly pointed front with commander and gunner on right and loader left. 105mm gun is stabilised and elevates from -10° to +20° with turret traverse through 360°. Main armament has 105mm gun which fires APFSDS, APDS, HESH, HEAT and smoke projectiles, 7.62mm MG mounted coaxial to left and 12.7mm AA MG in commander's cupola. M60A3 has computerised fire-control system, laser rangefinder and thermal night vision equipment. Roller-type mine-clearing devices or dozer blade can be fitted at front of hull.

Above: M60A1 with dozer blade (US Army)

General Dynamics Land Systems Division M60A3 MBT (USA)

Variants

M60, first production model, turret similar to M48 series, originally with searchlight over main armament.

M60A1, replaced M60 in production from 1962, has new turret. An explosive reactive armour package was developed for US Army M60 series MBTs but was not fielded. It was however installed on M60A1 MBTs of the US Marine Corps for operations in the Middle east in 1991.

M60A2, withdrawn from service.

M60A3, final production model for US Army. Many M60A1s were brought up to M60A3 standard with thermal night vision equipment.

M728, combat engineer vehicle.

M60 AVLB.

In Israel, most M60s fitted with Blazer reactive armour, new commander's cupola with external 7.62mm MG, 7.62mm MG for loader, 12.7mm MG over 105mm gun and smoke grenade dischargers each side of main armament. More recently Israel has developed a further upgraded version of the M60 series called the **MAGACH-7** which has many further improvements including a new passive armour package, Matador computerised fire control system and 908hp diesel engine.

Below: M60A1

Status

Production complete. In service with Austria, Bahrain, Egypt, Greece, Iran, Israel, Italy, Jordan, Oman, Saudi Arabia, Spain, Sudan, Taiwan, Thailand, Tunisia, Turkey and Yemen. They are no longer used by the US although large quantities are still held in reserve, many are now being passed to other countries.

Manufacturer

General Dynamics Land Systems Division, Detroit, Michigan, USA.

Above: M60A1 (USMC)

Above: Israeli M60A1 with reactive armour

M48A5 MBT (USA)

Key recognition features

● Well sloped glacis plate with driver centre, turret centre of hull, slightly raised engine compartment at rear which is almost identical to M60 MBT series

● Main armament has non-concentric fume extractor, no thermal sleeve, mounted in large external mantlet with rounded corners. Large infra-red/white light searchlight often mounted above mantlet. Turret has curved sides and bustle has stowage basket running around rear. Raised commander's cupola on right with external 7.62mm MG with similar weapon for loader on left

● Suspension each side has six road wheels, drive sprocket rear, idler front and five return rollers. US vehicles did not have skirt, South Korean vehicles have

Specifications

Crew: 4
Armament: 1 x 105mm gun, 1 x 7.62mm MG (coaxial), 1 x 7.62mm MG (commander's), 1 x 7.62mm MG (loader), 2 x 6 smoke grenade dischargers
Ammunition: 54 x 105mm, 10,000 x 7.62mm
Length gun forwards: 9.306m
Length hull: 6.419m
Width: 3.63m
Height overall: 3.086m
Power-to-weight ratio: 15.89hp/tonne
Ground pressure: 0.88kg/cm²
Ground clearance: 0.419m
Weight combat: 48,987kg
Weight empty: 46,287kg
Engine: Teledyne Continental AVDS-1790-2D diesel developing 750hp at 2,400rpm
Maximum road speed: 48.2km/hr
Maximum road range: 499km
Fuel capacity: 1,420 lit
Fording: 1.219m
Fording with preparation: 2,438m
Vertical obstacle: 0.915m
Trench: 2.59m
Gradient: 60%
Side slope: 40%
Armour: 120mm (maximum)
Armour type: Steel
NBC system: None
Night vision equipment: Yes

Development

M48 was developed from 1950 with first prototypes completed in 1951 and first production vehicles in 1952. By the time production was completed in 1959, 11,703 vehicles were built. M48 series replaced M47 in US Army and in the mid-1970s many were upgraded to M48A5 standard with 105mm gun and other improvements. Further development of M48 resulted in M60 (qv) series of MBTs. The M48A5 is no longer in front line US Army service. Diver sits front centre, commander and gunner on right side of turret and loader left. 105mm gun is mounted in turret with powered traverse through 360° and powered elevation from -9° to +19°. M48s can also be fitted with dozer blade.

Variants

M48, original model, 90mm gun, petrol engine, commander has external 12.7mm MG, five track-return rollers.
M48C, mild steel hull and turret, training only.
M48A1, 90mm gun, petrol engine, commander has cupola with internally mounted 12.7mm MG.
M48A2/M48A2C, 90mm gun, fuel injection system for petrol engine, five track-return rollers.
M48A3, rebuild of early vehicle with petrol engine replaced by diesel, 90mm gun, vision blocks between commander's cupola and roof, three track-return rollers.
M48A4 was cancelled project.
M48A5. Over 2,000 earlier M48s, rebuilt to M48A5 standard from mid-1970s, have many improvements including 105mm gun, new commander's cupola and diesel engine.
M48A2GA2 is German rebuilt M48A2 with 105mm gun with thermal sleeve. German smoke grenade dischargers, new mantlet, passive night vision equipment, retained petrol engine.

Turkish M48A5T1 with 105mm gun

M48A5 MBT (USA)

M48A2 (90mm gun)

M48A5 of South Korean Army with skirts (105mm gun)

Israeli M48s. All have 105mm gun, diesel engine, low profile commander's cupola. Many have explosive reactive armour like Israeli M60 tanks (qv).
South Korean M48s. Many brought up to M48A5 standard but also have side skirts.
Spain has upgraded many M48s with 105mm gun and many other improvements with the M48A5E1 and M48A5E2 remaining in service.

Right: M48A5 (105mm gun) (US Army)

and laser rangefinder.
Turkish M48s. 170 upgraded to German M48A2GA2 standard but also have MTU diesel engine. Much larger number upgraded with US assistance to M48A5 standard (known as M45A5T1 in Turkish Army).
M48 AVLB has scissors bridge.
M48 mine-clearing tank with flails is for German Army.
M67/M67A/M67A2, flamethrower tanks, no longer in service.

Status
Production complete. In service with Greece, Iran, Israel, Jordan, South Korea, Lebanon, Morocco, Norway, Pakistan, Portugal, Spain, Taiwan, Thailand, Tunisia, Turkey.

Manufacturers
Chrysler Corporation, Delaware; Ford Motor Company, Michigan; Fisher Body Division of General Motors Corporation, Michigan; and Alco Products, Schenectady, USA.

Taiwan also has model called M48H which is M60A1 chassis and M48A5 type turret with computerised fire control system

Above: M48A2

M47 Medium Tank (USA)

Key recognition features

● Well sloped glacis plate with 7.62mm MG in right bow, two hatches on opposite sides of hull immediately behind glacis plate, one for driver and one for bow gunner, turret in hull centre and engine compartment rear. Hull rear is vertical

● Cast turret with well sloped sides and bustle extending to rear with stowage box far rear, commander's cupola right side of turret roof, ventilation dome centre of roof at rear. 90mm gun has mantlet and T type or cylindrical muzzle brake with bore evacuator to immediate rear

● Suspension each side has six road wheels, idler front, drive sprocket rear and three track-return rollers, small track tensioning wheel between sixth rear wheel and drive sprocket, no skirts

Specifications

Crew: 5
Armament: 1 x 90mm, 1 x 7.62mm MG (coaxial), 1 x 7.62mm MG (bow), 1 x 12.7mm MG (AA)
Ammunition: 71 x 90mm, 4,125 x 7.62mm, 440 x 12.7mm
Length gun forwards: 8.508m
Length hull: 6.307m
Height to commander's cupola: 3.016m
Height with AA MG: 3.352m
Width: 3.51m
Height to turret top: 2.954m
Ground clearance: 0.469m
Power-to-weight ratio: 17.54hp/tonne
Weight, combat: 46,170kg
Weight, empty: 42,130kg
Ground pressure: 0.935kg/cm²
Engine: Continental AV-1790-5B series V-12 air-cooled petrol developing 810hp at 2,800rpm
Maximum road speed: 48km/hr
Maximum range: 130km
Fuel capacity: 875 lit
Fording: 1.219m
Vertical obstacle: 0.914m
Trench: 2.59m
Gradient: 60%
Side slope: 40%
Armour: 101mm (maximum)
Armour type: Steel
NBC system: None
Night vision equipment: Yes (infra-red for driver)

Right: Italian M47

Development

M47 was developed in the early 1950s, essentially the turret of the T42 medium tank fitted to the chassis of the M46 tank. A total of 8,676 vehicles was produced. In the US Army the M47 was soon replaced by the M48 and most M47s were then supplied to other countries under the Mutual Aid Program; in most of these (eg France and Germany) it has long since been replaced by more modern vehicles.

The driver sits front in left side, bow machine gunner to right, turret centre and engine and transmission rear. The commander and gunner sit right of the turret, loader left. The turret power-traverses through 360˚ and the 90mm gun elevates from -5˚ to +19˚ and fires APC-T, APERS-T, AP-T, canister, HE, HE-T, HEP-T, HEAT, HVAP-T, HVTP-T and smoke rounds. 7.62mm MG is mounted coaxial to left of main armament, with a similar weapon in the bow; many countries removed this weapon to accommodate additional ammunition. A 12.7mm M2 HB MG is mounted on the roof for air defence.

Right: M47

Variants

Many countries and companies have upgraded M47s at various times, but only Iran have them in any quantity. The Iranian vehicles retain their 90mm guns but have many automotive components (eg, engine and transmission) of the M48A3/M60A1; these are designated M47M.

South Korea has an M47 ARV in service, essentially an M47 with 90mm gun removed and winch in turret.

Status

Production complete. In service with Greece, Iran, Pakistan, South Korea, Turkey and Former Yugoslavia.

Manufacturers

Detroit Tank Plant and American Locomotive Company, USA

Below: M47
(US Army)

M551 Sheridan Light Tank (USA)

Key recognition features

● Well sloped glacis plate with driver's half-circular hatch cover rear, turret centre, engine rear with back sloping downwards
● Turret sides pointed and slope inwards bottom and bottom, short-barrelled 152mm gun/missile launcher with some machine gun ammunition boxes stowed externally on turret
● Suspension has five road wheels, idler front, drive sprocket rear, no track-return rollers

Specifications

Crew: 4
Armament: 1 x 152mm gun/launcher, 1 x 7.62mm MG (coaxial), 1 x 12.7mm MG (AA), 2 x 4 smoke grenade dischargers
Ammunition: 20 x 152mm, 10 x missiles, 3,080 x 7.62mm, 1,000 x 12.7mm
Length: 6.299m
Width: 2.819m
Height: 2.946 (overall), 2,272m (turret top)
Ground clearance: 0.48m
Weight, combat: 15,830kg
Weight, empty: 13,589kg
Power-to-weight ratio: 18.95bhp/tonne
Ground pressure: 0.49kg/cm²
Engine: Detroit Diesel 6V-53T 6-cylinder water-cooled turbocharged diesel developing 300bhp at 2,800rpm
Maximum road speed: 70km/hr
Maximum road range: 600km
Maximum water speed: 5.8km/hr
Fuel capacity: 598 lit
Fording: Amphibious with preparation
Vertical obstacle: 0.838m
Trench: 2.54m
Gradient: 60%
Side slope: 40%
Armour: Classified
Armour type: Hull aluminium, turret steel
NBC system: Yes
Night vision equipment: Yes (infra-red for commander, gunner and driver). For Operation Desert Shield/Desert Storm, front line M551s were fitted with thermal night vision equipment for the gunner and driver.

Development

M551 Sheridan was developed in the 1960s as the Armored Reconnaissance/Airborne Assault Vehicle and replaced the 90mm armed M41 light tank in the US Army. A total of 1,700 vehicles were built between 1966 and 1970. By 1995 less than 100 M551 Sheridan light tanks remained operational with the US Army. Over 300 have been assigned to the National Training Center (see variants).

The driver sits front with remaining three crew members in turret, engine and transmission rear. Flotation screen is collapsed round hull top and, when erected, the M551 is propelled in water by its tracks.

Main armament comprises a 152mm weapon that fires a wire guided Shillelagh missile or HEAT-T-MP, white phosphorous or canister projectile. The 152mm weapon is stabilised and elevates from -8° to +19.5°, with turret traverse 360°.

Variants

M551A1 has laser rangefinder.
M551s used by National Training Center have been modified to resemble the Soviet 122mm 2S1 self-propelled howitzer, ZSU-23-4 self-propelled anti-aircraft gun, T-72 MBT, BMP-1 IFV, BMD-1 airborne combat vehicle and ASU-85 airborne self-propelled anti-tank gun.

Status

Production complete. In service with US Army only.

Manufacturer

Allison Division of General Motors, Cleveland Tank-Automotive Plant, Cleveland, Ohio, USA.

Top: M551 Sheridan

Left: M551 Sheridan modified for National Training Center to resemble a Soviet BMP-1 IFV (US Army/Michael Green)

M41 Light Tank (USA)

Key recognition features

● Well sloped glacis plate with horizontal top, driver front left, turret centre, engine rear, exhaust pipe each side of upper hull rear

● Welded turret with sloping sides, bustle overhanging rear, stowage box far rear, commander's cupola on right side, 76mm gun has T-shaped muzzle brake with fume extractor to immediate rear

● Suspension has five road wheels, drive sprocket rear, idler front, three return rollers, no skirts

Specifications

Crew: 4
Armament: 1 x 76mm, 1 x 7.62mm MG (coaxial), 1 x 12.7mm MG (AA)
Ammunition: 57 x 76mm, 5,000 x 7.62mm, 2,175 12.7mm
Length gun forwards: 8.212m
Length hull: 5.819m
Height with 12.7mm MG: 3.075m
Height to turret top: 2.726m
Ground clearance: 0.45m
Weight, combat: 23,495kg
Weight, empty: 18,457kg
Power-to-weight ratio: 21.26hp/tonne
Engine: Continental AOS-895-3, 6-cylinder air-cooled supercharged petrol developing 500bhp at 2,800rpm
Maximum road speed: 72km/hr
Maximum range: 161km
Fuel capacity: 530 lit
Fording: 1.016m
Fording with preparation: 2.44m
Vertical obstacle: 0.711m
Trench: 1.828m
Gradient: 60%
Side slope: 30%
Armour: 31.75mm (maximum)
Armour type: Steel
NBC system: None
Night vision equipment: Optional

Development

M41 was developed shortly after the Second World War to replace the M24 Chaffee light tank. First production vehicles were completed in mid-1951 and 5,500 vehicles were completed by the late 1950s. In US Army service it was replaced by the M551 Sheridan light tank.

Driver sits front left, turret in centre and engine and transmission rear. Commander sits on turret right with gunner in front and loader on left side of turret.

The 76mm gun power-elevates from -9° to +19° with turret traverse 360°, and fires HE, HEAT, HVAP-DS-T, HVAP-T, HVTP-T, smoke and training rounds. A 7.62mm MG is mounted coaxial to left and a 12.7mm M2 HB MG is mounted on turret roof for anti-aircraft defence.

Variants

M41 was followed in production by the slightly different **M41A1, M41A2** and **M411A3.**
Bernardini of Brazil has rebuilt over 400 M41s for the Brazilian Army and Marines, with modifications including new engine, additional armour and gun bored out to 90mm; these are designated M41/B or M41/C.
Denmark has upgraded its vehicles to DK-1 standard with many improvements including new engine, NBC system, thermal

M41

*Left: Danish Army
upgraded M41 which
is called the DK-1*

sights and skirts. Some of the vehicles used by Uruguay have
new 90mm Cockerill Mk IV gun.

Status

Production complete. In service with Brazil, Chile, Denmark,
Dominican Republic, Guatemala, Taiwan, Thailand and Uruguay.

Manufacturer

Cadillac Motor Car Division, General Motors Corporation,
Cleveland Tank Plant, Ohio, USA.

Cadillac Gage Stingray Light Tank (USA)

Key recognition features

● Well sloped glacis plate with driver's hatch in upper part, hull top horizontal with two slight steps to raised engine compartment at rear of hull. Sides and rear of hull vertical with exhaust outlet in upper part of hull rear

● Turret in centre of hull with pointed front, sides slope inwards with turret basket at rear, bank of four smoke grenade dischargers on either side of the turret. 12.7mm MG mounted on right side of turret roof

● Suspension either side has six small road wheels with idler front, drive sprocket rear and three track return rollers, no side skirts

Specifications

Crew: 4
Armament: 1 x 105mm gun, 1 x 7.62mm MG coaxial, 1 x 12.7mm MG AA, 2 x 4 smoke grenade dischargers
Ammunition: 32 x 105mm, 2,400 x 7.62mm, 1,100 x 12.7mm
Length gun forwards: 9.30m
Length hull: 6.448m
Width: 2.71m
Height overall: 2.55m
Ground clearance: 0.46m
Weight, combat: 21,205kg
Weight, empty: 19,387kg
Power-to-weight ratio: 25.9hp/tonne
Ground pressure: 0.72kg/cm²
Engine: Detroit Diesel Model 8V-92TA developing 535hp at 2,300rpm
Maximum road speed: 67km/hr
Maximum range: 483km
Fuel capacity: 757 lit
Fording: 1.07m
Vertical obstacle: 0.76m
Trench: 2.13m
Gradient: 60%
Side slope: 40%
Armour: Classified
Armour type: Steel
NBC system: Yes (optional)
Night vision equipment: Yes (passive)

Development

The Stingray light tank was designed by Textron Marine & Land Systems (previously Cadillac Gage Textron) as a private venture

Above: Cadillac Gage Stingray light tank

with the first prototype being completed in 1985. Following trials in Thailand this country placed an order for a total of 106 Stingray vehicles which were delivered between 1988 and 1990. To reduce procurement and life cycle costs, standard components have been used wherever possible in the design of the vehicle, for example engine, transmission, suspension and tracks.

The driver is seated at the front of the vehicle in the centre with the turret in the centre of the hull and the powerpack at the rear. The commander and gunner are seated on the right of the turret with the loader on the left. Main armament comprises a Royal Ordnance Nottingham 105mm Low Recoil Force gun that is fitted with a thermal sleeve, fume extractor and muzzle brake, this can fire the full range of NATO ammunition including APFSDS types. Turret traverse is a full 360° with weapon elevation from -7.5° to +20° under full power control with manual controls being provided for emergency use.

The commander and gunner are provided with day/night sights with the gunner's sight incorporating a laser rangefinder, a HR Textron gun control and stabilisation system is fitted as is a Marconi Digital Fire Control System for improved first round hit probability. Various other types of fire control and night vision equipment can be fitted as can additional armour protection, land navigation system and fire detection and suppression system.

Variants

Chassis can be adopted for other roles. Further development has resulted in Stingray II with a number of improvements including additional armour protection.

Status

Production as required. In service with Thailand.

Manufacturer

Textron Marine & Land Systems, New Orleans, Louisiana, USA.

Above:
Cadillac
Gage
Stingray
light tank

Top right:
Cadillac
Gage
Stingray
light tank

Right:
Cadillac
Gage
Stingray
light tank

M-84 MBT (Former Yugoslavia)

Key recognition features

● Well sloped glacis plate with driver's position top centre, distinctive V splash plate on glacis, turret centre of hull, engine and transmission at rear, exhaust outlet on left side hull above last road wheel station

● Circular turret, raised cupola with external 12.7mm MG on right of roof, stowage box rear and right, snorkel left side, infra-red searchlight right of 125mm gun which has thermal sleeve and fume extractor. Unditching beam and long-range fuel drums sometimes fitted at rear. Mounted on forward part of turret roof is distinctive pole type sensor for the fire control system which is not seen on the Russian T-72 MBT

● Suspension each side has six road wheels, drive sprocket rear, idler front and three track return rollers. Upper part usually covered by rubber skirts

Specifications

Crew: 3
Armament: 1 x 125mm, 1 x 7.62mm (coaxial), 1 x 12.7mm MG (AA), 12 smoke grenade dischargers (one bank of five and one of seven)
Ammunition: 42 x 125mm, 2000 x 7.62mm, 300 x 12.7mm
Length gun forwards: 9.53m
Length hull: 6.86m
Width: 3.57m
Height (turret roof): 2.19m
Ground clearance: 0.5m
Weight, combat: 42,000kg
Power-to-weight ratio: 23.8hp/tonne
Ground pressure: 0.81kg/cm^2
Engine: V-12 water-cooled, supercharged diesel developing 780hp at 2,000rpm
Maximum road speed: 65km/hr
Range: 700km
Fuel capacity: 1,200 lit (estimate)
Fording: 1.2m (without preparation), 5m (with snorkel)
Vertical obstacle: 0.85m
Trench: 2.8m
Gradient: 60%
Side slope: 30%
Armour: Classified
Armour type: Composite/steel
NBC system: Yes
Night vision equipment: Yes (commander, gunner and driver)

Development

The M-84 is essentially the Russian T-72 manufactured under licence in Yugoslavia with a number of Yugoslav designed sub-systems, for example the fire control system. The first prototypes of the M-84 were completed in 1982-83 with production commencing in 1983-84 and first production vehicles being completed in 1984. It is estimated that by early 1992 over 600 had been built for the home and export markets. Following the Yugoslav war, production of the M-84 stopped although more recently Croatia has unveiled an MBT called the M-95 Degman which is similar to M-84 but has a new armour package.

The layout of the M-84 is identical to that of the T-72 with the driver being seated at the front of the vehicle in the centre, two man turret in the centre of the hull with the gunner on the left and commander on the right with the powerpack at the rear. The M-84 has no loader as the vehicle is fitted with an automatic loader for the 125mm gun, which has an elevation of +13˚ and a depression of -6˚ with turret traverse a full 360˚, turret controls are powered with manual controls for emergency use. Types of 125mm ammunition fired include HE-FRAG, HEAT-FS and APFSDS-T.

Variants

ARV, believed to exist although no firm details are available.
M-84A, latest production model with a number of improvements including a more powerful 1,000hp engine that gives a higher speed and improved power-to-weight ratio, it also has improved armour protection.

Status

Production complete. In service with Kuwait and parts of the former Yugoslavia.

Manufacturer

Former Yugoslav state factories.

Close up of turret of M-84 MBT

TRACKED APCs/ WEAPONS CARRIERS

Steyr 4K 7FA G 127 APC (Austria)

Key recognition features

● Almost identical to 4K 4FA series (qv) with low profile hull, well sloped glacis plate leading up to horizontal hull top, hull rear slopes sharply inwards, hull sides above tracks slope inwards, horizontal louvres each side of hull front

● Driver front left, engine right, weapon station to his immediate rear (normally cupola with 12.7mm MG)

● Suspension with five road wheels which all have small holes between hub and rim, drive sprocket front, idler rear, three track-return rollers, no skirts

Specifications

Crew: 2+8
Armament: 1 x 12.7mm MG, 1 x 4 smoke grenade dischargers
Ammunition: 500 x 12.7mm (estimate)
Length: 5.87m
Width: 2.5m
Height without MG: 1.611m
Ground clearance: 0.42m
Weight, combat: 14,800kg
Power-to-weight ratio: 21.62hp/tonne
Ground pressure: 0.55kg/cm^2
Engine: Steyr 7FA 6-cylinder liquid-cooled turbocharged diesel developing 320hp at 2,300rpm
Maximum road speed: 70.6km/hr
Maximum road range: 520km
Fuel capacity: 360 lit
Fording: 1m
Vertical obstacle: 0.8m
Trench: 2.1m
Gradient: 75%
Side slope: 40%
Armour: 25mm (maximum)
Armour type: Steel
NBC system: Yes
Night vision equipment: Yes (passive for driver)

Development

The Steyr 4K 7FA G 127 is a further development of the earlier 4K 4FA series (see following entry). The first prototype was completed in 1976 and first production vehicles in 1977. Main improvements over earlier Saurer 4K 4FA are better armour protection over frontal arc and improved power-to-weight ratio

from more powerful engine. Many automotive components also used in SK 105 tank destroyer.

Driver sits front left, engine compartment to his right, cupola with externally mounted 12.7mm M2 HB MG to his rear. Cupola has front and side armour protection for gunner, rear has bank of four electrically operated smoke grenade dischargers firing to rear. Troop compartment is rear of hull, has roof hatches that open each side and twin doors in rear. Four sockets around top of troop compartment allow quick installation of pintle-mounted MGs.

Standard equipment includes ventilation system and crew compartment heater. Optional equipment includes passive NVE, NBC system, air conditioning and fire detection/suppression system for engine and crew compartments.

Variants

4K 7FA-KSpZ MICV has two ball-type firing ports in each side of troop compartment with periscope for rifle fired from inside.
4K 7FA MICV essentially as above with one-man turret and 12.7mm MG and 7.62mm MG, prototype only.
4K 7KA FSCV 90 fire support vehicle has GIAT 90mm TS-90 turret fitted, prototype only.
4K 7FA MICV 30/1 with one-man turret and 30mm RARDEN cannon and 7.62mm coaxial MG, prototype only.
4K 7FA-F$_c$ command post vehicle has additional communications equipment.
4K 7FA-San is armoured ambulance.
4K 7FA AMC 81 is 81mm mortar carrier.
4K 7FA FLA 1/2.20 twin 20mm SPAAG, prototype only.
4K 7FA FLA 3/2.30 twin 30mm SPAAG, prototype only.

Status
Production complete. In service with Bolivia, Cyprus, Greece and Nigeria.

Manufacturers
Steyr-Daimler-Puch AG, Vienna, Austria; Steyr Hellas SA, Greece.

*Right: Steyr
4K 7FA G 127*

Saurer 4K 4FA APC (Austria)

Key recognition features

● Low profile hull with well sloped glacis plate leading up to horizontal hull top, hull rear slopes sharply inwards, hull sides above tracks slope slightly inwards, horizontal louvres each side of hull front
● Driver front left, engine right, weapon station to immediate rear (turret with 20mm cannon or 12.7mm MG)
● Suspension with five road wheels which all have small holes between hub and rim, drive sprocket front, idler rear, two track-return rollers, no skirts

Specifications

Crew: 2+8
Armament: 1 x 20mm cannon or 1 x 12.7mm MG
Length: 5.4m
Width: 2.5m
Height with 12.7mm MG: 2.1m
Height hull top: 1.65m
Ground clearance: 0.42m
Weight, combat (20mm cannon): 15,000kg
Weight, combat (12.7mm MG): 12,500kg
Power-to-weight ratio (20mm model): 16.66hp/tonne
Power-to-weight ratio (12.7mm model): 20hp/tonne
Ground pressure: 0.52kg/cm^2
Engine: Saurer model 4FA 4-stroke 6-cylinder diesel developing 250hp at 2.400rpm
Maximum road speed: 65km/hr
Maximum road range: 370km
Fuel capacity: 184 lit
Fording: 1m
Vertical obstacle: 0.8m
Trench: 2.2m
Gradient: 75%
Side slope: 50%
Armour: 20mm (maximum)
Armour type: Steel
NBC system: None
Night vision equipment: None

Development

In the mid-1950s Saurer-Werke designed and built a full tracked armoured personnel carrier, further development of which resulted in 4K 4F which entered production for Austrian Army in 1961. Replaced in production by 4K 3FA (230hp engine) and 4K 4FA (250hp engine) with final deliveries in 1968 after about 450 had been built. Further development resulted in the similar 4K 7FA APC (qv).

All vehicles have similar layout with driver front left, engine compartment to his immediate right. Main armament is to rear of driver, troop compartment extending to rear with roof hatches. Troops enter via twin doors in rear.

Variants

4K 4FA-G1 has cupola with 12.7mm MG.
4K 4FA-G2 has a one-man Oerlikon-Contraves turret armed with one Oerlikon-Contraves 20mm 204GK cannon. Turret traverse is a full 360° with weapon elevation from -12° to +70°.
4K 3FA-F,1 is brigade command post vehicle.
4K 3FA-F1A is artillery command post vehicle.
4K 3FA-F,/FIA is anti-aircraft command post vehicle.
4K 3FA-FS is wireless teleprinter vehicle.
4K 4FA-San is armoured ambulance.
4K 4F GrW1 is 81mm mortar carrier.
81mm multiple rocket launcher is used in small numbers.

Status

Production complete. In service with Austrian Army only.

Manufacturer

Saurer-Werke (now Steyr-Daimler-Puch), Vienna, Austria.

Saurer 4K 4FA-G2 with 20mm cannon

Right: Saurer 4K 4FA-G2 with 20mm cannon (Austrian Army)

Below right: Saurer 4K 4FA-G1 with 12.7mm MG (Austrian Army)

Below: Saurer 4K 4FA-San armoured ambulance (Austrian Army)

BMP-23 Infantry Combat Vehicle (Bulgaria)

Key recognition features

● Chassis has nose sloping back under hull with almost horizontal glacis plate, horizontal hull top, vehicle hull rear and sides are vertical with chamfer between sides and hull top

● Turret mounted in centre of vehicle with sloping front, 23mm cannon has muzzle suppressor and slots. Sagger ATGW mounted on left side of turret roof

● Chassis is similar to Russian 2S1 122mm SPG with seven road wheels, drive sprockets at front, idler at rear and no track return rollers

Specifications

Crew: 3+7
Armament: 1 x 23mm cannon, 1 x 7.62mm MG (coaxial), 1 x AT-3 Sagger ATGW launcher
Ammunition: 600 x 23mm, 2,000 x 7.62mm and 4 x AT-3 Sagger ATGW
Length: 7.285m
Width: 2.85m
Height: 2.53m
Ground clearance: 0.40m
Weight, combat: 15,200kg
Power-to-weight ratio: 20.72hp/tonne
Ground pressure: 0.498kg/cm^2
Engine: Diesel developing 315hp
Maximum road speed: 61.5km/hr
Maximum road range: 550-600km
Fuel capacity: 500 to 560 lit
Fording: Amphibious
Vertical obstacle: 0.8m
Trench: 2.5m
Gradient: 60%
Side slope: 30%
Armour: Classified
Armour type: Steel
NBC system: Yes
Night vision equipment: Yes

Development

The BMP-23 ICV was developed by the Bulgarian defence industry to meet the requirements of the Bulgarian Army and uses a number of components of the Russian MT-LB multi-purpose armoured vehicle and 2S1 122mm self-propelled artillery system that have been manufactured under licence in Bulgaria for some time.

The driver is seated at the front left with one of the infantrymen on the opposite side of the vehicle with the engine to their rear, the two man turret is in the centre of the vehicle with gunner on the left and commander on the right. The 23mm cannon has a maximum range of 2,000m with the 7.62mm MG being mounted coaxial to the right. The AT-3 ATGW has a maximum range of 3,000m. The infantry compartment is at the rear with three men being seated either side back to back, the infantry enter the BMP-23 via doors in the hull rear. The troop compartment is provided with firing ports, associated vision devices and roof hatches.

The BMP-23 is fully amphibious being propelled in the water by its tracks and before entering the water a trim vane is erected at the front of the hull, which when not required folds back onto the glacis plate. Standard equipment includes heater, fire detection and suppression system and navigation system. It can also lay its own smoke screen by injecting diesel fuel into the exhaust outlet on the right side of the hull.

Variants

BMP-23A, is BMP-23 with three smoke grenade dischargers either side of turret and launcher on roof for AT-4 Spigot ATGW launcher.
BRM-23 is a reconnaissance vehicle with a similar layout and weapon fit but has a five-man crew and additional surveillance equipment.

BMP-30 is essentially BMP-23 fitted with complete turret of Russian BMP-2 ICV which is armed with a 30mm cannon, 7.62mm coaxial machine gun, launcher for AT-4/AT-5 ATGW and a bank of three smoke grenade dischargers mounted either side of the turret.

BMR-23 reconnaissance vehicle

Status
Production as required. In service with Bulgarian Army.

Manufacturer
Bulgarian state factories.

Above right: BMR-23 reconnaissance vehicle

Right: BMP-23 ICV

133

NORINCO YW 531 H APC (China)

Key recognition features

● Well sloped glacis plate with nose sloped back under front of vehicle, horizontal hull top with distinctive domed hatch cover for driver at front left of vehicle, 12.7mm MG on roof provided with lateral and rear protection
● Hull sides slope slightly inwards, vertical hull rear with single large door, either side of which is a large box that protrudes to the rear
● Suspension either side consists of five road wheels with drive sprocket at the front, idler at the rear and track-return rollers, the upper part of which are covered by a light steel skirt with horizontal ribs

Specifications

Crew: 2+13
Armament: 1 x 12.7mm MG
Ammunition: 1,120 x 12.7mm
Length: 6.125m
Width: 3.06m
Height: 2.586m (inc 12.7mm MG), 1.914m (hull roof)
Ground clearance: 0.46m
Weight, combat: 13,600kg
Power-to-weight ratio: 23.5hp/tonne
Ground pressure: 0.546kg/cm²
Engine: BF8L 413F air-cooled diesel developing 320hp
Maximum road speed: 65km/hr
Maximum road range: 500km
Fuel capacity: Not available
Fording: Amphibious
Vertical obstacle: 0.6m
Trench: 2.2m
Gradient: 60%
Side slope: 40%
Armour: Classified
Armour type: Steel
NBC system: Yes
Night vision equipment: Yes

Development

The YW 531 H APC was developed by NORINCO at the same time as the very similar YW 534, the main difference being that the YW 531 H is slightly lighter, shorter, narrower and does not have the bank of four electrically operated smoke grenade dischargers either side of the turret. The driver is seated at the front of the vehicle on the left with another crew member to his rear, to their right is the engine compartment. The troop compartment is to the rear of the hull and is provided with four small roof hatches and a single door in the rear, firing ports and observation devices are provided. On the basic vehicle armament comprises a ring-mounted 12.7mm MG with lateral and side protection. The YW 531 is fully amphibious being propelled in the water by its tracks and before entering the water the trim vane is erected on the glacis plate and the bilge pumps are switched on.

Variants

YW 309 ICV with turret of WZ 501 (the Chinese equivalent of the Russian BMP-1).
Type 85 armoured command post vehicle, similar to basic vehicle but has additional communications equipment, Type 85 armoured command vehicle is almost identical.
Type WZ 751 armoured ambulance, has raised rear compartment.
Type 85 120mm self-propelled mortar.
Type 85 82mm self-propelled mortar.
122mm self-propelled howitzer, uses mount and ordnance of Chinese produced version of the Russian 122mm D-30 howitzer.
Type 85 ARV, fitted with hydraulic crane.
Type 85 maintenance engineering vehicle, has raised hull like Type 85 ambulance.

Status

Production. In service with China and Thailand (these have US M2 type 12.7mm MGs in place of Chinese MGs).

Manufacturer

Chinese state factories. Marketed by NORINCO.

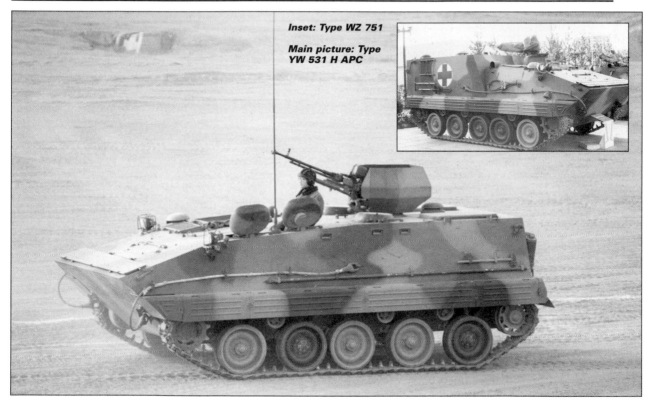

Inset: Type WZ 751

Main picture: Type YW 531 H APC

NORINCO YW 531C APC (China)

Key recognition features

● Nose slopes back under forward part of hull, well sloped glacis plate up to hull top that slopes slightly upwards towards rear. Vertical hull rear with large door that opens right

● Hull sides slope slightly inwards, driver front left, similar hatch cover front right, air inlet louvres in roof on right side, oblong hatches in roof over rear troop compartment

● Suspension each side has four road wheels, idler rear, drive sprocket front, no track-return rollers, upper part of track covered by sheet metal guard

Specifications

Crew: 2+13
Armament: 1 x 12.7mm MG
Ammunition: 1,120 x 12.7mm
Length: 5.476m
Width: 2.978m
Height with MG: 2.58m
Height to hull top: 1.887m
Ground clearance: 0.45m
Weight, combat: 12,600kg
Power-to-weight ratio: 25.39hp/tonne
Ground pressure: $0.57kg/cm^2$
Engine: BF8L 413F 4-cycle turbocharged, V-8 diesel developing 320hp at 2,500rpm
Maximum road speed: 65km/hr
Maximum water speed: 6km/hr
Maximum range: 500km
Fuel capacity: 450 lit
Fording: Amphibious
Vertical obstacle: 0.6m
Trench: 2m
Gradient: 60%
Side slope: 40%
Armour: 10mm (maximum)(estimate)
Armour type: Steel
NBC system: None
Night vision equipment: None

Development

The YW 531 series was developed in the late 1960s. (It has been referred to as K-63, M1967, M1970 and Type 63 at various times.) Driver sits front left with vehicle commander to rear,

another crew member sits front right with engine compartment to rear, 12.7mm MG is mounted in centre of roof, no protection for gunner. Troop compartment at rear of hull with two hatches above, large door in rear and single firing port in each side of hull.

YW 531 is fully amphibious, propelled by its tracks. Before entering the water a trim vane is erected at front of vehicle and bilge pumps switched on.

Variants

YW 531C (modified) has shield for 12.7mm MG.
YW 531C, YW 531D, YW 531E, all have additional communications.
WZ 701 command post vehicle has higher roof line at rear.
YW 750 ambulance is similar to above.
Type 54-1 122mm self-propelled howitzer uses components of YW 531.
130mm Type 70 self-propelled rocket launcher uses components of YW 531.
YW 304 82mm mortar carrier, mortar can be dismounted.
YW 381 120mm mortar carrier, mortar can be dismounted.
Anti-tank vehicle with turret armed with four Red Arrow 8 ATGWs in ready-to-launch position.
Further development has resulted in the NORINCO Type YW 531H (or Type 85 as it is also referred to)(qv). The NORINCO WZ 501 IFV is essentially a Chinese-built version of the Russian BMP-1 vehicle.

Status

Production complete. In service with Albania, China, Iraq, North Korea, Sudan, Tanzania, Vietnam and Zaire.

Type YW 531

Manufacturer
Chinese state arsenals

Above right: Type YW 304 82mm self-propelled mortar

Right: Type YW 531 (Paul Handel)

Left: Type YW 701 command post vehicle

NORINCO Type 77 APC (China)

Key recognition features

● Similar in appearance to the Russian BTR-50PK and Czechoslovak OT-62 with high nose sloping back under forward part of hull, almost horizontal glacis plate, forward part of crew compartment slopes rear, half-circular commander's position in right side, hull top horizontal to mid-way along vehicle then drops vertically to engine compartment at rear

● Hull rear and sides vertical, upper part of hull sides slope inwards, door in right side of hull opens forwards

● Suspension each side has six road wheels, idler front, drive sprocket rear, no track-return rollers

Specifications

Crew: 2+16
Armament: 1 x 12.7mm MG
Ammunition: 500 x 12.7mm
Length: 7.4m
Width: 3.2m
Height: 2.436m
Weight, combat: 15,500kg
Power-to-weight ratio: 25.8hp/tonne
Engine: Type 12150L-2A 4-cycle, compression ignition, direct injection water-cooled diesel developing 400hp at 2,000rpm
Maximum road speed: 60km/hr
Maximum water speed: 11 to 12km/hr
Maximum road range: 370km
Fuel capacity: 416 lit
Fording: Amphibious
Vertical obstacle: 0.87m
Trench: 2.9m
Gradient: 60%
Side slope: 40%
Armour: 8mm (maximum)(estimate)
Armour type: Steel
NBC system: None
Night vision equipment: None

Development

Although very similar to Russian BTR-50PK and Czechoslovak OT-62 APCs, the Chinese Type 77 has a more powerful engine which gives higher road and water speeds and a higher power-to-weight ratio. Many automotive components of Type 77 are also used in the Type 63 APC. Fully enclosed crew and troop compartments are situated at the front, with entry via a door in right side and roof hatches. Engine and transmission are at the rear. Troop compartment has three firing ports, several vision blocks, ventilation system and a white light searchlight for use from inside vehicle.

The Type 77 is fully amphibious, propelled by two waterjets mounted one each side at hull rear. Before entering the water, a trim board is erected at front of vehicle and two bilge pumps switched on. The Type 77 can be used as command post, fuel resupply vehicle, ambulance and load carrier. The Type 77-2 has three loading ramps that can be positioned at rear to carry 85mm Type 56 gun or 122mm Type 54 howitzer. Type 77-2 has no ramps.

Variants

The only known variant is a lengthened chassis with seven road wheels which is to transport and launch the HQ-2J SAM which is the Chinese equivalent of the Russian SA-2 Guideline SAM system.

Status

Production complete. In service with Chinese Army.

Manufacturer

Chinese state arsenals.

Above left: Type 77-1 with ramps lowered at rear

Left: 77-2 with side door open

Above: Type 77-1 from front

OT-62B APC (Former Czechoslovakia)

Key recognition features

● Similar to Russian BTR-50PK but latter has distinct chamfer to hull roof. Glacis plate almost horizontal then slopes upwards to crew compartment, flat roof with distinct step down to engine compartment mid-way along top
● Small turret on right side of roof at front, large square door in each side of troop compartment (do not appear on BTR-50PK)
● Suspension ha six rubber-tyred road wheels, idler front, drive sprocket rear, no track-return rollers

Specifications

Crew: 2+18
Armament: 1 x 7.62mm MG, 1 x 82mm recoilless rifle
Ammunition: 1,250 x 7.62mm, 12 x 82mm
Length: 7.08m
Width: 3.14m
Height: 2.23m (including turret)
Ground clearance: 0.37m
Weight, combat: 15,000kg
Power-to-weight ratio: 20hp/tonne
Ground pressure: 0.53kg/cm²
Engine: PV-6 6-cylinder supercharged water-cooled diesel developing 300hp at 1,800rpm
Maximum road speed: 58.4km/hr
Maximum water speed: 10.8km/hr
Maximum road range: 460km
Fuel capacity: 417 lit
Fording: Amphibious
Vertical obstacle: 1.1m
Trench: 2.8m
Gradient: 65%
Side slope: 40%
Armour: 10mm (maximum)
Armour type: Steel
NBC system: Yes
Night vision equipment: Yes (driver, infra-red)

Development

The OT-62 was developed jointly by former Czechoslovakia and Poland as their equivalent of Russian BTR-50PK and entered service with Czechoslovakia in 1964 and Poland in 1966. Main improvements over Russian vehicles are fully enclosed troop

OT-62B APC with turret-mounted MG

compartment, NBC system, higher road and water speeds, fully enclosed weapon stations. Some of these features were incorporated in late production BTR-50 series. Commander, gunner and driver sit at far front with troops to immediate rear. Troops enter and leave via roof hatches or side doors. One-man manually operated turret has 7.62mm MG with elevation from -10 degrees to +20 degrees, turret traverses 360 degrees. An 82mm T-21 Tarasnice recoilless rifle is mounted externally on right side.

All members of OT-62 family are fully amphibious, propelled by two waterjets at rear. Before entering the water a trim vane is erected at front and bilge pumps switched on.

Variants

OT-62AS is basic vehicle with no MG turret.
OT-62B fitted with 7.62mm MG turret as described above.
OT-62C, also known as TOPAS-2AP, has turret of OT-64C(2)(8x8).

APC on roof with one 14.5mm and one 7.62mm MG.
WPT-TOPAS recovery vehicle, Polish developed and fitted with winch and crane.
DPT-62 repair, Czechoslovakian OT-62 used in repair role.
Radio, Czechoslovakia has a number of radio versions designated the OT-62 R-3MT, OT-62 R-4MT, OT-62 R2 and OT-62 R-2M.

Status

Production complete. In service with Angola, Bulgaria, Czech Republic, Egypt, India, Iraq, Israel, Libya, Morocco (status uncertain), Poland (Army and Marines), Slovakia, and Sudan.

Manufacturer

Former Czechoslovakian state arsenals.

Above: OT-62A APC as used by Polish Marines

141

AMX VCI Infantry Combat Vehicle (France)

Key recognition features

● Well sloped glacis plate which often has trim vane across front with spare road wheel above, flat hull top to rear of second road wheel station, almost vertical hull front and horizontal roof that extends to rear of vehicle, vertical hull with twin doors
● Armament mounted on left side of forward superstructure with commander to right. Hull sides vertical for first half of troop compartment sides then slope inwards, four firing ports each side
● Suspension each side has five road wheels, drive sprocket front, idler rear, up to four return rollers, no skirts

Specifications

Crew: 3+10
Armament: 1 x 12.7mm MG
Ammunition: 1,000 x 12.7mm
Length: 5.7m
Width: 2.67m
Height with turret: 2.41m
Height hull top: 2.1m
Ground clearance: 0.48m
Weight, combat: 15,000kg
Weight, empty: 12,500kg
Power-to-weight ratio: 16.67hp/tonne
Engine: SOFAM model 8Gxb 8-cylinder water-cooled petrol developing 250hp at 3,200rpm
Maximum road speed: 60km/hr
Maximum road range: 350km
Fuel capacity: 410 lit
Fording: 1m
Vertical obstacle: 0.65m
Trench: 1.6m
Gradient: 60%
Side slope: 30%
Armour: 30mm (maximum)
Armour type: Steel
NBC system: Optional
Night vision equipment: Optional

Development

The AMX VCI (Véhicule de Combat d'Infanterie) was developed in the 1950s and is based on the AMX-13 light tank chassis. First prototype completed in 1955, first production vehicles completed at Atelier de Construction Roanne (ARE) in 1957.

Once AMX-30 production was under way at the ARE production of the whole AMX-13 light family was transferred to Creusot Loire, Chalon sur Saone. This vehicle has been replaced in front line French Army service by the GIAT Industries AMX-10P series.

Layout of all versions is similar with driver front left, engine compartment to his right, commander and gunner in raised superstructure to his rear, troop compartment which extends right to rear of vehicle, troop entry via two doors in hull rear. Ten infantry sit five each side back to back, two two-piece hatch covers in each side of troop compartment (lower part of each has two firing ports and folds forwards into horizontal, upper part folds upwards through 180o to rest on troop compartment roof).

Wide range of optional equipment includes NBC system, night vision devices and turrets and cupolas armed with 7.62mm or 12.7mm MGs, 20mm cannon or 60mm breech-loaded mortar. Original petrol engine can be replaced by fuel-efficient Detroit Diesel 6V-71T developing 280hp at 2,800rpm or Baudouin 6F11SRY turbo-charged diesel developing 280hp at 3,200rpm.

Variants

Ambulance (VTT/TB) transports four seated and three stretcher patients.
Command post vehicle (VTT/PC) has extensive communications equipment.
Cargo (VTT/cargo) with 3,000kg capacity.
Anti-tank, AMX VCI fitted with MILAN, SS-11 or TOW ATGWs.
Fire-control vehicle (VTT/LT), battery command post vehicle for artillery units.
RATAC radar carrier (VTT/RATAC) with RATAC battlefield surveillance radar on roof.
155mm Support Vehicle (VTT/VCA) operates with 155mm Mk

F3 self-propelled gun and carries remainder of gun crew and ammunition. Also tows ammunition trailer.

81mm mortar carrier (VTT/PM) has 81mm mortar in rear firing through roof.

120mm mortar carrier (VTT/PM) has 120mm mortar in rear firing through roof.

Status

Production complete. In service with Argentina, Cyprus (VTT/VCA and command post), Ecuador, France, Indonesia, Italy, Kuwait, Lebanon, Mexico, Morocco, Sudan, Venezuela and United Arab Emirates.

Manufacturer

Creusot-Loire Industrie at Chalon sur Saone, France.

AMX VCI with 12.7mm MG

Right: AMX VCI

Key recognition features

● Pointed hull front with nose directed back under hull, well sloped glacis plate with driver's position on upper left side, horizontal roof with hull rear sloping slightly inwards, large power-operated ramp

● Turret mounted centre of roof, 20mm cannon mounted externally with 7.62mm MG to right, two outward-opening roof hatches to rear of turret. Hull sides vertical, no firing ports in sides of rear troop compartment, circular exhaust outlet in right side of hull above second/third roadwheel

● Suspension each side has five road wheels, drive sprocket front, idler rear, three track-return rollers. Upper part of track covered by skirt

Specifications

Crew: 3+8
Armament: 1 x 20mm cannon, 1 x 7.62mm MG (coaxial), 2 x 2 smoke grenade dischargers
Ammunition: 760 x 20mm, 2,000 x 7.62mm
Length: 5.90m
Width: 2.83m
Height overall: 2.83m
Height hull top: 1.95m
Ground clearance: 0.45m
Weight, combat: 14,500kg
Weight, empty: 12,700kg
Power-to-weight ratio: 17.93hp/tonne
Ground pressure: 0.53kg/cm²
Engine: Hispano-Suiza HS-115 V-8 water-cooled supercharged diesel developing 300hp at 3,000rpm
Maximum road speed: 65km/hr
Maximum water speed: 7km/hr
Maximum road range: 500km
Fuel capacity: 528 lit
Fording: Amphibious
Vertical obstacle: 0.7m
Trench: 2.1m
Gradient: 60%
Side slope: 30%
Armour: Classified
Armour type: Aluminium
NBC system: Yes
Night vision equipment: Yes (driver, commander and gunner)

Development

The AMX-10P was developed from 1965 by Atelier de Construction d'Issy-les-Moulineaux to meet requirements of French Army with first prototype completed in 1968 and first production vehicles in 1973. AMX-10 RC (6x6) armoured car (qv) uses automotive components of this vehicle. The driver sits front left, with engine compartment to right and troop compartment extending right to rear. A two-man (commander and gunner) power-operated turret is armed with 20mm cannon and 7.62mm coaxial MG. Turret traverses through 360°, weapons elevate from -8° to +50°. Troop compartment has roof hatches and periscopes, two firing ports in rear ramp.

AMX-10P is fully amphibious, propelled by its waterjets, one mounted each side at hull rear. Before entering the water a trim vane is erected at front of vehicle and bilge pumps switched on.

Variants

AMX-10P 25 ICV, one-man 25mm turret, trials only.
AMX-10 ambulance is unarmed.
AMX-10P driver training vehicle has no turret.
AMX-10 ECH repair vehicle has one-man turret and hydraulic crane.
AMX-10P HOT (anti-tank) has turret with four HOT ATGWs.
AMX-10 PC (command vehicle) has additional communications equipment.
AMX-10P with RATAC (radar for field artillery fire) on roof.
AMX-10 SAO (artillery observation vehicle) has turret with 7.62mm MG.
AMX-10 SAT (artillery survey vehicle).
AMX-10 TM (mortar tractor) tows 120mm TDA mortar.
AMX-10 VOA (artillery observer vehicle).
AMX-10Ps used in Atila artillery fire-control system include AMX-10 VFA, AMX-10 VLA and AMX-10 SAF.
AMX-10P Marines has been developed specifically for

AMX-10P ICV

Left: AMX-10 PAC 90 fire support vehicle

Right: AMX-10P HOT anti-tank vehicle

amphibious operations. Singapore has vehicle with 90mm TS-90 turret and 25mm Dragar turret while Indonesia has vehicle with TS-90 turret and 12.7mm MG turret.

Status

Production as required. In service with France, Greece, Indonesia (Marines version), Iraq, Qatar, Saudi Arabia, Singapore (Marines version), and the United Arab Emirates.

Manufacturer

GIAT Industries, Roanne, France

Right: AMX-10P Marine with 12.7mm MG

Marder 1 Infantry Combat Vehicle (Germany)

Key recognition features

● Well sloped glacis plate with driver on left leading up to horizontal roof with vertical hull rear, hull sides slope inwards above suspension, power-operated ramp in hull rear
● Large turret with sloping front, sides and rear on roof with externally mounted 20mm cannon and smoke grenade dischargers on left
● Suspension with six rubber-tyred road wheels, drive sprocket front, idler rear, three track-return rollers. Upper part of suspension normally covered by track guard

Specifications

Crew: 3+6
Armament: 1 x 20mm cannon, 1 x 7.62mm MG (coaxial), 1 x 6 smoke grenade dischargers
Ammunition: 1,250 x 20mm, 5,000 x 7.62mm
Length: 6.79m
Width: 3.24m
Height over turret top: 2.985m
Height hull top: 1.9m,Ground clearance:
Ground clearance: 0.44mWeight, combat:
Weight, empty: 29,200kg
Power-to-weight ratio: 20.54hp/tonne
Ground pressure: 0.83kg/cm^2
Engine: MTU MB 833 Ea-500 6-cylinder liquid-cooled diesel developing 600hp at 2,200rpm
Maximum road speed: 75km/hr
Maximum road range: 520km
Fuel capacity: 652 lit
Fording: 1.5m, 2m with preparation
Vertical obstacle: 1m
Trench: 2.5m
Gradient: 60%
Side slope: 30%
Armour: Classified
Armour type: Steel
NBC system: Yes
Night vision equipment: Yes (for commander, gunner and driver) but see text

Development

In the 1960s development of an infantry combat vehicle to meet requirements of Germany Army was undertaken by three companies and after trials with three series of prototypes, pre-production vehicles were completed in 1967/68. In 1969 Rheinstahl was appointed prime contractor for its production vehicle (then known as Marder) with MaK as major sub-contractor.

First production vehicles were delivered to the German Army in December 1970 and production continued until 1975. The chassis remained in production for Roland surface-to-air missile system until 1983. The driver sits front left, with one infantryman behind him, and the engine compartment to his right. Turret is to rear with commander right and gunner left. 20mm cannon and 7.62mm MG mounted externally above turret, powered elevation from -17˚ to +65˚, traverse 360˚. Troop compartment rear with three infantrymen seated each side. Vehicle fords to depth of 2m with preparation, and many vehicles have a Euromissile MILAN above commander's hatch on right side of turret.

Variants

Countless trials versions of Marder 1 but only variant in service is Radarpanzer T₍R which is Marder 1 chassis with turret replaced by hydraulically operated arm on which radar scanner is mounted for air defence.

Marder 1 A1(+), double feed for 20mm cannon, image intensification night sight with thermal pointer, new water can racks and flaps for periscopes.

Marder 1 A1(-), as above but prepared for but not fitted with thermal pointer.

Marder 1 A1A, upgraded in all areas except passive night vision equipment.

Marder 1 A2, all Marders upgraded to this standard and includes modified chassis and suspension.

Marder 1 A3, all earlier Marders are being upgraded to this standard with improved armour and new roof hatch arrangement.

Driving Training Tank, has turret replaced by fixed cupola.

German and Brazilian armies use Marder IFV chassis as basis for their Roland surface-to-air missile system (see SPAAMs).

Argentina has built an IFV designated VCTP, based on the TAM tank chassis, which is similar to Marder but has simple two-man turret with 20mm cannon.

Right:
Marder 1 IFV

Below:
Marder 1A3
IFV

Status

Production complete. In service with German Army only.

Manufacturers

Thyssen Henschel (previously Rheinstahl), Kassel and MaK of Kiel, Germany.

Thyssen Henschel Jagdpanzer Jaguar 1 SP ATGW Vehicle (Germany)

Key recognition features

- Fighting compartment front with drop-down engine compartment rear, applique armour on front and sides of fighting compartment
- HOT ATGW launcher on left side of fighting compartment roof but can be retracted into vehicle
- Suspension has five road wheels, idler front, drive sprocket rear, return rollers covered by skirts

Specifications

Crew: 4
Armament: 1 x HOT ATGW launcher, 1 x 7.62mm coaxial MG, 1 x 7.62mm AA MG, 8 smoke grenade dischargers
Ammunition: 20 HOT ATGW, 3,200 x 7.62mm
Length: 6.61m
Width: 3.12m
Height: 2.54m (including missiles), 1.98m (hull top)
Ground clearance: 0.45m (front), 0.44m (rear)
Weight, combat: 25,500kg
Power-to-weight ratio: 19.6hp/tonne
Ground pressure: 0.7kg/cm^2
Engine: Daimler Benz MB 837 8-cylinder water-cooled diesel developing 500hp at 2,000rpm
Maximum road speed: 70km/hr
Maximum road range: 400km
Fuel capacity: 470 lit
Fording: 1.2m
Vertical obstacle: 0.75m
Trench: 2m
Gradient: 58%
Side slope: 30%
Armour: 50mm max (estimate)
Armour type: Steel
NBC system: Yes
Night vision equipment: Yes (driver and gunner)

Development

During 1967/68 370 Jagdpanzer Raketes were built, 185 by Hanomag and 185 by Henschel. They have the same chassis as 90mm Jagdpanzer Kanone (JPZ 4-5) self-propelled anti-tank gun built earlier by the same companies. The 90mm version is no longer in service with Belgian or German armies.

Between 1978 and 1983 316 of the original 370 Raketes were rebuilt and their SS-11 ATGW system replaced by the more advanced and effective Euromissile K3S HOT ATGW system with maximum range of 4,000m. At the same time applique armour was added to glacis plate and fighting compartment sides for increased protection against HEAT attack. The rebuilt vehicles are known as Jaguar 1s.

Mounted in front right side of hull is 7.62mm MG3 bow machine gun with traverse of 15° left and right and elevation from -8° to +15°. A second 7.62mm MG3 is mounted on commander's cupola for use in anti-aircraft role and a bank of eight electrically operated smoke grenade dischargers is mounted over hull rear firing forwards.

Variants

Jagdpanzer with HOT Compact Turret and four HOT ATGWs in ready-to-launch position (prototype). Jaguar 2 is Jagdpanzer Kanone with 90mm gun removed, applique armour and roof-mounted TOW ATGW launcher. A total of 162 vehicles were converted to the Jaguar 2 configuration with prime contractor being Thyssen-Henschel, conversions were carried out between 1983 and 1985.

Status

Production complete. In service with German Army only.

Jaguar 1 with HOT ATGW launcher raised

Manufacturer

Original builders were Henschel and Hanomag but conversion was by Thyssen Henschel with Euromissile providing complete HOT ATGW system.

Above right: Jaguar 1 with HOT ATGW launcher retracted

Right: Jaguar 1 with HOT ATGW launcher tube retracted

149

MaK Wiesel Airportable Armoured Vehicle (Germany)

Key recognition features

● Well sloped glacis plate with engine front left and driver right, TOW ATGW on pedestal mount over open horizontal roof at hull rear
● Suspension each side has three large road wheels, drive sprocket front, large idler and one track-return roller above first and second road wheels
● Hull sides slope inwards to above track guards with air outlet on left side, horizontal louvres with exhaust pipe to immediate rear with gauze-type cover. Right side of hull above tracks has spade

Specifications (TOW version)

Crew: 3
Armament: 1 x TOW ATGW
Ammunition: 7 x TOW ATGW
Length: 3.31m
Width: 1.82m
Height overall: 1.897m
Height to hull top: 1.352m
Ground clearance: 0.302m
Weight, combat: 2800kg
Power-to-weight ratio: 30.7hp/tonne
Engine: VW 5-cylinder turbocharged diesel developing 86hp at 4,500rpm
Maximum road speed: 75km/hr
Maximum road range: 300km
Fuel capacity: 80 lit
Vertical obstacle: 0.4m
Trench: 1.2m
Gradient: 60%
Side slope: 30%
Armour: Classified
Armour type: Steel
NBC system: None
Night vision equipment: Optional

Development

The Wiesel airportable light armoured vehicle was developed for the German airborne units by Porsche but production is undertaken by MaK with the first of 345 vehicles being delivered to the German Army late in 1989. The order comprises 210 with TOW ATGW and 135 with 20mm cannon. Wiesel with TOW, designated TOW A1 by German Army, has Hughes TOW ATGW launcher in rear with traverse of 45° left and right and total of seven missiles. The other version selected by the German Army is MK 20 A1 with two-man crew and KUKA turret armed with Rheinmetall 20mm MK 20 Rh 202 cannon with traverse of 110° left and right. It has 160 rounds of ready-use ammunition.

Variants

In 1995 the German Army ordered an air defence version of Wiesel with four Stinger SAM in ready to launch position.

Wiesel 2 Extended Base Vehicle has additional road wheel either side and will be used for some elements of the German Army air defence system which includes the Stinger mounted on standard Wiesel 1 chassis.

The Wiesel is suitable for a wide range of other roles including command and control vehicle, battlefield surveillance vehicle with radar, fitted with Euromissile HCT turret with HOT ATGWs, reconnaissance vehicle with SAMM BTM 208 turret, resupply vehicle, recovery vehicle, ambulance, air defence with Bofors RBS-70 SAM, and armoured personnel carrier.

The United States Army has taken delivery of a small number of vehicles for use in extensive Robotic trials.

Status

Production. In service with the German and US Army.

Manufacturer

MaK, Kiel, Germany.

Above: Wiesel with BTM 208 turret (Michael Jerchel)

Left: Wiesel with TOW (TOW A1) (Christopher F Foss)

Above right: Wiesel with 20mm cannon (MK 20 A1)

Right: Wiesel 2 Extended Base Vehicle (Christopher F Foss)

OTOBREDA Infantry Armoured Fighting Vehicle (Italy)

Key recognition features

● Based on modified M113 hull with well-sloped glacis plate with trim vane, horizontal hull top, hull sides vertical but slope inwards at rear, two firing ports each with observation window above
● Cupola right with external 12.7mm MG, 7.62mm MG on ring mount rear. Hull ramp at rear between two external fuel tanks
● Suspension each side has five road wheels, drive sprocket front, idler rear, no track-return rollers, upper part of track covered by rubber skirt

Specifications

Crew: 2+7
Armament: 1 x 12.7mm MG, 1 x 7.62mm MG
Ammunition: 1,050 x 12.7mm, 1,000 x 7.62mm
Length: 5.041m
Width: 2.686m
Height over MG: 2.552m
Height over commander's cover: 2.032m
Hull to hull top: 1.828m
Ground clearance: 0.406m
Weight, combat: 11,600kg
Power-to-weight ratio: 18.53bhp/tonne
Ground pressure: 0.57kg/cm²
Engine: Detroit Diesel Model 6V-53 6-cylinder water-cooled diesel developing 215bhp at 2,800rpm
Maximum road speed: 64.4km/hr
Maximum water speed: 5km/hr
Maximum road range: 550km
Fuel capacity: 360 lit
Fording: Amphibious
Vertical obstacle: 0.61m
Trench: 1.68m
Gradient: 60%
Side slope: 30%
Armour: Classified
Armour type: Aluminium with layer of steel
NBC system: None
Night vision equipment: Yes (infra-red for driver)

Development

Infantry Armoured Fighting Vehicle was developed by Automotive Technical Service of Italian Army and is based on US M113A1, made under licence by OTOBREDA. Main improvements over M113A1 are increased firepower, improved armour protection (standard aluminium armour plus layer of steel armour added to hull front, sides and rear), improved seating arrangements, ability for some troops to aim and fire from inside the vehicle using firing ports and vision blocks. Infantry Armoured Fighting Vehicle is also referred to as VCC-1 by Italian Army. Final deliveries made in 1982.

Engine compartment is front right, 12.7mm MG gunner to rear. Driver sits front left with vehicle commander rear. Infantry compartment is rear of hull, infantry enter and leave via power-operated ramp. Over top of troop compartment is ring-mounted 7.62mm MG. For operations in Somalia, some vehicles were fitted with Enhanced Applique Armour Kit (EAAK). IAFV is fully amphibious, propelled by its tracks. Before entering the water a trim vane is erected at front of vehicle and bilge pumps switched on.

Variants

Saudi Arabia has taken delivery of 224 IAFVs with US Improved TOW system as fitted to M901 Improved TOW Vehicle.

Italian Army also uses large numbers of M113/M113A1s, some of which have appliqué armour and firing ports/vision blocks in rear troop compartment (known as VCC-2s). Italian Army has also used M113A1 as basis for SIDAM 4x25mm self-propelled anti-aircraft gun system. Full details of the SIDAM 25 are given in the Self-propelled Anti-aircraft Guns section.

Status

Production complete but can be resumed for further orders. In service with Italy and Saudi Arabia.

Manufacturer
OTOBREDA, La Spezia, Italy.

Top left: IAFV without rear 7.62mm MG

Above: IAFV from rear with all hatches open

Left: IAFV with ITV launcher for Saudi Arabia

IVECO/OTOBREDA VCC-80 IFV (Italy)

Key recognition features

● Well sloped glacis plate with driver's circular hatch in upper left side, horizontal roof, turret centre. Troop compartment rear with two outward-opening roof hatches, circular roof hatch between

● Hull sides above tracks slope inwards, large horizontal air louvres on forward right side of hull, two spherical firing ports with vision block above in each side of troop compartment, hull rear slopes inwards with integral power-operated ramp

● Turret sides slope inwards with commander's cupola on left, periscopic sight to his immediate front. Suspension each side has six road wheels, drive sprocket front, idler rear, three track-return rollers. Upper part covered by side skirts

Specifications

Crew: 3+6
Armament: 1 x 25mm cannon, 1 x 7.62mm MG (coaxial), 1 x 7.62mm MG (anti-aircraft), 2 x 3 smoke grenade dischargers
Length: 6.705m
Width: 3.00m
Height overall: 2.70m
Ground clearance: 0.4m
Weight, loaded: 21.700kg
Weight, empty: 20,200kg
Power-to-weight ratio: 24hp/tonne
Engine: IVECO 8260 V-6 turbocharged, intercooled diesel developing 520bhp at 2,300rpm
Maximum road speed: 70km/hr
Maximum cruising range: 500km
Fuel capacity: Not available
Fording: 1.5m
Vertical obstacle: 0.85m
Trench: 2.5m
Gradient: 60%
Side slope: 40%
Armour: Classified
Armour type: Aluminium/steel
NBC system: Yes
Night vision equipment: Yes (passive for commander, gunner and driver)

Development

The VCC-80 has been developed by Consortium IVECO/OTOBREDA to meet requirements of the Italian Army. The first of three prototypes was completed in late 1985. Hull is all aluminium armour with additional layer of steel for increased protection. Driver sits front left with powerpack to his right, two-man power-operated turret is centre and troop compartment rear. In action the vehicle commander would dismount with the six infantrymen, five of whom can aim and fire from inside the vehicle using two firing ports/vision blocks in each side of hull and one in rear ramp. Commander sits on turret left, gunner right. 25mm Oerlikon-Contraves KBA cannon power-elevates from -10° to +60° and is stabilised, turret traverses 360°. 7.62mm MG is mounted coaxial to left of 25mm cannon. Fire-control system includes laser rangefinder and thermal image night vision equipment.

Variants

OTOBREDA has proposed that the VCC-80 could be fitted with different turret, for example a two-man OTOBREDA turret armed with a 60mm weapon.

For trials purposes, a TOW ATGW has been mounted either side of the turret of one of the prototypes of the VCC-80.

Status

Entering production for Italian Army.

Manufacturer

Consortium IVECO/OTOBREDA, Italy.

Above: VCC-80 IFV
Right: VCC-80 IFV
Below: VCC-80 IFV
Below right: VCC-80 IFV

Mitsubishi Heavy Industries Type 89 Mechanised Infantry Combat Vehicle (Japan)

Key recognition features

- Well sloped glacis plate with driver front right, turret centre, troop compartment rear with two-part roof hatch opening left and right and three firing ports in each side
- Turret has vertical sides with ATGW mounted externally each side, 35mm cannon in forward part of turret with night sight right
- Suspension each side has six road wheels, drive sprocket front, idler rear, three track-return rollers, skirts

Specifications

Crew: 3+7
Armament: 1 x 35mm, 1 x 7.62mm MG (coaxial), 2 x ATGW, 2 x 3 smoke grenade dischargers
Length: 6.8m
Width: 3.2m
Height:2.50m
Ground clearance: 0.45m
Weight, combat:27,000kg
Power-to-weight ratio: 22.22hp/tonne
Ground pressure: 0.73kg/cm²
Engine: Diesel developing 600hp
Maximum road speed: 70km/hr (forwards), 42km/hr (reverse)
Maximum road range: 400km
Fuel capacity: Not available
Fording: 1m
Vertical obstacle: 0.8m
Trench: 2.4m
Gradient: 60%
Side slope: 30%
Armour: Classified
Armour type: Steel
NBC system: Yes
Night vision equipment: Yes

Development

Development of a new mechanised infantry combat vehicle started in 1984 and after trials it was type classified as the Type 89 with first production vehicles being completed in 1991.

Prime contractor is Mitsubishi Heavy Industries with Komatsu being major sub-contractor. The layout of the vehicle is conventional with the driver being seated at the front right with the powerpack to his left, two-man power-operated turret in the centre and the troop compartment at the rear which is provided with entry doors, roof hatches and firing ports.

The commander is seated on the right side of the turret with the gunner on the left with both crew members being provided with a single piece roof hatch, periscopes for observation and a sight for aiming main armament. Main armament consists of a 35mm Oerlikon-Contraves cannon with a 7.62mm machine gun mounted coaxial and a Jyu-MAT medium range wire-guided anti-tank missile being mounted either side of the turret. Once these have been launched new missiles have to be reloaded manually.

Variants

As far as it is known there are no variants of the Type 89 MICV although the vehicle can be fitted with mine clearing equipment at the front of the hull.

Status

In production. In service with the Japanese Ground Self Defence Force.

Manufacturer

Mitsubishi Heavy Industries, Tokyo, Japan.

Main picture: Type 89 MICV (Paul Beaver)

Inset: Type 89 MICV (Kensuke Ebata)

Mitsubishi Heavy Industries Type 73 APC (Japan)

Key recognition features

● Low profile hull with glacis plate at 45o, horizontal hull top, vertical rear with two doors, vertical hull sides

● Flotation screen on glacis plate, 7.62mm MG in left side of glacis plate, 12.7mm MG on raised cupola on right side of hull top, 2x3 smoke grenade dischargers at hull rear above twin doors

● Suspension each side has five road wheels, drive sprocket front, idler rear, no return rollers or skirt

Specifications

Crew: 3+9
Armament: 1 x 12.7mm MG (main), 1 x 7.62mm MG (bow), 2x3 smoke grenade dischargers
Length: 5.78m
Width: 2.8m
Height including MG: 2.2m
Height, hull top: 1.7m
Ground clearance: 0.4m
Weight, combat: 13,300kg
Power-to-weight ratio: 22.6hp/tonne
Engine: Mitsubishi 4ZF air-cooled 2-stroke V4 diesel developing 300hp at 2,200rpm
Maximum road speed: 70km/hr
Maximum water speed: 7km/hr
Maximum road range: 300km
Fuel capacity: 450 lit
Fording: Amphibious (with kit)
Vertical obstacle: 0.7m
Trench: 2m
Gradient: 60%
Side slope: 30%
Armour: Classified
Armour type: Aluminium
NBC system: Yes
Night vision equipment: Yes (infra-red for driver)

Development

Development of a new APC to succeed Type SU 60 in Japanese Ground Self Defence Force commenced in 1967. After extensive trials with competing designs, Mitsubishi vehicle was accepted for service as Type 73 APC with first production vehicles completed in 1974. Production was completed after 225 had been built. It was followed by the Type 89 mechanised infantry combat vehicle (qv).

Bow 7.62mm MG gunner sits front left with driver front right and vehicle commander slightly to right and rear of bow MG gunner. Engine compartment to rear of driver with 12.7mm MG cupola on right side of hull roof. 12.7mm MG can be aimed and fired from inside vehicle, elevation from -10° to +60°, turret traverse 360°. Roof hatches over troop compartment and six T-shaped firing ports, two in each side of hull and two in rear, allowing some troops to fire from inside.

The Type 73 is fully amphibious with the aid of a kit which includes trim vane on glacis plate, buoyancy aids for wheels, skirts over tracks and protection for air inlet and air outlet louvres on roof.

Variants

Only variant in service is command post vehicle with higher roof at rear. Automotive components of Type 73 are used in Type 75 self-propelled ground wind-measuring system and used with Type 75 130mm self-propelled rocket launcher which uses some components of the Type 73. Components of the Type 73 APC are also used in a new Japanese mineclearing vehicle.

Status

Production complete. In service with Japanese Ground Self Defence Force only.

Manufacturer

Mitsubishi Heavy Industries, Tokyo, Japan.

Above left: Type 73 APC

Above: Type 73 APC (Kensuke Ebata)

Left: Type 73 APC

Mitsubishi Heavy Industries Type SU 60 APC (Japan)

Key recognition features

● Glacis plate at about 60o with 7.62mm MG ball mounted on left side, horizontal roof, engine compartment on left side to rear of bow MG operator and commander, troop compartment rear with roof hatches opening left and right

● Vertical hull sides and rear, twin doors in rear open outwards

● Suspension has five road wheels, drive sprocket front, idler rear, three track-return rollers, no skirts

Specifications

Crew: 4+6
Armament: 1 x 12.7mm MG, 1 x 7.62mm MG (bow)
Length: 4.85m
Width: 2.4m
Height including 12.7mm MG: 2.31m
Height hull top: 1.7m
Ground clearance: 0.4m
Weight, combat: 11,800kg
Weight, empty: 10.600kg
Power-to-weight ratio: 18.64hp/tonne
Engine: Mitsubishi Model 8 HA 21 WT, V-8 air-cooled 4-cycle diesel developing 220hp at 2,400rpm
Maximum road speed: 45km/hr
Maximum road range: 300km
Fuel capacity: Not available
Fording: 1m
Vertical obstacle: 0.6m
Trench: 1.82m
Gradient: 60%
Side slope: 30%
Armour: Classified
Armour type: Steel
NBC system: None
Night vision equipment: None

Development

In the mid-1950s Japanese Ground Self Defence Force issued a requirement for a full tracked APC and after trials with various prototypes one was accepted for service as Type SU 60. Production subsequently undertaken by Komatsu and Mitsubishi from 1959 through to the early 1970s, an estimated 430 being built. As its successor, Type 73 has been built in smaller numbers. Type SU 60 will remain in service in declining numbers until well into the next decade.

Driver sits front right with bow machine gunner on left side, vehicle commander between them, 12.7mm M2 HB MG complete with shield on right side of roof to rear of commander. Troop compartment at hull rear with twin doors rear and roof hatches above. No provision for weapon-firing from inside.

Variants

Type SX 60 81mm mortar carrier has 81mm mortar mounted in hull rear which can also be deployed away from vehicle. Only 18 built.

Type SX 60 4.2 inch (107mm) mortar carrier has 107mm (4.2 inch) mortar mounted in rear which can also be deployed away from vehicle. Only 18 built. 107mm mortar carrier can be distinguished from 81mm version by distinct chamfer to top of hull rear.
SU 60 dozer, only two in service, front-mounted dozer blade.
NBC detection vehicle has device at rear for taking soil samples.
Anti-tank vehicle, a few Type SU 60s have been fitted with two KAM-3D anti-tank guided missiles on hull roof at rear.
For training, a few SU 60s have been modified to resemble Russian BMD 1 airborne combat vehicles.

Status

Production complete. In service with Japanese Ground Self Defence Force only.

Above: Type SU 60 APC

Manufacturer

Mitsubishi Heavy Industries, Tokyo; Komatsu Manufacturing Corporation, Japan

Above: Type SU 60 APC (Kensuke Ebata)

Left: Type SX 60 4.2 inch (107mm) mortar carrier

Komatsu Type 60 106mm SP Recoilless Gun (Japan)

Key recognition features

● Low profile hull with two 106mm recoilless rifles in right side with travelling lock on hull front
● Suspension has five road wheels, drive sprocket front, idler rear, three track-return rollers

Specifications

Crew: 3
Armament: 2 x 106mm recoilless rifles, 1 x 12.7mm MG
Ammunition: 8 x 106mm
Length: 4.3m
Width: 2.23m
Height: 1.59m
Ground clearance: 0.35m
Weight, combat: 7,000kg
Weight, empty: 7,600kg
Power-to-weight ratio: 18hp/tonne (150hp engine)
Ground pressure: 0.67kg/cm^2
Engine: Komatsu Model 6T 120-2 air-cooled, 6-cylinder diesel developing 120hp at 2,400rpm (late production vehicles have 150hp engine)
Maximum road speed: 45km/hr (early production model), 55km/hr (late production model)
Maximum road range: 130km
Fuel capacity: 77 lit
Fording: 1m
Vertical obstacle: 0.55m
Trench: 1.8m
Gradient: 60%
Side slope: 30%
Armour: 12mm max (estimate)
Armour type: Steel
NBC system: No
Night vision equipment: IR night sight (optional)

Development

Type 60 106mm was developed from the 1950s to meet requirements of Japanese Ground Self Defence Force with production under way in 1960. Three versions were built, the final Model C having more powerful engine. Production completed in 1979 after 223 had been built.

Main armament comprises two 106mm recoilless rifles in right side of hull with traverse of 10 degrees left and right and elevation from -5 to +10. The two rifles and mount can be raised with the aid of powered controls above roof of vehicle, when they have traverse of 30 degrees left and right, elevation from -20 to +15. Mounted over right recoilless rifle is 12.7mm ranging machine gun. The effectiveness of these 106mm recoilless rifles against the more modern armours is questionable. For improved mobility in snow extra wide tracks can be fitted.

The recoilless rifles fire fixed HEAT and HE ammunition. A rangefinder is carried on the vehicle and some vehicles have been fitted with infra-red night vision equipment.

Variants

No variants.

Status

Production complete. In service with Japanese Ground Self Defence Force only.

Manufacturer

Komatsu Seisakujyo, Tokyo, Japan.

Above left: Type 60 106mm. Dotted line shows position of raised weapon

Top right: Type 60 106mm with weapons raised (R Watanabe)

Right: Type 60 106mm with weapons lowered (Keiichi Nogi)

Left: Type 60 106mm from rear with weapons lowered (Keiichi Nogi)

163

MLVM Mountaineers Combat Vehicle (Romania)

Key recognition features

● Large box type hull with well sloped glacis plate, nose slopes back under front of vehicle, hull sides slope slightly inwards with chamfer either side of hull at front, vertical hull rear with two doors

● Suspension either side consists of six spoked road wheels, drive sprocket at front, idler at rear and three track-return rollers, upper part of track covered by shallow skirt

● Turret in centre of hull roof with flat top and conical sides, distinctive sight is on left of turret and is protected by a distinctive wire gage

Specifications

Crew: 2+7
Armament: 1 x 14.5mm MG, 1 x 7.62mm MG (coaxial)
Ammunition: 500 x 14.5mm, 2,000 x 7.62mm
Length: 5.85m
Width: 2.87m
Height: 1.95m (turret roof), 1.55m (hull top)
Ground clearance: 0.38m
Weight, combat: 9,800kg
Power-to-weight ratio: 15.7hp/tonne
Ground pressure: 0.47kg/cm^2
Engine: 4-stroke supercharged diesel developing 153hp
Maximum road speed: 48km/hr
Range: 370/440km (cross-country), 680/740km (road)
Fuel capacity: 480 lit
Fording: 0.6m
Vertical obstacle: 0.6m
Trench: 1.5m
Gradient: 60%
Side slope: 30%
Armour: Classified
Armour type: Steel
NBC system: Yes
Night vision equipment: Yes (infra-red)

Development

The MLVM Mountaineers Combat Vehicle was developed to meet the specific operational requirements of the Romanian Army for a vehicle capable of operating in mountainous terrain. The driver is seated at the front left with the vehicle commander to his rear and the powerpack to their right. The troop compartment is at the rear with the troops entering via two doors in the hull rear. The troop compartment is provided with firing ports and vision devices and each of the rear doors contains an integral fuel tank.

Variants

MLVM AR, this has a modified rear hull and is fitted with a 120mm mortar.
ABAL armoured vehicle for combat supply.

Status

Production as required. In service with Romania.

Manufacturer

Romanian state factories.

Right: MLVM Mountaineers Combat Vehicle
(Paul Beaver)

BTR-50PK APC (Russia)

Key recognition features

● Similar to Czechoslovak OT-62 but BTR-50PK has no turret, no side doors and distinct chamfer between vertical hull sides and roof

● Glacis plate almost horizontal then slopes upwards to crew compartment, flat roof with distinct step down to engine compartment mid-way along top

● Suspension has six rubber-tyred road wheels, idler front, drive sprocket rear, no track-return rollers

Specifications

Crew: 2+20
Armament: 1 x 7.62mm MG
Ammunition: 1,250 x 7.62mm
Length: 7.08m
Width: 3.14m
Height: 1.97m (without MG)
Ground clearance: 0.37m
Weight, combat: 14,200kg
Power-to-weight ratio: 16.9hp/tonne
Ground pressure: 0.51kg/cm^2
Engine: Model V-6 6-cylinder in-line water-cooled diesel developing 240hp at 1,800rpm
Maximum road speed: 44km/hr
Maximum road range: 400km
Fuel capacity: 400 lit
Fording: Amphibious
Vertical obstacle: 1.1m
Trench: 2.8m
Gradient: 60%
Side slope: 30%
Armour: 10mm (maximum)
Armour type: Steel
NBC system: Yes
Night vision equipment: Yes (infra-red for driver and commander)

Development

BTR-50KP was the first full tracked APC to enter service with Russian Army and was first seen in public in 1957. Today has been replaced in front-line units by BMP-1/BMP-2 ICV. First version has open-topped troop compartment, later BTR-50PK has fully enclosed troop compartment and NBC system. The BTR-50P series are all fully amphibious, propelled by two waterjets, one each side at rear. Before entering the water a trim vane is erected at front of hull. BTR-50 series uses automotive components of PT-76 light amphibious tank family.

Czechoslovakia produced improved version of BTR-50PK, the OT-62 (see separate entry). These lack distinct chamfer to hull top as on Russian vehicles. China has also produced similar vehicle, Type 77 (see also separate entry).

Variants

BTR-50, original version with open-topped crew compartment, pintle-mounted 7.62mm MG front, loading ramps on rear engine decking for 57mm, 76mm or 85mm gun.
BTR-50A as BTR-50P but with no loading ramps.
BTR-50PK, full overhead armour protection and NBC system, 7.62mm MG on pintle-mount on roof.
BTR-50PU (command), at least two models, Model 1 with one projecting bay and Model 2 with two projecting bays at front of hull; Model 2 is more common. Usually have additional antenna, stowage boxes and generator.
BTR-50PK(B) amphibious armoured recovery vehicle, developed to assist and recover vehicles at water obstacles.
MTP technical support vehicle based on BTR-50PK, used for repair and recovery of other AFVs, has distinctive raised roof for personnel to work upright. There is also a repair version called the MTR.
MTK mine-clearing vehicle is BTR-50PK with special launcher on roof to fire rockets with flexible tubes filled with explosive.

Status

Production complete. In service with Afghanistan, Albania, Algeria, Angola (and OT-62), Bulgaria (and OT-62), Russia, Congo, Czech Republic, Egypt (and OT-62), Finland, Guinea, India (and OT-62), Iran, Iraq (and OT-62), Israel (and OT-62), North Korea, Libya (and OT-62), Morocco (OT-62 only, status uncertain), Poland (OT-62 only), Romania, Slovakia, Somalia, Sudan (and OT-62), Syria, Vietnam and former Yugoslavia.

Manufacturer

Russian state arsenals.

Above: BTR-50P APC without armament

Above right: BTR-50PK APC (Finnish Army)

Right: BTR-50PK APC

MT-LB Multi-Purpose Tracked Vehicle (Russia)

Key recognition features

● Commander's and driver's compartment to immediate rear of glacis plate, small flat-topped turret right of driver

● Troop compartment extends from crew compartment to rear of vehicle, almost vertical sides with chamfered top, twin rear doors, single firing port in left hull side

● Six equally spaced ribbed road wheels, drive sprocket front, idler rear, no track-return rollers

Specifications

Crew: 2+11
Armament: 1 x 7.62mm MG
Ammunition: 2,500 x 7.62mm
Length: 6.45m
Width: 2.86m
Height: 1.865m
Ground clearance: 0.4m
Weight, combat: 11,900kg
Weight, empty: 9,700kg
Power-to-weight ratio: 20.16hp/tonne
Ground pressure: 0.46kg/cm²
Engine: YaMZ 238 V, V-8 diesel developing 240hp at 2,100rpm
Maximum road speed: 61.5km/hr
Maximum water speed: 5-6km/hr
Maximum road range: 500km
Fuel capacity: 450 lit
Fording: Amphibious
Vertical obstacle: 0.61m
Trench: 2.41m
Gradient: 60%
Side slope: 30%
Armour: 3-10mm
Armour type: Steel
NBC system: Yes
Night vision equipment: Yes (infra-red for commander and driver)

Development

The MT-LB was developed in the late 1960s to replace the AT-P armoured tracked artillery tractor which is no longer in front-line service. It is based on MT-L unarmoured tracked amphibious carrier. Typical roles include carrying 11 fully equipped troops, towing 122mm D-30 howitzers or 100mm T-12 anti-tank guns, command and radio vehicle, artillery fire-control vehicle and cargo carrier, and many specialised versions.

The vehicle is fully amphibious, propelled by its tracks. Basic version normally has 350mm wide tracks which give ground pressure of 0.46kg/cm², but these can be replaced by much wider 565mm tracks which lower ground pressure to 0.27/0.28kg/cm², giving vehicle improved mobility in snow or swamp. Turret is manned by commander and has single 7.62mm PKT MG with manual elevation from -5 degrees to +30 degrees and manual traverse through 360 degrees. No roof hatch.

Variants

MT-LBV is standard MT-LB with 565mm wide tracks.

MT-LB artillery tractor normally has fully enclosed box over troop compartment for gun equipment.

MY-LBU command has additional radios, generator, land navigation system and canvas cover that extends to rear for additional space.

MT-LB with Big Fred artillery/mortar locating radar mounted on roof; when travelling antenna folds forward. Russian designation is TT-LB.

MTP-LB repair vehicle has no turret, A-frame, stowage on vehicle roof, winch, tools and other specialised equipment.

MT-LB ambulance has stretchers in rear troop compartment.

MT-LB engineer vehicle has stowage box on roof and hydraulically operated blade at hull rear.

SA-13 Gopher SAM system is based on MT-LB chassis (see SPAAMs).

MT-LB with AT-6 ATGW, has launcher which is raised when required.

Above: Basic MT-LB

Right: MT-LB with AT-6 ATGW system

MT-LBs are used for a variety of artillery and air defence fire control vehicles.

RKhM chemical reconnaissance vehicle is based on MT-LB components.

There are numerous **Polish variants** of MT-LB.

There are numerous **Bulgarian variants** of MT-LB.

MT-LB mortar, includes 82mm Vasilek and 120mm.

MT-LB with WAT turret, used by Poland, has turret of OT-64C (2) (SKOT-2AP) turret.

MT-LB, Iraq, includes 120mm mortar in rear and another with four 120mm mortars mounted externally at rear.

Status

Production complete. In service with Bulgaria, Russia, Czech Republic, Finland, Hungary, Iraq, Poland, Slovakia, Sweden and former Yugoslavia.

Manufacturer

Russian state arsenals, possibly Kirov facility in Leningrad. Also Bulgaria and Poland.

Right: MT-LB towing 100mm T-12 anti-tank gun

BMP-3 Infantry Combat Vehicle (Russia)

Key recognition features

● Large box type hull with almost horizontal glacis plate, nose slopes back under front of hull, vertical hull sides rear with two small doors in hull rear. Mounted in either side of hull front is a 7.62mm MG firing forwards

● Circular turret in centre of hull with two hatches, over frontal 180o of the turret is another layer of armour, long-barrelled 100mm gun with 30mm cannon mounted coaxial to right, distinctive box over rear of main armament

● Suspension either side has six road wheels with idler at front, drive sprocket at rear and three track-return rollers, upper part of track covered by light steel cover similar to that on BMP-1 and BMP-2.

Specifications

Crew: 3+7
Armament: 1 x 100mm, 1 x 30mm cannon (coaxial), 1 x 7.62mm MG (coaxial), 2 x 7.62mm (hull front, one either side), 2 x 3 smoke grenade dischargers
Ammunition: 40 x 100mm, 500 x 30mm, 6,000 x 7.62mm, 6 x ATGW
Length: 7.14m
Width: 3.14m
Height: 2.30m (turret roof)
Ground clearance: 510mm (see text)
Weight, combat: 18,700kg
Power-to-weight ratio: 26.73hp/tonne
Ground pressure: 0.61kg/cm²
Engine: Diesel developing 500hp
Maximum road speed: 70km/hr
Maximum water speed: 10km/hr
Maximum road range: 600km
Fuel capacity: Not known
Fording: Amphibious
Vertical obstacle: 0.8m
Trench: 2.5m
Gradient: 60%
Side slope: 30%
Armour: Classified
Armour type: Steel
NBC system: Yes
Night vision equipment: Yes (commander, gunner and driver)

Development

The BMP-3 was developed to meet the requirements of the Russian Army and was first seen in public during a parade held in Moscow in 1990. Within NATO it has been referred to as the Soviet Infantry Fighting Vehicle (SIFV) M1990/1.

The driver is seated at the front of the vehicle in centre with an additional crew member to his left and right, all three being provided with a single piece hatch cover. The two man turret is in the centre of the hull with the commander being seated on the right and the gunner on the left, both with a roof hatch. Main armament consists of a 100mm rifled gun that in addition to firing conventional ammunition also fires a laser guided ATGW which has the NATO designation of the AT-10. Mounted to the right of this is a 30mm cannon that is attached to the 100mm gun. In addition there is a 7.62mm machine gun mounted to the right of the 30mm cannon with another 7.62mm machine gun being mounted in the front of the hull firing forwards. A total of seven infantrymen are carried, one either side of the driver with the remainder being seated to the sides and rear of the turret.

The engine is located at the rear of the vehicle on the right side with the fuel tanks being under the floor of the vehicle. The small troop compartment at the rear of the BMP-3 is provided with roof hatches and two doors in the rear that open outwards. As the floor of the troop compartment is so high from the ground, steps unfold as the rear doors are opened.

The vehicle is fully amphibious being propelled in the water by two waterjets mounted at the rear of the hull and before entering the water the trim vane is erected at the front of the vehicle and the bilge pumps are switched on. The suspension is of the adjustable type and the driver can adjust the suspension to suit the type of ground being crossed.

BMP-3 ICV (Steve Zaloga)

Right: BMP-3

Variants
BMP-3 reconnaissance, called BRM, or Rys (Lynx).
BMP-3 driver training vehicle.
BMP-3 recovery vehicle (BREM-L).
BMP-3K command vehicle.
BMP-3 anti-tank.
BMP-3 chassis can be used for wide range of other roles.

Right: BMP-3 reconnaissance vehicle (BRM)

Status
In production. In service with Abu Dhabi, Russia, Cyprus and Kuwait.

Manufacturer
Russian state factories.

171

BMP-2 Infantry Fighting Vehicle (Russia)

Key recognition features

● Pointed nose with almost horizontal ribbed glacis plate, driver front left, engine compartment louvres in roof to right, turret slightly to rear of vehicle, troop compartment rear with two roof hatches. Vertical hull rear with two bulged doors opening rear. Similar in appearance to BMP-1 but with different turret and wider hull

● Turret has long-barrelled 30mm cannon with muzzle brake, three forward-firing smoke dischargers each side of turret, ATGW launcher in centre of turret at rear. Four firing ports in left side of hull and three in right plus one in each rear door

● Suspension each side has six road wheels, drive sprocket front, idler rear, track-return rollers covered by skirts with horizontal ribs

Specifications

Crew: 3+7
Armament: 1 x 30mm cannon, 1 x 7.62mm MG (coaxial), 1 x Spandrel ATGW launcher, 2 x 3 smoke grenade dischargers
Ammunition: 500 x 30mm, 2,000 x 7.62mm, 4 x Spandrel ATGW
Length: 6.735m
Width: 3.15m
Height: 2.45m
Ground clearance: 0.42m
Weight, combat: 14,300kg
Power-to-weight ratio: 20.30hp/tonne
Engine: Model UTD-20 6-cylinder diesel developing 300hp at 2,600rpm
Maximum road speed: 65km/hr
Maximum water speed: 7km/hr
Maximum road range: 600km
Fuel capacity: 462 lit
Fording: Amphibious
Vertical obstacle: 0.7m
Trench: 2.5m
Gradient: 60%
Side slope: 30%
Armour: Classified
Armour type: Steel
NBC system: Yes
Night vision equipment: Yes (commander, gunner and driver)

Development

The BMP-2 IFV is a further development of BMP-1 and was first seen in public during a Moscow parade in 1982. In addition to a more powerful engine BMP has a new two-man turret with different weapons. Driver sits front left with one of the seven infantrymen to his rear, engine compartment to his right. Turret is slightly to rear with troop compartment far rear. Six infantrymen sit three each side back to back, each man with firing port in side of hull and periscope above. Two-man turret has commander on right, gunner on left, new 30mm cannon with powered elevation up to +75˚ for use against helicopters and slow-flying aircraft, turret traverse 360˚ and 30mm cannon fully stabilised. 7.62mm MG is mounted coaxial to left of 30mm cannon.

Mounted on turret roof rear is launcher for AT-5 Spandrel ATGW which has maximum range of 4,000m. Some vehicles have launcher for 2500mm AT-4 Spigot instead. Some BMP-2s have appliquÈ armour on turrets and hulls. BMP-2 is fully amphibious, propelled by its tracks. Before entering the water a trim vane is erected at front of hull and bilge pumps switched on.

Variants

BMP-2D, late production vehicle with appliquÈ armour and provision for fitting mine clearing equipment under nose of vehicle.
BMP-2K, command version with additional communications equipment.
BVP-2, Czechoslovakian designation for BMP-2.

Status

In production. In service with Afghanistan, Algeria, Angola, Russia, Czech Republic, Finland, India, Iraq, Jordan, Kuwait, Poland, Slovakia, Yemen.

Manufacturer

Russian state arsenals. Manufactured under licence in former Czechoslovakia and India.

**Above: BMP-2
(Steven Zaloga)**

Right: BMP-2

Below right: BMP-2 (Michael Jerchel)

Below: BMP-2

BMP-1 Infantry Combat Vehicle (Russia)

Key recognition features

● Pointed nose with almost horizontal ribbed glacis plate, driver front left, engine compartment louvres in roof to right, turret slightly to rear of vehicle, troop compartment rear with four roof hatches, two each side. Vertical hull rear with two bulged doors opening rear. Similar in appearance to BMP-2 but with different turret with long-barrelled 30mm cannon and wider hull

● Circular turret with well sloped sides has 73mm gun with launcher above for Sagger ATGW (not always installed in peacetime), single gunner's hatch on left side of roof. Four firing ports each side of hull and three in each rear door

● Suspension each side has six road wheels, drive sprocket at front, idler rear, and three track-return rollers. Upper part of track covered by skirts

174

Specifications

Crew: 3+8
Armament: 1 x 73mm, 1 x 7.62mm MG (coaxial), 1 x Sagger ATGW launcher
Ammunition: 40 x 73mm, 2,000 x 7.62mm, 1+4 Sagger ATGW
Length: 6.74m
Width: 2.94m
Height over searchlight: 2.15m
Ground clearance: 0.39m
Weight, combat: 13,500kg
Weight, empty: 12,500kg
Power-to-weight ratio: 22.22hp/tonne
Ground pressure: 0.6kg/cm^2
Engine: Type UTD-20 6-cylinder in-line water-cooled diesel developing 300hp at 2,000rpm
Maximum road speed: 65km/hr
Maximum water speed: 7km/hr
Maximum road range: 600km
Fuel capacity: 460 lit
Fording: Amphibious
Vertical obstacle: 0.8m
Trench: 2.2m
Gradient: 60%
Side slope: 30%
Armour: 33mm (maximum)
Armour type: Steel
NBC system: Yes
Night vision equipment: Yes (infra-red for commander, gunner and driver)

Development

BMP-1 was developed in the early 1960s to replace BTR-50P

series tracked APCs and was first seen in public during 1967. It was replaced in production by BMP-2 ICV (previous entry) which, although similar in appearance, has slightly different layout and new turret and weapon system.

In the BMP-1, driver sits front left with vehicle commander to rear, engine compartment is to right of driver with one-man turret centre and troop compartment rear. Turret power-traverses through 360° and 73mm gun elevates from -4° to +33° and fires HEAT or HE-FRAG rounds. 7.62mm MG is mounted coaxial to right of 73mm gun and mounted over gun is launcher for AT-3 Sagger wire-guided ATGW which has maximum range of 3,000m.

Troop compartment is at rear with eight infantry seated four each side back to back. In each side of troop compartment are four firing ports with periscope above, and in each of two rear doors is a further firing port and periscope.

BMP-1 is fully amphibious, propelled by its tracks. Before entering the water a trim vane is erected at front of vehicle and bilge pumps switched on.

As BMP-1 was produced for some 20 years there are minor detailed differences between production models.

Variants

BMP-1F, reconnaissance model used by Hungary.
BMP-1K, BMP-1 commander's model.
BMP-1K3, BMP-1 commander's model.
BMP-1P, BMP-1 with no Sagger and roof-mounted AT-4 ATGW fitted.
BMP-1PK, BMP-1P commander's model.
BRM-1K, BRM-1 basic reconnaissance - armoured cavalry.
BREM-1 and BREM-4, recovery vehicles.
BMP-1KShM, unarmed command version of BMP-1.

BWP, Polish version of BMP-1.

Czech BMP-1, many variants including OT-90 (BMP-1 with turret of OT-64C(1)).

Egyptian BMP-1, have new French diesel engine.

BMP-1 can be fitted with mine clearing equipment.

BMP-1 has been fitted with 30mm grenade launcher.

BRM and BRM-1 reconnaissance vehicles, new two-man turret.

PRP-3 Radar, two-man turret in radar in roof.

IRM, Amphibious reconnaissance vehicle.

BMP-POO, Mobile Training Centre, no turret, raised roof, Iraqi versions include ambulance and basic vehicle with applique armour.

BMP-1G, for export, no Sagger, roof-mounted Spandrel ATGW plus 30mm grenade launcher.

Status

Production complete. In service with Afghanistan, Algeria, Angola, Bulgaria, Russia, Cuba, Egypt, Ethiopia, Finland, Greece, Hungary, India, Iran, Iraq, North Korea, Libya, Mongolia, Poland, Romania, Sri Lanka, Sweden, Syria, Yemen and former Yugoslavia

Manufacturer

Former Czechoslovak and Russian state arsenals. China builds a version of BMP-1 designated WZ 501.

Top left: BMP-1 ICV (Steven Zaloga)

Above: BMP-1

Above left: BMP-1

175

BMD-3 Airborne Combat Vehicle (Russia)

Key recognition features

● Pointed nose with horizontal hull top extending to rear of hull, three hatches in hull top at the front, turret (as fitted to BMP-2) in the centre, louvres in hull top either side, vertical hull rear
● Turret has long barreled 30 mm cannon that overhangs front of vehicle, hull sides are vertical
● Suspension either side consists of five road wheels with idler at the front, drive sprocket at the rear and four track return rolers

Specifications

Crew:2 + 5
Armament: 1 x 30 mm cannon, 1 x 7.62 mm MG (coaxial), 1 x AT-4/ AT-5 ATGW launcher, 1 x 7.62 mm MG (bow), 1 x 40 mm grenade launcher (bow), 1 x 5.45 mm MG (bow)
Ammunition: 860 x 30 mm, 2000 x 7.62 mm, 2160 x 5.45 mm, 551 x 30 mm grenade, 4 x ATGW, 2 x 3 smoke grenade launchers
Length: 6.1 m
Width: 3.134 m
Height: 2.170 m
Ground clearance: 0.15 to 0.53 m
Weight, combat: 13 200 kg
Power-to-weight ratio: 34 hp/t
Engine: 2V-06 water-cooled diesel developing 450 hp
Maximum road speed: 71 km/h
Maximum road range: 500 km
Fuel capacity: 450 l
Fording: amphibious
Vertical obstacle:0.8 m (estimate)
Trench: 1.8 m (estimate)
Gradient: 60%
Side slope:30%
Armour: classified
Armour type: aluminium
NBC: yes
Night vision equipment: yes

Development

The BMD-3 has been developed as the follow-on to the earlier BMD-1 and BMD-2 airborne combat vehicles with the BMD-3 being larger and much heavier. Production commenced in 1989 and so far it has been identified only in service with Russian airborne units.

The driver is seated in the front of the hull in the centre with another person either side. Mounted in the left side of the hull is a 30 mm AG-17 automatic grande launcher while in the right side is mounted a 5.45 mm RPKS machine gun.

The two man power operated turret is mounted in the centre of the forward part of the hull and is the same as the fitted to the BMP-2 ICV and armed with a 30 mm 2A42 cannon with a 7.62 mm machine gun mounted coaxial. Turret traverse is 360 degrees with weapon elevation from -5 to +75 degees. Mounted on the turret roof is a launcher for the AT-4 or AT-5 ATGW.

An unusual feature of the BMD-3 is is hydropneumatic suspension system which allows the ground clearance to be varied from 150 mm to 530 mm, normal ground clearance is 450 mm. The standard tracks are 320 mm wide but these can be replaced by wider 480 mm tracks.

The BMD-3 is fully amphibious being propelled in the water at a speed of 10 km/h by two waterjets mounted at the rear of the hull. Before

Variants

There are no known variants but it is expected that specialised versions of the BMP-3 are under development along similar lines to those of the BMD-1 and BMD-2.

Status

In production. In service only with Russia.

Manufacturer

Volgograd Tractor Plant, Russia

Above:
BMD-3

Above right:
BMD-3

Right:
BMD-3

Far right:
BMD-3

BMD-1 Airborne Combat Vehicle (Russia)

Key recognition features

● Same turret as BMP-1 ICV mounted on forward part of hull roof with Sagger ATGW over 73mm gun

● Suspension each side has five small road wheels, drive sprocket rear, idler front, four track-return rollers (first and fourth support inside of track only)

● Pointed nose with trim vane on glacis plate, hull sides vertical with slight chamfer along two-thirds of hull side

Specifications

Crew: 3+4
Armament: 1 x 73mm (main), 1 x 7.62mm MG (coaxial), 1 x AT-3 Sagger launcher, 2 x 7.62mm forward-firing MG
Ammunition: 40 x 73mm, 2,000 x 7.62mm, 3 x Sagger
Length: 5.4m
Width: 2.63m
Height: 1.62m to 1.97m
Ground clearance: 0.1 to 0.45m
Weight, combat: 7,500kg
Power-to-weight ratio: 32hp/tonne
Ground pressure: 0.57kg/cm²
Maximum road speed: 70km/hr
Maximum water speed: 10km/hr
Maximum road range: 320km
Fuel capacity: 300 lit
Fording: Amphibious
Vertical obstacle: 0.8m
Trench: 1.6m
Gradient: 60%
Side slope: 30%
Armour: 15mm (max hull), 23mm (max turret)
Armour type: Aluminium
NBC system: Yes
Night vision equipment: Yes (commander, gunner and driver, infra-red)

Development

The BMD-1 was developed to meet requirements of the Russian Airborne forces and was first seen in public in 1973. It has been widely used in Afghanistan. Driver sits front centre, commander to his left and bow machine gunner to his right. Turret is identical to BMP-1 ICV's and has 73mm 2A28 smoothbore gun fed by automatic loader with 7.62mm PKT MG mounted coaxially to right. Guns power-elevate from -4˚ to +33˚, turret traverses through 360˚. Mounted over 73mm gun is an AT-3 Sagger wire-guided ATGW and in each corner of bow is a 7.62mm MG. To rear of turret sit remaining three crew members, engine is far rear of hull.

The vehicle is fully amphibious, propelled by two waterjets mounted at rear, and is fitted with smoke generating equipment and engine pre-heater. Hydropneumatic suspension allows height adjustment.

Variants

BMD-1P, BMD-1 with Sagger removed and fitted with pintle-mounted AT-4 Spigot ATGW on turret roof.
BMD-2, new turret armed with 30mm cannon as used in BMP-2, 7.62mm coaxial MG and pintle mount on roof for AT-4 Spigot or AT-5 Spandrel ATGW. Only one bow-mounted 7.62mm MG.
82mm mortar carrier, BMD-1 with 82mm mortar in rear, probably field expedient for Afghanistan.
BTR-D APC, longer chassis with no turret six road wheels, higher roof.
BMD-KShM, command version of above.
1V118, BMD artillery observation post vehicle.
1V119, BMD artillery fire direction centre vehicle.
BMD-1 with RPV, BMD-KShM is used as launcher for Shmel RPV.
BREM-D, BMD ARV.
BTR-D, BTR-D towing or carrying ZU-23 LAAG.
SO-120, BMD chassis is used as basis for SO-120 (or 2S9) 120mm self-propelled howitzer/mortar covered in Self-propelled Guns and Howitzers section.

Status

Production complete. In service with Russia, India (unconfirmed) and Iraq.

Manufacturer

Russian state arsenals, possibly Izhevsk.

Above left: Standard BMD-1.

Above: BMD-1 with suspension raised.

Left: BMD-2 which has new turret armed with 30mm cannon (Steven Zaloga)

120mm SO-120 SPH/Mortar (2S9) (Russia)

Key recognition features

● Hull similar to BMD 1 airborne combat vehicle but fitted with larger turret with sloped front, sides curve round to rear, 120mm weapon level with front of hull

● Well sloped glacis plate, horizontal hull top with driver's hatch in centre, second hatch to his left, turret in centre of hull

● Vertical hull sides and rear with six road wheels, idler front, drive sprocket rear, five track-return rollers

Specifications

Crew: 4
Armament: 1 x 120mm mortar
Ammunition: 25 x 120mm
Length: 6.02m
Width: 2.63m
Height: 2.3m (with max ground clearance)
Ground clearance (variable): 0.1 to 0.45m
Weight, combat: 8,700kg
Power-to-weight ratio: 37.5hp.tonne
Ground pressure: 0.5kg/cm²
Engine: Model 5D20 diesel developing 240hp
Maximum road speed: 60km/hr
Maximum water speed: 9km/hr
Maximum road range: 500km
Fuel capacity: 400 lit
Fording: Amphibious
Vertical obstacle: 0.8m
Trench: 1.8m
Gradient: 60%
Side slope: 33%
Armour: 15mm (max) (hull)
Armour type: Aluminium
NBC system: Yes
Night vision equipment: Yes (infra-red for driver)

Development

The 120mm SO-120 (industrial number 2S9) Anona (Anemone) self-propelled howitzer/mortar was developed in the early 1980s and first seen in public in 1985. It was originally developed for use by the then Soviet air assault divisions, but has since been deployed with other units.

It is essentially a modified BTR-D air assault transporter, which was itself developed from the BMD-1 airborne combat vehicle, with a modified hull and fitted with a new fully enclosed turret armed with a 120mm breech-loaded mortar. Turret traverse is 35 degrees left and right with weapon elevation from -4 degrees to +80 degrees, maximum range of the mortar is 8,855m.

An automatic rammer is fitted which enables a rate of fire of six to eight rounds a minute to be fired and after the breech opens when a round is fired the rammer bleeds compressed air into the chamber to force firing fumes from the muzzle.

The driver is seated at the front of the SO-120 in the centre with the commander being seated to the left, the turret is in the centre with the engine and transmission system that can be adjusted to give a ground clearance from 100 to 450mm. It is also fully amphibious being propelled in the water by two waterjets mounted at the rear of the hull. Before entering the water, bilge pumps are switched on and two splash vanes are erected to the immediate front of the driver's position.

Variants

There are no known variants of the 2S9 although its turret, in a slightly modified version, is installed on the 2S23 (8x8) self-propelled howitzer/mortar (qv).

The 1V118 artillery observation post vehicle and the 1V119 artillery fire detection vehicle used with the 2S9 are based on chassis of BMD-1 vehicle.

Status

Production complete. In service with Afghanistan and Russia.

Manufacturer

Russian state factories.

Above: 120mm SO-120 SPH/mortar (2S9) (Steven Zaloga)

Right: 120mm SO-120 SPH/mortar (2S9)

Below: 120mm SO-120 SPH/mortar (2S9)

Below right: 120mm SO-120 SPH/mortar (2S9)

Key recognition features

● Well sloped glacis plate with trim vane, driver front left, commander's cupola with external 7.62mm MG to rear of driver, gunner's cupola with shield, 12.7mm MG right
● Troop compartment rear with single roof hatch, ramp in hull rear, two firing ports with vision block in each side of troop compartment
● Suspension has five road wheels, drive sprocket front, idler rear, no track-return rollers

Specifications

Crew: 3+7
Armament: 1 x 12.7mm MG, 1 x 7.62mm MG, 1 x 6 smoke grenade dischargers
Length: 5.486m (overall)
Width: 2.846m
Height: 1.93m (hull top), 2.518m (MG shield)
Ground clearance: 0.41m
Weight, combat: 12,900kg
Weight, empty: 11,500kg
Power-to-weight ratio: 21.70hp/tonne
Ground pressure: 0.67kg/cm^2
Engine: MAN D-2848M V-8 diesel developing 280hp at 2,300rpm
Maximum road speed: 74km/hr
Maximum water speed: 6km/hr
Maximum cruising range: 480km
Fuel capacity: 400 lit
Fording: Amphibious
Vertical obstacle: 0.63m
Trench: 1.7m
Gradient: 60%
Side slope: 30%
Armour: Classified
Armour type: Aluminium and steel
NBC system: Yes
Night vision equipment: Yes (passive for commander and driver)

Development

Korean Infantry Fighting Vehicle was developed to meet requirements of South Korean Army by Special Products

Korean Infantry Fighting Vehicle without armament

Division of Daewoo Heavy Industries with hull very similar to US Armored Infantry Fighting Vehicle. KIFV has MAN engine, British Self-Changing Gears T-300 fully automatic transmission and different roof arrangement.

Commander has pintle-mounted 7.62mm M60 MG which cannot be fired from inside vehicle, gunner has full front, side and rear protection for 12.7mm M2 HB MG. Mounted on glacis plate is bank of six electrically operated smoke grenade dischargers firing forwards. KIFV is fully amphibious.

Variants

More recently Daewoo has offered an improved version of the KIFV with a new powerpack consisting of the D2848T turbocharged diesel developing 350hp coupled to an Allison X-200-5D series fully automatic transmission.

20mm SPAAG, basic KIFV fitted with locally produced Vulcan 20mm anti-aircraft gun system that is made in South Korea.
Mortar carrier, two versions, 81mm and 107mm.

Recovery, fitted with roof-mounted hydraulic crane and a winch for recovery operations.

TOW anti-tank, can be fitted with various TOW anti-tank systems including the Norwegian one-man turret with two TOW ATGW in ready-to-launch position.

NBC reconnaissance, no weapons stations and fitted with a complete range of NBC detection systems.

Command, would have higher roof similar to that of the US M577 vehicle.

New generation

In 1992 the company unveiled a new family of vehicles with a new and more powerful powerpack. These include an ammunition resupply vehicle and a twin 30mm self-propelled anti-aircraft gun system. So far none of these have entered production.

Status

In production. In service with South Korean Army and Malaysia.

Manufacturer

Daewoo Heavy Industries, Seoul, South Korea.

Above: Korean Infantry Fighting Vehicle

ASCOD MICV (Spain/Austria)

Key recognition features

● Hull has vertical sides with well sloped glacis plate leading up to horizontal hull top which extends right to rear of vehicle. Hull rear vertical but large stowage bin either side of rear door

● Driver front left with powerpack to right, turret in centre of hull and offset to right

● Suspension either side consists of seven road wheels, drive sprocket front, idler rear and track return rollers, upper part of suspension covered by wavy skirt

Specifications
Crew: 3 + 8
Armament: 1 x 25 mm cannon, 1 x 7.62 mm MG, 2 x 6 smoke grenade launchers
Ammunition: 402 x 25 mm, 2900 x 7.62 mm
Length: 6.224 m
Width: 3.002 m
Height: 1.775 m (hull top), 2.653 m (overall)
Ground clearance: 0.45 m
Weight, combat: 25,200 kg
Power-to-weight ratio: 23.80 hp/t
Engine: MTU 8V 183 TE22 8 V-90 V-8 diesel developing 600 hp at 2300 rpm Maximum road speed:70 km/h
Maximum road range: 600 km
Fuel capacity:650 l
Fording: 1.2 m
Vertical obstacle: 0.95 m
Trench: 2.3 m
Gradient: 75%
Side slope: 40%
Armour: classified
Armour type: steel
NBC: yes
Night vision equipment: yes

Development
The ASCOD (Austrian Spanish Co-Operative Development) mechanised infantry combat vehicle has been jointly developed by Steyr-Daimler-Puch of Austria and SANTA BARBARA of Spain with the latter country placing the first production order for a total of 144 vehicles under the local name of Pizarro early in 1996.

The driver is seated at front left with the powerpack to his right, turret in the centre and the troop compartment at the rear. The infantry enter and leave via a large door in the hull rear that opens to the right.

The two man power operated turret is armed with a stabilised Mauser 30 mm cannon with a 7.62 mm machine gun being mounted co-axial to the left. Turret traverse is through a full 360 degrees with weapon elevation from -10 to +50 degrees.

Standard equipment includes a NBC protection system, heater, applique armour and a computerised day/night fire control system.

Variants
Anti-tank with various ATGW
Armoured recovery and repair vehicle
Armoured command vehicle
Armoured engineer vehicle
Armoured mortar carrier
MICV, various alternative weapon fits
Light tank with 105 mm gun
SAM system
SPAAG

Status
Entering production for Spanish Army

Manufacturers
Austria, Steyr-Daimler-Puch
Spain, SANTA BARBARA

Above:ASCOD MICV

Above right: ASCOD MICV

Far right: ASCOD MICV

Right: ASCOD MICV

Hägglunds Vehicle Pbv 302 APC (Sweden)

Key recognition features

● Hull front slopes to rear and curves to join vertical sides, hull rear also vertical and curves to join sides, twin doors rear, hatches over rear troop compartment

● Driver's cupola at front with commander's cupola right and large 20mm gun turret left

● Suspension has five large road wheels, drive sprocket front, idler rear, no track-return rollers

Specifications

Crew: 2+10
Armament: 1 x 20mm cannon, 1 x 6 smoke grenade dischargers, 2 x Lyran launchers
Ammunition: 505 x 20mm
Length: 5.35m
Width: 2.86m
Height: 2.5m (turret top), 1.9m (hull top)
Ground clearance: 0.4m
Weight, combat: 13,500kg
Power-to-weight ratio: 20.74hp/tonne
Ground pressure: 0.6kg/cm²
Engine: Volvo-Penta model THD 100B horizontal 4-stroke turbocharged diesel developing 280hp at 2,200rpm
Maximum road speed: 66km/hr
Maximum water speed: 8km/hr
Maximum road range: 300km
Fuel capacity: 285 lit
Fording: Amphibious
Vertical obstacle: 0.61m
Trench: 1.8m
Gradient: 60%
Side slope: 40%
Armour: Classified
Armour type: Steel
NBC system: None
Night vision equipment: None

Development

Pbv 302 (Pansarbandvagn 302) was developed by the then Hägglund and Söner to meet requirements of Swedish Army with prototype completed in 1962 and production from 1965 to 1971. Hull is all-welded steel armour with spaced armour in the sides for increased protection. Engine is mounted under floor of vehicle with crew compartment front and infantry compartment rear. Ten infantrymen sit five each side facing, and enter and leave via two doors in rear. They can fire small arms via roof hatches.

Turret is manually operated and armed with 20mm cannon with elevation of +50° and depression of -10°, turret traverses 360°, cannon can be fed by belt containing 135 rounds of HE ammunition or box magazine holding 10 rounds of AP ammunition. Pbv 302 is fully amphibious, propelled by its tracks. Before entering the water trim vanes are erected at front of vehicle and bilge pumps switched on.

Further development resulted in the Pbv 302 Mk 2 and the Product Improved Pb 302, but none of these entered production. Hägglunds and S˙ is now known as H‰oogglunds Vehicle. For operations in the former Yugoslavia, some Pbv 302s were fitted with additional armour protection.

Variants

Stripbv 3021 armoured command vehicle has four radio antennas compared to Pbv 302's two, and additional communications equipment.
Epbv 3022 is an armoured observation post vehicle and has commander's hatch replaced by cupola with rangefinding devices, three radio antennas, additional buoyancy aids on trim vanes.
Bplpbv 3023 is armoured fire direction post vehicle with four antennas and fire-control/communications equipment inside.

Status
Production complete. In service with Swedish Army only.

Manufacturer
Hägglunds Vehicle AB, Örnsköldsvik, Sweden.

Above: Pbv 302 APC

Above right: Pbv 302 APC
(Christopher F Foss)

Right: Pbv 302 APC
(Christopher F Foss)

Combat Vehicle 90 (Stridsfordon 90) (Sweden)

Key recognition features

● Hull has well sloped glacis plate with turret in centre that is offset slightly to left of hull. The sides and rear of hull are vertical with large door in hull rear

● Suspension either side consists of seven road wheels very close together, drive sprocket front, idler rear and upper part of suspension covered by skirt with wavy bottom

● Turret of 40mm version has sloped front, vertical sides and rear, 40mm cannon has distinctive muzzle with large gunner's sight in the right of turret roof

Specifications

Crew: 3+8
Armament: 1 x 40mm, 1 x 7.62mm MG (coaxial), 2 x 3 smoke grenade dischargers
Length: 6.471m
Width: 3.01m
Height: 2.5m (turret roof), 1.73m (hull top)
Ground clearance: 0.45m
Weight, combat: 22,800kg
Power-to-weight ratio: 24.12hp/tonne
Ground pressure: 0.53kg/cm^2
Engine: Scania DS 14 diesel developing 550hp
Maximum road speed: 70km/hr
Maximum road range: Not available
Fuel capacity: 525 lit
Fording: Not available
Vertical obstacle: 1.2m
Trench: 2.9m
Gradient: 60%
Side slope: 40%
Armour: Classified
Armour type: Steel
NBC system: Yes
Night vision equipment: Yes (passive)

Development

In 1985 HB Utveckling, a small holding company jointly established by Bofors and Hägglunds and Söner (now Hägglunds Vehicle), were awarded a contract by the Swedish Defence Material Administration for the construction of five prototypes of the Stridsfordon 90 (or Combat Vehicle 90) family of armoured vehicles for the Swedish Army. Before this, under separate contracts, an automotive test rig and a two-man 40mm turret had been funded. In 1986 a further contract was awarded for four two-man turrets, three with the 40mm cannon and one with a 25mm cannon.

Early in 1991 the first production order was placed for the Combat Vehicle 90 (CV 9040) with first production vehicles delivered in October 1993. Hägglunds Vehicle will build all of the chassis and send these to Bofors who will build the 40mm turrets and integrate this with the chassis and then deliver the complete system to the Swedish Army.

The driver is seated at the front of the vehicle on the left side with the powerpack to his right, the two-man turret is in the centre with the troop compartment at the rear. The infantry are seated either side facing inwards and enter and leave via a door in the rear. Roof hatches are also provided but there is no provision for the infantry to use their weapons from within the vehicle.

The 40mm gun has an elevation of +35° and a depression of -8° with turret traverse a full 360°, the CV 9040 has fully powered traverse and elevation with manual controls for emergency use.

Variants

CV 9025 IFV, two man turret, 25mm cannon, prototype only.
TriAD 40mm self-propelled anti-aircraft gun, Swedish Army.
CV 90 Forward Command Vehicle, Swedish Army.
CV 90 Forward Observation Vehicle, Swedish Army.
CV 90 Armoured Recovery Vehicle, Swedish Army.
CV 90 anti-tank, concept.
CV 9030, two man 30mm turret, for Norway.
CV 90105 TML, 105mm turret, trials.

Status
Production. In service with Norway and Sweden.

Manufacturer
Bofors, Sweden (turret) and Hägglunds Vehicle, Örnsköldsvik, Sweden (chassis) (but see text).

Above: CV 9040 IFV

Above right: CV 9030 IFV

Right: TriAD 40mm SPAAG

Hägglunds Vehicle Pvrbv 551 Anti-tank Missile Carrier (Sweden)

Key recognition features

- High superstructure with glacis plate at about 70o, commander's and driver's cupolas front
- TOW missile launcher retracts into vehicle when not in action
- Suspension has six road wheels, idler front, drive sprocket rear, two track-return rollers. Front part of suspension covered by wavy skirt

Specifications

Crew: 4
Armament: 1 x TOW ATGW launcher
Length: 4.81m
Width: 2.54m
Height: 2.46m (missile and launcher up), 1.97m (hull top)
Ground clearance: 0.33m
Weight, combat: 9,700kg
Power-to-weight ratio: 14hp/tonne
Ground pressure: 0.4kg/cm²
Engine: Ford model 2658E V-6 petrol developing 136hp at 5,200rpm
Maximum road speed: 41km/hr
Maximum road range: 300km
Fuel capacity: 240 lit
Fording: 0.9m
Vertical obstacle: 0.61m
Trench: 1.5m
Gradient: 60%
Side slope: 40%
Armour: Classified
Armour type: Steel
NBC system: No
Night vision equipment: Optional for TOW ATGW launcher

Development

Pvrbv 551 is the old Ikv-102/Ikv-103 self-propelled infantry cannon extensively rebuilt, including new engine fitted in unarmoured Bv 206 all-terrain vehicle. Conversion work undertaken by Hägglund and Sˆner (now Hägglunds Vehicle AB) with production vehicles delivered to Swedish Army between 1984 and 1986.

In centre of hull roof is large two-part circular opening under which is Hughes TOW ATGW launcher raised above roof when in action. Reserve missiles stowed in hull rear above engine and transmission compartment with access to these via hatches in roof that open each side. Range of the TOW missile depends on model but maximum is 3,750m.

Variants

Swedish Lvrbv 701 RBS-70 low altitude surface-to-air missile system uses similar chassis to Pvrbv 551s with conversion work also carried out by Hägglund and Söner. (Details given under SPAAGs.)

Status

Production complete. In service with Swedish Army only.

Manufacturer

AB Hägglund and Söner (now Hägglunds Vehicle AB), Örnsköldsvik, Sweden.

Right: Pvrbv 551 anti-tank vehicle with Hughes TOW ATGW launcher raised (FMV)

Hägglunds Vehicle Bv 206S APC (Sweden)

Key recognition features

● Unique vehicle consisting of two fully-tracked units joined together. Both units have wide rubber band type tracks
● Front unit has vertical hull front and bonnet that slopes up to the two-part windscreen.
● Front unit has single side door with window above in each side, smaller window to rear. Rear unit normally has two rectangular windows with large door at the back.

Specifications

Crew: 4 + 8
Armament: 1 x 12.7 mm MG (typical)
Length: 6.86 m
Width: 2 m
Height: 1.9 m without armament
Ground clearance: 0.35 m
Weight, combat: 7000 kg
Weight, empty: 5300 kg
Power-to-weight ratio: 19.42 hp/tonne
Engine: Mercedes-Benz 603A 6-cylinder in-line diesel developing 136 hp at 4600 rpm
Maximum road speed: 50 km/hr
Maximum road range: 370 km
Fording: amphibious
Vertical obstacle: not available
Trench: not available
Gradient: 100 %
Side slope: 60%
Armour: Classified
Armour type: Steel
NBC system: Optional
Night vision equipment: Optional

Development

The Bv206S is the Hägglunds BV206 all terrain vehicle (of which over 11,000 have been made) fitted with two new all-welded steel bodies to protect the occupants from small arms fire and shell splinters.

The front unit has the engine at the front and seats for the commander and driver in the centre, plus two for passengers in the back. The rear unit has seats for eight people, four down either side. The units are linked by a steering unit. Steering is accomplished by two hydraulic cylinders, servo-controlled from a conventional steering wheel.

The Bv206S is fully amphibious, propelled in the water by its tracks. Before entering the water, a trim vane is erected. A wide range of equipment can be fitted, including an NBC system, winch and night vision aids. A ring-mounted machine gun can be carried on the front unitis roof.

Variants

The Bv206S can be adapted for use as an ambulance, command post or weapons carrier

Status

In production. In service with Sweden and the UK

Manufacturer

Hägglunds Vehicle AB, Örnsköldsvik, Sweden

Right: Bv 206S

Below: Bv 206S

Below right: Bv 206S

FMC/NUROL Turkish Infantry Fighting Vehicle (Turkey)

Key recognition features

● Glassis plate with trim vane at 45 degrees, hull roof horizontal to hull at rear, angled downwards with hull rear sloping inwards
● Driver front left, commander rear, with engine compartment on right. Turret has vertical sides and rear, offset to right of hull. Large ramp in hull rear
● Hull sides vertical with curve to top, upper part of rear troop compartment slopes inwards, two firing ports with vision block above in each side. Suspension has five road wheels, drive sprocket at front, idler in rear. No return track rollers.

Specifications

Crew: 3+10
Armament: 1 x 25 mm cannon, 1 x 7.62 mm MG, 2 x 3 smoke grenade dischargers
Ammunition: 230 x 30mm, 1610 x 7.62mm
Length: 5.26m
Width: 2.82m
Height: 2.01m (turret roof), 2.62m (hull roof)
Ground clearance: 0.43m
Weight, combat: 13,687kg
Power-to-weight ratio: 21.91bhp/tonne
Ground pressure: 0.67kg/cm²
Engine: Detroit Diesel Model 6V53T developing 300 hp
Maximum road speed: 70km/hr
Maximum water speed: 6.3km/hr
Maximum road range: 490km
Fuel capacity: 416 lit
Fording: amphibious
Vertical obstacle: 0.74m
Trench: 1.83m
Gradient: 60%
Side slope: 30%
Armour: Classified
Armour type: Aluminium/steel
NBC system: Optional
Night vision equipment: Optional

Development

The Turkish Infantry Fighting Vehicle has been developed by FMC and Nurol as a joint venture for the Turkish army. It is based on the United Defense Armored Infantry Fighting Vehicle (qv). A total of 1998 vehicles are being built, of which 650 are the AIFV version fitted with a one-man power-operated turret with a 25 mm cannon and 7.62mm co-axial machine gun. The vehicle is fully amphibious, propelled in the water by its tracks.

Variants

AAPC (Advanced Armored Personnel Carrier) with 12.7 mm machine gun turret
81 mm mortar carrier
120 mm mortar carrier (private ventures from TDA of France and Lockheed Martin in the USA)
ATGW carrier (two TOWs in launch position)

Status

Production. In service with the Turkish army

Manufacturer

FMC-Nurol, Savunma Sanayii AS, Ankara, Turkey

FOLLOWING PAGE:
Above left: AIFV

Above right: Mortar carrier

Below Right: AIFV

Below left: ATGW carrier

GKN Defence Warrior Mechanised Combat Vehicle (U

Key recognition features

● High hull with well sloped glacis plate, driver's hatch in upper left side and louvres to right, horizontal hull top with turret centre, vertical hull rear with stowage boxes each side of single door. No firing ports

● Turret has vertical sides with long barrel 30mm RARDEN cannon with flash eliminator and mounted in external mantlet. Commander and gunner have hatches opening to rear and distinctive roof-mounted periscopes to their front, stowage basket on turret rear

● Troop compartment at rear has chamfered sides with stowage basket above. Suspension each side has six road wheels, drive sprocket front, idler rear and three track-return rollers covered by skirt

Specifications
Crew: 3+7
Armament: 1 x 30mm cannon, 1 x 7.62mm MG, 2 x 4 smoke grenade dischargers
Ammunition: 250 x 30mm, 2,000 x 7.62mm
Length: 6.34m
Width: 3.034m
Height: 2.791m (turret roof), 1.93m (hull roof)
Ground clearance: 0.49m
Weight, combat: 25,700kg
Power-to-weight ratio: 21.4bhp/tonne
Ground pressure: 0.65kg/cm²
Engine: Perkins CV8 TCA V-8 diesel developing 550hp at 2,300rpm
Maximum road speed: 75km/hr
Maximum road range: 660km
Fuel capacity: 770 lit
Fording: 1.3m
Vertical obstacle: 0.75m
Trench: 2.5m
Gradient: 60%
Side slope: 40%
Armour: Classified
Armour type: Aluminium (hull), steel (turret)
NBC system: Yes
Night vision equipment: Yes (passive for commander, gunner and driver)

Development
Warrior (previously known as MCV-80) was developed from mid-1970s by GKN Defence for the British Army. Following prototype trials it was accepted for service in November 1984 with first production vehicles completed in December 1986. The British Army took delivery of 789 Warrior MCV and variants with final deliveries in 1995.

In 1933 Kuwait placed an order for 254 Desert Warrior vehicles and variants with the first of these being completed in 1994. Desert Warrior has US Delco turret armed with 25mm cannon, 7.62mm coaxial machine gun and a launcher for TOW ATGW either side of turret. It also has a different armour package and an air conditioning system. Kuwaiti variants include command vehicles, repair and recovery and high mobility trailers. For operations in the Middle East the Warrior was fitted with additional armour protection.

Driver sits front left with engine to right, two-man turret in centre and troop compartment rear.

Variants
The British Army has following versions: section vehicle with two-man turret armed with 30mm RARDEN cannon and 7.62mm coaxial MG, command vehicle (three versions, platoon, company and battalion all with same turret as section vehicle but with different communications equipment), Warrior Repair and Recovery Vehicle, Warrior Combat Repair Vehicle, Warrior Mechanised Artillery Observation Vehicle, Battery Command Vehicle (for Royal Artillery) and MILAN ATGW carrier. For export the company is proposing other versions including 105mm light tank, Desert Fighting Vehicle with firing ports, 80mm mortar carrier, fitted with various anti-tank missile systems, anti-aircraft, load carrier, and fitted with other turrets such as 25mm or 90mm.

Status
Production. In service with Kuwait (Desert Warrior), and UK.

Manufacturer
GKN Defence, Telford, Shropshire, England, UK.

Above: Warrior MCV with applique armour

Above right: Desert Warrior

Far right: Warrior MCV (Richard Stickland)

Right: Warrior mechanised combat repair vehicle

GKN FV432 APC (UK)

Key recognition features

- Glacis plate slopes at about 60o with horizontal hull roof extending to rear, vertical hull rear with large door opening left
- Driver front right, engine to his left and machine gunner to his rear, troop compartment rear with four-part circular roof hatch above, two parts opening left and right. Vertical hull sides with exhaust pipe on left side and NBC pack protruding on right side
- Suspension each side has five road wheels, drive sprocket front, idler rear, two track-return rollers. Upper part sometimes covered by skirt

Specifications

Crew: 2+10
Armament: 1 x 7.62mm MG, 2 x 3 smoke grenade dischargers
Ammunition: 1,600 x 7.62mm
Length: 5.251m
Width: 2.8m
Height including MG: 2.286m
Height hull top: 1.879m
Ground clearance: 0.406m
Weight, combat: 15,280kg
Weight, empty: 13,740kg
Power-to-weight ratio: 15.7bhp/tonne
Ground pressure: $0.78kg/cm^2$
Engine: Rolls-Royce K60 No 4 Mk 4F 2-stroke 6-cylinder multi-fuel developing 240bhp at 3,750rpm
Maximum road speed: 52.2km/hr
Maximum road range: 480km
Fuel capacity: 454 lit
Fording: 1.066m
Vertical obstacle: 0.609m
Trench: 2.05m
Gradient: 60%
Side slope: 30%
Armour: 12mm (maximum)
Armour type: Steel
NBC system: Yes
Night vision equipment: Yes (passive for driver)

Development

FV432 series was developed to meet requirements of British Army in the late 1950s with first prototype completed in 1961. Production undertaken by Sankey, now GKN Defence from 1962 with first production vehicles completed in 1963 and over 3,000 built by production completion in 1972. FV432 was sometimes referred to as Trojan. The FV432 has now been supplemented by the GKN Defence Warrior MCV although the FV432 is expected to remain in service in specialised roles such as mortar, ambulance and signals for many years. FV432 has many common automotive components with FV433 Abbot 105mm self-propelled gun.

FV432 is all-welded steel with engine front left, driver front right and hatch to his rear, 7.62mm GPMG or 7.62mm Bren LMG. Troops sit on bench seats, five each side facing, and enter via large door in rear. Four-part circular roof hatch over top of troop compartment.

Variants

Many FV432s have Peak one-man turret mounted above rear troop compartment armed with 7.62mm GPMG.
Ambulance model is unarmed and carries both seated and stretcher patients.
Command, has extensive communications equipment and optional tent erected at rear.
Maintenance carrier (FV434) has different hull and crane for removing powerpacks in field.
Mortar carrier has turntable-mounted 81mm mortar in rear firing through roof.
Minelayer, tows Bar minelayer rear with Ranger anti-personnel mine system on roof. Engineers also use FV432 to tow mine-clearing system such as Giant Viper.
Two versions of FV432 are in service in radar role, one with Z8 298 ground surveillance radar, the other with Cymbeline mortar-locating radar.
Recovery, has winch mounted in vehicle rear.

Artillery command has Field Artillery Computer Equipment. Royal Artillery also uses it with sound ranging system. **FV439** is specialised Royal Signals vehicle. Some of the FV438 Swing-fire ATGW vehicles were converted into Wavell electronics carriers.

Status

Production complete. In service with India (command post for Abbot 105mm SPG) and UK.

Manufacturer

GKN Defence, Telford, Shropshire, England, UK.

Above: FV432 APC with turret-mounted 7.62mm MG

Above right: FV432 APC used in artillery command post role (Christopher F Foss)

Right: FV432 APC with 7.62mm GPMG turret

199

Alvis Stormer APC (UK)

Key recognition features

● Blunt nose with sloping glacis plate, driver's position on left side, engine to right, horizontal hull top with vertical hull rear, large door opening right. Sides vertical, chamfer between sides and roof
● Weapon station normally on forward part of roof with hatches to immediate rear
● Suspension each side has six road wheels with drive sprocket front, idler rear, track return rollers which are sometimes covered by skirt

Specifications

Crew: 3+8
Armament: See text
Ammunition: Depends on above
Length: 5.33m
Width: 2.4m
Width over stowage boxes: 2.69m
Height with 7.62mm MG: 2.27m
Ground clearance: 0.425m
Weight, combat: 12,700kg
Power-to-weight ratio: 19.68bhp/tonne
Ground pressure: 0.42kg/cm²
Engine: Perkins T6/3544 water-cooled 6-cylinder turbocharged diesel developing 250bhp at 2,600rpm
Maximum road speed: 80km/hr
Maximum water speed (tracks): 5km/hr
Maximum road range: 650km
Fuel capacity: 405 lit
Fording: 1.1m, amphibious with preparation
Vertical obstacle: 0.6m
Trench: 1.75m
Gradient: 60%
Side slope: 35%
Armour: Classified
Armour type: Aluminium
NBC system: Optional
Night vision equipment: Optional

Development

In the 1970s a British Government research and development establishment built FV4333 armoured personnel carrier prototype using components of Alvis Scorpion CVR(T) range.

Further development by Alvis resulted in Stormer which entered production in 1981 for export with three sold to USA for evaluation in Light Armored Vehicle (LAV) competition (subsequently won by Diesel Division, General Motors of Canada) and 25 to Malaysia, 12 of which had Helio FVT900 turret, 20mm Oerlikon-Contraves cannon and 7.62mm MG and remaining vehicles had Thyssen Henschel TH-1 turret with twin 7.62mm MG. Late in 1986 British Army selected Stormer to mount Shorts Starstreak High Velocity Missile (HVM) system. This has an unmanned turret with a total of eight Starstreak SAM in ready to launch position, four either side.

All versions have similar layout with driver front left, engine compartment right, troop compartment extending right to rear. Wide range of weapon stations for hull top including turrets with 7.62mm and 12.7mm MG, 20mm, 25mm or 30mm cannon up to 76mm or 90mm guns. Wide range of optional equipment including NBC system, night vision devices, flotation screen, firing ports/vision blocks, automatic transmission, land navigation system.

Variants

Alvis has proposed wide range of roles for Stormer including air defence (with guns or missiles), engineer vehicle, recovery vehicle, ambulance, minelayer, 81mm or 120mm mortar carrier, and command/control.

For Operation Desert Storm, Alvis designed and built a flatbed version of the Stormer to carry the GIAT Minotaur mine scattering system.

Status

In production. In service with Indonesia, Malaysia, Oman and the UK.

Manufacturer
Alvis Vehicles Limited, Coventry, West Midlands, England, UK.

Above: Alvis Stormer APC

Above right: Alvis Stormer in command post role

Below right: Alvis Stormer APC with FVT 900 turret

Right: Alvis Stormer APC with Shorts Starstreak HVM

201

Alvis Striker SP ATGW Vehicle (UK)

Key recognition features

● Same hull as Alvis Spartan APC but with launcher box for five Swingfire ATGWs on roof rear

● Well sloped glacis plate to roof with commander's cupola in front of Swingfire ATGW launcher box at hull rear

● Suspension has five road wheels, drive sprocket front, idler rear, no track-return rollers

Specifications

Crew: 3
Armament: Launcher with 5 Swingfire ATGW, 1 x 7.62mm MG, 2 x 4 smoke grenade dischargers
Ammunition: 10 x Swingfire ATGW, 3,000 x 7.62mm
Length: 4.826m
Width: 2.28m
Height: 2.28m
Ground clearance: 0.356m
Weight, combat: 8,346kg
Power-to-weight ratio: 22.77bhp/tonne
Ground pressure: 0.345kg/cm^2
Engine: Jaguar J60 No 1 Mk 100B 4.2 litre 6-cylinder petrol developing 190hp at 4,750rpm
Maximum road speed: 80.5km/hr
Maximum road range: 483km
Fuel capacity: 350 lit
Fording: 1.067m
Vertical obstacle: 0.5m
Trench: 2.057m
Gradient: 60%
Side slope: 30%
Armour: Classified
Armour type: Aluminium
NBC system: Yes
Night vision equipment: Yes, commander, gunner and driver

Development

Striker was developed to meet requirements of British Army, Alvis being responsible for chassis and the now Dynamics Division of British Aerospace Defence Limited for Swingfire ATGW missile system. First production vehicles delivered in 1975 and used in British Army service by Royal Armoured Corps. Striker (FV102) is member of the Scorpion family Combat Vehicle Reconnaissance (Tracked).

Mounted roof rear is a launcher box for five wire-guided British Aerospace Dynamics Swingfire ATGWs with HEAT warhead and range of 4,000m. They can be launched from inside or outside vehicle with the aid of a separation sight and controller, in day and night conditions. When travelling, launcher box is horizontal but elevated to 35o prior to missile launch. After the five Swingfire ATGWs are fired new missiles must be loaded externally.

The flotation screen on the Alvis Striker has now been removed and the vehicle has been withdrawn from service with the Belgian Army.

Most of the British Army Alvis Striker vehicles have now been upgraded with the Swingfire Improve Guidance (SWIG) system, the actual missile and chassis have not been upgraded. The British Army did deploy two other systems with the Swingfire ATGW system, the Ferret Mk 5 and the FV438 based on the FV432 chassis, but both of these have been phased out of service.

Variants

No variants.

Status

Production complete.

Manufacturer

Alvis Vehicles Limited, Dynamics Division, Coventry, West Midlands, England, UK (chassis), British Aerospace Defence Limited, Dynamics Division, Stevenage, Hertfordshire, England, UK (missile system).

Above: Alvis Striker ATGW vehicle launching Swingfire ATGW

Above right: Alvis Striker ATGW vehicle with launcher box raised

Right: Alvis Striker ATGW vehicle launching Swingfire ATGW

Alvis Spartan APC (UK)

Key recognition features

● Similar to Stormer but has narrower hull, blunt nose with sloping glacis plate, driver's position on left side with engine right, horizontal hull top with vertical hull rear, larger door opening right. Hull sides vertical, chamfer between sides and roof
● Cupola on hull top to rear of driver's position, 7.62mm MG on left side manned by vehicle commander, troop section commander has hatch to right which is flush with roof, two outward-opening roof hatches rear
● Suspension each side has five road wheels, drive sprocket front, idler rear, no return rollers, no skirts

Specifications

Crew: 3+4
Armament: 1 x 7.62mm MG, 2 x 4 smoke grenade dischargers
Ammunition: 3,000 x 7.62mm
Length hull: 5.125m
Width: 2.242m
Height overall: 2.26m
Ground clearance: 0.356m
Weight, combat: 8,172kg
Power-to-weight ratio: 23.25bhp/tonne
Ground pressure: 0.338kg/cm²
Engine: Jaguar J60 No 1 Mk 100B 4.2 litre 6-cylinder petrol developing 190hp at 4,750rpm
Maximum road speed: 80.5km/hr
Maximum road range: 483m
Fuel capacity: 386 lit
Fording: 1.067m, amphibious with preparation
Vertical obstacle: 0.5m
Trench: 2.057m
Gradient: 60%
Side slope: 35%
Armour: Classified
Armour type: Aluminium
NBC system: Yes
Night vision equipment: Yes (passive)

Development

Alvis Spartan (FV103) is a member of Scorpion CVR(T) family and entered service with British Army in 1978 for specialised roles such as carrying Javelin SAM or Royal Engineer assault teams. It is not replacement for FV432 APC (qv).

Driver sits front left, engine compartment to right, vehicle commander/7.62mm MG gunner to his rear and section commander, who dismounts with four infantry, right of vehicle commander. Troops in rear with two-part roof hatch opening left and right, no firing ports. ZB 298 ground surveillance radar can be mounted on roof. Flotation screen can be fitted round top of hull which, when erected, makes Spartan fully amphibious, propelled by its tracks.

New production vehicles would have a number of improvements including upgraded suspension and the option of the more fuel efficient Perkins diesel engine which has already been installed in some export Scorpions. By 1995 total production of the Spartan APC amounted to over 960 vehicles for both home and export market.

Variants

Spartan/MILAN: British Army uses Spartan with two-man turret and two Euromissile MILAN ATGWs in ready-to-launch position.

Spartan can be fitted with other weapon systems including Hughes TOW ATGW, turret with four HOT ATGW in ready-to-launch position, turret with twin 20mm cannon.

Status

Production as required. In service with Belgium, Oman, UK.

Manufacturer

Alvis Limited, Coventry, West Midlands, England, UK.

Above: Alvis Spartan APC of British Army (Richard Stickland)

Above right: Alvis Spartan of Belgian Army (C R Zwart)

Right: Alvis Spartan

United Defense M2 Bradley IFV (USA)

Key recognition features

● High hull line with well sloped glacis plate, driver's hatch left side, horizontal hull top, turret centre of roof. Large ramp at hull rear, hatch above rear troop compartment

● Turret has twin TOW ATGW launcher on left side, extensive external stowage with 25mm cannon front and 7.62mm MG right, two spherical firing ports with periscope above in each side of hull

● Suspension each side has six road wheels, drive sprocket front, idler rear, two track-return rollers. Upper part of track and hull sides has appliquÈ armour

Specifications

Crew: 3+6
Armament: 1 x 25mm cannon, 1 x 7.62mm MG (coaxial), 2 x TOW ATGW launcher, 2 x 4 smoke grenade dischargers
Ammunition: 900 x 25mm, 2,200 x 7.62mm, 7 x TOW ATGW
Length: 6.55m
Width: 3.61m
Height gunners sight: 2.972m
Height turret roof: 2.565m
Ground clearance: 0.432m
Weight, combat: 22,940kg
Weight, empty: 19,005kg
Power-to-weight ratio: 20.38hp/tonne
Ground pressure: 0.54kg/cm²
Engine: Cummins VTA-903T turbocharged 8-cylinder diesel developing 500hp at 2,600rpm
Maximum road speed: 66km/hr
Maximum water speed: 7.2km/hr
Maximum cruising range: 483km
Fuel capacity: 662 lit
Fording: Amphibious with preparation
Vertical obstacle: 0.914m
Trench: 2.54m
Gradient: 60%
Side slope: 40%
Armour: Classified
Armour type: Aluminium/laminate/steel
NBC system: Yes
Night vision equipment: Yes (passive for commander, gunner and driver)

M2 Bradley with TOW launcher retracted

Development

M2 Bradley is the culmination of an early 1960s programme to provide the US Army with a supplement for M113 APC. First two prototypes of XM2 were completed by FMC Corporation (now United Defense LP) in 1978. After trials it was standardised as M2 in 1980 with first production vehicles in 1981, when it was named Bradley IFV.

Hull is welded aluminium with additional layer of spaced laminated armour for increased protection. Driver sits front left, engine to his right, troop compartment extending right to rear. Two-man power-operated turret armed with 25mm McDonnell Douglas Helicopters Chain Gun, 7.62mm M240 MG mounted coaxial to right, turret traverse 360˚, weapon elevation from -10˚ to +60˚. Mounted on left side of turret is twin launcher for Hughes TOW ATGW with range of 3,750m. M2 Bradley is fully amphibious with flotation screen erected (carried collapsed round top of hull).

Later production vehicles are M2A1/M2A2 and M3A1/M3A2 which have many improvements with the A3 models having increased armour protection and upgraded powerpack. Some Bradley vehicles have been fitted with explosive reactive armour to their turrets and hulls for increased battlefield survivability.

Variants

M3 Cavalry Fighting Vehicle (CFV) is similar to M2 but has no firing ports, five-man crew and more ammunition.
Bradley FIST for field artillery is under development.
Bradley Stinger SAM - carries Stinger teams.
Bradley Stinger Fighting Vehicle - under development.
Multiple Launch Rocket System (MLRS) uses Bradley components.
XM4 Command and Control Vehicle (MLRS chassis), development.
XM5 Electronic Fighting Vehicle Systems Carrier (MLRS chassis), development.
Stingray, basic M2 series Bradley with laser system to engage enemy electro-optical systems.

Status

Production complete. In service with Saudi Arabia and USA.

Manufacturer

United Defense LP, Ground Systems Division, San JosÈ, California 95108, USA.

Above: M2A2
Bradley Fighting
Vehicle

United Defense, LP, Armored IFV (USA)

Key recognition features

- Glacis plate with trim vane at 45o, hull roof horizontal to hull at rear, angled downwards at 45o, hull rear sloping inwards
- Driver front left, commander rear, engine compartment right, turret with vertical sides and rear offset right of hull. Troop compartment rear with hatch above, large ramp in hull rear
- Hull sides vertical with curve to top, upper part of rear troop compartment slopes inwards, two firing ports with vision block above in each side. Suspension has five road wheels, drive sprocket front, idler rear, no track-return rollers

Specifications

Crew: 3+7
Armament: 1 x 25mm cannon, 1 x 7.62mm MG (coaxial), 1 x 6 smoke grenade dischargers
Ammunition: 324 x 25mm, 1,840 x 7.62mm
Length: 5.258m
Width: 2.819m
Height to top of periscopes: 2.794m
Height to hull top: 2.007m
Ground clearance: 0.432m
Weight, combat: 13,687kg
Weight, empty: 11,405kg
Power-to-weight ratio: 19.29hp/tonne
Ground pressure: 0.67kg/cm²
Engine: Detroit Diesel 6V-53T V-6 liquid cooled diesel developing 264hp at 2,800rpm
Maximum road speed: 61.2km/hr
Maximum water speed: 6.3km/hr
Maximum road range: 490km
Fuel capacity: 416 lit
Fording: Amphibious with preparation
Vertical obstacle: 0.635m
Trench: 1.625m
Gradient: 60%
Side slope: 30%
Armour: Classified
Armour type: Aluminium/laminate
NBC system: Optional
Night vision equipment: Yes (gunner and driver)

Development

Armored Infantry Fighting Vehicle was developed as a private venture by former FMC Corporation in the late 1960s, originally named Product Improved M113A1. With further improvements it was renamed AIFV, Netherlands placing initial order for 880 in 1975, followed by Philippines. In 1979 Belgium ordered 514 AIFVs and 525 M113A2s which were produced under licence in Belgium. It is now being manufactured in Turkey by FMC-Nurol to meet the requirements of the Turkish Army.

The AIFV has many improvements over M113 series including improved firepower, mobility and armour protection. One-man power-operated turret armed with 25mm KBA cannon, 7.62mm FM MG coaxial to left, turret traverse 360°, weapon elevation from -10° to +50°. AIFV is fully amphibious, propelled by its tracks. Before entering the water a trim vane is erected at front of vehicle.

Variants

Basic vehicle is designated YPR 765 PRI by Netherlands Army and variants in service include YPR 765 PRCO-B command vehicle, YPR 765 PRCO-C1 to C5 command vehicles, YPR 765 PRRDR radar vehicle, YPR 765 PRRDR-C radar command vehicle, YPR 765 PRGWT ambulance, YPR 765 PRI/I squad vehicle with 12.7mm MG, YPR 765 PRMR mortar tractor towing 120mm mortar, YPR 765 PRVR-A and PRVR-B cargo vehicles, YPR 765 PRAT anti-tank vehicle twin TOW launcher as fitted to US M901 Improved TOW Vehicle, and YPR 806 PRBRG armoured recovery vehicle.

Taiwan also produces a similar vehicle to the AIFV with various weapon installations.

Philippines models are similar to Dutch AIFV but have 12.7mm MG in place of 25mm KBA cannon.

Belgian versions include AIFV-B which is similar to Dutch vehicles. AIFV with 12.7mm cupola weapon station

AIFV-B-CP command post vehicle.
Turkey, there is a separate entry for these vehicles.

Status
In production. In service with Belgium, Netherlands, Philippines and Turkey.

Manufacturer
United Defense LP, San JosÉ, California 95108, USA; Belgian Mechanical Fabrication SA, Grace-Hollogne, Belgium; FMC-Nurol, Ankara, Turkey.

Above: Armored Infantry Fighting Vehicle

Above right: Armored Infantry Fighting Vehicle (Michael Jerchel)

Right: AIFV of Dutch Army in command role (RNLA)

United Defense M113A2 APC (USA)

Key recognition features

● Box-shaped hull with front sloping at 60o to rear, horizontal roof, vertical hull rear with large power-operated ramp, vertical hull sides with no firing ports or vision devices
● Driver's circular hatch front left with air louvres to right, commander's cupola with externally mounted 12.7mm M2 HB MG in centre of roof with rectangular hatch to rear. External box-type fuel tanks each side of ramp on hull rear
● Suspension each side has five road wheels, drive sprocket front, idler rear, no track-return rollers, upper part of track normally covered by rubber skirt

Specifications

Crew: 2+11
Armament: 1 x 12.7mm MG
Ammunition: 2,000 x 12.7mm
Length: 4.863m
Width: 2.686m
Height overall: 2.52m
Height to hull top: 1.85m
Ground clearance: 0.43m
Weight, combat: 11,253kg
Weight, empty: 9,957kg
Power-to-weight ratio: 18.51hp/tonne
Ground pressure: 0.55kg/cm²
Engine: Detroit Diesel Model 6V-53, 6-cylinder water-cooled diesel developing 212bhp at 2,800rpm
Maximum road speed: 60.7km/hr
Maximum water speed: 5.8km/hr
Maximum cruising range: 480km
Fuel capacity: 360 lit
Fording: Amphibious
Vertical obstacle: 0.61m
Trench: 1.68m
Gradient: 60%
Side slope: 40%
Armour: 44mm (maximum)
Armour type: Aluminium
NBC system: Optional
Night vision equipment: Yes (passive or infra-red for driver)

Development

M113 series full tracked APC was developed in late 1950s and first vehicles completed in 1960, powered by petrol engine.

M113 was replaced in production by diesel-powered M113A1 in 1964 which in turn was replaced by M113A2 with a number of automotive improvements. Latest model is M113A3 which entered service in 1987 and has many improvements including more powerful engine, spall liners and optional appliquÈ armour. By 1992 over 76,000 M113s and its variants had been built, including about 4,500 built in Italy by OTOBREDA. Basic vehicle is fully amphibious, propelled in the water by its tracks. Before entering the water a trim vane is erected at front of hull and bilge pumps switched on.

Variants

There are countless local modifications of M113, for example Israeli vehicles have additional armour protection and German vehicles have smoke grenade dischargers on hull front and 7.62mm MG in place of standard 12.7mm M2 HB MG. The following list is by no means exhaustive (see separate entries in this section for United Defense Armored Infantry Fighting Vehicle (AIFV) and Italian Infantry Fighting Vehicle):
M113 with dozer blade, M106 107mm mortar carrier, M125 81mm mortar carrier, M113 A/A (Egypt 2 x 23mm), M163 20mm Vulcan air defence system (qv), M548 unarmoured cargo carrier, M577 command post vehicle with higher roof, M113 series recovery vehicle, M901 Improved TOW Vehicle (qv tank destroyers), M981 Fire Support Team Vehicle, M113 with Scorpion turret (Australia), M113 with Green Archer radar (Germany).
The Norwegian Army has a number of specialised versions of the M113 series including the NM135 which has a one-man turret armed with a 20mm cannon and a 7.62mm MG and the NM142 which has a one-man Armoured Launching Turret with two TOW ATGW in the ready to launch position. Italy has the

Left: M113A1 APC with 12.7mm M@2 HB MG

Right: M577 command post (Pierre Touzin)

Below: Israeli M113 with extra armour

SIDAM 4 x 25mm SPAAG on M113 series chassis (qv).
Chassis is also used as basis for ADATS air defence system (qv).
M548 used for many specialised vehicles including Tracked Rapier air defence system (qv), Chapparral air defence missile system (qv), minelayer (Germany) and electronic warfare carrier.

Status
In production. In service with Argentina, Australia, Belgium, Bolivia, Brazil, Canada, Chile, Costa Rica, Denmark, Ecuador, Egypt, Ethiopia, Germany, Greece, Guatemala, Iran, Israel, Italy, Jordan, Kampuchea, South Korea, Kuwait, Laos, Lebanon, Libya, Morocco, Netherlands, New Zealand, Norway, Pakistan, Peru, Philippines, Portugal, Saudi Arabia, Singapore, Somalia, Spain, Sudan, Switzerland, Taiwan, Thailand, Tunisia, Turkey, USA, Uruguay, Vietnam, Yemen and Zaire.

Manufacturer
United Defense Ground Systems Division, San JosÈ, California, USA. Also built by OTOBREDA in La Spezia, Italy and by BMF in Belgium for Belgian Army.

M901 Improved TOW Vehicle (USA)

Key recognition features

● M113 APC with elevating launcher for two TOW ATGWs on hull roof; when travelling it folds flat on hull top with launcher to rear, when elevated to launch TOWs it has T-shaped profile

● Glacis slopes at 45o with trim vane hinged at bottom, flat hull roof with vertical hull sides and rear, hull has ramp with external fuel tanks each side (did not appear on early vehicles)

● Suspension each side has five road wheels, drive sprocket front, idler rear, no track-return rollers. Upper part of suspension normally covered by rubber skirt

Specifications

Crew: 4 or 5
Armament: 1 x twin TOW ATGW launcher, 1 x 7.62mm MG, 2 x 4 smoke grenade dischargers
Ammunition: 2+10 TOW ATGW, 1,000 x 7.62mm
Length: 4.83m
Width: 2.686m
Height, launcher erected: 3.35m
Height, travelling: 2.91m
Weight, combat: 11,794kg
Power-to-weight ratio: 18.22hp/tonne
Ground pressure: 0.58kg/cm^2
Engine: Detroit Diesel model 6V-53, 6-cylinder water-cooled developing 215bhp at 2,800rpm
Maximum road speed: 67.59km/hr
Maximum water speed: 5.8km/hr
Maximum cruising range: 483km
Fuel capacity: 360 lit
Fording: Amphibious
Vertical obstacle: 0.61m
Trench: 1.68m
Gradient: 60%
Side slope: 30%
Armour: 38mm (maximum)
Armour type: Aluminium
NBC system: None
Night vision equipment: Optional (passive for gunner and driver)

Development

Following trials with prototype systems submitted by three manufacturers, Emerson (now known as Systems & Electronics Inc) was awarded low rate initial contract in 1976 for M901 Improved TOW Vehicle and by 1995 well over 3,200 had been built for home and export markets. M901 Improved TOW Vehicle (ITV) is essentially M113A2 APC with roof-mounted launcher for two Hughes TOW ATGWs. Further 10 missiles carried in reserve which are manually loaded via roof hatch to rear of launcher. Latest version of ITV launches all three versions of TOW, Basic TOW, Improved TOW(1-TOw) and TOW 2; TOW 2 has range of 3,750m. Actual launcher has powered traverse through 360˚, elevates from -30˚ to +34˚ and can be fitted to wide range of vehicles including Armored Infantry Fighting Vehicle (adopted by Dutch Army), Italian VCC-2 (adopted by Saudi Arabia). Has been installed on a number of chassis for trials, including M41 light tank and LAV-300 (6x6).

Variants

Fire Support Team Vehicle (FISTV) is M901 but used to locate and designate targets instead of anti-tank capability. Equipment includes AN/TVQ-2 GLLD with north-seeking gyro and line-of-sight sub-system, AN/TAS-4 sight, land navigation system and extensive communications equipment.

FISTV is designated M981 and entered service with US Army in 1984.

Egyptian version of FISTV is called the Artillery Target Location Vehicle.

Status

Production complete. In service with Egypt, Greece, Jordan, Kuwait, Netherlands (on AIFV chassis), Pakistan, Saudi Arabia (on VCC-2 chassis) and USA.

Manufacturer

Chassis, United Defense LP, San JosÈ, California, USA. Turret, Systems & Electronics Inc, St Louis, Missouri, USA.

Above: M901 ITV launching TOW missile

Right: M981 FISTV in operating configuration

United Defense LVTP7 AAAV (USA)
(now designated AAV7A1 by US Marine Corps)

Key recognition features

- Boat-shaped hull, nose sloping under forward part of hull to tracks, vertical front with glacis almost horizontal, hull sides vertical to rear of commander's cupola then slope inwards at an angle to troop compartment roof, large ramp at rear
- Suspension has six road wheels, drive sprocket front, idler rear, no track-return rollers, skirt over upper forward part of track
- Driver's cupola front left with commander's cupola rear, MG cupola on right side of hull to rear of engine compartment

Specifications

Crew: 3+25
Armament: 1 x 12.7mm MG*
Ammunition: 1,000 x 12.7mm*
Length: 7.943m
Width: 3.27m
Height: 3.263m (overall), 3.12m (turret roof)
Ground clearance: 0.406m
Weight, combat: 22,838kg
Weight, empty: 17,441kg
Power-to-weight ratio: 17.51hp/tonne
Engine: Detroit Diesel model 8V-53T, 8-cylinder, water-cooled, turbocharged diesel developing 400hp at 2,800rpm
Maximum road speed: 64km/hr
Maximum water speed: 13.5km/hr (waterjets), 7.2km/hr (tracks)
Maximum road range: 482km
Fuel capacity: 681 lit
Fording: Amphibious
Vertical obstacle: 0.914m
Trench: 2.438m
Gradient: 60%
Side slope: 60%
Armour: 45mm (maximum)
Armour type: Aluminium
NBC system: None
Night vision equipment: Yes (for driver only)

* US vehicles have new turret with 40mm grenade launcher and 12.7mm MG

Development

In the mid-1960s FMC Corporation (now United Defense, LP) was awarded a contract to design and build prototypes of a new armoured amphibious assault vehicle to replace the then current LVTP5 series. First prototypes were completed in September 1967 under the designation LVTPX12 and after trials it was accepted for service as LVTP7 (Landing Vehicle, Tracked, Personnel, Model 7). First production models completed in 1971 and final deliveries in late 1974.

Hull is all-welded aluminium, engine compartment to front right and MG turret to rear. Turret traverses through 360˚ and 12.7mm MG elevates from -15˚ to +60˚. Driver sits front left with periscope that extends through roof of cupola, commander sits to rear. Troop compartment extends to hull rear with normal means of entry and exit via power-operated ramp in rear, troops and supplies can be loaded via overhead hatches when alongside ship. LVTP7 is fully amphibious, propelled by its tracks or via two waterjets, one each side of hull above idler. Specialised kits include stretcher, navigation, visor and winterisation.

Variants (excluding prototypes)

LVTC7 (Landing Vehicle, Tracked, Command, Model 7), no MG cupola but extensive communications equipment.
LVTR7 (Landing Vehicle, Tracked, Recovery, Model 7), no MG turret but specialised equipment including winch and crane.
LVTP7A1 with mine-clearing kit, basic LVTP7A1 with mine-clearance kit inside troop compartment which is raised when required, fires rockets over front of vehicle into minefield. Other types of mine clearance system are being developed including plough.

LVTP7A1 with 40mm/12.7mm turret. From 1986/87 many vehicles have been fitted with a new turret called the Upgunned Weapons Station which is armed with a 40mm grenade launcher and a 12.7mm machine gun.

LVTP7A1 is LVTP7 rebuilt, improvements including new Cummins engine, smoke generating capability, passive night vision equipment and improved electric weapon station under Service Life Extension Program (SLEP). In addition to SLEP new vehicles were built to LVTP7A1 standard with final deliveries in 1986 to US Marine Corps and some export customers.

LVTP7A1 with applique armour, some US Marine Corps vehicles have been fitted with the Enhanced Applique Armor Kit (EAAK) as the replacement for the earlier P900 armour kit.

**Above:
LVTP7**

**Above right:
LVTP7A1
with
40mm/12.7m
m turret**

**Right:
AA741 with
Upgunned
Weapons
Station and
RAFAEL
applique
armour**

Status
Production complete. In service with Argentina, Brazil, Italy, South Korea, Spain, Thailand, Venezuela and USA.

Manufacturer
United Defense LP, San JosÈ, California, USA.

LVTP5A1 AAAV (USA)

Key recognition features

● Box-shaped hull with vertical sides and rear, forward-opening integral ramp with inverted V indentation
● MG cupola on raised plinth over forward part of hull top, commander's and driver's cupolas each side, hatches over troop compartment in centre of vehicle, engine compartment rear, grille in each side of hull
● Suspension has nine very small road wheels, idler front, drive sprocket rear, track-return rollers covered by skirts

Specifications

Crew: 3+34
Armament: 1 x 7.62mm MG
Ammunition: 2,000 x 7.62mm
Length: 9.042m
Width: 3.567m
Height: 2.921m (turret top), 2.565m (hull top)
Ground clearance: 0.457m
Weight, combat: 37,442kg
Weight, empty: 30,144kg
Power-to-weight ratio: 20.177hp/tonne
Engine: Continental LV-1790-1 V-12 water-cooled petrol developing 810hp at 2,800rpm
Maximum road speed: 48.28km/hr
Maximum water speed: 10.94km/hr
Fuel capacity: 1,726 lit
Fording: Amphibious
Vertical obstacle: 0.914m
Trench: 3.657m
Gradient: 70%
Side slope: 60%
Armour: 16mm (maximum)
Armour type: Steel
NBC system: None
Night vision equipment: Optional (infra-red)

Development

In 1950 Ingersoll Products Division of Borg-Warner Corporation was awarded a contract for design, development and construction of a new armoured amphibious assault vehicle to replace those built during Second World War. First prototype was completed in 1951 with production commencing 1952

under the designation LVTP5 (Landing Vehicle, Tracked, Personnel, Model 5). 1,124 were built by five manufacturers by production completion in 1957.

By 1974 all LVTP5 series vehicles had been phased out of service with US Marine Corps, replaced by the new LVTP7 series (qv). Some LVTP5s were transferred overseas. Three-man crew of LVTP5A1 consists of commander, machine gunner and driver, all of whom sit above troop compartment which extends from front almost to rear. Engine compartment at rear. Troops enter via power-operated ramp in forward part of hull, hatches in roof for loading cargo and troops when alongside ships. LVTP5A1 is fully amphibious, propelled by its tracks. Optional kits include infra-red, stretcher, navigation and winterisation.

Variants (excluding prototypes)

LVTH6 (Landing Vehicle, Tracked, Howitzer, Model 6) with turret-mounted 105mm howitzer on hull top.
LVTC5 (landing Vehicle, Tracked, Command, Model 5) with additional communications equipment for use in command role.
LVTR1 (Landing Vehicle, Tracked, Recovery, Model 1) with boom, winch, tools and other specialised equipment.
LVTE1 (Landing Vehicle, Tracked, Engineer, Model 1) with special dozer blade at front for clearing mines and roof-mounted rocket-propelled mine-clearance system.

Status

Production complete. In service with Chile, Philippines and Taiwan. Some of latter are fitted with a new diesel engine.

Manufacturer

Baldwin-Lima Hamilton, FMC Corporation, Ingersoll, Pacific Car and Foundry and St Louis Car Manufacturing Company, USA.

Above: LVTR1 with ramp closed (US Marine Corps)

Right: LVTH6A1 with turret-mounted 105mm howitzer (US Marine Corps)

United Defense LP Lynx Command and Reconnaissance Vehicle (USA)

Key recognition features

● Low profile hull with well sloped glacis plate leading up to horizontal roof, commander's cupola centre, vertical hull sides and rear, access door in hull rear opens to left

● Four road wheels each side, drive sprocket front, idler rear, no track-return rollers, upper part of track covered by rubber side skirts.

● Driver sits front left, commander/gunner rear and right of driver, radio operator left of commander/gunner

Specifications

Crew: 3
Armament: 1 x 12.7mm MG, 1 x 7.62mm MG, 2 x 3 smoke grenade dischargers
Ammunition: 1,155 x 12.7mm, 2,000 x 7.62mm
Length: 4.597m
Width: 2.413m
Height with armament: 2.18m
Height to hull top: 1.651m
Ground clearance: 0.41m
Weight, combat: 8,775kg
Weight, unloaded: 7,725kg
Power-to-weight ratio: 24.5hp/tonne
Engine: Detroit Diesel 6V-53, 6-cylinder, water-cooled diesel developing 215hp at 2,800rpm
Maximum road speed: 70.8km/hr
Maximum water speed: 6.6km/hr
Range (cruising): 523km
Fuel capacity: 303 lit
Fording: Amphibious
Vertical obstacle: 0.609m
Trench: 1.474m
Gradient: 60%
Side slope: 30%
Armour: 12-38mm (estimate)
Armour type: Aluminium
NBC system: None
Night vision equipment: Yes (infra-red for driver)

Development

The command and reconnaissance vehicle was developed as a private venture by FMC corporation (now United Defense, LP) and uses automotive components of M113 APC built by the same company. First prototype was completed in 1963 but it was not adopted by the US Army. The Canadian Armed Forces purchased 174, which they call Lynx, the first production vehicles being completed in 1968. The Netherlands ordered 250, the first of these completed in 1966.

The Commander/gunner has an M26 turret which is manually traversed through 360˚ and has an externally mounted 12.7mm M2 MG which is aimed and fired from inside the vehicle. Radio operator has pintle-mounted 7.62mm MG. Lynx is fully amphibious, propelled by its tracks. Before entering the water a trim vane is erected at the front, bilge pumps switched on and rectangular covers erected round the air inlet and exhaust louvres on top of the hull.

A wide range of optional equipment was offered for the vehicle including NBC detection and alarm system, different armament installations, windscreen and a capstan winch.

Variants

The Dutch version has a slightly different hull top with driver front left, radio operator/7.62mm MG gunner to his right and a cupola with externally mounted 12.7mm M2 HB MG centre. In the 1970s all these vehicles were fitted with a new one-man Oerlikon-B₁rle (now Oerlikon-Contraves) turret armed with a 25mm Oerlikon-B₁rle (now Oerlikon-Contraves) 25mm KBA cannon that is mounted externally.

Status

Under current plans, this vehicle is soon to be phased out of service with both Canada and the Netherlands.

Manufacturer

United Defense, LP, San JosÈ, California, USA.

Top left: Lynx

Above: Lynx with armament

Left: Dutch Army vehicle with 25mm one-man turret (C R Zwart)

219

M-60P APC (Former Yugoslavia)

Key recognition features

● Well sloped glacis plate with hatches for driver and assistant driver in upper part, cupola with externally mounted 12.7mm M2 HB MG on right side of hull, commander's cupola opposite
● Troop compartment has vertical sides with top half sloping inwards, vertical hull rear with two doors
● Suspension extends each side of hull with five road wheels, drive sprocket front, idler rear, three track-return rollers. Upper part of track covered by skirt

Specifications

Crew: 3+10
Armament: 1 x 12.7mm MG (AA), 1 x 7.92mm MG (bow)
Length: 5.02m
Width: 2.77m
Height: 2.385m (with 12.7mm MG), 1.86m (without armament)
Ground clearance: 0.4m
Weight, combat: 11,000kg
Power-to-weight ratio: 12.73hp/tonne
Ground pressure: 0.7kg/cm²
Engine: FAMOS 6-cylinder in-line water-cooled diesel developing 140hp
Maximum road speed: 45km/hr
Maximum road range: 400km
Fuel capacity: 150 lit
Fording: 1.35m (still water), 1.25m (running water)
Vertical obstacle: 0.6m
Trench: 2m
Gradient: 60%
Side slope: 40%
Armour: 25mm (maximum)
Armour type: Steel
NBC system: None
Night vision equipment: Yes (infra-red for driver)

Development

M-60P was developed to meet requirements of Yugoslav Army in late 1960s and made first appearance during parade in 1965. For a short period it was also referred to as M-590. Driver sits front left with co-driver to his right (who also operates bow mounted 7.92mm MG), engine and transmission below. Commander's cupola is to rear of driver and protrudes slightly over left side of hull, with similar machine gunner's cupola on opposite side. 12.7mm M2 HB MG can be used both in anti-aircraft and ground-to-ground roles, no provision for firing from inside vehicle. 12.7mm M2 HB MG can be dismounted and used in ground role.

The Troop compartment is at the rear and infantry enter and leave via two doors in rear, each of which has firing/observation port. Three firing/observation ports in each side of troop compartment. M-60P has no amphibious capability but board mounted on glacis plate deflects water rushing up glacis plate when fording.

Variants

Only known variant is M-60PB anti-tank which has twin 82mm recoilless rifles mounted on top left or top right of hull at rear, elevation of +6°, depression of -4°, traverse and elevation both manual. Ten 82mm HEAT projectiles are carried.

Other versions of M-60P are probably in service, such as ambulance, command and radio vehicles.

Status

Production complete. In service with former Yugoslavia.

Manufacturer

Former Yugoslavia state factories.

Above left: M-60P with 12.7mm MG
Left: M-60P with 12.7mm MG
Top: Infantry dismount from M-60P
Above: M-60P with 12.7mm MG

BVP M80A Infantry Combat Vehicle (former Yugoslavia)

Key recognition features

● Well sloped glacis plate leads up to hull top which is horizontal all way to rear, vertical back with hull sides above track sloping inwards, two doors in hull rear
● Circular turret with sloping sides slightly to rear of vehicle centre, 20mm cannon in front and twin launcher for Sagger ATGW externally at rear
● Suspension has five road wheels, drive sprocket front, idler rear, two track-return rollers. Rollers and upper part of track covered by sheet metal skirt

Specifications

Crew: 3+7
Armament: 1 x 20mm cannon, 1 x 7.62mm MG (coaxial), 2 x Sagger ATGW
Ammunition: 1,400 x 20mm, 2,000 x 7.62mm, 4 Sagger ATGW
Length: 6.42m
Width: 2.995m
Height: 2.67m (with ATGW)
Ground clearance: 0.4m
Weight, combat: 14,000kg
Power-to-weight ratio: 22.5hp/tonne
Ground pressure: 0.67kg/cm²
Engine: FAMOS 10V003 4-stroke 10-cylinder direct-injection diesel developing 315hp at 2,500rpm
Maximum road speed: 64km/hr
Maximum water speed: 7.8km/hr
Maximum road range: 500km
Fuel capacity: 510 lit
Fording: Amphibious
Vertical obstacle: 0.8m
Trench: 2.4m
Gradient: 60%
Side slope: 40%
Armour: Classified
Armour type: Steel
NBC system: Yes
Night vision equipment: Yes (commander, gunner and driver)

Development

The BVP M80A is a further development of M-80 and was seen in public for the first time during a military exhibition in Cairo in late 1984. Main improvement over M-80 is a more powerful engine which gives slightly higher speed and higher power-to-weight ratio.

Overall layout is very similar to earlier M-80 with driver front left, vehicle commander to his rear, engine compartment front right, turret centre and infantry compartment rear. Infantry sit back to back along centre of vehicle, enter and leave via two doors in hull rear each of which has firing port and vision block. In each side of personnel compartment are a further three firing ports with periscope above for aiming. Over top of troop compartment are two oval roof hatches. One-man turret traverses through 360°. 20mm cannon and 7.62mm MG mounted coaxially right elevate from -5° to +75° under power control, with manual controls provided for emergency use. Twin launcher for Sagger-type wire-guided anti-tank missiles mounted on turret rear (launched from inside turret).

The BVP M80A is fully amphibious, propelled by its tracks. Before entering the water a trim vane is erected on glacis plate and bilge pumps switched on. Engine compartment fire suppression system fitted as standard. Vehicle lays its own smoke screen by injecting diesel fuel into exhaust.

Variants

BVP M80AK, new one-man turret armed with 30mm cannon, 7.62mm coaxial MG and twin launcher for Yugoslav built Sagger ATGW.
BVP M80A1, two-man turret armed with twin 30mm anti-aircraft cannon.
BVP M80A KC, company commander's vehicle.
BVP M80A KB, battalion commandeer's vehicle.
BVP M80A LT anti-tank, new turret with six Sagger ATGW in ready-to-launch position.
BVP M80A Sn, ambulance, has no turret.

SAVA low altitude SAM system.

Status
Production complete. In service with the former Yugoslav Army and other countries/regions in this area.

Manufacturer
Former Yugoslav state factories.

Right: BVP M80AK which has 30mm cannon

M-80 Mechanised ICV (Former Yugoslavia)

Key recognition features

● Well sloped glacis plate with trim vane folded back on lower part, horizontal hull top to rear, hull rear slopes slightly inwards with two doors that open on outside

● Circular turret with sloping sides slightly to rear of vehicle centre with 20mm cannon in front, 7.62mm MG coaxial to right, twin launcher for Sagger ATGW right rear

● Suspension has five road wheels, drive sprocket front, idler rear, two track-return rollers. Rollers and upper part of track covered by sheet metal skirt. Hull sides at rear slope inwards, firing ports in sides and periscopes above

Specifications

Crew: 3+7
Armament: 1 x 20mm, 1 x 7.62mm MG (coaxial), twin launcher for Sagger ATGW
Ammunition: 400 x 20mm, 2,250 x 7.62mm, 4 x Sagger ATGW
Length: 6.4m
Width: 2.59m
Height over ATGW: 2.5m
Height over turret: 2.3m
Height hull roof: 1.8m
Ground clearance: 0.4m
Weight, combat: 13,600kg
Weight, empty: 11,700kg
Power-to-weight ratio: 18.97hp/tonne
Ground pressure: 0.64kg/cm^2
Engine: HS 115-2 V-8 water-cooled turbocharged diesel developing 260hp at 3,000rpm
Maximum road speed: 60km/hr
Maximum water speed: 7.5km/hr
Maximum road range: 500km
Fuel capacity: Not available
Fording: Amphibious
Vertical obstacle: 0.8m
Trench: 2.2m
Gradient: 60%
Side slope: 30%
Armour: 30mm (maximum) (estimate)
Armour type: Steel
NBC system: Yes
Night vision equipment: Yes (infra-red for commander, gunner, driver)

Development

M-80 was developed in the early 1970s and seen in public for the first time in May 1975. The vehicle was originally referred to by the Yugoslavs as the M-980, but this was subsequently changed to the M-80. Driver sits front left with commander to his rear, engine compartment to right. Turret is in centre with 20mm cannon and 7.62mm coaxial MG which elevates from -5° to +75°, turret traverses 360°. Mounted externally on right side of turret at rear is launcher with two Sagger-type wire-guided ATGWs which have maximum range of 3,000m. Troop compartment is at rear, three men sit each side back to back, each with firing port and periscope above. Two roof hatches above troop compartment with periscope above. Over top of troop compartment are two roof hatches hinged in centre. M-80 is fully amphibious, propelled by its tracks. Before entering the water the trim vane is erected and bilge pumps switched on.

Variants

No known variants.

Status
Production complete. In service
with former Yugoslavia.
Succeeded in production by
BVP M80A (qv).

Manufacturer
Former Yugoslav state arsenals.

Right: M-80

4x4 VEHICLES

BDX APC (Belgium)

Key recognition features

- Box-type hull, sloping glacis plate with large bullet-proof window in front of driver with smaller window each side
- Lower hull sides vertical with door between roadwheels, upper part of hull slopes inwards, vertical hull rear with door opening to right
- Horizontal roof with armament mounted centre, exhaust pipe and silencer mounted on each side of upper part of hull sides

Specifications

Crew: 2+10
Configuration: 4x4
Armament: See text
Length: 5.05m
Width: 2.5m
Height with turret: 2.84m
Height to hull top: 2.06m
Ground clearance: 0.4m
Wheelbase: 3.003m
Weight, combat: 10,700kg
Weight, unloaded: 9,750kg
Power-to-weight ratio: 16.82hp/tonne
Engine: Chrysler V-8 water-cooled petrol developing 180bhp at 4,000rpm
Maximum road speed: 100km/hr
Maximum road range: 500 to 900km
Fuel capacity: 248 lit
Fording: Amphibious
Vertical obstacle: 0.4m
Trench: Not applicable
Gradient: 60%
Side slope: 40%
Armour type: Steel
Armour: 12.7mm (maximum)
NBC system: Optional
Night vision equipment: Optional

Development

In 1976 the Engineering Division of Beherman Demoen obtained a licence to produce an improved version of the Irish Timoney (4x4) APC. In 1977 the Belgian Government ordered 123 vehicles, 43 for the Belgian Air Force for airfield protection and 80 for the Belgian gendarmerie, delivered between 1978 and 1981. Five vehicles were also delivered to Argentina, and more recently some of the Belgian vehicles have been transferred to Mexico. Further development of BDX resulted in the Vickers Defence Systems Valkyr, only two of these were sold to Kuwait before the Iraqi invasion.

The driver sits far front with engine to rear. Behind this is troop compartment with entry doors sides and rear. Variety of weapons can be mounted on roof including turret with twin 7.62mm MGs or turret with twin MILAN ATGWs in ready-to-launch position.

The BDX is fully amphibious, propelled by its wheels. Waterjets, NBC system, smoke grenade dischargers, air-conditioning system and front-mounted dozer blade available as optional extras. As an option the petrol engine fitted to all production vehicles could be replaced by the more fuel efficient Detroit Diesel Model 4V-53T developing 180hp at 2,800rpm.

Variants

Gendarmerie order comprised 41 APCs without turret, 26 with dozer blade and 13 81mm mortar carriers.
Technology Investments built 10 Timoney APCs for Irish Army, five Mk 4s and five Mk 6s which remain in service.

Status

Production complete. In service with Argentina, Belgium, Ireland (built in Ireland), and Mexico.

Manufacturer

Beherman Demoen Engineering (BDX), Mechelen, Belgium.

Top: BDX with twin 7.62mm turret
Above: BDX with twin 7.62mm MG turret
Above right: BDX of Belgian Air Force (C R Zwart)
Right: Timoney Mk 4 of Irish Army (Denis McCarthy)

ENGESA EE-3 Jararaca Scout Car (Brazil)

Key recognition features

● Nose slopes back under hull front, headlamps recessed, well sloped glacis plate with horizontal roof line, driver's position protruding from roof line over glacis plate

● Armament normally mounted on top of hull in centre (offset to right), engine rear, air louvres in vertical hull rear

● Vertical hull sides with chamfer between hull sides and roof, door in right hull side on late production models, two road wheels each side at extreme ends of vehicle

Specifications

Crew: 3
Configuration: 4x4
Armament: 1 x 12.7mm MG
Ammunition: 1000 x 12.7mm
Length: 4.163m
Width: 2.235m
Height (top of 12.7mm mount): 2.3m
Height (hull top): 1.56m
Ground clearance: 0.335m
Wheelbase: 2.6m
Weight, combat: 5,800kg
Power-to-weight ratio: 20.7hp/tonne
Engine: Mercedes-Benz OM 314A turbocharged, 4-cylinder water-cooled diesel developing 120hp at 2,800rpm
Maximum road speed: 100km/hr
Maximum road range: 700km
Fuel capacity: 140 lit
Fording: 0.6m
Vertical obstacle: 0.4m
Trench: Not applicable
Gradient: 60%
Side slope: 30%
Armour: Classified
Armour type: Steel (2 layers)
NBC system: Optional
Night vision equipment: Optional

Development

EE-3 Jararaca (4x4) was designed by ENGESA to complement its EE-9 (6x6) Cascavel armoured car and EE-11 Urutu (6x6) armoured personnel carrier. Like other ENGESA wheeled armoured vehicles the Jararaca has proven and common automotive components wherever possible. The driver sits front with machine gunner to his right rear and vehicle commander, who also operates communications equipment, to left rear. All three crew members have roof hatches and there is a large forward-opening door in the right side of the hull. Standard equipment includes central tyre pressure regulation system that allows driver to adjust tyre pressure to suit ground, and run flat tyres. Optional equipment includes smoke grenade dischargers, passive night vision equipment, NBC system, radios and intercom.

A wide range of armament can be installed on the roof including a pintle-mounted Euromissile MILAN ATGW system, and the standard 12.7mm M2 HB MG can be replaced by a 7.62mm MG or a 20mm cannon. Other armament installations include a 60mm breech-loaded mortar, ENGESA ET-MD one-man turret armed with one 20mm cannon and one 7.62mm MG

Variants
Apart from the different armament options the only Known variant is the NBC reconaissance version with raised roof and NBC monitoring equipment.

Status
Production complete. In service with Cyprus, Equador, Gabon, Jordan and Uruguay.

Manufacturer
ENGESA, Sao José dos Campos, Brazil.

Right: Engesa EE-3

Kader Fahd APC (Egypt)

Key recognition features

● Fully enclosed hull with front, sides and rear slightly sloping inwards

● Commander and driver sit front, each with large side door and large windscreen to immediate front which can be covered by armoured shutter hinged at top

● Radiator grille low down in nose of vehicle, firing ports in rear troop compartment, two-part rear entry hatch

Specifications

Crew: 2+10
Configuration: 4x4
Armament: 1 x 7.62mm MG (see text), 2 x 4 smoke grenade dischargers
Ammunition: 1,000 x 7.62mm (estimate)
Length: 6m
Width: 2.45m
Height: 2.1m (hull top)
Ground clearance: 0.31 to 0.37m
Wheelbase: 3.2m
Weight, combat: 10,900kg
Weight, empty: 9,100kg
Power-to-weight ratio: 15.4hp/tonne
Engine: Mercedes-Benz OM-352 A 6-cylinder direct injection water-cooled turbocharged diesel developing 168hp at 2,800rpm
Maximum road speed: 90km/hr
Maximum road range: 800km
Fording: 0.7m
Vertical obstacle: 0.5m
Trench: 0.9m
Gradient: 70%
Side slope: 30%
Armour: 10mm (maximum)(estimate)
Armour type: Steel
NBC system: Optional
Night vision equipment: Optional

Development

Fahd (4x4) was designed by Thyssen Henschel, Germany, under the designation TH 390 to meet requirements of the Egyptian Army. Production commenced in 1985, first deliveries in 1986. It consists of a modified truck chassis with an armoured body that provides complete protection from attack by 7.62 x 54mm armour-piercing projectiles and shell splinters.

Commander and driver sit front, engine below and between, troop compartment rear, normal means of entry and exit for 10 troops via two-part hatch in rear, top part opens upwards and lower part folds downwards to form step. Firing ports with vision block above in each side of troop compartment, another each side of rear entry hatch. Hatches in roof.

Standard equipment includes central tyre pressure regulation system allowing driver to adjust tyre pressure to suit ground, power-assisted steering. Options include NBC system, front-mounted winch, ventilation system, night vision equipment and smoke grenade dischargers.

Fahd 30 was shown for the first time in 1991 and is essentially the Fahd fitted with the complete turret of the Soviet BMP-2 IFV armed with 30mm cannon, 7.62mm coaxial machine gun and roof-mounted ATGW.

Variants

Fahd can be fitted with wide range of armaments ranging from pintle-mounted 7.62mm MG up to 20mm cannon. Variants suggested by manufacturer include ambulance, command post, multiple rocket launcher, recovery, minelayer and internal security. Latest production vehicles are powered by the Mercedes-Benz OM 352A 6-cylinder diesel developing 168hp at 2,800rpm.

Status

Production. In service with Egypt, Kuwait, Oman, Sudan and Zaire.

Manufacturer

Kader Factory for Developed Industries, Heliopolis, Egypt.

Top left: Fahd (4x4) without armament

Right: Fahd (4x4) fitted with BMP-2 turret

Kader Walid APC (Egypt)

Key recognition features

- Fully enclosed engine compartment front with horizontal armoured grille to protect radiator, troop compartment rear with vertical sides and rear with sides sloping slightly inwards, three circular firing ports each side
- Commander's and driver's doors open forwards, rear door with spare wheel and tyre open to left, firing port each side
- Similar in appearance to former Soviet BTR-40 (4x4) APC but Walid is larger with rear wheel arches straight rather than curved, as in BTR-40

Specifications

Crew: 2+8/10
Configuration: 4x4
Armament: 1 x 7.62mm MG
Ammunition: 1,000 x 7.62mm
Length: 6.12m
Width: 2.57m
Height: 2.3m
Ground clearance: 0.4m
Wheelbase: Not available
Weight, combat: 12,000kg (estimate)
Weight, empty: 9,200kg (estimate)
Power-to-weight ratio: 14hp/tonne (estimate)
Engine: 168hp diesel
Maximum road speed: 86km/hr
Maximum range: 800km
Fuel capacity: Not available
Fording: 0.8m (estimate)
Vertical obstacle: 0.5m (estimate)
Trench: Not applicable
Gradient: 60%
Side slope: 30%
Armour: 8mm (maximum) (estimate)
Armour type: Steel
NBC system: None
Night vision equipment: None

Development

Walid (4x4) was developed in the 1960s and used for the first time in the 1967 Middle East campaign. Consists of a German Magirus Deutz chassis made in Egypt and fitted with open-topped armoured body. Walid 2 was introduced in 1981 and is based on Mercedes-Benz automotive components. It has now been succeeded in production by Fahd (4x4) APC (qv).

Commander and gunner sit to rear of engine, troop compartment at rear, 7.62mm MG normally mounted on forward part of hull roof firing forwards. Additional weapons can be mounted round top of hull. Walid has no amphibious capability and no central tyre pressure regulation system.

Variants

Only known variants are minelayer with ramp at rear for laying mines on surface, and multiple rocket launcher with 12 rockets in ready-to-launch position. The latter has 12 80mm D-3000 rockets with a maximum range of 2,500m. There is also a six round version with six 122mm D-6000 smoke rockets with a maximum range of 6000m.

Status

Production complete. In service with Algeria, Burundi, Israel, Sudan and Yemen.

Manufacturer

Kader Factory, Cairo, Egypt.

Above: Walid with all hatches closed (Kensuke Ebata)

Above right: Walid with launcher for smoke rockets (Egyptian Army)

Right: Walid in mine-clearing role with doors open (Christopher F Foss)

ACMAT APC (TPK 4.20 VSC) (France)

Key recognition features

● Engine front with radiator grilles under nose, sloped windscreen with two windows covered by armoured shutters hinged at top, side door to immediate rear of windscreen which opens forwards
● Horizontal roof line that extends to rear, two doors in hull rear, troop compartment at rear has three square bullet-proof windows each side
● Two road wheels each side with hull sides sloping inwards from just above road wheels

Specifications

Crew: 2+8/10
Configuration: 4x4
Armament: See text
Length: 5.98m
Width: 2.1m
Height hull top: 2.205m
Ground clearance (axle): 0.273m
Ground clearance (hull): 0.5m
Wheelbase: 3.6m
Weight, combat: 7,300kg
Weight, empty: 5,880kg
Power-to-weight ratio: 18.49hp/tonne
Engine: Perkins Model 6.354.4 6-cylinder diesel developing 135hp at 2,800rpm
Maximum road speed: 95km/hr
Maximum range: 1,600km
Fuel capacity: 360 lit
Fording: 0.8m
Trench: Not applicable
Gradient: 60%
Side slope: 40%
Armour: 5.8mm (maximum)
Armour type: Steel
NBC system: None
Night vision equipment: None

Development

TPK 4.20 VSC was designed as a private venture by ACMAT and is a VLRA (4x4) 2,500kg long-range reconnaissance vehicle with an armoured body. First prototype completed in 1980 and production commenced same year. Engine is at far front with driver and commander to its immediate rear and troop compartment extending right to rear of vehicle. Troops sit at rear on bench seats down each side. One version has fully enclosed roof with three sliding bullet-proof windows each side allowing some occupants to use small arms from inside. Other model has open roof and sides hinged outwards and downwards at mid-point for rapid exit or return fire.

Optional equipment on open-topped version includes 81mm TDA mortar firing to rear, 7.62mm or 12.7mm pintle-mounted MGs or Euromissile MILAN ATGW. Fully enclosed version can have air-conditioning system and be used as command or radio vehicle.

Variants

VBL light armoured car is essentially the fully enclosed APC with one-man turret on roof armed with 7.62mm or 12.7mm MG. The VBL can be fitted with different radios and an air conditioning system and be modified for more specific roles such as an ambulance or command post vehicle.
6x6 version still at prototype stage, designated TPK 6.40 VBL.

Status

In production. In service with a number of countries including Gabon and Ivory Coast.

Manufacturer

ACMAT, Ateliers de Construction Mécanique de l'Atlantique, Saint-Nazaire, France.

Above: ACMAT VBL light armoured car with one-man turret armed with 12.7mm M2 HB and 7.62mm MGs

Panhard VBL Scout Car (France)

Key recognition features

● Almost vertical hull front, sloping glacis plate with large access panel in upper part, forward part of rear crew compartment slopes to rear, horizontal roof with three hatches, single door in hull rear

● Two large road wheels, hull above wheel arches slope inwards, single forward-opening door in each side with bullet-proof window in upper part

● Heavy armament, eg 12.7mm M2 HB MG or MILAN, is mounted on circular hatch at rear

Specifications
Crew: 3
Configuration: 4x4
Armament: 1 x 7.62mm MG, 1 x MILAN ATGW launcher
Ammunition: 3000 x 7.62mm, 6 x MILAN ATGW
Length: 3.87m
Width: 2.02m
Height: 1.7m (hull top), 2.14m (with 7.62mm MG)
Ground clearance: 0.37m
Wheelbase: 2.45m
Weight, combat: 3590kg
Weight, empty: 2890kg
Power-to-weight ratio: 26.76hp/tonne
Engine: Peugeot XD3T, 4-cylinder turbocharged diesel developing 95hp at 4150rpm
Maximum road speed: 95km/hr
Maximum water speed: 4.5km/hr
Maximum road range: 600km, 800km with onboard fuel cans
Fording: 0.9m (see text)
Trench: 0.50m
Gradient: 50%
Side slope: 30%
Armour: 11.5mm (maximum)
Armour type: Steel
NBC system: Yes
Night vision equipment: Yes (passive for driver)
(Above relates to French Army VBL in combat/anti-tank role)

Development
In 1978 the French Army issued a requirement for a new light reconnaissance/anti-tank vehicle, the Véhicule Blindé Léger (VBL). Panhard and Renault each built prototypes for competitive evaluation and in February 1985 the Panhard VBL was selected, although at this time the vehicle was already in production for Mexico. The exact number of vehicles required by the French Army is still uncertain but the first order was for 569 vehicles with the first production vehicles for the French Army being completed late in 1990. The French Army will have two basic versions of the VBL, combat/anti-tank with a three-man crew armed with a MILAN ATGW launcher and 7.62mm MG, and intelligence/scout with a two-man crew and armed with one 7.62mm and one 12.7mm MG. The 1000th VBL vehicle was completed at the Panhard production facility at Marolles in October 1995.

All versions have engine front and crew compartment rear with three roof hatches and three doors. It is fully amphibious, with propeller at hull rear, and standard equipment includes central tyre pressure system. Options include heater, powered steering and air-conditioning system.

Variants
Panhard has proposed over 20 models of the VBL for the export market including radar (battlefield and air defence), anti-aircraft (Mistral SAMs), anti-tank (MILAN, HOT or TOW ATGWs) and internal security to name but a few. There is also a long wheelbase version of the VBL.

Status
In production. In service with Cameroon, Djibouti, France, Gabon, Mexico, Niger, Nigeria, Portugal, Qatar, Rwanda and Togo.

Manufacturer
Societe de Constructions Mecaniques Panhard et Levassor, Paris, France.

Top: Panhard VBL with 7.62mm ring mount

Top right: Panhard VBL

Right: Panhard VBL with 7.62mm MG ring mount

Panhard M3 APC (France)

Key recognition features

- Pointed front with well sloped glacis plate, driver's position in upper part, horizontal roof with main armament normally centre, secondary armament rear
- Vertical hull sides with upper part sloping inwards, three observation/firing hatches each side, vertical hull rear with two outward-opening doors each with firing port
- Two large road wheels each side with forward-opening door between, wheels outside hull envelope with mudguards which blow off if vehicle runs over mine

Specifications

Crew: 2+10
Armament: See text
Length: 4.45m
Width: 2.4m
Height: 2.48m (with twin 7.62mm MG turret)
Height to hull top: 2m
Ground clearance: 0.35m
Wheelbase: 2.7m
Weight, combat: 6,100kg
Weight, unloaded: 5,300kg
Power-to-weight ratio: 14.75hp/tonne
Engine: Panhard Model 4 HD 4-cylinder air-cooled petrol developing 90hp at 4,700rpm
Maximum road speed: 90km/hr
Maximum water speed: 4km/hr
Maximum road range: 600km
Fuel capacity: 165 lit
Fording: Amphibious
Vertical obstacle: 0.3m
Trench (1 channel): 0.8m
Trench (5 channels): 3.1m
Gradient: 60%
Side slope: 30%
Armour: 12mm (maximum)
Armour type: Steel
NBC system: Optional
Night vision equipment: Optional

Development

M3 (4x4) was developed by Panhard as a private venture, first prototype completed in 1969 and first production vehicles in 1971. Well over 1,200 have been built for export with sales made to some 35 countries. Ninety-five per cent of automotive components are identical to those of the Panhard AML range 4x4 armoured cars. Panhard M3 is used for a wide range of roles including internal security, ambulance and command post.

Driver sits front, engine to his rear, troop compartment occupies remainder of vehicle. Troops enter and leave via single door in sides and twin doors in rear. Eight firing ports. Wide range of turrets, mounts and cupolas can be mounted on roof armed with cannon, machine guns and ATGWs such as MILAN.

Vehicle is fully amphibious, propelled by its wheels. Wide range of optional equipment including front-mounted winch, air-conditioning system and two electrically operated smoke grenade dischargers.

Variants

M3/VDA anti-aircraft vehicle with one-man power-operated turret armed with twin 20mm cannon. Before firing four outriggers are lowered to ground for a more stable firing platform. This version known to be in service with Ivory Coast, Niger and United Arab Emirates (Abu Dhabi).
M3/VAT repair vehicle with lifting gear at rear.
M3/VPC command vehicle with extensive communications equipment.
M3/VLA engineer vehicle with front-mounted obstacle-clearing blade.
M3/VTS ambulance which carries four stretcher patients or six walking wounded, or a mixture, plus its crew.
M3 radar can be fitted with wide range of radars including **RASIT battlefield surveillance radar** or RA 20S surveillance radar.
Buffalo APC which in 1986 replaced Panhard M3 in production.

**Left:
Panhard M3
(4x4) with
twin
7.62mm MG
turret**

**Right:
Panhard
M3/VLA
engineer
vehicle**

Essentially a Panhard M3 with additional external stowage spaces and original petrol engine replaced by 146hp V-6 petrol or 95hp diesel. This model now in production and in service with Benin, Colombia and Rwanda. The 95hp diesel is the same Peugeot XD3T that is fitted to the Panhard VBL (4x4) light armoured vehicle and can be bracketed to the Panhard AML.

Status
Production complete, replaced in production by Buffalo. M3 known to be in service with Algeria, Bahrain, Burkina Faso, Burundi, Chad, Gabon, Iraq, Ireland, Ivory Coast, Kenya, Lebanon, Malaysia, Mauritania, Morocco, Niger, Nigeria, Portugal, Rwanda, Saudi Arabia, Senegal, Spain, Togo, United Arab Emirates and Zaire.

Manufacturer
Société de Constructions Mecaniques Panhard et Levassor, Paris, France.

241

Panhard AML Light Armoured Car (France)

Key recognition features

● Well sloped inverted V glacis plate with driver's hatch in upper part, horizontal hull top with engine rear, stowage boxes project forward of rear wheels. Diesel engine version has different hull rear
● Turret has bustle that extends over hull rear, vertical sides slope slightly inwards. 90mm gun has prominent double-baffle muzzle brake, no fume extractor or thermal sleeve. Two smoke grenade dischargers each side at turret rear
● Two large road wheels each side with large rearward-opening door to rear of first road wheel. Left door has spare wheel and tyre. Sand channels normally carried across lower hull front

Specifications (H 90 version)

Crew: 3
Configuration: 4x4
Armament: 1 x 90mm, 1 x 7.62mm MG coaxial, 2 x 2 smoke grenade dischargers
Ammunition: 20 x 90mm, 2,000 x 7.62mm
Length gun forwards: 5.11m
Length hull: 3.79m
Width: 1.97m
Height overall: 2.07m
Ground clearance: 0.33m
Wheelbase: 2.5m
Weight, combat: 5,500kg
Power-to-weight ratio: 16.36hp/tonne
Engine: Panhard Model 4 HD 4-cylinder air-cooled petrol developing 90hp at 4,700rpm. Current production models have Peugeot XD 3T diesel developing 98hp and operating range of 700 to 800km
Maximum road speed: 90km/hr
Maximum road range: 600km
Fuel capacity: 156 lit
Fording: 1.1m
Vertical obstacle: 0.3m
Trench with one channel: 0.8m
Trench with three channels: 3.1m
Gradient: 60%
Side slope: 30%
Armour: 8-12mm (hull)
Armour type: Steel
NBC system: None
Night vision equipment: Optional

Development

Panhard AML (Automitrailleusse Legere) was developed for the French Army with first prototypes completed in 1959 and first production vehicles in 1961. By 1996 over 4,800 vehicles had been built for home and export (including those build under licence in South Africa by Sandock-Austral). Panhard M3 (4x4) armoured personnel carrier (qv) shares 95 per cent automotive components of AML and has also been built in large numbers.

All AMLs have similar layout with driver front, turret centre and engine rear. The Hispano-Suiza two-man H90 turret traverses through 360° and the 90mm gun elevates from -8° to +15°. Main armament comprises 90mm gun which fires HE, HEAT, canister and smoke projectiles. 7.62mm machine gun is mounted coaxial with left of main armament, and 7.62mm or 12.7mm machine gun can be mounted on turret roof.

Variants

AML with Lynx 90 turret. Replaced H90 turret, similar armament but can have powered traverse, laser rangefinder and night vision equipment, commander's cupola raised on left side.
AML with HE-60-7 turret, 60mm mortar and twin 7.62mm MGs.
AML with HE60-12 turret, 60mm mortar and 12.7mm MG.
AML with HE60-20 turret, 60mm mortar and 20mm cannon.
AML with HE60-20 Serval turret, replaced above in production.
AML with S 530 turret, twin 20mm anti-aircraft cannon, used only by Venezuela.
AML with diesel engine, current production AMLs have Panhard diesel replaced by more fuel efficient Peugeot diesel which is also installed in the Panhard VBL (4x4) (qv) light armoured vehicle. Panhard also now offer an upgrade package

that can include the new diesel engine, improved
automotives, new exhaust and upgraded weapons. For the
H90 turret, for example, the 90mm gun can be modified to
fire APFSDS ammunition, a laser rangefinder added for
improved first round hit probability and passive night vision
equipment installed.

South African-built vehicle is known as Eland and ran
through to Mk 7 in two basic versions: Eland 60 with 60mm
mortar and 7.62mm MG and Eland 90 with 90mm gun and
7.62mm coaxial MG. Both have roof-mounted 7.62mm MG,
different engine and detailed differences to French-built
vehicles.

Status

Production as required. In service with Algeria, Argentina,
Bahrain, Benin, Burkina Faso, Burundi, Chad, Djibouti,
Ecuador, El Salvador, France, Gabon, Iraq, Ireland, Ivory Coast,
Kenya, Malaysia, Mauritania, Morocco, Niger, Nigeria,
Polisario guerrillas, Portugal, Rwanda, Saudi Arabia,
Senegambia, Somalia, South Africa, Spain, Sudan, Togo,
Tunisia, United Arab Emirates, Venezuela, Yemen, Zaire and
Zimbabwe.

Manufacturers

Societe de Constructions Mecaniques Panhard and Levassor,
Paris, France; Sandock Austral, South Africa.

*Above: Panhard AML
with HE60-20 Serval
turret*

*Right: Panhard AML
with H90 90mm
turret*

Berliet VXB-170 APC (France)

Key recognition features

- Four large road wheels, hull has pointed nose with driver far front, large windscreen to front and sides
- Lower half of hull vertical, top half sloping slightly inwards, single door in each hull side
- Engine compartment left rear with grilles in roof, entry door in right hull rear

Specifications

Crew: 1+11
Configuration: 4x4
Armament: 1 x 7.62mm MG, 2 x 2 smoke grenade dischargers (optional)
Ammunition: 1,000 x 7.62mm
Length: 5.99m
Width: 2.5m
Height: 2.05m (without armament)
Ground clearance: 0.45m
Wheelbase: 3m
Weight, combat: 12,700kg
Weight, empty: 9,800kg
Power-to-weight ratio: 13.38hp/tonne
Engine: Berliet model V800 M V-8 diesel developing 170hp at 3,000rpm
Maximum road speed: 85km/hr
Maximum water speed: 4km/hr
Road range: 750km
Fuel capacity: 220 lit
Fording: Amphibious
Vertical obstacle: 0.3m
Trench: Not applicable
Gradient: 60%
Side slope: 30%
Armour: 7mm
Armour type: Steel
NBC system: None
Night vision equipment: Optional

Development

VXB-170 was developed as a private venture by Société des

VXB-170 (4x4) without armament

Automobiles Berliet under the designation BL-12, first prototype completed in 1968. With a number of improvements it was adopted by the French Gendarmerie for internal security, the first of 155 vehicles delivered in 1973. In 1975 Berliet became part of the Renault Group which also included Saviem, so production of VXB-170 was phased out after completion of existing orders; the French Army had adopted the VAB to meet its future requirements.

VXB-170 has an all-welded steel hull, driver front and troop compartment extending right to rear of vehicle, except for engine compartment on left side at rear. In addition to the three doors there are give hatches in roof, one for driver with larger circular hatch to rear on which main armament is normally mounted.

French Gendarmerie vehicles are blue and normally have hydraulically operated obstacle clearing blade at hull front and are fitted with roof-mounted SAMM BTM 103 light turret armed with 7.62mm MG and 40mm grenade launcher. Turret traverse is 360° and weapon elevation from -15° to +60°.

VXB-170 is fully amphibious, propelled by its wheels, and optional equipment includes heater, night vision equipment, NBC system, front-mounted winch and bullet-proof tyres.

Variants
Wide range of variants were projected and prototypes of some were built, for example with a two-man turret from the AML armed with 60mm mortar and 7.62mm MGs. None entered production.

Status
Production complete. In service with France (Gendarmerie), Gabon and Senegal.

Manufacturer
Société des Automobiles Berliet, Bourge, France.

Above: VXB-170 (4x4) with cupola-mounted MG

Right: VXB-170 (4x4) with 7.62mm MG

Left: VXB-170 (4x4) showing amphibious capabilities

Thyssen TM 170 APC (Germany)

Key recognition features

- Box-type engine compartment front, radiator grille under nose with slightly sloping glacis plate, almost vertical windscreen which can be covered by two armoured shutters hinged at bottom, horizontal roof with hull rear sloping inwards
- Two road wheels each side, bullet-proof window in upper part of hull front which can be covered by hinged shutter, single door in each side of hull and hatch in hull rear
- Troop compartment has firing ports in sides and rear, hull sides are welded midway up then slope inwards at top and bottom

Specifications

Crew: 2+10
Configuration: 4x4
Armament: Optional
Length: 6.14m
Width: 2.47m
Height: 2.32m (hull top)
Ground clearance: 0.48m
Wheelbase: 3.25m
Weight, combat: 11,650kg
Weight, unloaded: 8800kg
Power-to-weight ratio: 18hp/tonne
Engine: Daimler-Benz OM366 supercharged diesel developing 240hp at 1400rpm
Maximum road speed: 100km/hr
Maximum water speed: 9km/hr
Maximum road range: 870km
Fuel capacity: 200 lit
Fording: Amphibious
Vertical obstacle: 0.6m
Trench: Not applicable
Gradient: 80%
Side slope: 40%
Armour: 8mm (estimate)
Armour type: Steel
NBC system: Optional
Night vision equipment: Optional

Development

TM 170 (4x4) was developed as a private venture by Thyssen Henschel and entered production in 1979. It consists of a UNIMOG cross-country truck chassis with an all-welded steel body for protection from small arms fire and shell splinters.

Engine compartment is front with commander and driver to its immediate rear and troop compartment extending right to rear of vehicle. Wide range of weapon stations can be mounted on top of hull to rear of commander's and driver's position, such as turret with twin 7.62mm MGs or one-man turret with 20mm cannon.

Basic vehicle is fully amphibious, propelled by its wheels or two waterjets which give maximum speed of 9km/hr. Before entering the water a trim vane is erected at the front and bilge pumps switched on. Wide range of optional equipment available including NBC system, night vision equipment, obstacle clearing blade, smoke grenade dischargers, winch, flashing lights, fire extinguishing system, heater, spherical firing ports and loudspeaker.

Variants

TM 170 can be adapted for a wide range of roles including communications and workshop vehicles. More recent version is TM 170 Hardliner with a number of detailed improvements.

Thyssen Henschel also built prototypes of TM 125 and TM 90 (4x4) armoured personnel carriers, but they did not enter production and are no longer being offered.

Status

In production. In service with German Border Guard, under designation SW4, and State Police and other undisclosed countries.

Manufacturer

Thyssen Maschinenbau, Witten-Annen, Germany.

246

Above: TM 170 (4x4) with 20mm turret

Top right: TM 170 (4x4) with cupola

Left: TM 170 Hardliner

Right: TM 170 (4x4) with obstacle clearing blade

Thyssen UR-416 APC (Germany)

Key recognition features

● Box-shaped hull with front sloping to rear, horizontal roof, sloping rear which sometimes has spare wheel, hull sides slope inwards from above wheel arches
● Radiator grilles on lower hull front with observation flaps at top which hinge upwards for normal use, firing ports in sides and rear of hull
● Armament normally mounted on forward part of roof, two road wheels each side with single door in each side and one rear

Specifications

Crew: 2+8
Configuration: 4x4
Armament: 1 x 7.62mm MG
Ammunition: 1,000 x 7.62mm
Length: 5.1m
Width: 2.25m
Height: 2.52m (with turret), 2.25m (hull top)
Ground clearance: 0.44m
Wheelbase: 2.9m
Weight, combat: 7,600kg
Weight, empty: 5,700kg
Power-to-weight ratio: 16.5hp/tonne
Engine: Daimler-Benz OM 352 6-cylinder water-cooled diesel developing 120hp at 2,800rpm
Maximum road speed: 81km/hr
Maximum road range: 600 to 700km
Fuel capacity: 150 lit
Fording: 1.3m
Vertical obstacle: 0.55m
Trench: Not applicable
Gradient: 70%
Side slope: 35%
Armour: 9mm
Armour type: Steel
NBC system: None
Night vision equipment: Optional

Development

UR-416 was developed by Rheinstahl Maschinenbau (now Thyssen Henschel) as a private venture, first prototype completed in 1965. Production commenced in 1969, since when over 1,000 have been built, mostly for export where it is normally used in internal security by police or other paramilitary units.

UR-416 is a Mercedes-Benz (4x4) UNIMOG cross-country truck chassis with an all-welded body that provides protection from small arms fire and shell splinters.

Commander and driver sit front with engine forward and below, leaving the whole of the rear clear for troops. Basic model has three doors, one each side and one in rear, and is fitted with various weapons on the roof ranging from simple pintle-mounted 7.62mm MG to turret armed with 20mm cannon.

Optional equipment includes spherical firing ports with vision devices, fire detection and extinguishing system, air-conditioning system, heater, run-flat tyres, smoke grenade dischargers and 5,000kg capacity winch.

Variants

UR-416 can be adopted for wide range of roles including ambulance, anti-tank (recoilless rifle or missile), internal security (with wide range of equipment including obstacle-clearing blade front), reconnaissance and workshop. Latest version is UR-416 M which has many detailed improvements including better visibility and armoured flaps.

Status

Production complete. Known users include Ecuador, El Salvador, Germany, Kenya, South Korea, Morocco, Netherlands, Nigeria, Peru, Philippines, Qatar, Saudi Arabia, Spain, Togo, Turkey, Venezuela and Zimbabwe.

Manufacturer

Thyssen Maschinenbau, Witten-Annen, Germany.

Top left: UR-416 (4x4) with 7.62mm MG

Above: UR-416 (4x4) without armament

Left: UR-416 (4x4) without armament

Thyssen Condor APC (Germany)

Key recognition features

● Box-type hull with driver's position far front left side, distinctive windows to front and sides, nose slopes back under hull and glacis slopes up to horizontal hull roof that extends right to rear, all four corners of hull angled
● Two large road wheels each side with forward-opening door in each side and another door in rear
● Hull sides slope inwards top and bottom with external wheel arches

Specifications

Crew: 2+12
Configuration: 4x4
Armament: 1 x 20mm, 1 x 7.62mm MG (coaxial), 2 x 3 smoke grenade dischargers
Ammunition: 220 x 20mm, 500 x 7.62mm
Length: 6.13m
Width: 2.47m
Height: 2.79m (turret top), 2.18m (hull top)
Ground clearance: 0.475m
Wheelbase: 3.275m
Weight, combat: 12,400kg
Weight, empty: 9,200kg
Power-to-weight ratio: 13.54hp/tonne
Engine: Daimler-Benz OM 352A 6-cylinder supercharged water-cooled diesel developing 168hp
Maximum road speed: 100km/hr
Maximum water speed: 10Km/hr
Maximum road range: 900km
Fuel capacity: 280 lit
Fording: Amphibious
Vertical obstacle: 0.55m
Trench: Not applicable
Gradient: 60%
Side slope: 30%
Armour: Classified
Armour type: Steel
NBC system: Optional
Night vision equipment: Optional

Development

Condor was developed by Thyssen Henschel as a private venture, first prototype completed in 1978. Wherever possible standard commercial components have been used in the design to keep procurement and life-cycle costs to a minimum. Largest order for Condor was placed by Malaysia in 1981 and consisted of 459 vehicles including ambulance, APC with twin 7.62mm MG, fitter's vehicle with crane, command post vehicle and APC with FVT900 one-man turret with 20mm cannon, 7.62mm MG coaxial with main armament and smoke grenade dischargers each side.

Driver sits front left, engine compartment to his right and troop compartment extending right to rear. Condor is fully amphibious, propelled by a propeller mounted under hull rear. Before entering the water a trim vane is erected at front of hull. Optional equipment includes heater and winch. The latter has 50m of cable and can be used to the front or rear of the vehicle.

Variants

Thyssen Henschel offers wide range of armament including Thyssen turret with twin 7.62mm MGs, pintle-mounted 7.62mm and 12.7mm MGs and ATGWs such as HOT, MILAN and TOW.

Status

Production complete. In service with Indonesia, Malaysia, Portugal, Turkey, Uruguay and other countries.

Manufacturer

Thyssen Henschel, Kassel, Germany.

Above: Condor (4x4) with 20mm turret

Above right: Condor (4x4) with 20mm turret

Below: Condor (4x4) ambulance

Right: Condor (4x4) with 20mm turret

FUG Amphibious Scout Car (Hungary)

Key recognition features

● Glacis plate slopes up to crew compartment which has sloping front and sides, roof hatches are only means of entry
● Engine compartment rear, roof almost parallel to crew compartment, exhaust pipe on right side
● Twin belly wheels each side which are raised when travelling on roads

Specifications

Crew: 2+4
Configuration: 4x4
Armament: 1 x 7.62mm MG
Ammunition: 1250 x 7.62mm
Length: 5.79m
Width: 2.5m
Height: 1.91m (hull top), 2.25m (OT-65A turret top)
Ground clearance: 0.34m
Wheelbase: 3.3m
Power-to-weight ratio: 15.87hp/tonne
Engine: Csepel D.414.44 4-cylinder in-line water-cooled diesel developing 100hp at 2,300rpm
Maximum road speed: 87km/hr
Maximum water speed: 9km/hr
Road range: 600km
Fuel capacity: 200 lit
Fording: Amphibious
Vertical obstacle: 0.4m
Trench: 1.2m
Gradient: 60%
Side slope: 30%
Armour: 13mm (maximum)
Armour type: Steel
Night vision equipment: Yes (driver only, infra-red)

Development

FUG (Felderito Uszo Gepkosci) entered service with the Hungarian Army in 1964 and fulfils a similar role to the Russian BRDM-1 (4x4) amphibious scout car. Major differences are that FUG has engine rear and is propelled by two water jets at rear (BRDM-1 has one). Before entering water bilge pumps are switched on and trim vane, stowed under nose when not required, is erected. A 7.62mm SGMG MG is pintle-mounted on forward part of roof.

When travelling across rough country, two powered belly wheels are lowered each side to improve mobility. All FUGs have central tyre pressure regulation system.

Variants

Ambulance, but probably limited to walking wounded only as sole means of entry and exit is via roof hatches.
Radiological-chemical reconnaissance vehicle; mounted on each side of hull rear is a rack that dispenses lane marking poles.
OT-65A is a Czechoslovak modification, a basic FUG fitted with OT-62B turret (full tracked APC armed with 7.62mm M59T machine gun). 82mm T-21 Tarasnice recoilless rifle on right side of turret.
PSZH-IV APC, there is a separate entry in the wheeled Armoured personnel carriers section for the PSZH-IV (4x4) vehicle which has been called the FG-66 and FUG-70 in the past.

Status

Production complete. In service with Czech Republic, Hungary (basic FUG is OT-65), Poland (limited use), and Slovakia.

Manufacturer

Hungarian state arsenals.

Top: FUG (4x4) without armament

Above: FUG (4x4) without armament

Above right: FUG (4x4) radiological-chemical reconnaissance vehicle with trim vane erected

Right: FUG (4x4)

PSZH-IV APC (Hungary)

Key recognition features

● Turret with no roof hatches over forward part of hull, 14.5mm MG right and 7.62 MG left

● Forward-opening door in each side of hull to rear of first road wheel station

● Trim vane for amphibious operations stowed on glacis plate

Specifications

Crew: 3+6
Configuration: 4x4
Armament: 1 x 14.5mm MG (main), 1 x 7.62mm MG (coaxial)
Ammunition: 500 x 14.5mm, 2,000 7.62mm
Length: 5.695m
Width: 2.5m
Height: 2.308m
Ground clearance: 0.42m
Wheelbase: 3.3m
Weight, combat: 7,600kg
Power-to-weight ratio: 13.15hp/tonne
Engine: Csepel D.414.44 4-cylinder in-line water-cooled diesel developing 100hp at 2,300rpm
Maximum road speed: 80km/hr
Maximum water speed: 9km/hr
Road range: 500km
Fuel capacity: 200 lit
Fording: Amphibious
Vertical obstacle: 0.4m
Trench: 0.6m (with channels)
Gradient: 60%
Side slope: 30%
Armour: 14mm (maximum)
Armour type: Steel
NBC system: Yes
Night vision equipment: Yes (infra-red for gunner and driver)

Development

PSZH-IV APC was developed in Czechoslovakia after the FUG (4x4) armoured amphibious scout car. PSZH-IV used to be called the FUG-66 or FUG-70 as it was originally thought to be a reconnaissance vehicle, not an APC.

Commander and driver sit front with one-man manually operated turret to rear. The 14.5mm KPVT and 7.62mm PKT MGs have manual elevation from -5° to +30°, turret traverse is manual through 360°. Commander and driver can leave via their roof hatches but the only means of entry and exit for troops and gunner is the small two-part door in each side of hull.

Unlike the former Soviet BRDM-2 (4x4) amphibious reconnaissance vehicle, PSZH-IV does not have belly wheels to improve cross-country mobility. It is, however, fully amphibious, propelled by two waterjets mounted to rear of hull. Standard equipment includes central tyre pressure regulation system and NBC system.

Variants

There are at least two command post versions of PSZH-IV, one with turret and one without turret. There is also an ambulance and radiological-chemical reconnaissance vehicle.

The latter is very similar to the former Soviet BRDM-2 vehicle designated the BRDM-2RKhb and is distinguishable by the two rectangular racks positioned one either side of the hull rear that dispense lane marking pennants into the ground.

Status

Production complete. In service with Bulgaria, Czech Republic (OT-66), Hungary, Iraq and Slovakia.

Manufacturer

Hungarian state arsenals.

Above: PSZH-IV

Above right: PSZH-IV

Right: PSZH-IV

RAM Family of Light AFVs (Israel)

Key recognition features

● spare tyre in horizontal position at front, open-topped crew compartment centre with four upward-opening hatches in forward part (two front, one each side), engine compartment rear. No side doors
● Two large wheels each side at extreme ends of vehicle, high ground clearance, extensive external stowage

Specifications (RAM-V-1 short)

Crew: 2+4
Configuration: 4x4
Armament: Depends on role
Ammunition: Depends on role
Length: 5.02m
Width: 2.03m
Height overall: 1.72m
Ground clearance (hull): 0.575m
Ground clearance (axles): 0.31m
Wheelbase: 3.4m
Weight, combat: 5,400kg
Weight, unloaded: 4,100kg
Power-to-weight ratio: 24.44hp/tonne
Engine: Deutz air-cooled 6-cylinder diesel developing 132bhp
Maximum road speed: 96km/hr
Maximum road range: 600km
Fuel capacity: 120 lit
Fording: 0.75m
Vertical obstacle: 0.8m
Trench: Not applicable
Gradient: 70%
Side slope: 35%
Armour: 8mm
Armour type: Steel
NBC system: None
Night vision equipment: Optional

Development

In the early 1970s RAMTA Structures and Systems, a subsidiary of Israel Aircraft Industries, designed and built as a private venture the RBY Mk1 light armoured reconnaissance vehicle

RAM V-1 with twin 7.62mm MG

which was subsequently built for home and export markets. It could be used for a wide range of roles and with various weapon systems including pintle-mounted 7.62mm MGs up to a 106mm recoilless rifle. In 1979 the RAM family of light AFVs was announced by the same company and this has now replaced the RBY in production. The RAM family has been expanded into two basic groups: RAM V-1 open top and RAM V-2 closed top. Both are produced in two wheelbases, 3.4m and 3.8m respectively, and designated V-1 short and V-1L, V-2 short and V-2L. Main improvements on the original RBY Mk1 are increased ground clearance owing to larger tyres, increased range of action (original petrol engine replaced by diesel), and automatic transmission.

Variants

Infantry fighting vehicle has three pintle-mounted 7.62mm MGs, one anti-tank rocket launcher.
Infantry combat vehicle as above but also carries 52mm mortar and night vision equipment.

TCM-20 AA fitted with one-man power-operated turret, armed with twin 20mm cannon, to provide more stable firing platform. Stabilisers lowered to ground before firing.
Close-range anti-tank has 106mm M40 recoilless rifle.
Long-range anti-tank has Hughes TOW ATGW launcher and two 7.62mm MGs.
RAM V-2 AFV has fully enclosed troop compartment for crew of eight or ten, and can be fitted with wide range of weapon stations including 7.62mm and 12.7mm MGs and 40mm grenade launcher.

Status

Production completed. Known users are Israel, Guatemala, Honduras and Lesotho. RAM series is in current production but only known user is Morocco.

Manufacturer

RAMTA Structures and Systems, Israel Aircraft Industries, Beer Sheba, Israel.

Above left: RAM V-2L with twin 7.62mm MG

Above: RAM TCM-20 AA (anti-aircraft)

FIAT OTOBREDA Type 6616 Armoured Car (Italy)

Key recognition features

● Nose slopes back under hull, well sloped glacis plate with driver's half-circular position on right side, turret centre
● Square turret with sides sloping slightly inwards, commander's cupola on left extends slightly over turret side, chamfer between turret front and sides
● Two large road wheels each side, horizontal louvres above both rear wheel stations, spare wheel often on hull rear, small hatch in lower part of hull side between wheels

Specifications
Crew: 3
Configuration: 4x4
Armament: 1 x 20mm, 1 x 7.62mm MG (coaxial), 2 x 3 smoke grenade dischargers
Ammunition: 400 x 20mm, 1,000 x 7.62mm
Length gun forwards: 5.37m
Length hull: 5.37m
Width: 2.5m
Height: 2.035m (turret roof)
Ground clearance: 0.44m (hull centre), 0.37m (axles)
Wheelbase: 2.75m
Weight, combat: 8,000kg
Power-to-weight ratio: 20.20hp/tonne
Engine: Model 8062.24 supercharged liquid-cooled in-line diesel developing 160hp at 3,200rpm
Maximum road speed: 100km/hr
Maximum water speed: 5km/hr
Maximum road range: 700km
Fuel capacity: 150 lit
Fording: Amphibious
Vertical obstacle: 0.45m
Trench: Not applicable
Gradient: 60%
Side slope: 30%
NBC system: Optional
Night vision equipment: Optional

Development
Type 6616 (4x4) is a joint development by FIAT and OTOBREDA and shares many components with Type 6614 (4x4) armoured personnel carrier. FIAT is responsible for the hull, automotive components and final assembly; OTOBREDA for the complete two-man turret.

First prototype was completed in 1972 and first order placed by the Italian Carabinieri. Production was completed after about 300 vehicles had been built for the home and export markets.

The turret has full power traverse through 360° and the 20mm Rheinmetall MK 20 Rh 202 cannon elevates from -5° to +35°. The 7.62mm MG is mounted coaxial above the 20mm cannon. Type 6616 is fully amphibious, propelled by its wheels. Optional equipment includes 4,500kg capacity winch, NBC system, air-conditioning system and fire extinguishing system. A 106mm M40 recoilless rifle can be mounted on turret roof.

Variants
For trials purposes, the FIAT-OTOBREDA Type 6616 armoured car has been fitted with a number of different weapon systems as listed below but so far none of these has entered production for the Type 6616:
OTOBREDA OTO T 90 CKL turret armed with 90mm gun.
OTOBREDA turret armed with OTOBREDA 60mm High Velocity Gun System.

Status
Production complete. In service with Italian Carabinieri, Peru, Somalia and other countries.

Manufacturer
IVECO-FIAT, Bolzano, Italy.

Above: Type 6616 (4x4)

Above right: Type 6616 (4x4)

Right: Type 6616 (4x4)

IVECO/OTOBREDA Puma APC (Italy)

Key recognition features

● Lower part of hull is vertical, well sloped glacis plate that leads up to horizontal roof, vertical hull rear with lower part sloping inwards. Upper sides of hull slope inwards. Headlamps are recessed into front of hull
● Driver's hatch front left of roof with commander's cupola in centre and small rectangular roof hatch at rear. Large door in hull rear
● Two large road wheels either side with large door in centre that opens forwards, all doors have firing port and associated vision block above

Specifications

Crew: 1+6
Configuration: 4x4
Armament: 1 x 7.62mm or 12.7mm MG, 2 x 3 smoke grenade dischargers
Length: 4.65m
Width: 2.085m
Height hull top: 1.67m
Ground clearance: 0.392m
Weight, combat: 5,500kg
Power-to-weight ratio: 32.72hp/tonne
Engine: FIAT Type 8042 TCA 4-cylinder diesel developing 180hp at 3,000rpm
Maximum road speed: 105km/hr
Range: 800km
Fuel capacity: 150 lit
Fording: Not available
Vertical obstacle: Not available
Trench: Not available
Gradient: 60%
Side slope: 30%
Armour: Classified
Armour type: Steel
NBC system: Yes
Night vision equipment: Yes (passive)

Development

IVECO/OTOBREDA has considerable experience in the design, development and production of wheeled armoured vehicles and the Puma family has been developed to meet the requirements of the Italian Army for a vehicle to operate with the IVECO/OTOBREDA B1 Centauro (8x8) tank destroyer/armoured car (qv).

The first prototype of the Puma was completed in 1988 and by 1990 a total of five vehicles had been built. The Italian Army subsequently awarded the company a contract to build six specialised versions of the Puma, one each for the MILAN and TOW ATGW system, one for the Mistral SAM system, one 81mm mortar carrier, one ambulance and one command post vehicle. In 1966 the Italian Army placed an order for 150 Puma in 4x4 configuration.

The engine is at the front of the vehicle with the driver being seated towards the front on the left side and the troop compartment at the rear. Doors are provided in the sides and rear and on the roof is the commander's cupola that can be fitted with a 12.7mm or 7.62mm machine gun.

Standard equipment includes an integrated air conditioning system, fire detection and suppression system, power-operated winch, powered steering and run-flat tyres.

Variants

The 4x4 version of the Puma can be adopted for a wide range of roles in addition to those ordered by the Italian Army, for example NBC reconnaissance and internal security. More recently a 6x6 version of the Puma has been developed, this has the same automotive components as the Puma 4x4 including engine, automatic transmission and suspension and has a combat weight of 7,500kg. This version can carry eight men plus the driver and can be fitted with a wider range of armament stations. Its fuel capacity has been increased to 270 litres.

Status

Entering production for Italian Army.

Manufacturer

IVECO/OTOBREDA, Bolzano, Italy.

Above: Puma (4x4) APC

Top right: Puma (4x4) APC with TOW

Right: Puma (6x6) APC

FIAT/OTOBREDA Type 6614 APC (Italy)

Key recognition features

● Two large road wheels each side with entry door between, large ramp at rear opens downwards

● Pointed hull front, driver's position front left, hull roof to rear in line with driver's roof

● Hull sides above wheel arches slope inwards, large rectangular louvres above first wheel station on each side

Specifications

Crew: 1+10
Configuration: 4x4
Armament: 1 x 12.7mm MG
Ammunition: 1,000 x 12.7mm
Length: 5.86m
Width: 2.5m
Height: 1.78m (hull top), 2.18m (MG mount)
Ground clearance: 0.37m (axles)
Wheelbase: 2.9m
Weight, combat: 8,500kg
Power-to-weight ratio: 18.82hp/tonne
Engine: Model 8062.24 supercharged liquid-cooled in-line diesel developing 160hp at 3,200rpm
Maximum road speed: 100km/hr
Maximum water speed: 4.5km/hr
Maximum road range: 700km
Fuel capacity: 142 lit
Fording: Amphibious
Vertical obstacle: 0.4m
Trench: Not applicable
Gradient: 60%
Side slope: 30%
Armour: 6 to 8mm
Armour type: Steel
NBC system: None
Night vision equipment: Optional

Development

Type 6614 is a joint development between FIAT and OTOBREDA, former responsible for hull and automotive components, latter for weapons installation. The vehicle shares many components with the FIAT/OTOBREDA Melara Type 6616 armoured car, for which there is a separate entry.

Driver sits front left, engine compartment to his right, whole remaining area to rear for 10 fully equipped troops, each with individual seats, and one manning the externally mounted 12.7mm HB MG. Gun is mounted on an M113 type cupola with no provision for aiming the weapon from inside the vehicle. Ten circular firing ports, each with vision block above, in troop compartment, four in each side of hull and one each side of rear ramp.

Type 6614 is fully amphibious, propelled by its wheels. Standard equipment includes ventilation system, electrically operated bilge pumps. Optional equipment includes front-mounted winch, night vision equipment, air-conditioning system, fire extinguishing system for wheel arches, smoke grenade dischargers and different armament installations such as turret with twin 7.62mm MG.

Variants

Type 6614 can be used for a wide range of roles such as internal security and reconnaissance. Projected variants included ambulance, cargo carrier, command post and mortar carrier.

Status

Production as required. In service with Argentina, Italy (Police and Air Force), South Korea (licensed production), Peru, Tunisia and Venezuela.

Manufacturers

FIAT/OTOBREDA, Bolzano, Italy; Asia Motors Company, Seoul, South Korea.

Above: Type 6614 with 12.7mm MG

Above right: Type 6614 without armament (Paul Handel)

Right: Type 6614 without armament (Paul Handel)

DAF Multipurpose carrier/LBV (Netherlands)

Key recognition features

● Nose slopes back under vehicles with front of vehicle angled back at 45 degrees, horizontal roof extends to rear, vertical hull rear. Upper hull sides slope inwards.

● Large driver's windscreen at front with another window either side sloping to rear. Roof hatches in forward part of roof with engine louvres in roof at rear.

● Two large road wheels either side with large forward opening door in either side

Specifications

Crew: 3-5
Configuration: 4 x 4
Armament: 1 x 7.62mm MG
Ammunition: 1000 x 7.62mm
Length: 5.3 m
Width: 2.5m
Height: 1.7m
Weight, combat: 9600kg
Weight, empty: 6900kg
Power-to-weight ratio: 25hp/t
Engine: 6-cylinder turbocharged intercooled diesel developing 240hp
Maximum road speed: 115km/hr
Maximum range: n/a
Fuel capacity: m/a
Fording: n/a
Vertical obstacle: n/a
Trench: n/a
Gradient: 60%
Side slope: 40%
Armour: classified
Armour type: aluminium
NBC system: optional
Night vision equipment: optional

Development

The Multipurpose carrier (MPC) has been developed as a private venture by Daf Special Products with the first prototype being completed in 1992. It is designed to undertake a wide range of military and paramilitary roles, with the former including command and control and battlefield surveillance.

The driver is seated at the front with bulletproof windows to his front and rear, providing the same level of protection as the hull. The other crew members, typically the commander and radio operator are seated in the centre. The powerpack is at the rear. A variety of weapons can be mounted on the roof, including machine guns, grenade launchers and ATGWs. Optional equipment includes an NBC system and an amphibious kit. A long wheelbase version is being studied.

Variants

The LBV, another version of the MPC is being developed as a new reconnaissance vehicle for the Royal Netherlands army and the German army. Four prototypes are being built, two for each army. It is expected that the Dutch will take 164 vehicles and the Germans will order 224. Daf Special Products will build the vehicles, with Wegmann installing the reconnaissance equipment including an elevated mast with day/thermal cameras and a laser rangefinder.

Status

Prototypes. Not yet in production or service.

Manufacturer

Daf Special Products BV, Geldrop, Netherlands

Above: DAF MPC

Above right: DAF MPC

Right: DAF MPC

BRAVIA Chaimite APC (Portugal)

Key recognition features

● Similar in appearance to Cadillac Gage (4x4) range with four large road wheels, single two-part hatch in each side of hull between wheels, nose angled inwards, glacis well sloped then almost vertical to horizontal hull top that extends to rear

● Hull rear angled inwards at an angle of about 45o, engine in left hull rear with additional entry hatch to right

● Top half of hull above wheel hatches slopes slightly inwards, rectangular vision blocks with firing ports beneath

Specifications

Crew: 11
Configuration: 4x4
Armament: See text
Ammunition: See text
Length: 5.606m
Width: 2.26m
Height: 2.26m (turret top), 1.84m (hull top)
Ground clearance: 0.61m (hull)
Wheelbase: 2.667m
Weight, combat: 7,300kg
Power-to-weight ratio: 32hp/tonne
Engine: Model M75 V-8 water-cooled petrol developing 210hp at 4,000rpm (or V-6 diesel)
Maximum road speed: 99km/hr
Maximum water speed: 7km/hr
Maximum road range: 804 to 965km
Fuel capacity: 300 lit
Fording: Amphibious
Vertical obstacle: 0.9m
Trench: Not applicable
Gradient: 65%
Side slope: 40%
Armour: 7.94mm (maximum)
Armour type: Steel
NBC system: None
Night vision equipment: Optional

Development

Chaimite range of 4x4s was designed by BRAVIA to meet requirements of the Portuguese armed forces, first prototype completed in 1966 and production commencing soon afterwards. In appearance Chaimite is very similar to the Cadillac Gage (now Textron Marine & Land Systems) LAV-150 and AV Technology Corporation Dragoon families of 4x4 vehicles. Both of these have their own entry in this section.

Crew number depends on mission but typically could be 11: commander, driver, gunner and eight fully equipped infantry. Chaimite is fully amphibious, propelled by its wheels. Standard equipment includes a front-mounted winch with capacity of 4,530kg, optional equipment includes infra-red night vision equipment.

Variants

V-200 is basic vehicle normally fitted with a one-man MG turret, twin 7.62mm MG with 500 rounds of ready-use ammunition (250 per gun), 9,000 carried in reserve in hull, or turret with one 12.7mm and one 7.62mm MG.

V-300 can be fitted with variety of 20mm turrets.

V-400 can be fitted with 90mm turrets.

V-500, command and communications vehicle.

V-600, 81mm or 120mm mortar carrier.

V-700, ATGW vehicle.

V-800, unarmed ambulance.

V-900, crash rescue vehicle.

V-1000, riot control/internal security vehicle.

A 6x6 version, **BRAVIA Mk II**, was projected but as far as is known this never entered production or service.

BRAVIA has also stated that there is an 8x8 **BRAVIA Mk III** APC but this has never entered production or service. BRAVIA has also designed and built the Tigre Mk II (6x6) APC which is essentially a truck with an armoured body.

Status

Production as required. Known to be in service with Lebanon (status uncertain), Libya (status uncertain), Peru, Philippines and Portugal.

Manufacturer

BRAVIA SARL, Lisbon, Portugal.

Top: Chaimite V-200 with twin 7.62mm MG turret

Right: Chaimite V-400 with 90mm MECAR gun

Above right: Chaimite V-200 with 12.7mm and 7.62mm MG turret

BRAVIA Commando Mk III APC (Portugal)

Key recognition features

● Similar in appearance to British Shorland armoured patrol vehicle with engine compartment front, crew compartment centre, forward-opening door in each side

● MG turret on roof which then drops down at 45o to hull rear which is in line with bonnet

● Two wheels each side, spare tyre and wheel carried almost horizontally on hull rear

Specifications

Crew: 3+5
Configuration: 4x4
Armament: 1 x 12.7mm MG, 1 x 7.62mm MG (coaxial)
Length: 4.975m
Width: 1.93m
Height: 2.42m (turret top), 2.05m (hull top)
Ground clearance: 0.21m
Wheelbase: 3.03m
Weight, combat: 4,855kg
Weight, unladen: 4,330kg
Power-to-weight ratio: 16.68hp/tonne
Engine: Perkins 4-cylinder in-line diesel developing 81hp at 2,800rpm or Dodge H225 6-cylinder in-line petrol developing 150hp at 4,000rpm
Maximum road speed: 90km/hr (diesel engine), 110km/hr (petrol)
Maximum road range: 800km (diesel engine), 600km (petrol engine)
Fuel capacity: 160 lit
Fording: 0.6m (estimate)
Gradient: 70%
Side slope: 35%
Armour: 7.94mm (maximum)
Armour type: Steel

Development

Commando Mk III was originally developed by BRAVIA SARL from 1977 to meet requirements of the Portuguese National Guard, first prototype completed late in 1977 and first production vehicles in 1978. It is a short wheelbase version of the BRAVIA Gazela (4x4) 1 tonne truck chassis with a fully armoured body.

Basic vehicle normally carries eight men, three-man crew (commander, gunner and driver) and five troops. The BRAVIA-designed manually operated turret is mounted centre and armed with one 7.62mm and one 12.7mm MG, elevation from -15o to +60o and 360o traverse. Can also be fitted with device for launching five 60mm anti-personnel, anti-tank, smoke, illuminating or incendiary grenades.

Variants

It is also available in a 4x2 configuration and with an extended troop compartment with an additional door in each side of the hull. It can also be supplied without the turret.

Status

Production as required. In service with Portuguese National Guard and at least two other countries.

Manufacturer

BRAVIA SARL, Lisbon, Portugal.

Above: Commando Mk III

TABC-79 APC (Romania)

Key recognition features

● Box type hull with nose sloping back under hull front, trim vane folds back onto glacis plate, two windows in hull front with shutters above, horizontal hull top, vertical hull rear
● Upper part of hull slopes slightly inwards as does lower half, two large wheels either side with door in lower half of hull
● Turret mounted towards front of vehicle has flat top and well sloped sides

Specifications

Crew: 3+4
Configuration: 4x4
Armament: 1 x 14.5mm MG, 1 x 7.62mm MG
Ammunition: 600 x 14.5mm, 2,500 x 7.62mm
Length: 5.64m
Width: 2.805m
Height: 2.335m (with turret)
Ground clearance: 0.485m
Wheelbase: 2.9m
Weight, combat: 9275kg
Weight, empty: 8575kg
Power-to-weight ratio: 16.66hp/tonne
Engine: Turbocharged diesel developing 154hp
Maximum road speed: 85km/hr
Maximum road range: 600km (estimate)
Fuel capacity: Not available
Fording: Amphibious
Vertical obstacle: 0.3m
Trench: 0.70m
Gradient: 60%
Side slope: 30%
Armour: 8mm (maximum)(estimate)
Armour type: steel
NBC system: Yes
Night vision equipment: Yes

Development

The TABC-79 (4x4) APC was developed specifically to meet the requirements of the Romanian Army and uses some automotive components of the TAB-77 (8x8) APC.

The driver is seated at the front of the vehicle on the left with the vehicle commander to his right. Mounted on the roof to the rear of the commander's and driver's position is the one-man manually operated turret which is the same as that fitted to the TAB-71M (8x8), TAB-77 (8x8) and the Mountaineers Combat Vehicle. This is armed with one 14.5mm and one 7.62mm machine gun with total ammunition capacity being 500 rounds of 14.5mm and 2,000 rounds of 7.62mm.

The engine compartment is at the rear of the vehicle on the left side and in addition to the entry doors in either side there is also a door in the hull rear on the right side as well as a single roof hatch.

Standard equipment includes infra-red night vision equipment and an NBC system. The TABC-79 (4x4) APC is fully amphibious being propelled in the water by a single waterjet mounted at the rear of the hull. Before entering the water the bilge pumps are switched on and the trim vane erected at the front of the hull. When not required this lays back on the glacis plate.

Variants

TAB-79A PCOMA, TABC-79 armoured artillery observation post vehicle, armed with 7.62mm machine gun.
TAB-79R, TABC-79 self-propelled 82mm mortar system which can also be deployed away from the vehicle if required.
TABRCH-84, armoured chemical and radiological reconnaissance vehicle, no turret, fitted with racks of pennants to mark contaminated areas. Armed with 7.62mm pintle-mounted machine gun.
TCG-80, this is an unidentified variant, may be a recovery vehicle.

The chassis is used as basis for Romanian equivalent of the Russian SA-9 SAM, the A95.

Status
Production complete. In service with Romania.

Manufacturer
Romanian state factories.

Right: TABC-79 (4x4) APC

BRDM-1 Amphibious Scout Car (Russia)

Key recognition features

● Pointed nose containing engine slopes upwards towards crew compartment that extends almost to rear of vehicle. Only mens of entry and exit via roof hatches
● Hull sides and rear vertical, but front, sides and rear of crew compartment slope inwards with two armoured covers on front and two firing ports in sides
● On each side of hull between roadwheels are two belly wheels that are raised when travelling on roads. Trim vane under nose when not in use

Specifications

Crew: 5
Configuration: 4x4
Armament: 1 x 7.62mm MG
Ammunition: 1,250 x 7.62mm
Length: 5.7m
Width: 2.25m
Height: 1.9m (without MG)
Ground clearance: 0.315m
Wheelbase: 2.8m
Weight, combat: 5,600kg
Power-to-weight ratio: 16.7hp/tonne
Engine: GAZ-4oP 6-cylinder water-cooled in-line petrol developing 90hp at 3,400rpm
Maximum road speed: 80km/hr
Maximum water speed: 9km/hr
Road range: 500km
Fuel capacity: 150 lit
Fording: Amphibious
Vertical obstacle: 0.4m
Trench: 1.22m
Gradient: 60%
Side slope: 30%
Armour: 10mm (maximum)
Armour type: Steel
NBC system: None
Night vision equipment: Yes (infra-red for driver only)

Development

BRDM-1 (4x4) was developed in the mid-1950s and entered service with the Russian Army in 1957, but it has been replaced in all front-line Russian units by the later BRDM-2 (4x4) amphibious reconnaissance vehicle.

BRDM-1 is fully amphibious, propelled by a single waterjet mounted at hull rear. Before entering a trim vane is erected at hull front and bilge pumps switched on. On each side of hull, between road wheels, is a set of powered belly wheels that are lowered to the ground to improve cross-country mobility. Tyre pressure regulation system is fitted as standard.

Typical armament comprises 12.7mm DShKM MG at front and 7.62mm SGMB MG at rear of crew compartment.

Variants

BRDM-1 Model 1957 had open roof, but only a few were built.
BRDM-1 Model 1958 is the most common, with enclosed roof and hatches.
BRDM-U is command model with four radio antennas compared with one in standard vehicle.
BRDM-RKhh radiological-chemical reconnaissance vehicle has two rectangular packs at rear for dispensing poles with pennants.
BRDM-1 with three Snapper ATGWs which are raised from inside for launching; rarely seen today.
BRDM-1 with four Swatter ATGWs which are raised from inside for launching; rarely seen today.
BRDM-1 with six Sagger ATGWs which are raised from inside, complete with overhead armour protection; rarely seen today.

Status

Production complete. In service with Albania, Bulgaria, RUSSIA, Congo, Cuba, Guinea, Mozambique, Sudan and Zambia. In most of these countries the vehicle is now found in reserve units.

Manufacturer

Molotov GAZ plant, Gorkiy, former USSR.

Right: BRDM-1 (4x4)

Below: BRDM-1 (4x4) amphibious scout car with 7.62mm MGs installed

BRDM-2 Amphibious Scout Car (Russia)

Key recognition features

● Lower part of hull has vertical sides and rear, upper part slopes inwards, engine compartment roof slopes down to rear

● Belly wheels raised when travelling on roads, trim vane under nose when not required

● Turret on centre of hull roof with flat top. Only means of entry and exit via two circular hatches forward of turret

Specifications

Crew: 4
Configuration: 4x4
Armament: 1 x 14.5mm MG (main), 1 x 7.62mm MG (coaxial)
Ammunition: 500 x 14.5mm, 2,000 7.62mm
Length: 5.75m
Width: 2.35m
Height: 2.31m
Ground clearance: 0.43m
Wheelbase: 3.1m
Weight, combat: 7,000kg
Power-to-weight ratio: 20hp/tonne
Engine: GAZ-41 V-8 water-cooled petrol developing 140hp at 3,400rpm
Maximum road speed: 100km/hr
Maximum water speed: 10km/hr
Road range: 750km
Fuel capacity: 290 lit
Fording: Amphibious
Vertical obstacle: 0.4m
Trench: 1.25m
Gradient: 60%
Side slope: 30%
Armour: 3-7mm
Armour type: Steel
NBC system: Yes
Night vision equipment: Yes (driver and commander, infra-red)

BDRM-2 (4x4)

Development

BRDM-2 was developed as the replacement for the BRDM-1 (4x4) and was first seen in public during 1966. Main improvements are better road and cross-country performance, heavier armament in fully enclosed turret, more powerful rear-mounted engine, improved amphibious capabilities, NBC system and night vision equipment.

Commander and driver sit side-by-side at front with roof hatch behind. Turret is the same as on the OT-64 Model 2A (8x8), BTR-70 and BTR-60PB (8x8) armoured personnel carriers and has no roof hatch. The 14.5mm KPVT MG is mounted on left with 7.62mm PKT MG right; both have manual elevation from -5° to +30° and manual traverse through 360°.

Standard equipment on all BRDM-2s includes central tyre pressure system, decontamination kit, winch and land navigation system. Two powered belly wheels can be lowered to the ground each side to improve cross-country mobility.

Variants

BRDM-2-RKhb radiological-chemical reconnaissance vehicle has two rectangular racks, one each side at rear, which dispense lane marking poles with pennants.

BRDM-1U command vehicle retains turret of BRDM-2 but has additional communications equipment.
BRDM-2U command vehicle normally has turret replaced by small roof-mounted generator and two roof-mounted antennas.
SA-9 Gaskin SAM system is based on BRDM-2 chassis (see SPAAMs).
BRDM-2 with Sagger ATGWs (see TDs).
BRDM-2 with Spandrel ATGWs (see TDs).
BRDM-2 with Swatter ATGWs (see TDs).

Status
Production complete. In service with Afghanistan, Algeria, Angola, Benin, Bulgaria, Cape Verde Islands, RUSSIA, Congo, Croatia, Cuba, Czech Republic, Egypt, Equatorial Guinea, Estonia, Ethiopia, Guinea, Guinea-Bissau, Hungary, India, Iraq, Latvia, Libya, Madagascar, Malawi, Mali, Mauritania, Mongolia, Mozambique, Namibia, Nicaragua, Peru, Poland, Romania, Seychelles, Slovakia, Somalia, Sudan, Syria, Tanzania, Vietnam, Yemen, former Yugoslavia and Zambia

Manufacturer
Molotov GAZ Plant, Gorkiy, former USSR.

Above: BRDM-2 with commander's and driver's hatches open

Key recognition features

● Hull identical to BRDM-2 (4x4) amphibious scout car except turret replaced by retractable launcher for six Sagger ATGWs

● When in action six-round Sagger launcher complete with overhead armour protection is raised above hull roof

● Gunner's sight protrudes from hull roof to right of driver

Specifications (BRDM-2 Sagger)

Crew: 2-3
Configuration: 4x4
Armament: Launcher with 6 Sagger ATGW
Ammunition: 14 x Sagger ATGW (total)
Length: 5.75m
Width: 2.35m
Height: 2.01m (launcher retracted)
Ground clearance: 0.43m
Wheelbase: 3.1m
Weight, combat: 7,000kg
Power-to-weight ratio: 20hp/tonne
Engine: GAZ-41 V-8 water-cooled petrol developing 140hp at 3,400rpm
Maximum road speed: 100km/hr
Maximum water speed: 10km/hr
Maximum road range: 750km
Fuel capacity: 290 lit
Fording: Amphibious
Vertical obstacle: 0.4m
Trench: 1.25m
Gradient: 60%
Side slope: 30%
Armour: 14mm (maximum)
Armour type: Steel
NBC system: Yes
Night vision equipment: Infra-red (driver)

Development

BRDM-2 Sagger was developed in the late 1960s to replace versions of the earlier BRDM-1 with Snapper, Swatter of Sagger ATGWs. First used operationally by Egypt and Syrian Army in 1973 Middle East conflict. Automotively, BRDM-2 (Sagger) is identical to standard BRDM-2 amphibious scout vehicle. Fully amphibious, propelled by single waterjet mounted in hull rear, central tyre pressure regulation system, and between road wheels each side are two powered belly wheels lowered to ground when vehicle is crossing rough ground.

When in firing position the six-round Sagger launcher, complete with overhead armour protection, is raised above roof of vehicle and missiles can be launched from inside vehicle or up to 80 m away with the aid of a separation sight and cable. Further eight missiles carried internally for manual reloading. Sagger has maximum range of 3,000rpm. In 1977 Sagger was being converted from its normal wire command guidance system to a semi-automatic infra-red system.

Variants

BRDM-2 with Spandrel ATGWs, first seen in 1977, has five AT-5 Spandrel ATGWs in ready-to-launch position on roof, a further 10 being carried internally. AT-5 Spandrel has range of 4,000 m; gunner keeps cross-hair of sight on target to ensure a hit. Some BRDM-2s (Spandrel) have been seen with two AT-4 Spigot (right) and three AT-5 Spandrel (left) ATGW in the ready-to-launch position.

BRDM-2 with Swatter-C ATGW, first seen in 1973, has quadruple launcher for AT-2 Swatter converted from original radio-to-line-of-sight to semi-active infra-red command guidance.

Status

Production complete. Known users of BRDM-2 Sagger include Algeria, Czech Republic, Egypt, Hungary, Iraq, Libya, Morocco, Nicaragua, Poland, Romania, Russia, Slovakia, Syria and former Yugoslavia.

Manufacturer
Molotov GAZ plant, Gorkiy, former
USSR.

Right: BRDM-2 (Spandrel)

Below: BRDM-2 (Spandrel)

*BRDM-2 Sagger with
launcher raised*

BTR-40 APC (Russia)

Key recognition features

● Engine front with open-topped troop compartment rear, firing ports each side and entry door at rear which normally has spare wheel and tyre
● Armoured air intake grille under nose, engine compartment roof sloping up towards commander's and driver's flap that can be locked in horizontal open position

Specifications

Crew: 2+8
Configuration: 4x4
Armament: 1 x 7.62mm MG
Ammunition: 1,250 x 7.62mm
Length: 5m
Width: 1.9m
Height: 1.75m (without armament)
Ground clearance: 0.275m
Wheelbase: 2.7m
Weight, combat: 5,300kg
Power-to-weight ratio: 15hp/tonne
Engine: GAZ-40 6-cylinder water-cooled in-line petrol developing 80hp at 3,400rpm
Maximum road speed: 80km/hr
Range: 285km
Fuel capacity: 120 lit
Fording: 0.8m
Vertical obstacle: 0.47m
Trench: 0.7m (with channels)
Gradient: 60%
Side slope: 30%
Armour: 8mm (maximum)
Armour type: Steel
NBC system: None
Night vision equipment: Yes (driver only, infra-red)

Development

BTR-40 was developed from 1944, essentially a lengthened and modified GAZ-63 (4x4) truck chassis with fully armoured body. Entered service with the former Soviet Army in 1950 and used both as APC and command and reconnaissance vehicle; in the latter role it was replaced in the late 1950s by BRDM-1 (4x4) which had better cross-country mobility and was fully amphibious. Three pintle mounts for MGs round hull top.

In the former Soviet Army the BTR-40 was often referred to as the Sorokovke. As far as it is known, none remain in front line service with the former Soviet Army.

Variants

Original version did not have firing ports. Models built from the 1950s were designated BTR-40V and have central tyre pressure regulation system. Some BTR-40s have 4,500kg winch mounted at front of vehicle.

BTR-40A anti-aircraft vehicle has same turret as BTR-152A armed with twin 14.5mm MGs; no longer in front line Soviet service.

BTR-40B APC has overhead armour protection for troop compartment, carries six troops plus two-man crew.

BTR-40Kh is chemical reconnaissance vehicle with equipment at rear to dispense marking pennants.

BTR-40 zhd has steel wheels for running on railway lines.

Status

Production complete. In service with Afghanistan, Albania, Bulgaria, Burundi, Chi9na, RUSSIA, Cuba, Ethiopia, Equatorial Guinea, Guinea, Guinea-Bissau, Indonesia, Iran, Kampuchea, North Korea, Laos, Mozambique, Nicaragua, Somalia, Syria, Tanzania, Uganda, Vietnam, Yemen, former Yugoslavia and Zaire. In many of these countries the vehicle is in second line use, often with militia units.

Manufacturer

Russian state arsenals.

Above: BTR-40

Reumech OMC Mamba Mk II APC (South Africa)

Key recognition features

● Vertical hull front with grill in centre, long horizontal bonnet which slopes slightly upwards, then almost vertical bullet proof windscreen, horizontal roof with eight hatches
● Hull sides vertical with large bullet proof windows in sides and rear, large door in rear. Side and rear windows have firing ports
● Two large road wheels either side with spare wheel carried on left side of hull

Specifications

Crew: 2 + 9
Configuration: 4 x 4
Armament: 1 x 12.7 mm MG (optional)
Length: 5.46 m
Width: 2.205 m
Height: 2.495 m
Ground clearance: 0.39 m
Wheelbase: 2.90 m
Weight, combat: 6800 kg
Weight, empty: 5710 kg
Power-to-weight ratio: 18.08 hp/t
Engine: Daimler-Benz OM 352 6-cylinder water-cooled diesel developing 123 hp at 2800 rpm
Maximum road speed: 102 km/h
Maximum road range: 900 km
Fuel capacity: 200 l
Fording: 1 m
Vertical obstacle: 0.4 m
Trench: 0.9 m
Gradient: 60%
Side slope: 40%
Armour: classified
Armour type: steel
NBC: no
Night vision equipment: no

Development

The first Mamba was a 4 x 2 vehicle and was produced in significant numbers for a variety of missions. Further development by Reumech OMC resulted in the Mamba Mk II which has a number of improvements including 4 x 4 drive and a higher ground clearance. The hull of the Mamba Mk II is V-shaped to provide a high level of protection against anti-tank mines. Wherever possible stsndard UNIMOG components are used in the design of the vehicle.

The engine compartment is at the front with the commander and driver in the centre and the troop compartment extending right to the rear. Only means of entry is via the large door in the rear of the hull and the roof hatches. Bullet proof windows are fitted all round and these provide the same level of protection as the armoured hull.

The basic model is unarmed although various weapon systems can be fitted. Alvis has a licence to produce a similar version which they call the Alvis 8 with short wheelbase version being Alvis 4.

Variants

Projected roles include ambulance, command post vehicle, utility vehicle, recovery, VIP transport and logistics support. Can be fitted with various weapons including machine guns.

Status

In production. In service with South African National Defence Force.

Manufacturer

Reumech OMC, Benoni, South Africa.

Top left: Mamba II (4 x 4) APC
Left: Mamba II (4 x 4) APC (Christopher F Foss)
Above: Mamba II (4 x 4) APC (Christopher F Foss)

TFM Casspir Mk III APC (South Africa)

Key recognition features

- Lower part of hull is V-shaped with upper part of hull sides and rear vertical, single wheel at each end of the vehicle outside of the armour envelope
- Bonnet type engine compartment at the front with horizontal engine louvres with chamfer between sides and top, large bullet-proof windows at front and along sides of hull. The bullet-proof windows along sides towards rear have firing ports below
- Horizontal hull top with forward part armoured and often mounting a 7.62mm machine gun, early models had open roof but late production models had fully enclosed rear troop compartment, twin doors in rear

Specifications

Crew: 1 + 12
Configuration: 4x4
Armament: 1 to 3 7.62mm MGs
Length: 6.87m
Width: 2.5m
Height: 2.85m
Ground clearance: 0.41m (axles)
Weight, combat: 12,580kg
Weight, empty: 11,040kg
Power-to-weight ratio: 13.51hp/tonne
Engine: ADE-352T, 6-cylinder diesel developing 170hp at 2,800rpm
Maximum road speed: 90km/hr
Maximum road range: 850km
Fuel capacity: 220 lit
Fording: 1.0m
Vertical obstacle: 0.5m
Trench: 1.06m
Gradient: 65%
Side slope: 40%
Armour: Classified
Armour type: Steel
NBC system: None
Night vision equipment: None

Development

The original Casspir family of vehicles was developed in the late 1970s but from 1981 production was undertaken by TFM which has since developed the Casspir Mk II and Mk III vehicles of which well over 2,000 have been built. Although designed mainly for internal security operations, it has been used for offensive operations in Southern Africa. A unique feature of the Casspir is that it has been designed to give its crew a high degree of protection against anti-tank mines and for this reason the vehicle has a very high ground clearance with the hull having a V-shape to help deflect the blast from any mines. The large cross-country wheels are outside of the main armour envelope.

There have been three main models of the Casspir, the Mk I, Mk II and Mk III, all of which have incorporated improvements as a result of operational experience. Wherever possible standard commercial components are used in the construction of the Casspir family of vehicles.

The engine compartment is at the front, commander and driver to the immediate rear with the troop compartment extending right to the rear. The troops are seated six either side facing each other. There are minor differences between production runs and there are a number of local modifications.

Standard equipment includes long range fuel tank, drinking water tank, two spare wheels and tyres and fire extinguishers.

Optional equipment includes floodlights, searchlights and obstacle clearing equipment. As well as the 7.62mm MGs, a rubber bullet launcher can be fitted.

Variants

Blesbok, this is a cargo carrier and retains the fully armoured cab.
Duiker, this is a 5,000 litre fuel tanker and retains the fully armoured cab.
Gemsbok, recovery vehicle with recovery equipment at very rear of hull and fitted with extended armoured cab.
Ambulance, similar to Casspir Mk III APC but modified for ambulance role.

Police, increased visibility.
Artillery fire control.
Mine clearing, two versions.
Mine sensor vehicle.

Status

Production as required. In service with Peru, South Africa and other undisclosed countries.

Manufacturer

TFM (Pty) Limited, Olifantsfontein 1663, South Africa.

Above:
Casspir Mk
III APC
(Christopher
F Foss)

Top right:
Casspir Mk
III APC
(Christopher
F Foss)

Right:
Casspir Mk
III APC
(Christopher
F Foss)

TFM RG-12 Patrol APC (South Africa)

Key recognition features

● Box type hull with sloping windscreen at front, vertical hull sides and rear, horizontal radiator grille in centre of hull front

● Large square windows in front, sides and rear of vehicle that are usually covered by wire mesh screens, two doors in each side of vehicle, one over first road wheel and one between road wheels

● Total of four road wheels which are at extreme ends of vehicle, horizontal roof raised for air conditioning system

Specifications

Crew: 2+6
Configuration: 4x4
Length: 5.2m
Width: 2.45m
Height: 2.64m
Ground clearance: 0.322m
Weight, combat: 9,200kg
Weight, empty: 7,420kg
Power-to-weight ratio: 18.4hp/tonne
Engine: ADE 366 diesel developing 170hp
Maximum road speed: 100km/hr
Range: 1000km
Fuel capacity: 260 lit
Fording: Not available
Vertical obstacle: Not available
Trench: Not available
Gradient: 50%
Side slope: 40%
Armour: Classified
Armour type: Steel
NBC system: None
Night vision equipment: None

RG-12 APC

Development

The RG-12 patrol armoured personnel carrier was developed as a private venture by the TFM company which also manufactures the Casspir (4x4) range of armoured personnel carriers (qv). The first prototypes were completed early in 1990 with first production vehicles being completed later the same year.

The RG-12 is designed mainly for internal security operations and wherever possible standard commercial components are used in the construction of the vehicle. Both 4x4 and 4x2 versions of the RG-12 are manufactured.

The complete powerpack is mounted at the front of the vehicle with the commander being seated on the left and the driver on the right, each being provided with a forward opening door. The three troops are seated either side facing outwards and enter and leave the vehicle via door in the side that can be rapidly opened. In addition there is a door in the rear that gives access to the spare wheel and storage. A tropical roof is fitted and a roof hatch is provided above the commander's seat.

Standard equipment includes an air conditioning system, powered steering, protection against 7.62mm ball attack, floodlights, flashing beacons, hand held spotlight, siren, public address system, fire extinguishers and drinking water tank. All windows are covered by wire mesh screens and a barricade removal device is provided at the front of the hull.

Variants

There are no variants of the RG-12. Reumech OMC, another private South African company, has manufactured a similar vehicle called the RCV 9. This carries 9 men, including the driver and has a combat weight of 6,900kg. This has been built in production quantities and sold to Colombia as well as within South Africa. It is no longer being marketed.

Status

Production. In service in South Africa.

Manufacturer

TFM (Pty) Limited, Olifantsfontein 1663, South Africa.

RG-12 APC

SANTA BARBARA BLR APC (Spain)

Key recognition features

● Box-type hull with sloping nose, flat roof, vertical hull rear, vertical hull sides with top sloping slightly inwards
● Two large road wheels each side with forward-opening door between, two doors rear, one each side of central engine compartment which has louvres in roof and hull rear
● Depending on model, has various types of observation/firing device in hull sides, normally has cupola or turret on forward part of hull top to rear of commander's and driver's position

Specifications

Crew: 1+12
Configuration: 4x4
Armament: 1 x 7.62mm MG
Ammunition: 1,000 x 7.62mm
Length: 5.65m
Width: 2.5m
Height: 2m (hull top)
Ground clearance: 0.32m
Wheelbase: 3.15m
Weight, combat: 12,000kg
Weight, unloaded: 9,600kg
Power-to-weight ratio: 17.5hp/tonne
Engine: Pegaso 6-cylinder turbo-charged in-line diesel developing 210hp at 2,100rpm
Maximum road speed: 93km/hr
Maximum range: 570km
Fuel capacity: 200 lit
Fording: 1.1m
Vertical obstacle: Not available
Trench: Not applicable
Gradient: 60%
Side slope: 30%
Armour: 8mm (maximum)(estimate)
Armour type: Steel
NBC system: None
Night vision equipment: None

Development

BLR (Blindado Ligero de Ruedas), also known previously as Pegaso BLR 3545, has been designed mainly for use in internal security. Its hull gives the crew complete protection from small

BLR without armament

arms fire and shell splinters, commander and driver sit front and whole of rear is occupied by troop compartment with exception of engine compartment which is centre of hull at rear. To reduce procurement and life cycle costs, standard commercial components are used in the vehicle wherever possible.

Armament depends on role, but typically is one-man cupola with externally mounted 7.62mm MG. Standard equipment includes ventilation system, choice of manual or automatic transmission, fire suppression system for both engine compartment and wheels, bullet-proof tyres and 4,500kg capacity winch.

Wide range of optional equipment includes smoke/CS gas dischargers, PTO, specialised riot control equipment and various communications systems.

Variants

Manufacturer has suggested alternative weapon systems including 12.7mm MG, 20mm or 25mm cannon and turret-mounted 90mm gun. More specialised versions could include ambulance and command.

Status

Production as required. In service with Ecuador, Spanish Marines and Guardia Civil.

Manufacturer

SANTA BARBARA, Madrid, Spain.

Right: BLR with 7.62mm MG

MOWAG Eagle Armoured Recon Vehicle (Switzerland)

Key recognition features

● Vertical hull front with radiator grille in centre, horizontal bonnet leading up to windscreen with two large windows that slopes slightly to the rear. Horizontal roof with turret in centre, hull slops sharply down with lower part vertical

● Lower part of hull sides vertical with upper part sloping slightly inwards. Two doors in each side with windows in upper part

● Two large road wheels either side

Specifications

Crew:4
Configuration:4 x 4
Armament:1 x 7.62 mm MG, 1 x 6 smoke grenade launchers
Ammunition:1000 x 7.62 mm
Length:4.90 m
Width:2.28 m
Height: 1.75 m (hull top)
Ground clearance:0.4 m
Wheelbase:3.30 m
Weight, combat:4800 kg
Weight, empty:3800 kg
Power-to-weight ratio:33.3 hp/t
Engine:General Motors Type 6.5 1 NA V-8 diesel developing 160 hp at 1700 rpm
Maximum road speed:125 km/h
Maximum road range:450 km
Fuel capacity:95 l
Fording:0.76 m
Vertical obstacle:n/avail
Trench:n/app
Gradient: 60%
Side slope:40%
Armour: classified
Armour type:steel
NBC:yes
Night vision equipment:none (optional)

Development

The Eagle Armoured Reconnaissance Vehicle was developed by MOWAG to meet the requirements of the Swiss Army and following trials with three prototype vehicles a production order was placed for 156 units with the first of these being delivered early in 1995.

The Eagle essentially consists of the chassis of the US AM General High Mobility Multi-purpose Wheeled Vehicle (HMMWV), of which over 130 000 have been built for the US Army and for export, fitted with a armoured body that provides the occupants with protection from small arms fire and shell splinters.

The engine is at the front, driver and commander in the centre and another two people to the rear. Mounted on the hull top is a one man turret with a 7.62 mm machine gun mounted on the right side. Turret traverse is through 360 degrees with weapon elevation from -12 to +20 degrees. A day/night thermal imaging device is fitted on the forward part of the turret. The bullet proof windows provide the same level of protection as the hull.

Standard equipment includes a NBC system, power steering and run-flat tyres. A wide range of optional equipment can be fitted including central tyre pressure system, heater and a winch.

Variants

There are no variants of the MOWAG Eagle although it can be adopted for a wide range of roles and missions.

Status

Production. In service with Denmark and Switzerland.

Manufacturer

MOWAG Motorwagenfabrik, Kreuzlingen, Switzerland.

Right: MOWAG Eagle (4 x 4)

MOWAG Piranha APC (Switzerland)

Key recognition features

- Pointed hull front with lower part sloping back to first road wheel station and upper part sloping up to horizontal hull top that extends to rear. Trim vane normally folded up under nose.
- Driver sits front left with engine compartment to right, troop compartment extends right to rear with troops entering via two doors in rear. Hull sides slope inward top and bottom just above road wheels
- MOWAG Piranha produced in 4x4, 6x6 and 8x8 versions but all have similar layout. In 6x6 rear two road wheels are close together, in 8x8 road wheels are equally spaced

Specifications

Model:	4x4	6x6	8x8
Crew: (max)	10	14	15
Length:	5.32m	5.97m	6.365m
Width:	2.5m	2.5m	2.5m
Height (hull top):	1.85m	1.85m	1.85m
Weight, combat:	7,800kg	10,500kg	12,300kg
Weight, empty:	6,700kg	8,000kg	8,800KG
Power-to-weight ratio:	25hp/t	28.6hp/t	24.4hp/t
Engine type:(all diesel)	6BTA 5.9	6V-53T	6V-53T
hp/rpm:	195/2800	300/2800	300/2800
Maximum road speed:	100km/hr	100km/hr	100km/hr
Maximum water speed:	9.5km/hr	10.5km/hr	10.5km/hr
Maximum road range:	700km	600km	780km
Fuel capacity: (lit)	200	200	300
Fording:	All fully amphibious		
Vertical obstacle:	0.5m	0.5m	0.5m
Gradient: 70%	70%	70%	
Side slope: 35%	35%	35%	
Armour (maximum):	10mm	10mm	10mm
NBC system:	Standard on all vehicles		
Night vision equipment:	Optional on all vehicles		

Development

In the early 1970s MOWAG started development of a range of 4x4, 6x6 and 8x8 armoured vehicles which have many common components and a wide range of roles. The family was subsequently called Piranha, first prototype completed in 1972 and first production vehicles in 1976.

In addition to being manufactured by MOWAG in Switzerland the Piranha family is also manufactured under licence in Canada (Diesel Division, General Motors of Canada),

Chile (FAMAE), and the UK (GKN Defence). In the latter case they are all for export (Oman and Saudi Arabia).

There are separate entries for the Canadian (6x6), Canadian (8x8) LAV-25 and Bison (8x8) APCs.

All Piranhas have similar layout with driver front left, Detroit Diesel right, rear taken by troop compartment which has roof hatches and twin doors in rear. Troop compartment can have firing ports and vision devices and a wide range of weapon systems can be installed on roof.

Piranha is fully amphibious, propelled by two propellers under hull at rear. Before entering water a trim vane is erected at front and bilge pumps switched on.

Vehicle can be used for wide range of roles including ambulance, anti-tank armed with ATGWs, cargo, command, internal security, mortar carrier, recovery, reconnaissance and radar carrier.

Standard equipment includes NBC and air-conditioning system, optional equipment includes winch and night vision equipment.

Variants

4x4 can have various weapon stations up to turret-mounted 20mm cannon.

6x6 can have various turrets up to two-man turret armed with 90mm gun. Swiss Army has ordered 310 in anti-tank role with Norwegian Kvaerner-Eureka turret and twin TOW ATGW in ready-to-launch position.

8x8 version can have wide range of turrets and weapon systems including Euromissile Mephisto launcher with four HOT ATGWs, 90mm turret, 105mm turret with low recoil force gun, and multiple rocket launchers.

In 1994 the prototype of a MOWAG 10x10 Piranha was built

Right: MOWAG Piranha (8x8) APC of the Swiss Army

Left: MOWAG Piranha (8x8) Generation III with 25mm turret

Below: MOWAG Piranha (6x6) fitted with Kvaerner-Eureka ATGW turret

and fitted with a 105mm gun. In 1996 the MOWAG Piranha Generation III of 6x6, 8x8 and 10x10 vehicles was launched with increased armour and mobility.

Status
In production. Australia (8x8), Canada (6x6 and 8x8), Chile (6x6), Ghana (4x4, 6x6 and 8x8), Liberia (4x4), Nigeria (6x6 and 8x8), Oman (8x8), Saudi Arabia (8x8), Sierre Leone, Switzerland (6x6 and 8x8), and USA (8x8). Unconfirmed reports indicate Taiwan ordered 50 MOWAG Piranhas (6x6) in 1984.

Manufacturer
MOWAG Motorwagenfabrik AG, Kreuzlingen, Switzerland (but see text).

MOWAG Roland APC (Switzerland)

Key recognition features

● Nose slopes back under vehicle, well sloped glacis plate with driver's hatch in upper part, flat roof with engine compartment in left side, vertical rear with louvres in left side and door in right side

● Hull side welded in middle with upper and lower parts sloping inwards. Some vehicles have air louvres over left rear wheel

● Two wheels each side, sides of wheel arches outside armour envelope, door mid-way between wheel arches is hinged at top

Specifications

Crew: 3+3
Configuration: 4x4
Armament: 1 x 7.62mm MG
Ammunition: 1,000 x 7.62mm
Length: 4.44m
Width: 2.01m
Height turret top: 2.03m
Ground clearance: 0.4m
Wheelbase: 2.5m
Weight, combat: 4,700kg
Weight, empty: 3,900kg
Power-to-weight ratio: 42.9hp/tonne
Engine: V-8 4-stroke water-cooled petrol developing 202hp at 3,900rpm
Maximum road speed: 110km/hr
Maximum road range: 550km
Fuel capacity: 154 lit
Fording: 1m
Vertical obstacle: 0.4m
Trench: Not applicable
Gradient: 60%
Side slope: 30%
Armour: 8mm (maximum) (estimate)
Armour type: Steel
NBC system: None
Night vision equipment: Optional

Development

Roland was designed by MOWAG in the early 1960s for a wide range of roles including internal security, armoured personnel carrier and reconnaissance vehicle. First prototypes completed

in 1963, first production vehicles in 1964. Driver sits front left with crew compartment to rear. Each side of hull has entry hatch with firing port and observation hatch. Additional door in right rear side, engineer compartment left rear.

Roland normally has three-man crew consisting of commander, machine gunner and driver and carries three fully equipped troops. A 7.62mm or 12.7mm MG can be mounted on top of hull on simple pintle mount, or turret armed with similar weapon can be installed.

Standard model has manual transmission with four forward and one reverse gears, but was also available with fully automatic transmission with three forward and one reverse gears.

Wide range of optional equipment available including smoke grenade dischargers, night vision equipment, MOWAG-designed firing ports allowing some occupants to aim and fire from inside, obstacle-clearing blade at full front, searchlights and MOWAG bullet-proof cross-country wheels consisting of metal discs each side of tyre to support tyre when punctured and give additional traction when moving across country.

Late production vehicles had a fully automatic transmission in place of the manual transmission and a slightly longer wheelbase. This model has a combat weight of 4,900kg and power-to-weight ratio of 41hp/tonne.

Variants

No variants except for different armament installations.

Status

Production complete. In service with many countries including Argentina, Bolivia, Chile, Greece, Mexico and Peru.

Manufacturer

MOWAG Motorwagenfabrik AG, Kreuzlingen, Switzerland.

Right: MOWAG Roland with remote-controlled 7.62mm machine gun

Otakar APC (Turkey)

Key recognition features

● Conventional layout, with armour-plated engine compartment front with horizontal louvres in centre, bonnet slopes slightly upwards to windscreen which slopes to rear

● Front of roof has sloping front with searchlight on top, hull top horizontal and rear hull vertical. Machinegun mount on roof with spare wheel to rear. Forward-opening door in each side has bullet-proof window in upper part. Three small firing ports with window above in either side of troop compartment.

● Two wheels each side with extended wheel arches above. Lower hull sides are vertical, upper part slopes slightly inwards.

Specifications

Crew: 2 + 6
Configuration: 4 x 4
Armament: 1 x 7.62mm MG, 1 x 6 smoke grenade launchers
Ammunition: 1000 x 7.62mm
Length: 4.155m
Width: 1.81m
Height: 2.26m (hull top) 2.75m with MG
Weight, combat: 3600kg
Weight, empty: 3000kg
Power-to-weight ratio: 37hp/t
Engine: Land Rover V-8 3.5 litre petrol developing 134hp at 5000rpm or Rover 300 Tdi 4-cylinder turbocharged diesel developing 111hp at 4000rpm
Maximum road speed: 125km/hr
Maximum range: 500km
Fuel capacity: 85l
Fording: 0.6m
Vertical obstacle: 0.315m
Trench: n/a
Gradient: 80%
Side slope: 70%
Armour: classified
Armour type: Steel
NBC system: No
Night vision equipment: No

Development

The Otakar APC was developed for the Turkish army with first prototypes completed in 1993 and production vehicles in 1994. In many respects it is similar to the British Shorland S55 (qv). It consists of a modified Land Rover Defender 4 x 4 chassis, fitted with a fully-armoured body that provides protection from small arms fire. The engine is at the front as in a normal Land Rover, with the commander and driver behind it, each provided with a forward-opening side door with window. The six troops are seated three to either side, facing each other. They enter and exit via door doors in the hull rear. Firing ports and vision devices are provided in the sides and rear of the troop compartment, and a 7.62mm machinegun mount is fitted on the forward part of the roof. The mount can be traversed through 360° and elevated from -12° to +65°.

Variants

None, although the vehicle can be adapted for a variety of roles. The similar Otakar Akrep (Scorpion) light reconnaissance vehicle, also based on the Land Rover Defender, has a crew of three and has a remotely-controlled 7.62mm machinegun on the roof.

Status

In production. In service with Turkey and other undisclosed countries.

Manufacturer

Otakar Otobus Karoseri Sanayi AS, Istanbul, Turkey

Otakar APC with 7.62mm MG

Shorland Armoured Patrol Car (UK)

Key recognition features

● Land Rover chassis with armoured engine compartment front, crew compartment centre, commander and driver each have forward-opening side door with drop-down vision port in upper part and windscreen to front, which can be covered by two armoured shutters hinged at top

● One-man six-sided turret on hull roof, turret rear in line with rear of crew compartment which then drops down to back of vehicle which is almost in line with engine compartment

● Two large road wheels each side that extend from hull side, extended wheel arches above

Specifications

Crew: 3
Configuration: 4x4
Armament: 1 x 7.62mm MG
Ammunition: 1600 x 7.62mm
Length: 4.49m
Width: 1.8m
Height: 1.8m (roof)
Ground clearance: 0.324m
Wheelbase: 2.79m
Weight, combat: 3,600kg
Power-to-weight ratio: 37.8bhp/tonne
Engine: Rover 4-stroke V-8 petrol developing 134bhp at 5000rpm
Maximum road speed: 120km/hr
Maximum road range: 630km
Fuel capacity: 136 lit
Fording: 0.5m
Vertical obstacle: 0.23m
Trench: Not applicable
Gradient: 60%
Side slope: 30%
Armour: 8mm
Armour type: Steel
NBC system: None
Night vision equipment: None
(Above relates to current production S52 vehicle)

Development

Shorland was originally developed in 1965 to meet the requirements of Royal Ulster Constabulary for Northern Ireland. First production vehicles were completed in 1965 since when well over 1,000 have been built, mostly for export. The original vehicles have now been taken over by the British Army. Shorland is a modified long wheelbase Land Rover chassis with a fully armoured body for protection from small arms fire and shell splinters.

First production vehicles were Mk 1s, followed by the Mk 2, 3, 4 and 5, the main difference being the Land Rover chassis used. Mk 5 has improved coil suspension and wider wheel track. Current production models are known as the Series 5 with the Armoured Patrol Car being designated the S52.

The 7.62mm MG mounted in turret has manual traverse and elevation and four electrically operated smoke grenade dischargers can be mounted each side, firing forwards. Optional equipment includes various radios, air-conditioning system and loud hailer. Different vision arrangements are also available as is a version powered by a 107bhp diesel engine. Latest production vehicles have a redesigned rear angled 45 degrees and a slightly different hull front.

Variants

S52 is the basic Shorland armoured patrol car.
S53 is mobile air defence vehicle. Mounted on the turret roof is a lightweight mounting with three Javelin SAMs in the ready-to-launch position.
S54 is an anti-hijack vehicle with a special turret fitted with a mounting for a sniper's rifle.
S55 is the APC and covered in the APC section.

Status

In production. In service with 40 countries including Argentina, Bahrain, Botswana, Brunei, Burundi, Cyprus, Guyana, Kenya, Lesotho, Libya, Malayia, Mali, Portugal, Syria, Thailand, United Arab Emirates and UK (Northern Ireland only).

Manufacturer
Short Brothers, Belfast,
Northern Ireland, UK.

Right: Shorland S52

Below: Shorland S52

Above: Shorland S54

Shorland Mk 5

297

Daimler Ferret Scout Cars (UK)

Key recognition features

● Driver front, turret centre, engine compartment rear with roof that slopes down slightly each side with louvres at far rear top. Top half of hull rear vertical, lower half slopes back under hull rear
● Well sloped glacis plate, driver has hatch hinged at top that opens upwards and similar smaller hatch each side. Upper part of hull front, sides and rear slope inwards
● Two large road wheels each side with spare wheel and tyre on left side of hull

Specifications

Crew: 2
Armament: 1 x 7.62mm MG, 2 x 3 smoke grenade dischargers
Ammunition: 1,000 x 7.62mm
Length: 3.835m
Width: 1.905m
Height: 1.879m
Ground clearance: 0.33m
Wheelbase: 2.286m
Weight, combat: 4,400kg
Weight, empty: 3,640kg
Power-to-weight ratio: 29.35bhp/tonne
Engine: Rolls-Royce B60 Mk 6A 6-cylinder in-line water-cooled petrol developing 129bhp at 3,750rpm
Maximum road speed: 93km/hr
Maximum road range: 306km
Fuel capacity: 96 lit
Fording: 0.914m
Fording with preparation: 1.524m
Vertical obstacle: 0.406m
Trench with channels: 1.22m
Gradient: 46%
Side slope: 30%
Armour: 8-16mm
Armour type: Steel
NBC system: None
Night vision equipment: None

Development

Ferret series 4x4 scout car was developed by the Daimler company shortly after the Second World War for the British Army. First prototypes completed in 1949 with production running from 1952 to 1971. Total production amounted to 4,409 vehicles for home and export. It is no longer used by the British Army.

Ferret Mk 2/3 has driver at front, commander centre and engine rear. Turret has manual traverse through 360˚, 7.62mm machine gun with manual elevation from -15˚ to +45˚. Turret is identical to that on many Alvis Saracen (6x6) APCs. Spare wheel carried on left side of hull, emergency hatch on opposite side. Channels were often carried across front of hull for crossing ditches or sandy terrain.

Variants

Ferret Mk 1 has no turret and open top, normally has pintle-mounted 7.62mm MG.
Mk 1/2 has crew of three and low profile turret with 7.62mm machine gun.
Mk 2 is similar to Mk 2/3, with turret.
Mk 2/2 was for Far East, no longer in service.
Mk 2/4 had additional armour.
Mk 2/5 is Mk 2 brought up to Mk 2/4 standard.
Mk 2/6 is Mk 2/3 with Vigilant ATGW mounted each side of turret. No longer used by British Army but may be found in Middle East.
Mk 2/7 is Mk 2/6 with missiles removed and equals Mk 2/3.
Mk 3 is Mk 1 with same modifications as Mk 4.
Mk 4 is Mk 2/3 rebuilt with many improvements including larger wheels and flotation screen.
Mk 5 had Swingfire ATGWs. No longer in service.

Further development of Mk 4 (or 'big wheeled Ferret') resulted in Fox (qv). A number of companies, including Alvis Limited (now design authority for the Ferret) offer upgrade packages for the Ferret including a more fuel-efficient diesel engine. Alvis has already sold its repower package to Malaysia.

Left: Daimler Ferret Mk 1

Right: Ferret Mk 1

Left: Daimler Ferret Mk 4

Status

Production complete. In service with Bahrain, Burkina Faso, Burma, Cameroon, Central African Republic, India, Indonesia, Jordan, Kenya, Lebanon, Madagascar, Malaysia, Nepal, Portugal, South Africa, Sri Lanka, Sudan, and United Arab Emirates.

Manufacturer

Daimler Limited, Coventry, England, UK.

Fox Light Armoured Car (UK)

Key recognition features

● Two large road wheels each side with stowage box between, flotation screen carried on hull top
● Well sloped glacis plate with large driver's hatch opening to right in upper part
● Turret in hull centre with two hatch covers opening to rear, long 30mm RARDEN cannon with day/night sight on right, turret welded in middle and upper and lower parts sloping inwards

Specifications

Crew: 3
Configuration: 4x4
Armament: 1 x 30mm cannon, 1 x 7.62mm MG (coaxial), 2 x 4 smoke grenade dischargers
Ammunition: 99 x 30mm, 2,600 x 7.62mm
Length gun forwards: 5.08m
Length hull: 4.166m
Width: 2.134m
Height overall: 2.2m
Height to turret top: 1.981m
Ground clearance: 0.3m
Wheelbase: 2.464m
Weight, combat: 6120kg
Weight, empty: 5733kg
Power-to-weight ratio: 30.04bhp/tonne
Engine: Jaguar XK 4.2 litre 6-cylinder petrol developing 190bhp at 4,500rpm
Maximum road speed: 104km/hr
Maximum water speed: 5.23km/hr
Maximum road range: 434km
Fuel capacity: 145 lit
Fording: 1m, amphibious with preparation
Vertical obstacle: 0.5m
Trench with channels: 1.22m
Gradient: 46%
Side slope: 30%
Armour: Classified
Armour type: Aluminium
NBC system: None
Night vision equipment: Yes (passive for driver and gunner)

Development

Combat Vehicle Reconnaissance (Wheeled) was developed in the 1960s by the then Fighting Vehicles Research and Development Establishment (FVRDE) at the same time as the Combat Vehicle Reconnaissance (Tracked) Scorpion. The prototypes were built by Daimler, Coventry, the first completed in 1967. Production was undertaken by the then Royal Ordnance Factory, Leeds, first production vehicles completed in 1973. In 1986 Royal Ordnance Leeds was taken over by Vickers Defence Systems. The production line for Fox was however closed some time ago.

Driver sits front, two-man turret centre, engine and transmission rear. Turret has manual traverse through 360° and 30mm RARDEN cannon elevates from -14° to +40°. Ammunition consists of APDS-T, APSE-T, HEI-T and training.

The Fox light armoured car is fitted with a flotation screen and when this is erected the vehicle is propelled and steered in the water by its wheels.

Variants

Many variants of the Fox were projected but none of these entered service. The Fox has been phased out of service with the British Army and their turrets have been fitted onto the Scorpion chassis to produce the Sabre reconnaissance vehicle.

Status

Production complete. In service with Malawi and Nigeria.

Manufacturer

Vickers Defence Systems, Leeds, England, UK.

Fox (4x4)

Above right: Fox (4x4) without flotation screen

Right: Fox (4x4) without flotation screen (MoD)

GKN Saxon APC (UK)

Key recognition features

● Box-shaped hull with front sloping to rear and driver's position offset to right, horizontal louvres on front and left side of hull, single door in right side of hull and twin doors rear
● Flat roof with commander's fixed cupola on forward part with rear-opening hatch, vision block in each side and 7.62mm MG on external DISA mount
● Two large road wheels each side with stowage bins on left side of hull and wire stowage box on roof
(Note: left-hand drive model available; export vehicles have door in left side of hull)

Specifications

Crew: 2+8 (or 10)
Configuration: 4x4
Armament: 1 x 7.62mm MG
Ammunition: 1,000 x 7.62mm
Length: 5.169m
Width: 2.489m
Height: 2.628m (commander's cupola)
Ground clearance: 0.41m (hull), 0.29m (axles)
Wheelbase: 3.073m
Weight, combat: 11,660kg
Weight, empty: 9,940kg
Power-to-weight ratio: 14.06bhp/tonne
Engine: Bedford 500 6-cylinder diesel developing 164bhp at 2,800rpm
Maximum road speed: 96km/hr
Maximum road range: 480km
Fuel capacity: 153 lit
Fording: 1.12m
Vertical obstacle: 0.41m
Trench: Not applicable
Gradient: 60%
Side slope: 30%
Armour: Classified
Armour type: Steel
NBC system: None
Night vision equipment: None

Development

Saxon (4x4) was developed as a private venture by GK Defence, first prototype completed in 1976 and first production vehicles in 1976. In 1983 it was adopted by the British Army for infantry battalions based in UK but deployed to Germany in wartime.

Driver sits front left or front right, engine in lower part of hull and troop compartment extending right to rear. Troops on bench seats down both sides and enter via side doors or two doors at rear. Commander has fixed cupola or turret with single or 7.62mm twin MGs.

Optional equipment includes air-conditioning system, front-mounted winch, heater, grenade launchers, barricade remover, searchlights, front-mounted winch and replacement of Bedford engine by Perkins T6.3544 diesel developing 195hp at 2,500rpm.

Latest production vehicles for the British Army are powered by a Cummins 6BT 5.91 litre turbocharged 6-cylinder diesel engine developing 160hp coupled to a fully automatic transmission.

By late 1995 total production of the Saxon APC amounted to almost 800 vehicles with the British Army being largest customer. Late production models for British Army are called Saxon Patrol and were for Northern Ireland. Some British Army Saxon APCs have one-man 7.62mm machine gun turret fitted.

Variants

Command vehicle - fitted with additional communications equipment.
Ambulance - ordered by British Army in 1991.
Recovery - in service with British Army, has winch with capacity of 16 tonnes.
Incident control vehicle - prototype only for IS applications.
Water cannon - prototype only.

Status

Production complete. In service with Bahrain, Hong Kong, Kuwait (status uncertain), Malaysia, Nigeria, Oman, United Arab Emirates and UK.

GKN Saxon (4x4) with MG turret

Manufacturer
GKN Defence, Telford, Shropshire, England, UK.

Right: GKN Saxon (4x4) APC of British Army

Far right: GKN Saxon (4x4) in ambulance configuration

Top right: GKN Saxon (4x4) APC of British Army (Richard Stickland)

303

Shorland S 55 APC (UK)

Key recognition features

● Conventional layout with armour plated engine compartment front, angled windscreen with armoured louvres hinged at top, hull top above commander. Driver has integral spotlight, horizontal roof over rear troop compartment, vertical hull rear
● Single forward-opening door each side with outward-opening observation panel in upper part, two rectangular firing ports in hull sides that slope slightly inwards, two doors rear each with firing port
● Two road wheels each side with rounded front and square cut rear wheel arches
(See variants)

Specifications

Crew: 2+6
Configuration: 4x4
Armament: 2 x 4 smoke grenade dischargers
Length: 4.25m
Width: 1.8m
Height: 2.28m
Ground clearance: 0.324m
Wheelbase: 2.795m
Weight, combat: 3,600kg
Power-to-weight ratio: 37.2hp/tonne
Engine: Rover V-8 water-cooled petrol developing 134bhp at 5,000rpm
Maximum road speed: 120km/hr
Maximum range: 630km
Fuel capacity: 136 lit
Fording: 0.50m
Vertical obstacle: 0.23m
Trench: Not applicable
Gradient: 60% (estimate)
Side slope: 30% (estimate)
Armour: 8mm (estimate)
Armour type: Steel
NBC system: None
Night vision equipment: None

Development

In the early 1970s Short Brothers developed an APC based on a Land Rover (4x4) chassis to work with its Shorland Armoured Patrol Vehicle on a similar chassis. First prototype completed in 1973 under the designation SB 301.

This was followed in production by SB 401 with improved armour protection and more powerful engine, and in 1980 SB 501 was introduced, based on new Land Rover One-Ten chassis with wider wheelbase and improved coil spring suspension. Depending on year of manufacture there are minor exterior differences between vehicles, especially hull front; for example, on early vehicles radiator grille was short distance back from front mudguards whereas on SB 501 it is slightly forward of radiator.

Layout of all versions virtually identical with engine front, commander and driver to its rear (left-hand and right-hand drive models available), and troop compartment rear, three men each side facing.

Wide range of optional equipment including long-range fuel tank, smoke grenade dischargers, flashing lamps, air-conditioning system and roof-mounted 7.62mm MG.

Variants

No variants but see also Shorland Armoured Patrol Vehicle (ACRVs). Current production models have different hull front, three small vision blocks with associated firing ports in either side of hull and integral bullet-proof windows for commander and driver.

Status

In production. In service with more than 20 countries including Malaysia, Papua New Guinea Defence Force, Pakistan, and Turkey.

Manufacturer

Short Brothers, Belfast, Northern Ireland, UK.

Shorland SB 501 (4x4) APC

Below: Latest production S55 (4x4)

Above: Shorland S55 (4x4) APC with roof-mounted MG

Right: Shorland S55 (4x4) APC on One-Ten chassis

305

Glover Webb Armoured Patrol Vehicle (UK)

Key recognition features

● Conventional layout with armour plated engine compartment front with wire mesh screen across front, bonnet horizontal to windscreen which can be provided with wire mesh screen that hinges forward onto bonnet when not required

● Front part of roof has slightly sloping front with searchlight above, hull top horizontal and hull rear vertical. Hatch in roof of British Army vehicles. Forward opening door in each side has bullet proof window in upper part. Troops enter and leave via twin doors in rear each of which has vision block

● Two wheels each side with arches above, lower part of hull sides are vertical with upper part sloping slightly inwards

Specifications

Crew: 2 + 6
Configuration: 4 x 4
Armament: nil
Ammunition: nil
Length: 4.55 m
Width: 1.79 m
Height: 2.08 m
Ground clearance: 0.32 m
Wheelbase: 2.794 m
Weight, combat: n/avail
Weight, empty: n/avail
Power-to-weight ratio: n/avail
Engine: Rover V-8 petrol developing 114 hp
Maximum road speed: 120 km/h
Maximum road range: n/avail
Fuel capacity: n/avail
Fording: n/avail
Vertical obstacle: 0.23 m
Trench: n/app
Gradient: 60%
Side slope: 30%
Armour: classified
Armour type: steel
NBC: none
Night vision equipment: none

Development

The Glover Webb Armoured Patrol Vehicle (APV) was originally developed to meet the requirements of the British Army for use in Northern Ireland with the first of about 100 vehicles being completed in 1986. Glover Webb has now been taken over by GKN Defence but the company retains its name.

The vehicle is essentially a Land Rover chassis fitted with an armoured body that provides the occupants with protection from small arms fire and shell splinters. The engine is at the front, commander and driver in the centre and the troop compartment at the rear. The troops are seated three down each side facing each other.

Variants

Can be provided with firing ports in rear troop compartment and roof mounted 7.62 mm machine gun. Glover Webb have also built quantities of Hornet (4 x 4) armoured car based on a modified Land Rover chassis, this is fitted with a roof mounted turret armed with a 7.62 mm machine gun.

Many other companies build light armoured vehicles based on the Land Rover (4 x 4) Defender chassis including Courtaulds Aerospace of the UK who have built over 1000 of the CAV 100 vehicles, many for the British Army.

Status

Production as required. In service with British Army, Police and other undisclosed users.

Manufacturer

Glover Webb, Hamble, Hampshire, UK.

Above: Glover Webb Armoured Patrol Vehicle

Right: Glover Webb Hornet

Above: Glover Webb Armoured Patrol Vehicle

Glover Webb Tactica APC (UK)

Key recognition features

● Conventional layout with armour plated engine compartment front with horizontal louvres in the centre, bonnet slopes slightly upwards to windscreen which slopes to rear

● Front part of roof has slightly sloping front with hull top horizontal and hull rear vertical, lower part of hull rear slopes inwards. Forward opening door in each side has bullet proof window in upper part. Three firing ports with bullet proof window above in either side of rear troop compartment

● Two wheels each side, lower part of hull sides slope slightly inwards, upper part of hull are vertical, twin door in hull rear with two firing ports with vision blocks above

Specifications

Crew: 2 + 12
Configuration: 4 x 4
Armament: nil (see text)
Ammunition: nil (see text)
Length: 5.6 m
Width: 2.2 m
Height: 2.35 m
Ground clearance: 0.3 m
Wheelbase: n/avail
Weight, combat: 10 000 kg
Weight, empty: 6500 kg
Power-to-weight ratio: see text
Engine: Mercedes, Perkins or Renault turbocharged diesel engine
Maximum road speed: 120 km/h
Maximum road range: 650 km
Fuel capacity: 167 l
Fording: n/avail
Vertical obstacle: n/avail
Trench: n/app
Gradient: 60%
Side slope: 30%
Armour: classified
Armour type: steel
NBC: none
Night vision equipment: none

Development

The Tactica APC (4 x 4) was developed as a private venture by Glover Webb who were taken over by GKN Defence in 1994. First prototype of the Tactica was completed in 1988 with first production vehicles being completed the following year.

Two versions of the Tactica are currently offered, one with a forward control type hull which can carry up to 14 men and the other with a conventional bonnet type hull which can carry up to 10 men. Different wheelbase models are available as are different engines.

The conventional bonnet type has the engine at the front, commander and driver in the centre and the troop compartment at the rear. The troops normally enter and leave via two doors in the hull rear. The basic model is unarmed but can be fitted with a variety of roof mounted weapon stations including a pintle mounted 7.62 mm or 12.7 mm machine gun or one man turret armed with similar weapons.

Standard equipment includes power steering and a wide range of optional equipment is available according to mission requirements.

Variants

The vehicle can be adopted for a wide range of roles, for example fitted with a water cannon and for use in command post role. The UK uses the vehicles to transport EOD teams.

Status

Production. In service with Indonesia, Kuwait, Mauritius, Singapore, UK and other countries.

Manufacturer

Glover Webb, Hamble, Hampshire, UK.

Above: Tactica water cannnon

Top right: Forward control Tactica

Right: Two versions of Tactica

GKN Simba APC (UK)

Key recognition features

● Box-shaped hull sloping up to raised drivers position on left side, engine compartment on right side with louvres on lower part of glacis plate. Horizotal roof extends to rear, vehicle hull rear with large door

● Upper part of hull slopes inwards with two part door in left side of hull and single hatch in right side of hull. Various armament options can be mounted on roof

● Two large road wheels each side, lower part of hull slopes inwards

Specifications

Crew: 3 + 8/10
Configuration: 4 x 4
Armament: 1 x 7.62 mm MG
Ammunition: 1000 x 7.62 mm
Length: 5.35 m
Width: 2.50 m
Height: 2.19 m (low profile cupola)
Ground clearance: 0.45 m (hull), 0.33 m (axles)
Wheelbase: 2.972 m
Weight, combat: 11 200 kg
Weight, empty: 9500 kg
Power-to-weight ratio: 18.75 bhp/t
Engine: Perkins 210Ti turbocharged intercooled diesel developing 210 bhp at 2500 rpm
Maximum road speed: 100 km/h
Maximum road range: 660 km
Fuel capacity: 296 l
Fording: 1 m
Vertical obstacle: 0.45 m
Trench: n/app
Gradient: 60%
Side slope: 40%
Armour: 8 mm (maximum) (estimate)
Armour type: steel
NBC: none (optional)
Night vision equipment: none (optional)

Development

The Simba light combat vehicle was designed as a private venture by GKN Defence specifically for the export market and following trials was selected by the Philippines Armed Forces who placed an order for 150 vehicles.

Of these 150 vehicles, eight vehicles were delivered complete. two in knowcked down kit form and the remaining 138 are being assembled in the Philippines at a facility owned by the joint venture company Asian Armoured Vehicle Technologies Corporation.

The driver is seated front left with the powerpack to his right and the troop compartment extending to the rear. The troops sit on seats down either side and can leave the vehicle via the door in the rear or the door in left side of the hull. Most vehicles used by the Philippines have a one man turret armed with a 12.7 mm M2 machine gun.

A wide range of optional equipment can be fitted including front mounted winch, heater and/or air conditioning system and various weapon systems.

Variants

AIFV, two man 20 mm or 25 mm turret
Fire support vehicle, two man 90 mm turret
Internal security, wide range of equipment
Anti-tank, HOT or TOW ATGW
Mortar, 81 mm on turntable

Status

In production. In service with Philippines Armed Forces.

Manufacturer

GKN Defence, Telford, Shropshire, England, UK.

Top left: GKN Simba

Top right: GKN Simba

Left: GKN Simba fitted for 7.62 mm MG (Christopher F Foss)

Right: GKN Simba fitted for 7.62 mm MG (Christopher F Foss)

Vickers Defence Systems Valkyr Family (UK)

Key recognition features

● Short glacis plate, driver has three large windows (one front and one each side), flat roof and vertical hull rear
● Large door in left side of hull, two doors rear, small door in right side, commander's cupola offset to left side of hull
● Two large road wheels each side with rounded wheel arches, hull sides vertical to just above wheels, then slope slightly inwards

Specifications

Crew: 2+8
Configuration: 4x4
Armament: 1 x 7.62mm MG
Ammunition: 1,000 x 7.62mm
Length: 5.6m
Width: 2.5m
Height: 2.27m (hull top)
Ground clearance: 0.4m
Wheelbase: 3.1m
Weight, combat: 11,500kg
Power-to-weight ratio: 17.5hp/tonne
Engine: Detroit Diesel 4-53T developing 300hp at 2,800rpm
Maximum road speed: 100km/hr
Maximum range: 700km
Fuel capacity: 200 lit
Fording: Amphibious
Vertical obstacle: 0.4m
Trench: Not applicable
Gradient: 60%
Side slope: 30%
Armour: Classified
Armour type: Steel
NBC system: Optional
Night vision equipment: Optional
(Above relates to APC model)

Development

Valkyr family of 4x4s has been developed by Vickers Defence Systems as a private venture in association with Beherman-Demoen of Belgium which previously developed the BDX (4x4)(qv). First prototype of Valkyr completed in 1982, first pre-production vehicle followed in 1984. Two versions of Valkyr are offered: fire support vehicle with lower hull top with a wide range of weapons and high-roof APC with distinctive air-inlet louvres above driver's position.

In APC version driver sits front, engine to right rear, passageway to left rear where vehicle commander normally sits Above this is a cupola with externally mounted 7.62m MG, troop compartment rear and firing ports/vision devices if required.

Valkyr is fully amphibious, propelled by its wheels. Options include waterjets, air-conditioning system, increased armour protection and run flat tyres.

Variants

Fire Support Vehicle model has wide range of turrets for single or twin 7.62mm MGs, up to two-man turret with 90mm gun. The latter is the Cockerill CM90 two-man power operated turret armed with a 90mm gun, 7.62mm coaxial machine gun, 7.62mm anti-aircraft machine gun and two banks of smoke grenade dischargers.

Other roles include internal security, 81mm mortar, command post, ambulance, cargo carrier, ATGW carrier, recovery, workshop and state vehicle.

Status

Production as required. Two were delivered to Kuwait before the Iraqi invasion.

Manufacturer

Vickers Defence Systems Limited, Newcastle-upon-Tyne, England, UK.

Above: Vickers Valkyr (4x4) without armament

Top right: Vickers Valkyr (4x4) in IS role

Left: Vickers Valkyr (4x4) in APC role

Right: Vickers Valkyr (4x4) with 90mm turret

Cadillac Gage Ranger APC (USA)

Key recognition features

● Vertical hull front with horizontal armoured radiator louvres, horizontal bonnet top which then slopes upwards to crew compartment, horizontal roof and almost vertical hull rear

● Single door in each hull side with firing port and vision block, twin doors in rear each with firing port, left door also has vision block and ventilator

● Two road wheels each side with hull sides above road wheels sloping slightly inwards

Specifications

Crew: 2+6
Configuration: 4x4
Armament: 1 x 7.62mm MG
Ammunition: 1,000 x 7.62mm
Length: 4.699m
Width: 2.019m
Height: 1.981m
Ground clearance: 0.203m
Wheelbase: 2.641m
Weight, combat: 4,536kg
Power-to-weight ratio: 40hp/tonne
Engine: Dodge 360 CID V-8 liquid-cooled petrol developing 180hp at 3,600rpm
Maximum road speed: 112.65km/hr
Maximum road range: 482km
Fuel capacity: 121 lit
Fording: 0.60m
Vertical obstacle: 0.254m
Trench: Not applicable
Gradient: 60%
Side slope: 30%
Armour: 7mm (maximum)(estimate)
Armour type: Steel
NBC system: None
Night vision equipment: None

Development

Ranger was developed as a private venture in the late 1970s and following completion was selected by the US Air Force for a Security Police Armored Response/Convoy Truck to patrol air bases and other high value targets. First production vehicles completed in 1980 and by 1995 over 700 were built.

It is essentially a Chrysler truck chassis with a shorter wheelbase fitted with armoured body for protection from small arms fire and shell splinters. Engine is front, commander and driver to rear and crew compartment far rear.

Basic vehicle is fitted with roof-mounted 7.62mm MG which normally has a shield, but a wide range of other weapon systems can be installed including turret with twin 7.62mm MG or turret with one 7.62mm and 12.7mm MG. The turret has manual traverse through a full 360° with weapon elevation being from -14° to +55°. Luxembourg has five vehicles with this turret armed with twin 7.62mm MGs.

Standard equipment includes air-conditioning system and heater, optional equipment includes grenade launchers, flashing lights, spotlight and front-mounted winch.

Variants

In addition to different weapon stations, Ranger can be used as command post vehicle, ambulance and light reconnaissance vehicle.

Status

Production complete. In service with Indonesia, Luxembourg and USA (Air Force and Navy).

Manufacturer

Textron Marine & Land Systems, New Orleans, Louisiana, USA.

Main picture: Ranger in command post role

Inset: Ranger in police role

Cadillac Gage LAV-150 AFV Range (USA)

Key recognition features

● Very similar in appearance to Dragoon (qv) except engine is left side at rear, not right
● Pointed hull front with horizontal roof, hull sides above curved wheel arches slope inwards, hull back cut off top and bottom and points rear
● Two large road wheels each side with two-part hatch between, similar hatch right rear, armament mounted on hull roof centre of vehicle

Specifications

Crew: 3+2
Configuration: 4x4
Armament: 1 x 20mm, 1 x 7.62mm MG (coaxial), 1 x 7.62mm MG (anti-aircraft), 2 x 6 smoke grenade dischargers
Ammunition: 400 x 20mm, 3,200 x 7.62mm
Length: 5.689m
Width: 2.26m]
Height: 2.54m (turret roof), 1.981m (hull roof)
Ground clearance: 0.381m (axles), 0.648m (hull)
Wheelbase: 2.667m
Weight, combat: 9,888kg
Power-to-weight ratio: 20.42bhp/tonne
Engine: V-504 V-8 diesel developing 202bhp at 3,300rpm
Maximum road speed: 88.54km/hr
Maximum water speed: 5km/hr
Maximum range: 643km
Fuel capacity: 303 lit
Fording: Amphibious
Vertical obstacle: 0.609m
Trench: Not applicable
Gradient: 60%
Side slope: 30%
Armour: Classified
Armour type: Steel
NBC system: None
Night vision equipment: Optional

Development

In 1962 Cadillac Gage (now Textron Marine & Land Systems) started private venture development work on a 4x4 which became known as LAV-100, first prototype completed in 1963

and first production vehicle in 1964. It was powered by a Chrysler petrol engine and used on a large scale in South Vietnam. A scaled-up version, LAV-200, was also built but was sold only to Singapore.

In 1971 LAV-100 and LAV-200 were replaced in production by LAV-150 with a number of improvements including replacement of petrol engine by diesel. In 1985 LAV-150 was replaced in production by LAV-150S which has longer wheelbase and therefore greater weight. So far over 3,200 vehicles have been built.

In all versions commander and driver are at front with troop compartment extending to rear except for engine compartment left rear. All versions are fully amphibious, propelled by their wheels, have a front-mounted winch and run-flat tyres. A wide range of armament can be fitted as well as other specialised equipment.

Variants

These are many and include turret with twin 7.62mm or one 7.62mm and one 12.7mm MG, turret with 20mm cannon and 7.62mm MG (one- or two-man versions), two-man turret with 25mm cannon and 7.62mm MG, one-man turret with 40mm grenade launcher and 12.7mm MG, anti-aircraft with 20mm Vulcan cannon, two-man turret with 90mm gun and 7.62mm coaxial and 7.62mm AA MG, 81mm mortar carrier, TOW ATGW, command or APC with pod, recovery, base security, ambulance and emergency rescue vehicle.

US Army designation is M706 and some are used as surrogate Soviet systems such as SA-9.

There is also a 6x6 version, Commando LAV-300 (qv).

Singapore has a number of variants of LAV-200 including recovery and air defence with RBS-70 SAM.

Status

In production. In service with Bolivia (LAV100), Botswana (LAV-150), Cameroon (LAV-150), Chad (LAV-150S), Dominican Republic (LAV-150), Gabon (LAV-150), Guatemala (LAV-150), Haiti (LAV-150), Indonesia (LAV-150), Jamaica (LAV-150), Kuwait (LAV-150S)*, Malaysia (LAV-100 and LAV-150), Mexico (LAV-150 ST), Philippines (LAV-150), Saudi Arabia (LAV-150), Singapore (LAV-150 and LAV-200), Somalia, Sudan (LAV-150 and LAV-150 S), Taiwan (LAV-150), Thailand (LAV-150), Turkey (LAV-150), USA (LAV-100), Venezuela (LAV-150) and Vietnam (LAv-100)*. (* status uncertain)

Manufacturer

Textron Marine & Land Systems, New Orleans, Louisiana, USA.

Above: Cadillac Gage LAV-150 Commando with two-man 20mm turret

Above right: Cadillac Gage LAV-200 Commando mortar carrier

Right: Cadillac Gage LAV-150 Commando with roof-mounted pod

AV Technology Dragoon Armoured Vehicle (USA)

Key recognition features

● Similar in appearance to Cadillac Gage (now Textron Marine & Land Systems) LAV-100/LAV-150 (4x4) vehicles except that engine is on right side rear, not left
● Pointed front with almost horizontal roof, hull sides above curved wheel arches slope inwards, hull back slopes to rear at about 60o
● Two large road wheels each side with two-part hatch between similar hatch left rear, armament mounted on hull roof centre of vehicle

Specifications
Crew: 3+6
Configuration: 4x4
Armament: 1 x 20mm cannon, 1 x 7.62mm MG (coaxial)
Length: 5.89m
Width: 2.49m
Height: 2.819m overall
Ground clearance: 0.685m (hull centre), 0.381m (axles)
Wheelbase: 3.10m
Weight, combat: 12,700kg
Weight, empty: 11,204kg
Power-to-weight ratio: 23.62bhp/tonne
Engine: Detroit Diesel 6V-53T 6-cylinder liquid-cooled turbocharged diesel developing 300bhp at 2,800rpm
Maximum road speed: 115.9km/hr
Maximum water speed: 5.6km/hr
Maximum road range: 885km
Fuel capacity: 350 lit
Fording: Amphibious
Vertical obstacle: 0.609m
Trench: Not applicable
Gradient: 60%
Side slope: 30%
Armour: Classified
Armour type: Steel
NBC system: Optional
Night vision equipment: Optional

Development
Dragoon AFV family was originally developed by the Verne Corporation to meet requirements of the US Army Military Police. The requirement subsequently lapsed and the company built two prototypes first shown in 1978. A small quantity of vehicles was built for the US Army and Navy in 1982. The US Army vehicles were supplied to the 9th Infantry Division High Technology Test Bed in two versions, electronic warfare and optical surveillance. The US Navy uses them for patrolling nuclear weapon storage sites in Alaska and the US east coast.

To reduce life-cycle and procurement costs Dragoon uses components of M113A2 full-tracked APC and M809 5-ton (6x6) truck.

Commander and driver sit front with troops carried to rear, wide range of weapon stations mounted on hull top up to 90mm KEnerga gun with 7.62mm coaxial MG in power-operated turret.

Dragoon is fully amphibious, propelled by its wheels, standard equipment includes front-mounted winch and wide range of optional equipment.

In 1984 the Verne Corporation and the Arrowpointe Corporation merged to form AV Technology Corporation and since then the vehicle has been further developed into the following basic versions: APC, Patroller armoured security vehicle, armoured command vehicle, 81mm armour mortar carrier, 90mm turret, 40mm/12.7mm turret, armoured maintenance vehicle, electronic warfare, armoured logistic support vehicle and TOW ATGW carrier.

Variants
Dragoon can be used for wide range of roles including APC, reconnaissance, recovery, command/communications, riot control, engineer, security/escort, 81mm mortar carrier, anti-tank with TOW, ambulance and logistics.

Status
Production as required. In service with US forces, Thailand, Turkey, Venezuela and a number of civil authorities.

Manufacturer
AV Technology Corporation, Troy, Michigan, USA.

Above left: Dragoon with two-man 90mm turret

Above: Dragoon APC with 7.62mm MG

Left: Dragoon Patroller armoured security vehicle

Right: Dragoon with two-man 90mm turret

Cadillac Gage Scout (USA)

Key recognition features

● Nose slopes back at 45o to first road wheel station, well sloped glacis plate which extends half way along to horizontal roof at rear on which turret is mounted
● Driver's hatch upper left side of glacis plate with air louvres to right, exhaust pipe right side of hull, two-part hatch in hull rear
● Two large road wheels each side with hull sides sloping inwards top and bottom

Specifications

Crew: 1+1 or 1+2
Configuration: 4x4
Armament: 2 x 7.62mm MG
Ammunition: 2,600 x 7.62mm
Length: 5.003m
Wheelbase: 2.743m
Width: 2.057m
Track: 1.660m
Height: 2.159m
Weight, combat: 7240kg
Power-to-weight ratio: 20.58hp/tonne
Engine: Cummins V-6 diesel developing 149hp at 3,300rpm
Maximum road speed: 96km/hr
Maximum road range: 1,287km
Fuel capacity: 378 lit
Fording: 1.168m
Vertical obstacle: 0.609m
Trench: 1.14m
Gradient: 60%
Side slope: 30%
Armour: 8mm (maximum)(estimate)
Armour type: Steel
NBC system: None
Night vision equipment: None

Development

Commando Scout (4x4) was developed as a private venture by Cadillac Gage (now part of Textron Marine & Land Systems), the first prototype shown in 1977. Although its main role is reconnaissance it is suitable for a wide range of roles with little modification, such as anti-tank and command post. In 1983

Indonesia ordered 28 Commando Scouts and in 1986 Egypt ordered 112, all of which were delivered by mid-1987.

The fuel tank is at the front, driver to immediate rear on left side, engine to his right. The turret is mounted rear, gunner enters via turret hatch cover or via two-part hatch in hull rear, upper part opens upwards and lower part downwards.

Standard equipment includes run-flat tyres, power steering, and air compressor with 15.24m hose. Optional equipment includes siren/public address system, various radio installations, slave cable, auxiliary cable, smoke grenade system and fragmentation grenade system as well as a wide range of turrets.

Variants

40mm/12.7mm turret armed with 40mm grenade launcher and 12.7mm MG as fitted to US Marine Corps AAV7A1 vehicles.
Twin/combination MG (1m) Cadillac Gage turret with twin 7.62mm or twin 12.7mm MG or combination of both. Turret traverses 360°, weapon elevates from -10° to +55°.
Command pod with three-man crew (driver, commander and radio operator) and raised pod o0n which a 7.62mm or 12.7mm MG is mounted.
Anti-tank with Hughes TOW ATGW launcher with one missile in ready-to-launch position and six missiles in reserve.

Status

Production complete. Can be placed back into production. In service with Egypt and Indonesia.

Manufacturer

Textron Marine & Land Systems, New Orleans, Louisiana, USA.

Above: Commando Scout with Command Pod and 7.62mm MG

Top right: Commando Scout with 1m turret and twin 7.62mm MG

Right: Commando Scout with 1m pod and one 7.62mm/one 12.7mm MG

BOV-VP APC (Yugoslavia)

Key recognition features

● Nose angled at 45o with slightly sloped glacis plate leading up to almost vertical windscreen for commander and driver, horizontal roof for crew compartment drops down to rear in line with back wheels

● Cupola in middle of roof with externally mounted 12.7mm MG, upper part of troop compartment sides has rectangular windows with circular firing ports between

● Two large road wheels each side with hull sides sloping inwards from just above wheel arches

Specifications

Crew: 2+8
Configuration: 4x4
Armament: 1 x 7.62mm MG, 2 x 3 smoke grenade dischargers
Length: 5.7m
Width: 2.534m
Height: 2.335m
Ground clearance: 0.325m
Wheelbase: 2.75m
Weight, combat: 5,700kg (estimate)
Power-to-weight ratio: 25.96hp/tonne (estimate)
Engine: Deutz type F 6L 413 F 6-cylinder diesel developing 148hp at 2,650rpm
Maximum road speed: 95km/hr
Range: 500km
Fuel capacity: 220 lit
Fording: 1.1m
Vertical obstacle: 0.54m
Trench: 0.64m
Gradient: 55%
Side slope: 30%
Armour: 8mm (Maximum)(estimate)
NBC system: No
Night vision equipment: Yes (infra-red for driver)

Development

In the early 1980s Yugoslavia introduced the first of what was to become a family of 4x4 armoured vehicles using many commercial automotive components such as engine, transmission and suspension. In many respects this series, known as BOV, is similar to the US LAV-150 series multi-mission vehicle developed in the 1960s and since built in large numbers, mainly for export.

BOV-VP APC has commander and driver front, each provided with a roof hatch, raised troop compartment centre, engine and transmission rear. T roops normally enter and leave via door in side of hull between road wheels. Armament comprises 7.62mm pintle-mounted MG with bank of three electrically operated smoke grenade dischargers mounted on hull side firing forwards.

Standard equipment includes day/night vision equipment, heater and communications equipment. Some BOV-VP vehicles have been fitted with wire mesh screens along side of the hull that folds forwards through 90 degrres when required.

Variants

BOV-1 is anti-tank version. Mounted on hull roof are two pods, each containing three ATGWs based on Soviet AT-3 Sagger but fitted with semi-automatic guidance system.
BOV-3 triple 20mm SPAAG system (see SPAAGs).
BOV-30 twin 30mm SPAAG system (see SPAAGs).

Status

Production complete. In service with former Yugoslavia.

Manufacturer

Former Yugoslav state factories.

Above: BOV-VP APC

6x6 VEHICLES

Steyr-Daimler-Puch Pandur APC (Austria)

Key recognition features

● Box-like hull with nose sloping back under front of vehicle, well sloped glacis plate with driver to left rear and engine compartment to the right. Horizontal hull top extends to rear
● Upper part of hull sides above road wheels slope inwards with optional firing ports/vision devices in either side
● Three road wheels either side with equal space between them

Specifications

Crew: 2 + 8
Configuration: 6 x 6
Armament: 1 x 12.7 mm MG, 2 x 3 smoke grenade launchers
Ammunition: 1000 x 12.7 mm
Length: 5.697 m
Width: 2.5 m
Height: 1.82 m
Ground clearance: 0.43 m
Wheelbase: 1.53 m + 1.53 m
Weight, combat: 13 000 kg
Weight, empty: 9800 kg
Power-to-weight ratio: 26.6 hp/t
Engine: Steyr WD 612.95 6-cylinder turbocharged diesel, developing 260 hp at 2400 rpm
Max road speed: 100 km/h
Maximum road speed: 650 km
Fuel capacity: 275 l
Fording: 1.2 m
Vertical obstacle: 0.5 m
Trench: 1.1 m
Gradient: 70%
Side slope: 40%
Armour: 8 mm (estimate)
Armour type: steel
NBC system: yes
Night vision equipment: yes

Development

The Pandur 6 x 6 armoured personnel carrier was developed as a private venture by Steyr-Daimler-Puch. The first prototypes were shown in 1985 and in 1994 the Austrian army ordered 68 Pandurs for use by Austrian forces serving with the UN. Deliveries began in 1995.

The driver is seated front left, with the commander to his rear and the engine compartment to the right. The troop compartment extends to the rear and has roof hatches and firing ports/vision devices. The version for the Austrian army has a raised rear troop compartment with spall liners, mine protection mats and a heater. The commander/gunner has a 12.7 mm machine gun in a protected position.

Standard equipment includes power steering, fire detection and suppression systems and a central tyre pressure regulation system. An amphibious version has been developed.

Variants

Ambulance
Anti-aircraft
Anti-tank (HOT or TOW)
Armoured reconnaissance scout vehicle (30 mm)
Armoured reconnaissance fire support vehicle (90 mm)
Command and control vehicle
Mechanised Infantry Combat Vehicle
Reconaissance vehicle

Status

In production. In service with the Austrian army.

Manufacturer

Steyr-Daimler-Puch

Above: Pandur

Above right: Pandur with 25mm turret

Right: ARSV 30

Far right: Pandur (unarmed)

Cougar Diesel Division, General Motors of Canada, Armoured Vehicle General Purpose (Canada)

Key recognition features

● Pointed hull front with nose sloping under hull to front wheel station, well sloped glacis plate leads up to horizontal hull top which extends to vertical hull rear with two doors. Turret mounted centre of hull roof

● Hull side welded mid-way up then slopes inwards at top and bottom, two firing ports with vision block above each over second and third road wheel station

● Three road wheels each side with distinct gap between first and second, propeller to immediate rear of third road wheel

Specifications

Crew: 3+6
Configuration: 6x6
Armament: 1 x 12.7mm MG, 1 x 7.62mm MG (coaxial), 2 x 4 smoke grenade dischargers
Ammunition: 1,000 x 12.7mm, 4,400 x 7.62mm
Length: 5.968m
Width: 2.53m
Height overall: 2.53m
Height hull top: 1.85m
Ground clearance: 0.392m
Wheelbase: 2.04m + 1.04m
Weight, combat: 10,500kg
Power-to-weight ratio: 20.46hp/tonne
Engine: Detroit Diesel 6V-53T, 6-cylinder diesel developing 215hp
Maximum road speed: 101.5km/hr
Maximum water speed: 7km/hr
Maximum road range: 603km
Fuel capacity: 204 lit
Fording: Amphibious
Vertical obstacle: 0.381m to 0.508m
Trench: Not applicable
Gradient: 60%
Side slope: 30%
Armour: 10mm (maximum)
Armour type: Steel
NBC system: None
Night vision equipment: Yes (passive for driver)

Note: Above relates to Wheeled Armoured Personnel Carrier Grizzly

Development

In 1974 the Canadian Armed Forces issued a requirement for an Armoured Vehicle General Purpose and after evaluating three prototype vehicles selected the Swiss MOWAG Piranha 6x6. Production was undertaken in Canada by Diesel Division, General Motors of Canada, first production vehicles completed in 1979. By the time production was completed in 1982, 491 had been built in three versions. More recently the Diesel Division, General Motors of Canada has built the Light Armored Vehicle (LAV) family of vehicles for Australia, Canada, the US Marine Corps and Saudi Arabia and the Bison (8x8) for the Canadian Armed Forces (qv).

Grizzly Wheeled Armoured Personnel Carrier (WAPC) has driver front left, commander to rear, engine compartment front right and turret in centre. Turret has one 12.7mm and one 7.62mm MG with manual traverse through 360° and elevation from -8° to 55°. Six infantrymen sit rear and enter and leave via two doors in hull rear. All three versions fully amphibious with two propellers, one each side at rear. Before entering the water a trim vane is erected at front and bilge pumps switched on.

Variants

Cougar 76mm Gun Wheeled Fire Support Vehicle (WFSV) is fitted with complete Alvis Scorpion turret with 76mm gun and 7.62mm coaxial MG. A total of 195 was built.
Husky Wheeled Maintenance and Recovery Vehicle, of which

27 were built, has roof-mounted hydraulic crane and crew of three.

All Canadian Armed Forces 6x6 vehicles are now fitted with the upgraded suspension fitted to the 8x8 vehicles which gives improved cross-country mobility.

Status
Production complete. In service with Canadian Armed Forces only.

Manufacturer
Diesel Division, General Motors of Canada Limited, London, Ontario, Canada.

Above: Canadian army Grizzly on exercise in Norway

Right: Husky Wheeled Maintenance and Recovery vehicle

NORINCO WZ 523 APC (China)

Key recognition features

● Long box-shaped hull similar to Belgian SIBMAS (6x6) APC, trim vane mounted on glacis plate, windscreen above covered by shutters hinged at top, horizontal hull top, vertical hull rear with single door opening to right
● Hull sides almost vertical, door in each side to rear of first road wheel, 12.7mm roof-mounted MG, roof hatches above rear troop compartment
● Three road wheels each side, second and third road wheels close together

Specifications

Crew: 2+10
Configuration: 6x6
Armament: 1 x 12.7mm MG
Ammunition: 600 x 12.7mm
Length: 6.02m
Width: 2.55m
Height with MG: 2.73m
Weight, combat: 11,200kg
Power-to-weight ratio: 14.73hp/tonne
Engine: EQ 6105 water-cooled petrol developing 165hp
Maximum road speed: 80km/hr
Maximum water speed: 7km/hr
Maximum range: 600km
Fuel capacity: 255 lit
Fording: Amphibious
Gradient: 60%
Side slope: 30%

Development

During a parade in Beijing in October 1984 a new Chinese 6x6 APC was seen in public for the first time. It is very similar to the Belgian SIBMAS and South African Ratel (6x6) and is believed to have the Chinese designation WZ 523; US Army refers to it as M1984. It is fully amphibious, propelled by two waterjets mounted one each side of hull at rear. Main armament comprises roof-mounted 12.7mm Type 54 MG with lateral protection for gunner.

Variants

No known variants, but other models could include command post vehicle, ambulance, mortar carrier and anti-tank vehicle with missiles.

Status

Production probably complete.

Manufacturer

Chinese state arsenals.

Right: Type WZ 523 (6x6) (via G Jacobs)

NORINCO WZ 551 APC (China)

Key recognition features

● Box type hull with nose sloping back under hull front, almost horizontal glacis plate leading to well sloped hull front with two large windows with flaps above. Horizontal hull roof and almost vertical hull rear with one large door
● Upper part of hull slopes inwards with firing ports in either side towards rear, exhaust pipe runs alongside upper part of left hull side. When armed, turret is normally on centre of hull roof
● Three large rubber tyred road wheels each side with shrouded propeller at rear each side

Specifications

Crew: 3 + 9
Configuration: 6 x 6
Armament: 1 x 25 mm cannon, 1 x 7.62 mm MG, 2 x 4 smoke grenade dischargers
Ammunition: 400 x 25 mm, 1000 x 7.62 mm
Length: 6.65 m
Width: 2.8 m
Height: 1.95 m (hull top), 2.89 m (turret top)
Ground clearance: 0.41 m
Wheelbase: 1.9 m + 1.9 m
Weight, combat: 15 300 kg
Weight, empty: 13 300 kg
Power-to-weight ratio: 16.73 hp/t
Engine: Deutz BF8L413F V8 diesel developing 256 hp at 2500 rpm
Maximum road speed: 85 km/h
Maximum road range: 600 km
Fuel capacity: 300 l (estimate)
Fording: amphibious
Vertical obstacle: 0.5 m
Trench: 1.2 m
Gradient: 60%
Side slope: 30%
Armour: 8 mm (maximum) (estimate)
Armour type: steel
NBC system: yes
Night vision equipment: yes

Development

The NORINCO (Chinese North Industries Corporation) WZ 551 (6 x 6) APC is very similar in appearance to the French VAB (4 x 4 and 6 x 6) series which are covered in the previous entry and was first observed in the mid-1980s. Although the 6 x 6 version is the most common a quantity of 4 x 4 models have been built and there is also a projected 8 x 8 version.

The layout is similar to the VAB with the commander and driver at the front, engine compartment to rear of the driver and troop compartment extending to the rear. The latter has roof hatches, firing ports and a large door that opens to the right.

The specification above relates to the model armed with a one man turret armed with a 25 mm externally mounted cannon and a 7.62 mm co-axial machine gun. Turret traverse is 360° with weapon elevation from -8° to +55°.

The WZ 551 is fully amphibious being propelled in the water by a single shrouded propeller mounted at the rear of the hull and standard equipment includes run-flat tyres and a fire detection and suppression system.

Variants

Ambulance, raised roof
Anti-tank (4 x 4) with Red Arrow 8 ATGW
APC, armed with 12.7 mm MG
IFV, turret armed with 25 mm cannon and 7.62 mm MG
IFV, turret of WZ 501 IFV (similar to Russian BMP-1)
NGV-1 IFV, fitted with Giat Industries Dragar turret 122 mm 8 x 8 SPG, projected
SAM, with four fire and forget missiles

Status

In production. In service with Bosnia-Herzegovina and China.

Manufacturer

Chinese state factories.

Left:
WZ 551 with 25 mm turret

Right:
WZ 551 with 25 mm turret

Below left:
WZ 551 with 25 mm turret

Below right
WZ 551 with French Dragar turret

SIBMAS APC (Belgium)

Key recognition features

● Long box-shaped hull, driver front, large windows to front and sides, horizontal roof, hull rear slopes inwards with engine compartment left and entry door right rear
● Hatch over driver's position, turret to immediate rear of driver's position, three rectangular roof hatches to turret rear, one left and two right. Externally mounted 7.62mm anti-aircraft MG on roof at right rear
● Three large road wheels, forward-opening door each side of hull to rear of first road wheel station, two rear road wheels close together

Specifications

Crew: 3+11
Configuration: 6x6
Armament: Depends on role
Ammunition: Depends on role
Length, hull: 7.32m
Width: 2.5m
Height, turret top: 2.77m
Height, hull top: 2.24m
Ground clearance: 0.4m
Wheelbase: 2.8m + 1.4m
Weight, combat: 14,500 to 18,500kg (depends on role)
Weight, unloaded: 13,200kg (eg without turret)
Power-to-weight ratio (at 16,000kg): 20hp/tonne
Engine: MAN D 2566 MK 6-cylinder in-line water-cooled turbocharged diesel developing 320hp at 1,900rpm
Maximum road speed: 100km/hr
Maximum water speed (wheels): 4km/hr
Maximum water speed (propellers): 11km/hr
Maximum road range: 1,000km
Fuel capacity: 400 lit
Fording: Amphibious
Vertical obstacle: 0.7m
Trench: 1.5m
Gradient: 70%
Side slope: 40%
Armour: Classified
Armour type: Steel
NBC system: Optional
Night vision equipment: Optional

Development

SIBMAS (6x6) wheeled armoured vehicle range was designed as a private venture from 1975 by BN Constructions Ferroviaires et MÈtalliques, first prototype completed in 1976. In appearance SIBMAS is similar to the South African Ratel (6x6) infantry fighting vehicle (qv).

In 1981 Malaysia ordered 196 SIBMAS vehicles, delivered between 1983 and 1985 in two versions, 162 Armoured Fire Support Vehicle 90s (AFSV-90) with CM 90 turret, and 24 ARVs. In mid-1985 the SIBMAS Division of BN was transferred to Belgian Mechanical Fabrication. The SIBMAS production line was closed some time ago and the vehicle is no longer being marketed.

Drivers sits front with weapon station on roof to his rear, troop compartment extends to rear of hull, engine compartment is left rear of vehicle. Three entry doors, one in each side and one at rear, and three roof hatches. Troop compartment has firing ports and vision devices.

Standard equipment includes run-flat tyres, optional equipment includes night vision equipment, propellers, winch, heater, air-conditioning system and NBC pack. Wide range of turrets including twin 7.62mm MG, 20mm cannon, twin 20mm anti-aircraft, up to two-man turret with 90mm gun.

Variants

SIBMAS can be adapted for a wide range of roles including mortar carrier, cargo vehicle, command post, ambulance, and recovery (used by Malaysia, with 20,000kg winch, 10,500kg crane and front and rear stabilising blades).
AFSV-90 has two-man CM 90 turret armed with 90mm Cockerill gun with 7.62mm coaxial and 7.62mm anti-aircraft MG and eight smoke/fragmentation grenade launchers each side of turret.

Status

Production complete. In service with Malaysia only.

Manufacturer

Cockerill Mechanical Industries.

Above: SIBMAS (6x6)

Above right: SIBMAS (6x6) with CM 90 turret

Right: SIBMAS (6x6) with CM 90 turret

ENGESA EE-11 Urutu APC (Brazil)

Key recognition features

● Nose slopes back to just forward of front road wheels at 60o, recessed headlamps, glacis plate has driver's position left and engine compartment right, horizontal roof and vertical hull rear, large door in rear opening to left

● Hull sides vertical half-way up then slope slightly inwards to hull roof, single door on left side of hull to rear of first road wheel station, earlier Mks have door in each side, four outward-opening roof hatches over rear troop compartment

● Three road wheels each side with rear wheels close together, ENGESA boomerang suspension which keeps both wheels in contact with ground

Specifications (Mk VII)

Crew: 1+12
Configuration: 6x6
Armament: 1 x 12.7mm MG, 2 x 2 smoke grenade dischargers
Ammunition: 1,000 x 12.7mm
Length: 6.1m
Width: 2.65m
Height top of MG mount: 2.9m
Height hull top: 2.125m
Ground clearance: 0.38m
Wheelbase: 3.05m
Weight, combat: 14,000kg
Weight, unloaded: 11,000kg
Power-to-weight ratio: 18.6hp/tonne
Engine: Detroit Diesel 6V-53T 6-cylinder water-cooled diesel developing 260hp at 2,800rpm
Maximum road speed: 105km/hr
Maximum water speed: 8km/hr
Maximum road range: 850km
Fuel capacity: 380 lit
Fording: Amphibious
Vertical obstacle: 0.6m
Trench: Not applicable
Gradient: 60%
Side slope: 30%
Armour: Classified
Armour type: Steel (2 layers)
NBC system: Optional
Night vision equipment: Optional

Development

EE-11 Urutu (6x6) was developed to meet the requirements of Brazilian Army with first prototype completed in 1970 and first production vehicles in 1974. It shares many automotive components with ENGESA EE-9 Cascavel (6x6) armoured car developed at the same time. ENGESA is no longer trading.

All vehicles have same basic layout with driver front left, engine to right and troop compartment extending back to rear. Troops enter and leave via door in each side and one in rear (except on Mk V which has no door in right side owing to larger engine compartment). Armament is usually mounted to rear of driver and ranges from pintle-mounted 7.62mm or 12.7mm MG to turret with 60mm breech-loaded mortar or 25mm cannon. Over top of troop compartment are four roof hatches.

EE-11 Urutu has had seven marks, I, II, III, IV, V, VI and VII, main difference being the engine (Mercedes-Benz or Detroit Diesel) and transmission (manual or automatic). Late production vehicles have run-flat tyres and central tyre pressure regulation system. The Mark VII has the turbocharged diesel in place of the standard 6V-53 developing 212hp installed in the Mk III. Vehicle is fully amphibious, propelled by its wheels. Before entering the water a trim vane is erected at front of hull. Wide range of optional equipment available including firing ports, vision blocks, 5,000kg capacity winch, NBC system and night vision devices.

Variants

In addition to armament options, the following versions are available: 81mm mortar carrier, ambulance with higher roof, cargo carrier, armoured fire support vehicle with 90mm turret as fitted to EE-9 Cascavel armoured car, command post vehicle, recovery vehicle, anti-aircraft vehicle with twin 20mm cannon, and internal security vehicle with obstacle-clearing blade at front of hull.

Status

Production complete. Known users include Angola, Bolivia, Brazil (Army and Marines), Chile, Colombia, Cyprus, Gabon, Guyana, Iraq, Jordan, Libya, Morocco, Surinam, Tunisia, United Arab Emirates, Uruguay and Venezuela.

Manufacturer

ENGESA, Sao JosÈ dos Campos, Brazil.

Above: ENGESA EE-11 Urutu (6x6) APC

Above right: ENGESA EE-11 Urutu (6x6) with 90mm turret

Right: ENGESA EE-11 Urutu (6x6) with one-man machine gun turret

ENGESA EE-9 Cascavel Armoured Car (Brazil)

Key recognition features

● Nose slopes back under hull with recesses in upper part for headlamps, well-sloped glacis plate leads up to horizontal hull top which extends to rear, driver's position front left, turret centre, engine rear. Vertical hull rear with horizontal air louvres

● Turret has flat sides and rear which slope slightly inwards, smoke grenade dischargers mounted each side at rear, 90mm barrel has muzzle brake with three vertical slots, commander's cupola on left side of turret roof

● Three road wheels each side (rear two mounted close together on boomerang suspension to maintain contact with ground)

Specifications (Mk IV)

Crew: 3
Configuration: 6x6
Armament: 1 x 90mm, 1 x 7.62mm MG (coaxial), 1 x 7.62mm or 12.7mm MG (anti-aircraft), 2 x 3 smoke grenade dischargers
Ammunition: 44 x 90mm, 2,200 x 7.62mm
Length gun forwards: 6.2m
Length hull: 5.2m
Width: 2.64m
Height to top of commander's cupola: 2.68m
Height to turret roof: 2.28m
Ground clearance: 0.34m (front axle)
Ground clearance: 0.5m (hull centre)
Wheelbase: 2.343m + 1.414m
Weight, combat: 13,400kg
Weight, empty: 10,900kg
Power-to-weight ratio: 15.82hp/tonne
Engine: Detroit Diesel model 6V-53N 6-cylinder water-cooled diesel developing 212hp at 2,800rpm
Maximum road speed: 100km/hr
Maximum range: 880km
Fuel capacity: 390 lit
Fording: 1m
Vertical obstacle: 0.6m
Trench: Not applicable
Gradient: 60%
Side slope: 30%
Armour: Classified
Armour type: Steel (2 layers)
NBC system: None
Night vision equipment: Optional (passive for commander, gunner and driver)

Development

EE-9 Cascavel (6x6) was developed by ENGESA to meet the requirements of the Brazilian Army and shares many common components with EE-11 Urutu (6x6) APC developed about the same time. First prototypes of EE-9 were completed in November 1970, pre-production vehicles following in 1972/73 and first production vehicles in 1974.

First production vehicles for the Brazilian Army had 37mm guns, while those for export had a French 90mm turret as installed on the AML 90 (4x4) armoured car. For some years all production EE-9s have had an ENGESA ET-90 turret armed with an ENGESA EC-90 gun.

Marks I, II, III, IV and V of EE-9 Cascavel have been built so far by ENGESA. Layout of all vehicles is similar with driver front left, two-man turret centre, engine and transmission rear. Turret has a 90mm gun which elevates from -8° to 15° under manual control, turret traverses manually through 360°. A 7.62mm MG is mounted coaxial to left of main armament, plus a cupola with externally mounted 12.7mm M2 HB MG which can be aimed and fired from inside the vehicle.

Standard equipment includes central tyre pressure regulation system and run-flat tyres. A wide range of optional equipment includes different sights, laser rangefinder, fire detection and suppression system, fire-control system, power traverse and different engines, 190hp Mercedes-Benz diesel or 212hp Detroit Diesel.

Variants

No variants except for models mentioned above.

Status

Production complete. In service with Bolivia, Brazil (Army and Marines), Burkina Faso, Chile, Colombia, Cyprus, Ecuador, Gabon, Iran, Iraq, Libya, Nigeria, Paraguay, Surinam, Togo, Tunisia, Uruguay, Zimbabwe and other countries.

Manufacturer

ENGESA, Sao Jose dos Campos, Brazil.

Above: ENGESA EE-9 Cascavel

Above Right: ENGESA EE-9 Cascavel

Right: ENGESA EE-9 Cascavel with 7.62mm AA MG

339

SISU XA-180 APC (Finland)

Key recognition features

● Hull sides and rear almost vertical with flat roof and pointed nose, trim vane on nose top
● Commander and driver at far front, each with side door, large windscreen covered by shutter hinged at top
● Three equally spaced road wheels each side, two doors in hull rear, shrouded propeller under each hull side at rear

Specifications

Crew: 2+10
Configuration: 6x6
Armament: 1 x 12.7mm MG, 1 x 4 smoke grenade dischargers
Ammunition: 1,000 x 12.7mm (estimate)
Length: 7.35m
Width: 2.9m
Height: 2.3m
Ground clearance: 0.4m
Weight, combat: 15,500kg
Weight, empty: 12,500kg
Power-to-weight ratio: 15.22hp/tonne
Engine: Valmet 6-cylinder, water-cooled, turbocharged diesel developing 236hp
Maximum road speed: 95km/hr
Maximum water speed: 10km/hr
Fuel capacity: 290 lit
Fording: Amphibious
Vertical obstacle: 0.6m
Trench: 1m
Gradient: 70%
Side slope: 60%
Armour: 10mm (maximum) (estimate)
Armour type: Steel
NBC system: Optional
Night vision equipment: Optional

Development

To replace Russian-supplied BTR-60PB (8x8) APCs in service with Finnish Army, SISU and Valment each built prototypes of a new 6x6 APC in 1982. Following extensive trials with both vehicles SISU XA-180 was selected in 1983 and is now in production and service with Finnish Army. XA-180 uses many automotive components of the SISU SA-150 VK (4x4) 6,500kg truck, also in service with Finnish Army.

Hull is all-welded armour with commander and driver front, engine compartment to rear of driver on left side and troop compartment rear. Troops sit five each side at rear on bench seats, and enter and leave via twin doors in hull rear, one of which has firing port and vision block. Two roof hatches over troop compartment and three vision blocks in each side with firing port beneath. Steering power-assisted on front two axles and vehicle fully amphibious, propelled by two propellers under hull rear. Before entering water a trim vane is erected at front of hull. Standard equipment includes front-mounted winch with 50m of 16mm cable and capacity of 10 tonnes, engine compartment fire suppression system. Armament normally comprises a roof-mounted 7.62mm or 12.7mm MG, the latter can be ring or turret mounted.

The SISU XA-180 has now been followed in production by the improved SISU XA-185 which has a more powerful engine.

Variants

Air defence, armed with Thomson-CSF Crotale New Generation SAM system, used by Finland only.
Radar, Finland has a number of vehicles with the Giraffe air surveillance radar.
Other versions are believed to include command post with projected versions including anti-tank, mortar carrier, ambulance and repair and recovery.

Status

In production. In service with Finnish Army, and used by Austria, Finland, Ireland, Norway and Sweden when operating as part of United Nations forces.

Manufacturer
SISU Defence OY, Hameenlinna, Finland.

Above: SISU XA-180 (6x6)

*Above right: SISU XA-180
(6x6)*

*Below right: SISU XA-180
(6x6)*

Panhard ERC 90 F4 Sagaie Armoured Car (France)

Key recognition features

● Well sloped glacis plate with driver's hatch in upper part which cannot be seen from side owing to large sheet metal covering, rear-opening side door between first and second wheel stations
● Turret centre of hull, long-barrelled 90mm gun with thermal sleeve and single baffle muzzle brake, two smoke grenade dischargers each side of turret towards rear
● Three road wheels each side with largest gap between first and second road wheel, sheet metal sides above rear road wheels ribbed horizontally

Specifications

Crew: 3
Configuration: 6x6
Armament: 1 x 90mm, 1 x 7.62mm MG (coaxial), 1 x 7.62mm MG AA (optional), 2 x 2 smoke grenade dischargers
Ammunition: 20 x 90mm, 2,000 x 7.62mm
Length gun forwards: 7.693m
Length hull: 5.098m
Width: 2.495m
Height: 2.254m (overall), 1.502m (hull top)
Ground clearance: 0.294m (road), 0.344m (cross-country)
Wheelbase: 1.63m + 1.22m
Weight, combat: 8,100kg
Power-to-weight ratio: 19.13hp/tonne
Engine: Peugeot V-6 petrol developing 155hp at 5,250rpm
Maximum road speed: 95km/hr
Maximum water speed (wheels): 4.5km/hr
Maximum water speed (hydrojets): 9.5km/hr
Maximum road range: 700km
Fuel capacity: 242 lit
Fording: Amphibious
Vertical obstacle: 0.8m
Trench: 1.1m
Gradient: 60%
Side slope: 30%
Armour: 10mm (maximum hull) (estimate)
Armour type: Steel
NBC system: Optional
Night vision equipment: Optional (passive)

Development

ERC (Engin de Reconnaissance Cannon) 6x6 armoured cars were developed as a private venture by Panhard from 1975, first production vehicles completed at its new Marolles factory in 1979. ERC shares many common component with the Panhard VCR 6x6 armoured personnel carriers developed at the same time. Although the ERC range was developed specifically for export it was adopted by the French Army, first vehicles delivered in 1984.

Drivers sits front, two-man turret centre, engine and transmission rear. GIAT TS 90 turret is armed with 90mm gun that fires canister, HE, HE long-range, HEAT, smoke and APFSDS ammunition. Turret has manual traverse through 360°, manual elevation from -8° to +15°. This is usually referred to as the ERC-1 Sagaie.

Basic vehicle is fully amphibious, propelled by its wheels, although waterjets can be fitted if required. Steering is power-assisted on front two wheels. Centre road wheel each side is normally raised when travelling. A wide range of optional equipment is available including NBC system, night vision, land navigation, air-conditioning system/heater.

Variants

ERC 90 F4 Sagaie TTB 190 has SAMM 90mm TTB 190 turret.
ERC 90 F4 Sagaie 2 is slightly larger with two engines.
ERC 90 F1 Lynx has Hispano-Suiza Lynx 90mm turret as on AML armoured car. This is usually referred to as the ERC-1 Lynx.
ERC 60-20 Serval has Hispano-Suiza Serval turret armed with 60mm breech loaded mortar, 20mm cannon and 7.62mm MG.
ERC anti-aircraft, Gabon has model with turret armed with twin 20mm cannon.
ERC anti-aircraft, can be fitted with turret with six Mistral SAMs in ready-to-launch position.

Status
In production. In service with Argentina (Lynx 90), Chad (Lynx 90), France (ERC 90 F4 Sagaie), Gabon (Sagaie 2 TTB 190 and twin 20mm TAB 220 turret), Ivory Coast (ERC 90 F4 Sagaie) and Mexico (Lynx).

Manufacturer
SociÈtÈ de Constructions Panhard et Levassor, Paris, France.

Above: Panhard ERC 90 F4 Sagaie

Above right: Panhard ERC 90 F4 Sagale

Right: Panhard ERC 90 F1 Lynx

GIAT AMX-10RC Reconnaissance Vehicle (France)

Key recognition features

● Pointed nose with trim vane folded back onto glacis plate, driver has half-circular cupola on left side of glacis, hull top to his rear horizontal, vertical hull rear

● Turret centre of hull, commander's cupola right and large periscopic sight to his front, 105mm gun with double baffle muzzle brake overhangs front of vehicle

● Three equally spaced road wheels each side which can be raised or lowered by driver. French Army vehicles have waterjet inlets to rear of last road wheels with outlet on hull rear

Specifications

Crew: 4
Configuration: 6x6
Armament: 1 x 105mm, 1 x 7.62mm MG (coaxial), 2 x 2 smoke grenade dischargers
Ammunition: 38 x 105mm, 4,000 x 7.62mm
Length gun forwards: 9.15m
Length hull: 6.357m
Width: 2.95m
Height: 2.66m (overall), 2.29m (turret top)
Ground clearance: 0.35m (normal)
Wheelbase: 1.55m + 1.55m
Weight, combat: 15,880kg
Weight, empty: 14,900kg
Power-to-weight ratio: 16.45hp/tonne
Engine: Baudouin Model 6F 11 SRX diesel developing 280hp at 3000rpm
Maximum road speed: 85km/hr
Maximum water speed: 7.2km/hr
Maximum road range: 1,000km
Fuel capacity: Not available
Fording: Amphibious
Vertical obstacle: 0.8m
Trench: 1.65m
Gradient: 50%
Side slope: 30%
Armour: Classified
Armour type: Aluminium
NBC system: Yes
Night vision equipment: Yes (passive for commander, gunner and driver)

Development

AMX-10RC was developed by the AMX to meet a French Army requirement to replace the Panhard EBR (8x8) armoured car. First prototype was completed in 1971, first production vehicles completed in 1978 and final deliveries made to French Army in 1987. The Moroccan vehicles are not fitted with a waterjet propulsion system.

Layout is conventional with driver front left, three-man turret centre, loader left, commander and gunner right, engine and transmission rear. The 105mm gun is mounted in a turret which traverses 360°, gun elevates from -8° to +20°. Computerised fire-control system includes laser rangefinder and LLLTV system for both commander and gunner. The 105mm gun fires HEAT, HE and practice rounds with an APFSDS round introduced in 1987.

AMX-10RC is fully amphibious, propelled by two waterjets. The driver can adjust suspension to suit terrain.

Variants

AMX-10RC driver training vehicle.
AMX-10RC 105 TML, still at prototype stage.
French Army AMX-10RC vehicles are to be upgraded in a number of key areas including installation of a 105mm gun that can fire NATO types of ammunition, thermal camera, decoy system, additional armour, central tyre pressure regulation system, electronic control system for the transmission and a Land Battlefield Management System.

Status

Production complete. In service with France, Morocco and Qatar.

Manufacturer
GIAT Industries, Roanne, France.

Above: AMX-10RC (6x6)

Above right: AMX-10RC (6x6)

Right: AMX-10RC (6x6)

Renault VBC 90 Armoured Car (France)

Key recognition features

● Very high hull with sloping glacis plate, driver sits front left, three bullet-proof windows, horizontal hull top, turret centre, vertical hull rear
● Three very large road wheels each side with equal spaces between, louvres on left side of hull at rear
● Turret has long-barrelled 90mm gun with single baffle muzzle brake and thermal sleeve that overhangs front of vehicle

Specifications

Crew: 3
Configuration: 6x6
Armament: 1 x 90mm, 1 x 7.62mm MG (coaxial), 1 x 7.62mm MG (anti-aircraft) (optional), 2 x 2 smoke grenade dischargers
Ammunition: 45 x 90mm, 4000 x 7.62mm
Length gun forwards: 8.085m
Length hull: 5.63m
Width: 2.5m
Height: 2.552m (turret top), 1.737m (hull top)
Ground clearance: 0.4m (axle), 0.5m (hull)
Wheelbase: 1.5m + 1.5m
Weight, combat: 13,500kg
Power-to-weight ratio: 16bhp/tonne
Engine: Renault MIDS 06.20.45 in-line water-cooled turbocharged diesel developing 220hp at 2,300rpm (or MAN developing 220bhp)
Maximum road speed: 92km/hr
Maximum road range: 1,000km
Fording: 1.2m
Vertical obstacle: 0.5m
Trench: 1m
Gradient: 50%
Side slope: 30%
Armour: Classified
Armour type: Steel
NBC system: Optional
Night vision equipment: Optional

Renault VBC 90 (6x6)

Development

VBC 90 (Vehicule Blindé de Combat) was designed by Renault Vehicles Industriels for export and has many automotive components of the VAB 4x4 and 6x6 APCs such as engine, transmission and suspension. The first prototype was completed in 1979, first production vehicles following in 1981. The French Gendarmerie took delivery of the first of 28 VBC 90s in 1983; these have a SOPTAC 11 fire-control system incorporating a laser rangefinder.

Driver sits front left, two-man turret centre, engine and transmission rear. The GIAT TS-90 turret is also installed on the Panhard ERC 90 F4 Sagaie (6x6) and has a 90mm gun with 7.62mm MG mounted coaxial to left with optional 7.62mm anti-aircraft MG on turret roof. Turret traverse is powered through 360°, manual elevation from -8° to +15°.

Standard equipment includes front-mounted winch with capacity of 6,000kg, heater, and wide range of optional equipment including NBC system, different fire-control systems and night vision devices.

Variants

There were many variants of the Renault VBC 90 (6x6) armoured car but apart from the standard production model with the GIAT Industries TS-90 turret, none of these ever went into production or service.

Status

Production complete. No longer being marketed. In service with France and Oman.

Manufacturer

Renault Vehicules Industriels/Creusot-Loire Industrie, Saint Chamond, France.

Right: Renault VBC 90 (6x6)

Panhard VCR APC (France)

Key recognition features

● Glacis plate at about 45o with driver's hatch in upper part, step up to hull roof which extends to vertical hull rear with large door opening right
● Commander's cupola rear of driver on left side, engine compartment right, main armament on forward part of roof and secondary armament on rear. Rear troop compartment has two upward-opening flaps in each side
● Three road wheels each side, second wheel normally raised while travelling on roads. Hull sides vertical except for rear troop compartment which slopes inwards mid-way up

Specifications

Crew: 3 + 9
Configuration: 6x6
Armament: Depends on role
Ammunition: Depends on role
Length: 4.875m
Width: 2.5m
Height with 7.62mm MG: 2.56m
Height hull top: 2.13m
Ground clearance: 0.315m (4 wheels), 0.37m (6 wheels)
Wheelbase: 1.66m + 1.425m
Power-to-weight ratio: 18.35hp/tonne
Engine: Peugeot PRV V-6 petrol developing 145hp at 5,500rpm
Maximum road speed: 90km/hr
Maximum water speed: 4km/hr
Maximum road range: 700km
Fuel capacity: 242 lit
Fording: Amphibious
Vertical obstacle: 0.8m
Trench: 1.1m
Gradient: 60%
Side slope: 30%
Armour: 12mm (maximum)
Armour type: Steel
NBC system: Optional
Night vision equipment: Optional (passive)

Development

VCR (VÉhicule de Combat ✝ Roues) was developed as a private venture by Panhard and shares many automotive components with Panhard ERC range of 6x6 armoured cars. VCR was first

Above left: Panhard VCR (6x6) APC without armament

shown in 1977 and entered production in 1979. Largest order to date is 100 VCT/TH anti-tank vehicles for Iraq. Panhard has also built prototypes of the improved VCR TT 2 (6x6) APC but this has yet to enter production.

VCR is fully amphibious, propelled by its wheels. Standard equipment includes run-flat tyres, optional equipment includes front-mounted winch, air-conditioning system, NBC system and passive night vision equipment. Wide range of weapon stations including turret-mounted 12.7mm MG at front and ring-mounted 7.62mm MG at rear. Other options include turret with 60mm breech-loaded mortar, turret- or ring-mounted 20mm cannon, turret with MILAN ATGWs in ready-to-launch position.

Variants

VCR/AT repair vehicle has block and tackle at rear, tools and spare parts.
VCR/AA anti-aircraft vehicle has Bofors RBS-70 SAM, prototype only.
VCR/TH anti-tank vehicle has Euromissile UTM 800 turret with

four HOT ATGW in ready-to-launch position, GIAT Mascot 7.62mm remote-controlled MG rear.

VCR/IS ambulance has higher roof and medical equipment.

VCR/PC command post vehicle has extensive communications equipment. Also variant in electronic warfare role.

VCR/TT (4x4) is essentially 6x6 with centre wheel removed each side and replaced by waterjet. Used only by Argentina.

Status

Production as required. In service with Argentina (4x4), Iraq (6x6), Mexico (6x6) and United Arab Emirates (6x6).

Manufacturer

Société de Constructions MÈcaniques Panhard and Levassor, Paris, France.

Above: Panhard VCR/IS (6x6) ambulance

Left: Panhard VCR/PC (6x6) command post with EW system

GIAT VAB APC (France)

Key recognition features

● Box-type hull with nose sloping back under hull front, almost horizontal glacis plate leading to well sloped hull front with two windows, horizontal roof and almost vertical hull rear with two large opening rear doors

● Upper part of hull sides slope inwards, single door with window in each side of forward part of hull, three upward-opening shutters in each side at rear, exhaust pipe on right side of hull

● Two large rubber-tyred road wheels each side in 4x4 model, also 6x6 version with three equally spaced road wheels each side, waterjets sometimes mounted under hull at rear. Light armament normally mounted over front right of vehicle.

Specifications (4x4)

Crew: 2+10
Configuration: 4x4
Armament: 1 x 12.7mm MG (typical)
Length: 5.98m
Width: 2.49m
Height (hull top): 2.06m
Ground clearance: (axles) 0.4m, (hull) 0.5m
Wheelbase: 3m
Weight, combat: 13,000kg
Weight, empty: 10,200kg
Power-to-weight ratio: 16.92hp/tonne
Engine: Renault MIDS 06.20.45 six-cylinder in-line water-cooled turbocharged diesel developing 220hp at 2,200rpm
Maximum road speed: 92km/hr
Maximum water speed: 7km/hr
Maximum road range: 1,000km
Fuel capacity: 300 lit
Fording: Amphibious
Vertical obstacle: 0.5m
Trench: Not applicable
Gradient: 50%
Side slope: 35%
Armour: Classified
Armour type: Steel
NBC system: Yes
Night vision equipment: Yes (passive for driver)

Development

Prototypes of both 4x4 and 6x6 versions were built by Renault and Panhard to meet requirements of French Army for a Forward Area Armoured Vehicle (Véhicule de l'Avant Blindé). The 4x4 configuration was selected with first production vehicles completed at Saint Chamond in 1976. By late 1995 over 5,000 had been built for French Army (4x4) and for export (6x6 and 4x4). Production and marketing of the VAB family is now carried out by Giat Industries.

All versions have a similar layout with driver front left, commander/machine gunner right, engine compartment rear of driver, small passageway on right and troop compartment rear with seats down each side, roof hatches, two doors at rear and three hatches in each side. Fully amphibious, propelled by its wheels or by waterjets mounted at rear of hull. Before entering water a trim vane is erected at front.

In 1991 the VAB New Generation (VAB NG) was launched with many improvements. As of early 1996 no firm orders for this vehicle had been placed.

Variants

Variants are numerous and include infantry combat vehicle (with various turrets mounting 25mm or 20mm cannon), VAB Echelon (repair vehicle), VCAC HOT anti-tank vehicle with Mephisto system with four HOT missiles, VCAC HOT anti-tank vehicle with UTM 800 turret with four HOT missiles, VCAC MILAN with MILAN MCT turret with two MILAN missiles, VAB PC (command vehicle), VAB Transmission (communications vehicle), VAB engineer vehicle, electronic warfare carrier (Bromure), VAB Sanitaire (ambulance), VMO (internal security vehicle), VTM 120 (mortar towing vehicle with 120mm mortar), VPM 81 (81mm mortar in rear), anti-aircraft (2 x 20mm cannon, used by Oman), NBC reconnaissance, recovery, TOW ATGW and anti-aircraft with Matra Mistral SAMs. VAB components also used in VBC-90 (6x6) armoured car (qv).

Status
Production as required. In service with Brunei, Central African Republic, Cyprus, France, Ivory Coast, Lebanon, Mauritius, Morocco, Oman, Qatar, United Arab Emirates and other undisclosed countries.

Manufacturer
Giat Industries, France

Above left: VAB (4x4) without armament

Above: VAB Sanitaire (4x4) ambulance

Left: VAB (4x4) ACAC anti-tank with Mephisto launcher raised

Thyssen Henschel Transportpanzer 1 (Fuchs) APC (Germany)

Key recognition features

● Long box-shaped hull with pointed front, trim vane retracted onto glacis plate above which is large one-piece window covered by armoured shutter hinged at top, forward-opening door each side at hull front
● Flat horizontal roof with two circular hatches over front of vehicle, three hatches over rear troop compartment, twin doors at rear
● Three large road wheels each side with hull above sloping inwards. Six forward-firing smoke grenade dischargers and exhaust pipe on left side of hull

Specifications

Crew: 2+10
Configuration: 6x6
Armament: 1 x 7.62mm MG, 1 x 6 smoke grenade dischargers
Ammunition: 1,000 x 7.62mm (estimate)
Length: 6.3m
Width: 2.98m
Height: 2.30m (hull top)
Ground clearance: 0.506m (hull), 0.406m (axle)
Wheelbase: 1.75m + 2.05m
Weight, combat: 17,000kg
Weight, empty: 14,400kg
Power-to-weight ratio: 18.82hp/tonne
Engine: Mercedes-Benz Model OM 402A V-8 liquid-cooled diesel developing 320hp at 2,500rpm
Maximum road speed: 105km/hr
Maximum water speed: 10.5km/hr
Maximum road range: 800km
Fuel capacity: 390 lit
Fording: Amphibious
Vertical obstacle: 0.6m
Trench: 1.1m
Gradient: 70%
Side slope: 35%
Armour: Classified
Armour type: Steel
NBC system: Yes
Night vision equipment: Yes (driver has passive periscope)

Development

After building numerous prototypes of 4x4 and 6x6 amphibious armoured load carriers, the 6x6 was placed in production as Transportpanzer 1 (Fuchs) with 996 delivered to the German Army between 1979 and 1986.

Since then production has been resumed for the NBC reconnaissance vehicle which has been adopted by the US Army as the M93. During the Middle East conflict of 1991, Thyssen Henschel supplied these vehicles to Israel, United Kingdom and the United States.

Commander and driver sit at far front, engine compartment to their immediate rear on left side, small passageway on right side. Troop compartment extends right to rear, troops enter and leave via twin doors in rear. Transportpanzer is fully amphibious, two propellers mounted on each side under hull rear. Standard equipment includes NBC system, power-assisted steering on front two axles, engine compartment fire extinguishing system. Normal armament for German Army vehicles is 7.62mm MG above hull front on right side.

Variants

Models in service with Germany Army:
RASIT radar carrier with radar retracted into hull for travelling.
Command and communications vehicle with extensive communications equipment.
NBC reconnaissance vehicle.
Engineer vehicle carrying demolitions.
Electronic warfare, TPz 1 Eloka.
Supply carrier.
EOD vehicle, developed to prototype stage.
Transportpanzer 1 could be adopted for a wide range of roles including ambulance, mortar vehicle (81mm or 120mm), ATGW carrier, ambulance, cargo carrier, recovery or maintenance vehicle and infantry fighting vehicle with various types of weapon stations and firing ports/vision blocks.

Transportpanzer 1 (6x6)

Venezuela has taken delivery of 10 Transportpanzer 1s with one 12.7mm MG and one 7.62mm MG on roof. Prototype of an 8x8 Transportpanzer has been built. Components also used in Wildcat 2 x 30mm self-propelled anti-aircraft gun which is still at prototype stage.

Status
Production. In service with Germany, Israel, Saudi Arabia, The Netherlands, Turkey, United Kingdom, United States and Venezuela.

Manufacturer
Thyssen Henschel, Kassel, Germany.

Above right: Transportpanzer 1 (6x6) armed with 7.62mm MG (Michael Jerchel)

Right: NBC reconnaissance Tpz 1 used by US Army in NBC role (Michael Jerchel)

Komatsu Type 87 Reconnaissance and Patrol Vehicle (Japan)

Key recognition features

● Box-shaped hull with flat nose, well sloped glacis plate with driver's position on right side, horizontal hull top, vertical rear with engine on right side
● Turret in centre of hull has eight sides, all of which are vertical, 25mm cannon in forward part with 7.62mm coaxial MG to right
● Three large equally spaced road wheels each side with forward-opening door in left side between second and third road wheels

Specifications
Crew: 5
Configuration: 6x6
Armament: 1 x 25mm cannon, 1 x 7.62mm MG (coaxial), 2 x 3 smoke grenade dischargers
Length: 5.99m
Width: 2.48m
Height: 2.8m
Ground clearance: 0.45m
Wheelbase: 1.5m + 1.5m
Weight, combat: 15,000kg
Power-to-weight ratio: 20.33hp/tonne
Engine: Isuzu 10PBI water-cooled diesel developing 305hp at 2,700rpm
Maximum road speed: 100km/hr
Maximum road range: 500km
Fuel capacity: Not available
Fording: 1m
Vertical obstacle: 0.6m
Trench: 1.5m
Gradient: 60%
Side slope: 30%
Armour: Classified
Armour type: Aluminium
NBC system: None
Night vision equipment: Yes

Development
Type 87 has been developed to meet the requirements of the Japanese Ground Self Defence Force by Komatsu and shares many automotive components with the Type 82 Command and Communications Vehicle developed by Mitsubishi Heavy Industries. It is believe that the total requirements is for 250 vehicles.

Driver sits front right with radio operator to his left, two-man turret centre, engine rear on right side, observer facing rear on left side.

Two-man power-operated turret sits commander on right and gunner on left and has Oerlikon-Contraves 25mm KBA cannon with 7.62mm Type 74 MG mounted coaxial to left. Type 87 has no amphibious capability.

Variants
No variants.

Status
Production. In service with Japanese Ground Self Defence Force.

Manufacturer
Komatsu Limited, Minato-Ku, Japan.

Above: Type 87 Reconnaissance and Patrol Vehicle (Paul Beaver)

Above right: Type 87 Reconnaissance and Patrol Vehicle (Kensuke Ebata)

Right: Type 87 Reconnaissance and Patrol Vehicle (Kensuke Ebata)

Mitsubishi Type 82 Command and Communications Vehicle (Japan)

Key recognition features

● Three closely spaced large road wheels each side with hull line above road wheels
● Snub nose with glacis plate sloping up towards windscreen that extends across front of vehicle with smaller windows to sides, all of which can be covered by hatch covers hinged top; 7.62mm MG above forward hull
● Front two-thirds of hull roof horizontal, then slopes upwards at an angle for remaining third on which 12.7mm MG is mounted, large door in hull rear opens to right

Specifications

Crew: 8
Configuration: 6x6
Armament: 1 x 12.7mm MG, 1 x 7.62mm MG
Length: 5.72m
Width: 2.48m
Height without armament: 2.38m
Ground clearance: 0.45m
Wheelbase: 1.5m 1.5m
Weight, combat: 13,500kg
Weight, empty: 12,000kg
Power-to-weight ratio: 22.4hp/tonne
Engine: Isuzu 10PBI water-cooled diesel developing 305hp at 2,700rpm
Maximum road speed: 100km/hr
Maximum range: 500km
Fuel capacity: Not available
Fording: 1m
Vertical obstacle: 0.6m
Trench: 1.5m
Gradient: 60%
Side slope: 30%
Armour: Classified
Armour type: Steel (not confirmed)
NBC system: None
Night vision equipment: Yes (driver)

Development

In the early 1970s the Japanese Ground Self Defence Force issued a requirement for a new wheeled reconnaissance vehicle and, following trials with both 4x4s and 6x6s, the latter was selected for further development. This was subsequently standardised as Type 82 command and communications vehicle, the first ten approved in the 1982 defence budget. Under current plans it is expected that 250 vehicles will be supplied to the Japanese Ground Self Defence Force.

Driver sits front right, another crew member on left (who also mans pintle-mounted 7.62m MG above his position). Engine compartment is towards hull front on left side with passageway to rear crew compartment on right.

Remainder of crew sit on individual seats at rear and enter via a large door in hull rear; there is also a door between the second and third road wheels on the left side and between the first and second road wheels on the right side. All doors have vision port which can also be used as firing port. There are extra two vision ports on the right side and one on the left. The 12.7mm M2 HB MG has a shield and is mounted on the forward right part of the rear crew compartment roof, commander's cupola on the left.

More recently some vehicles have been fitted with a new roof-mounted cupola armed with 12.7mm MG that can be aimed and fired from within the vehicle.

Variants

No variants of the Type 82, but its automotive components are also used in the Type 87 reconnaissance and patrol vehicles (qv).

Status
In production. In service with the Japanese Ground Self Defence Force.

Manufacturer
Mitsubishi Heavy Industries, Tokyo, Japan.

Right: Type 82 with roof mounted cupola with 12.7mm MG (Kensuke Ebata)

357

BTR-152 APC (Russia)

Key recognition features

- 6x6 chassis with rear wheels mounted close together, sides and rear of troop compartment vertical, with corners sloping inwards
- Engine front with open-topped troop compartment rear, firing ports each side, single door each side to rear of engine compartment, twin doors rear with spare wheel and tyre
- Nose of BTR-152 has armoured louvres for engine cooling

Specifications (BTR-152V1)

Crew: 2+17
Configuration: 6x6
Armament: 1 x 7.62mm MG
Ammunition: 1,250 x 7.62mm
Length: 6.55m
Width: 2.32m
Height: 2.36m (without armament)
Ground clearance: 0.295m
Wheelbase: 3.3m 1.13m
Weight, combat: 8,950kg
Power-to-weight ratio: 12.29hp/tonne
Engine: ZIL-123 6-cylinder in-line water-cooled petrol developing 110hp at 3,000rpm
Maximum road speed: 75km/hr
Road range: 600km
Fuel capacity: 300 lit
Fording: 0.8m
Vertical obstacle: 0.6m
Trench: 0.69m
Gradient: 55%
Side slope: 30%
Armour: 4mm to 13.5mm
Armour type: Steel
NBC system: None
Night vision equipment: Yes (driver only, infra-red, on BTR-152V3)

Development

BTR-152 was developed after the Second World War, basically a much modified truck chassis with armoured body. First production vehicles completed in 1950 but it was replaced many years ago in the Soviet Army by BTR-60P series 8x8 APCs.

Commander and driver sit to rear of fully enclosed engine compartment at front, open-topped troop compartment to rear. Around top of troop compartment are three sockets for mounting 7.62mm or 12.7mm MGs. Some vehicles have front-mounted winch with capacity of 5,000kg.

Late vehicles have the central tyre pressure regulation system that allows the driver to adjust tyre pressure to suit terrain being crossed.

Variants

BTR-152, first model, no winch or tyre pressure system.
BTR-152V has external central tyre pressure regulation system, command version is BTR-1521.
BTR-152V1 has front-mounted winch and central tyre pressure regulation system with external air lines.
BTR-152V2 has central tyre pressure regulation system with external air lines, no winch.
BTR-152V3 has front-mounted winch, infra-red driving lights, central tyre pressure regulation system with internal air lines.
BTR-152K, same as BTR-152V3 but with full overhead armour protection for troop compartment.
BTR-152U command vehicle with much higher roof for command staff to stand upright, often tows trailer with generator.
BTR-152A anti-aircraft vehicle with turret armed with twin 14.5mm MGs, also fitted in BTR-40P.
BTR-152 with 23mm ZU-23 LAAG, some of which were captured by Israel in Lebanon, summer 1982.
BTR-152 with 12.7mm MGs. Egypt used BTR-152s with former Czechoslovak Quad 12.7mm M53 turret in rear.

BTR-152K (6x6)

Status

Production complete. In service with Afghanistan, Albania, Algeria, Angola, Bulgaria, Central African Republic, China, CIS, Congo, Cuba, Egypt, Ethiopia, Guinea, Guinea-Bissau, Hungary, Indonesia, Iran, Iraq, North Korea, Laos, Mali, Mongolia, Mozambique, Nicaragua, Poland, Romania, Sri Lanka, Sudan, Syria, Tanzania, Uganda, Yemen, former Yugoslavia, Vietnam and Zimbabwe.

Manufacturer

Former Soviet state factories.

Right: BTR-152V1 (6x6) APC (Michael Jerchel)

Above Right: BTR-152K (6x6) APC

Reumech Sandock Ratel 20
Infantry Fighting Vehicle (South Africa)

Key recognition features

● Long box-shaped hull, driver front, large windows to his front and sides, horizontal roof and vertical rear with engine on left rear side, entry door on right rear side

● Circular turret with raised cupola for commander on left side of roof to rear of driver, externally mounted 7.62mm anti-aircraft MG on roof at right side

● Three large road wheels, forward-opening door to rear of first road wheel, four firing ports and vision blocks in each side, two rear wheels close together

Specifications
Crew: 4+7
Configuration: 6x6
Armament: 1 x 20mm cannon, 1 x 7.62mm MG (coaxial), 1 x 7.62mm MG (anti-aircraft), 1 x 7.62mm MG (anti-aircraft, rear), 2 x 2 smoke grenade dischargers
Ammunition: 1,200 x 20mm, 6,000 x 7.62mm
Length of hull: 7.212m
Width: 2.516m
Height overall: 2.915m
Height hull top: 2.105m
Ground clearance: 0.34m
Wheelbase: 2.809m + 1.4m
Weight, combat: 18,500kg
Weight, empty: 16,500kg
Power-to-weight ratio: 15.24hp/tonne
Engine: D 3256 BTXF 6-cylinder in-line turbocharged diesel developing 282hp at 2,200rpm
Maximum road speed: 105km/hr
Maximum road range: 1,000lkm
Fuel capacity: 430 lit
Fording: 1.2m
Vertical obstacle: 0.6m
Trench: 1.15m
Gradient: 60%
Side slope: 30%
Armour: 20mm (maximum)
Armour type: Steel
Night vision equipment: Optional

Development
Ratel range of 6x6s was developed to meet the requirements of South African Army, first prototype completed in 1974 and first production vehicles in 1979. Production continued until early 1987 with about 1,200 built in three marks (1, 2 and 3) for both home and export.

Driver sits front with three large bullet-proof windows for observation to front and sides; windows can be covered by armoured shutters hinged at bottom.

Mounted on roof to rear of driver is manual turret with commander left and gunner right, turret traverse 360°, 20mm cannon and 7.62mm coaxial MG elevating from -8° to +38°, second 7.62mm MG on turret roof for air defence.

Seven infantrymen sit centre of vehicle with firing ports, vision blocks and roof hatches. Engine compartment is left rear with passageway, 7.62mm anti-aircraft MG mounted above on the right side.

Variants
Ratel 60 IFV has crew of 11 and two-man turret armed with 60mm mortar, 7.62mm coaxial and 7.62mm anti-aircraft MG, second 7.62mm anti-aircraft MG at right rear.
Ratel 90 FSV (fire support vehicle) has 10-man crew and similar turret to Eland 90 (4x4) armoured car's with 90mm gun, 7.62mm coaxial and 7.62mm anti-aircraft MG right rear.
Ratel 12.7mm command has nine-man crew and two-man turret with 12.7mm MG, 7.62mm anti-aircraft MG and second 7.62mm anti-aircraft MG right rear.
Ratel repair, basic Ratel fitted with a front mounted jib for

Ratel 20 (6x6) IFV

Above: Ratel 20 (6x6) IFV

Far left: Ratel (6x6) with turret for launching Swift ATGWs (Christopher F Foss)

Left: Ratel 90 (6x6) FSV

carrying out repairs in the field.

Ratel 81mm mortar has no turret and 81mm turntable mounted mortar firing through roof hatches.

Ratel anti-tank, fitted with new turret armed with three Swift laser guided ATGWs in ready-to-launch position and 7.62mm machine gun. In service with South African Armoured Corps.

Status

Production complete. In service with Morocco and South Africa.

Manufacturer

Reumech Sandock, Boksburg, Transvaal, South Africa.

361

SANTA BARBARA BMR-600 IFV (Spain)

Key recognition features

● Long box-shaped hull with pointed front and driver's compartment offset to left side
● Three large road wheels each side with equal gap between, hull line above wheel arches slopes slightly inwards, exhaust pipe right side of hull, power operated ramp at rear
● Basic Spanish Army BMR-600 has cupola with externally mounted 12.7mm MG on hull top to rear of driver's position

Specifications

Crew: 2+11
Configuration: 6x6
Armament: 1 x 12.7mm MG
Ammunition: 2,500 x 12.7mm
Length: 6.15m
Width: 2.5m
Height: 2.36m (including armament), 2m (hull top)
Ground clearance: 0.4m
Wheelbase: 1.65m + 1.65m
Weight, combat: 14,000kg
Power-to-weight ratio: 22hp/tonne
Engine: Pegaso 9157/8 6-cylinder in-line diesel developing 310hp at 2,200rpm
Maximum road speed: 103km/hr
Maximum water speed: 9KM/HR
Maximum range: 1,000km
Fuel capacity: 400 lit
Fording: Amphibious
Vertical obstacle: 0.6m
Trench: 1.5m
Gradient: 60%
Side slope: 30%
Armour: 38mm (maximum) (estimate)
Armour type: Aluminium
NBC system: Optional
Night vision equipment: Optional

Development

BMR-600 (Blindado Medio de Ruedas) was designed by the Spanish Army and Pegaso, first prototype completed in 1975 and first production vehicles delivered in 1979. It shares many components with the VEC (see ACRVs). Company designation for BMR-600 was BMR 3560.50.

Driver sits front left, MG cupola to his immediate rear, engine compartment to right, troop compartment extends to rear and has roof hatches and ramp at rear.

BMR-600 is fully amphibious, propelled by waterjets one each side at rear of hull. Standard equipment includes power steering, engine compartment fir extinguishing system, run-flat tyres and winch. Optional equipment includes different tyres, communications equipment, firing ports/vision blocks, night driving equipment and air-conditioning system.

Spanish Army BMR-600s have cupola with externally mounted 12.7mm M2 HB MG which can be aimed and fired from inside. Wide range of weapon stations available including turret-mounted 20mm cannon.

Variants

Command vehicle (3560.51)
Radio communications vehicle (3560.56).
Missile launcher (eg HOT) (3560.57).
81mm mortar carrier (3560.53E).
Combat vehicle with heavier armament such as 90mm gun (3564, for export only).
Ambulance (3560.54).
Recovery and maintenance vehicle (3560.55), towing 120mm mortar.

There is also a version with the 120mm mortar mounted in the rear of the vehicle, this is designated the 3560.59E.

Status

Production as required. In service with Egypt, Peru, Saudi Arabia and Spain.

Manufacturer

SANTA BARBARA, Madrid, Spain.

Above: BMR-600 with 7.62mm MG

Above right: BMR-600 with 12.7mm MG as used by Spanish Army (Pierre Touzin)

Right: BMR-600 with 12.7mm MG (Francisco A Marin)

SANTA BARBARA VEC Cavalry Scout Vehicle (Spain)

Key recognition features

● High hull with well sloped glacis plate with central driver's position, horizontal hull top with sloping back
● Turret centre of hull with slightly sloping front and sides, distinct chamfer between turret front and sides
● Three equally spaced road wheels each side with hull above road wheels sloping inwards

Specifications

Crew: 5
Configuration: 6x6
Armament: 1 x 25mm, 1 x 7.62mm MG (coaxial), 2 x 3 smoke grenade dischargers
Ammunition: 170 x 25mm (turret), 250 x 7.62mm (turret)
Length: 6.1m
Width: 2.5m
Height: 2.51m (turret roof), 2.00m (turret top)
Ground clearance: 0.4m
Wheelbase: 1.65m + 1.65m
Weight, combat: 13,750kg
Power-to-weight ratio: 22.25hp/tonne
Engine: Pegaso Model 9157/8 6-cylinder in-line turbocharged diesel developing 310hp at 2,200rpm
Maximum road speed: 103km/hr
Maximum water speed (wheels): 3km/hr
Maximum water speed (waterjets): 9km/hr
Maximum road range: 800km
Fuel capacity: 400 lit
Fording: Amphibious
Vertical obstacle: 0.6m
Trench: 1.5m
Gradient: 60%
Side slope: 30%
Armour: Classified
Armour type: Aluminium
NBC system: Optional
Night vision equipment: Optional

Development

VEC (Vehiculo de Exploracion de Caballeria) was developed by Pegaso to meet the requirements of the Spanish Army and uses many common components of the BMR-600 (6x6) infantry fighting vehicle. First five prototypes were completed in 1977/78, with a total Spanish Army requirement for 235 vehicles. (VEC is also known as Pegaso VEC 3562.) Driver sits front centre, two-man turret centre (Italian OTOBREDA T25 made under licence in Spain), engine to turret rear on left side. Fourth crew man sits turret rear on right side, fifth crew man to his front.

The T25 turret has full powered traverse through 360°, elevation powered from -10° to +50°, and 7.62mm MG mounted above.

The Spanish designation for the T25 turret is the CETME TC-15/M242. The 25mm cannon is the US M242 Bushmaster from McDonnell Douglas Helicopter Company and is also installed in the Bradley M2/M3 used by the US Army.

VEC is fully amphibious, propelled by its wheels; waterjets are an optional extra. Steering is power-assisted on front and rear axles, suspension is adjustable.

Optional equipment includes NBC system, night vision equipment, winch with capacity of 4,500kg, fire extinguishing system, larger tyres and land navigation system.

Variants

VEC for the export market has a wide range of other turrets to meet different mission requirements, such as anti-tank missile, air-defence (gun or missile), or French Hispano-Suiza 90mm turret as fitted to Panhard AML armoured car.
Spanish Army has some vehicles fitted with 20mm turret and 90mm turret (from AML).

Status
Production complete. In service with the Spanish Army.

Manufacturer
SANTA BARBARA, Madrid, Spain.

Right: VEC (6x6)

Alvis Saracen APC (UK)

Key recognition features

● Engine compartment far front, horizontal radiator louvres which extend to rear of first road wheel station, raised troop compartment to rear, hull sides sloping slightly inwards
● Troop compartment has three rectangular firing ports in each side, two outward-opening doors in hull rear which each have rectangular firing port
● Three large equally spaced road wheels each side, MG turret on hull roof centre and 7.62mm MG on ring mount to immediate rear

Specifications

Crew: 2+10
Configuration: 6x6
Armament: 1 x 7.62mm MG (turret), 1 x 7.62mm MG 9ring), 2 x 3 smoke grenade dischargers
Ammunition: 3,000 x 7.62mm
Length: 5.233m
Width: 2.539m
Height: 2.463m (turret top), 2m (hull top)
Ground clearance: 0.432m
Wheelbase: 1.524m + 1.524m
Weight, combat: 10,170kg
Weight, empty: 8,640kg
Power-to-weight ratio: 15.73hp/tonne
Engine: Rolls-Royce B80 Mk 6A 8-cylinder petrol developing 160hp at 3,750rpm
Maximum road speed: 72km/hr
Maximum range: 400km
Fuel capacity: 200 lit
Fording: 1.07m, 1.98 with preparation
Vertical obstacle: 0.46m
Trench: 1.52m
Gradient: 42%
Side slope: 30%
Armour: 16mm (maximum)
Armour type: Steel
NBC system: None
Night vision equipment: None

Development

Alvis Saracen APC (FV603) was developed shortly after the Second World War and shares many components with Alvis

Alvis Saracen (6x6)

Saladin (6x6) armoured car. First prototype completed in 1952, 1,838 vehicles being built by the time production was completed in 1972. The Saracen APC was finally phased out of service with the British Army in 1993 and these have all now been disposed of.

Driver sits front of crew compartment, section commander to his left rear, radio operator right rear, four troops on each side facing. Turret has manual traverse through 360˚ and 7.62mm MG elevates from -12˚ to +45˚. A 7.62mm Bren LMG is normally mounted to rear of turret for anti-aircraft role.

Variants

Saracen with reverse-flow cooling has different front and top engine covers.
Saracen with open roof, built for Kuwait.
FV604 Saracen command vehicle is similar to FV603 but can have tent erected to rear of hull.
FV610 command vehicle has much higher roof and no MG turret.

FV611 is ambulance with same hull as above.

Alvis Vehicles Limited now offer an upgrade for the FV600 series, including the Saracen which includes the installation of a Perkins Phaser 180 MTi 180hp diesel engine. This is known to have been adopted by Indonesia.

Status

Production complete. In service with Indonesia, Jordan, Lebanon, Libya (probably non-operational), Nigeria and South Africa (for sale).

Manufacturer

Alvis Vehicles Limited, Coventry, West Midlands, UK.

Right: Alvis Saracen
(6x6) (MoD)

Hotspur Hussar APC (UK)

Key recognition features

● Vertical hull front with horizontal louvres, spare wheel on top, commander's and driver's windscreen slopes to rear with shutters hinged above, horizontal hull top extends to rear

● Forward-opening door in each side to immediate front of second road wheel station, three firing ports with vision block above in each side of troop compartment which slopes inwards top and bottom

● Twin doors in rear each with firing port and vision block, three road wheels each side, one front and two close together at rear

Specifications

Crew: 1+13
Configuration: 6x6
Armament: Optional
Length: 5.994m
Width: 2.489m
Height with turret: 2.833m
Height hull roof: 2.383m
Ground clearance: 0.21m
Wheelbase: 3.81m
Weight, combat: 5,350kg
Power-to-weight ratio: 25hp/tonne
Engine: Rover V-8 water-cooled petrol developing 134hp at 4,000rpm
Maximum road speed: 120km/hr
Maximum range: 300km
Fuel capacity: 98 lit
Armour: 8mm (maximum) (estimate)
Armour type: Steel
NBC system: None
Night vision equipment: Optional for driver (passive)

Development

Hussar was developed as a private venture by Hotspur Armoured Products and shown for the first time in 1984. Two prototypes were built followed by 25 production vehicles for two undisclosed countries. Since then additional orders have been placed.

Hussar is a modified Land Rover One Ten chassis with fully armoured body for complete protection from small arms fire and shell splinters. Engine is front, driver and commander to immediate rear, troop compartment extending to back of vehicle. Twelve troops sit six each side on bench seats facing. Standard equipment includes a full air-conditioning system.

Optional equipment includes turret on roof with single or twin 7.62mm MGs, winch, night vision equipment, 24V electrical system, smoke/grenade launchers, powered steering, diesel engine, spot lamps, siren, long-range fuel tanks and run-flat tyres.

Variants

Hussar can be used for a number of roles including ambulance and command post vehicle.

Other armoured vehicles designed and built by Hotspur Armoured Products include Borderer (4x4) scout car (prototypes only), Sandringham (6x6) APC (in service with Finland, Sri Lanka and a Gulf state), 4984 (4x4) vehicle based on Land Rover chassis, Polisec APC based on 6x6 Land Rover chassis and Skirmisher 4585 (4x4) APC.

Status

Production as required. In service with Bahrain (police), Egypt and at least two other undisclosed countries.

Manufacturer

Hotspur Armoured Products, a Division of Penman Engineering Limited, Heathall, Dumfries, Scotland, UK.

Above: Hotspur Hussar (6x6) with MG turret (Christopher F Foss)

Right: Hotspur Sandringham (6x6)

Alvis Saladin Armoured Car (UK)

Key recognition features

● Driver front, well sloped glacis plate, turret centre, engine rear. Engine has six rectangular covers on top, upper part of hull rear vertical, lower part sloping back under hull, cylindrical silencer on right side at rear
● Three equally spaced road wheels identical to those of Alvis Saracen APC
● Turret has flat sides and vertical rear with short-barrelled 76mm gun in external mantlet, 7.62mm MG on right side of roof, cable drum on turret rear

Specifications

Crew: 3
Configuration: 6x6
Armament: 1 x 76mm gun, 1 x 7.62mm MG (coaxial), 1 x 7.62mm MG (anti-aircraft), 2 x 6 smoke grenade dischargers
Ammunition: 42 x 76mm, 2,750 x 7.62mm
Length gun forward: 5.284m
Length hull: 4.93m
Width: 2.54m
Height to top of gunner's periscope: 2.39m
Height to turret top: 2.19m
Ground clearance: 0.426m
Wheelbase: 1.524m + 1.524m
Weight, combat: 11,590kg
Weight, empty: 10,500kg
Power-to-weight ratio: 14.66hp/tonne
Engine: Rolls-Royce B80 Mk 6A 8-cylinder petrol developing 170bhp at 3,750rpm
Maximum road speed: 72km/hr
Range: 400km
Fuel capacity: 24 lit
Fording: 1.07m
Vertical obstacle: 0.46m
Trench: 1.52m
Gradient: 46%
Side slope: 30%
Armour: 8-32mm
Armour type: Steel
NBC system: None
Night vision equipment: None

Development

Saladin (FV601) (6x6) armoured car was developed by Alvis of Coventry for the British Army and shares many components with Alvis Saracen (6x6) armoured personnel carrier. 1,177 vehicles were produced between 1959 and 1972. Has been replaced in British Army by Alvis Scorpion CVR(T).

Main armament comprises 76mm gun with 7.62mm machine gun mounted coaxial to right and similar weapon on right side of turret roof. Turret traverse is powered through 360° with weapon elevation from -10° to +20°. Gun fires same ammunition as 76mm gun on Alvis Scorpion, although actual gun is different.

Variants

No variants. Saladin turret has been fitted to some Australian M113A1 series APCs for fire support role but these now in reserve.

Alvis have developed an upgrade kit for the Saladin which includes the replacement of the petrol engine by a more fuel-efficient diesel. This has been sold to Indonesia.

Status

Production complete. In service with Bahrain, Honduras, Indonesia, Jordan, Lebanon, Mauritania, Nigeria, Portugal, Sri Lanka, Sudan, Tunisia, United Arab Emirates.

Manufacturer

Alvis Vehicles Limited, Coventry, England, UK.

AboveAlvis Saladin

Above right: Alvis Saladin (MoD)

Right: Alvis Saladin (MoD)

Cadillac Gage LAV-300 AFV Range (USA)

Key recognition features

● Long box-type hull with pointed front, horizontal hull top and vertical rear. Weapon station normally on hull top in line with second road wheel

● Three large road wheels each side with distinctive gap between first and second,, hull sides above road wheels slope inwards

● Twin doors at rear each with firing port and vision block above, small door in left side of hull to rear of first wheel station, firing ports with vision block above in hull sides

Specifications

Crew: 3+9
Configuration: 6x6
Armament: 1 x 90mm, 1 x 7.62mm MG (coaxial), 1 x 7.62mm MG (anti-aircraft), 2 x 6 smoke grenade dischargers
Length: 6.4m
Width: 2.54m
Height: 2.7m (turret roof), 1.98m (hull top)
Ground clearance: 0.533m (hull), 0.381m (axle)
Wheelbase: 2.209m + 1.524m
Weight, combat: 14,696kg
Power-to-weight ratio: 18.94bhp/tonne
Engine: Cummins 6 CTA 8.3 turbocharged, 6-cylinder in-line diesel developing 275hp at 2,500rpm
Maximum road speed: 100km/hr
Maximum water speed: 5km/hr
Maximum range: 700km
Fuel capacity: 302 lit
Fording: Amphibious
Vertical obstacle: 0.609m
Trench: Not applicable
Gradient: 60%
Side slope: 30%
Armour: Classified
Armour type: Steel
NBC system: Optional
Night vision equipment: Optional

Development

LAV-300 range of 6x6s was developed by Cadillac Gage as a private venture to complement its 4x4s. First prototypes completed in 1979, first production vehicles in 1982.

Driver sits front left, engine compartment to his right, troop compartment extending right to rear. Troops enter and leave via twin dors in hull rear, roof hatches also provided. LAV-300 is fully amphibious, propelled by its wheels. Standard equipment includes front-mounted winch with capacity of 9,072kg. Wide range of optional equipment includes air-conditioning system and heater.

Cadillac Gage vehicles are manufactured by Textron Marine & Land Systems.

Variants

LAV-300 can be fitted with wide range of turrets including one-man turret with twin 7.62mm or one 7.62mm and one 12.7mm MGs, ring mount with 7.62mm or 12.7mm MG, one- or two-man turret with 20mm cannon and 7.62mm MG, two-man turret with 25mm cannon and 7.62mm coaxial MG, two-man turret with 76mm or 90mm gun, 7.62mm coaxial and 7.62mm AA MG.

More specialised versions include TOW anti-tank, ambulance, 81mm mortar, recovery, cargo carrier, command post vehicle, and air defence vehicle (gun or missile), some of which have raised roof to rear of driver's position. The 81mm mortar carrier, for example, has the standard hull with hatches that open either side to enable mortar to be used.

Status
Production as required. Sales have been made to Kuwait, Panama and the Philippines.

Manufacturer
Textron Marine & Land Systems, New Orleans, Louisiana, USA.

Right: LAV-300 with 90mm two-man turret

373

8x8 VEHICLES

Diesel Division, General Motors of Canada, Bison APC (Canada)

Key recognition features

● Long hull with nose sloping back under front to first road wheel station, well sloped glacis plate leading to horizontal roof, above second/third road wheel roof is raised and extends to rear of vehicle. Hull rear is vertical with ramp that contains a door
● Four road wheels either side with slightly larger gap between second and third road wheels, upper part of hull slopes inwards on front half of vehicle, rear half almost vertical with extensive external stowage
● Raised commander's cupola in line with second road wheel on left side of hull, 7.62mm MG on ring type mount

Specifications

Crew: 2+9
Configuration: 8x8
Armament: 1 x 7.62mm MG, 2 x 4 smoke grenade dischargers
Ammunition: 2,000 x 7.62mm (estimate)
Length: 6.452m
Width: 2.5m
Height: 2.21m
Weight, combat: 12,936kg
Weight, empty: 11,072kg
Power-to-weight ratio: 21.25hp/tonne
Engine: Detroit Diesel Model 6V-53T 6-cylinder diesel developing 275hp at 2,800rpm
Maximum road speed: 100km/hr
Maximum water speed: 9.7km/hr
Maximum range: 665km
Fuel capacity: Not available
Fording: Amphibious
Vertical obstacle: 0.381 to 0.508m
Trench: 2.06m
Gradient: 60%
Side slope: 30%
Armour: Classified
Armour type: Steel
NBC system: Yes
Night vision equipment: Yes (commander and driver)

Development

In 1988, the Diesel Division of General Motors of Canada designed and built the prototype of an 8x8 APC as a private venture. This was based on the chassis and automotive components of the Light Armoured Vehicle (LAV) that it has built for the United States Marine Corps (qv). The Canadian Army subsequently placed an order for 199 of a modified version for the Militia called the Bison and first production vehicles wee completed in late 1990.

The driver is seated at the front of the vehicle on the left with the commander being seated to his rear with a raised cupola, the powerpack is to the right of the driver with the remainder of the hull being occupied by the troop compartment. The infantry are seated on seats on either side of the troop compartment and enter via a large hydraulic operated ramp in the rear. Over the top of the troop compartment are hatches that open either side of the roof. There is no provision for the troops to fire their weapons from within the vehicle.

The Bison is fully amphibious being propelled in the water by two propellers mounted at the rear of the hull and before entering the water a trim vane is erected at the front of the vehicle which, when not required, folds back under the nose. Steering is power assisted on the front four road wheels and standard equipment includes a winch and fire detection and suppression system.

Variants

The Canadian Armed Forces order comprises 149 APCs, 18 command post vehicles, 16 81mm mortar carriers and 16 maintenance and repair vehicles that are fitted with a hydraulic crane.

Status
In production. In service with Australia, Canada and the United States (National Guard).

Manufacturer
Diesel Division, General Motors of Canada, London, Ontario, Canada.

Right: Bison (8x8) APC

Diesel Division, General Motors of Canada, Light Armored Vehicle 25 (LAV-25) (Canada)

Key recognition features

- Long hull with nose sloping back under front to first road wheel station, well sloped glacis plate leading to horizontal roof, above second/third roaose sloping back under hull to first road wheel station, well sloped glacis plate leading to horizontal roof, vertical hull rear with two doors
- Four road wheels each side, upper part of hull sloping inwards, equal gap between first and second and third and fourth road wheels
- Turret to rear of vehicle and offset to left, flat front, sides and rear that slope inwards, basket rear

Specifications

Crew: 3+6
Configuration: 8x8
Armament: 1 x 25mm, 1 x 7.62mm MG (coaxial), 1 x 7.62mm MG (anti-aircraft, optional), 2 x 4 smoke grenade dischargers
Ammunition: 630 x 25mm, 1,620 x 7.62mm
Length: 6.393m
Width: 2.499m
Height overall: 2.692m
Ground clearance: 0.5m
Wheelbase: 1.1m + 1.135m + 1.04m
Weight, combat: 12,882kg
Weight, empty: 11,099kg
Power-to-weight ratio: 21.34hp/tonne
Engine: Detroit Diesel 6V-53T, 6-cylinder diesel developing 275hp at 2,800rpm
Maximum rod speed: 100km/hr
Maximum water speed: 9.656km/hr
Maximum range: 668km
Fuel capacity: 300 lit
Fording: Amphibious
Vertical obstacle: 0.5m
Trench: 2.057m
Gradient: 60%
Side slope: 30%
Armour: 10mm (estimate)
NBC system: None
Night vision equipment: Yes (passive, commander, gunner and driver)

Development

To meet a US Marine Corps requirement for a Light Armored Vehicle (LAV) prototypes were built by Diesel Division, General Motors of Canada, Alvis, and Cadillac Gage. In 1982 Diesel Division, General Motors of Canada 8x8 (based on Swiss MOWAG Piranha series) was selected and 758 ordered over a five-year period from FY82 to FY85 in six basic versions. US Army was also involved in the programme but subsequently withdrew. First production vehicles, LAV-25s, were delivered in October 1983 with final deliveries in 1987.

LAV has driver front left, engine compartment to right, two-man power-operated turret to rear, troop compartment at far rear Six troops sit three each side back to back, six firing ports and vision blocks. Vehicle is fully amphibious with two propellers mounted at rear. Before entering the water a trim vane is erected at front of vehicle and bilge pumps switched on. Turret is armed with 25mm McDonnell Douglas Helicopters Chain Gun as installed in M2 Bradley, with 7.62mm M240 MG mounted coaxial and optional 7.62mm or 12.7mm MG on turret roof for anti-aircraft defence. Turret traverse is 360°, weapon elevation from -10° to +60°.

Variants

LAV logistics has two-man crew, higher roof and crane. In service.
LAV mortar has 81mm mortar in rear. In service.
LAV maintenance/recovery has five-man crew, crane. In service.
LAV anti-tank has three-man crew, same turret as M901s.
Improved TOW vehicle has two TOW in ready-to-launch

position. In service.

LAV command and control is similar to logistics with higher hull. In service.

LAV Mobile Electronic Warfare Support System (MEWS), raised roof. In service.

Anti-aircraft (Marine Corps), fitted with turret armed with 25mm cannon and Stinger SAMs, prototype stage.

Assault Gun Vehicle, armed with 105mm gun, prototypes only.

LAV-25 (Recce), for Canada, plus APC and other versions.

Saudi Arabia has many variants including 120mm Armoured Mortar System, 90mm assault gun and anti-tank with HOT ATGW.

LAV can be fitted with many other weapon systems.

Bison (8x8) APC (qv).

Status

In production. In service with Australia, Canada, Saudi Arabia and United States (Army and Marine Corps).

Manufacturer

Diesel Division, General Motors of Canada Limited, London, Ontario, Canada. Also made under licence in UK by GKN Defence for export market.

Above right: LAV-25 (Barry Marriott)

Right: LAV with HOT ATGW for Saudi Arabia

OT-64C(1) (SKOT-2A) APC (Former Czechoslovakia)

Key recognition features

● 8x8 chassis with equal spaces between first/second and third/fourth wheels, larger gap between second/third
● Blunt nose with vertical hull sides sloping slightly inwards at top, rear slopes outwards, exhaust pipes on both sides of hull, trim vane front
● OT-64C(1) has flat topped turret on plinth just forward of third wheel station

Specifications

Crew: 2+15
Configuration: 8x8
Armament: 1 x 14.5mm MG (main), 1 x 7.62mm MG (coaxial)
Ammunition: 500 x 14.5mm, 2,000 x 7.62mm
Length: 7.44m
Width: 2.55m
Height: 2.71m (turret top), 2.06m (hull top)
Ground clearance: 0.46m
Wheelbase: 1.3m + 2.15m + 1.3m
Weight, combat: 14,500kg
Weight, unloaded: 12,800kg
Power-to-weight ratio: 12.41hp/tonne
Engine: Tatra 928 18 V-8 air-cooled diesel developing 180hp at 2,000rpm
Maximum road speed: 94.4km/hr
Maximum water speed: 9km/hr
Maximum road range: 710km
Fuel capacity: 320 lit
Fording: Amphibious
Vertical obstacle: 0.5m
Trench: 2m
Gradient: 60%
Side slope: 30%
Armour: 14mm (max turret), 10mm (max hull
Armour type: Steel
NBC system: Yes
Night vision equipment: Yes (infra-red for driver)

Development

OT-64 (Obrneny Transporter) series 8x8 was developed by Former Czechoslovakia and Poland from 1959, first production

vehicles completed in 1964. In these countries it is used in place of the similar Soviet-designed and built BTR-60 (8x8). Tatra of Czechoslovakia built the chassis and FSC/Lubin of Poland the armoured body.

OT-64 (designated SKOT by Poland) is fully amphibious with two propellers at the rear. Before entering the water a trim vane is erected at the front and bilge pumps switched on. All vehicles have powered steering on front four wheels and central tyre pressure regulation system.

Variants

OT-62A (SKOT), original model armed with pintle-mounted 7.62mm MG (Poland) or unarmed (Czechoslovakia). Some fitted with two Sagger ATGWs over rear troop compartment.
OT-64B (SKOT-2), used only by Poland. Square plinth with pintle-mounted 7.62mm or 12.7mm MG with shield.
OT-64C(1) (SKOT-2A) has same turret as fitted to Soviet BRDM-2, BTR-60PB and BTR-70 vehicles and armed with one 14.5mm KPVT and one 7.62mm PKT coaxial MG with elevation from -4° to +29°. Turret traverse is 360°. Both elevation and traverse are manual.
OT-64C(2) (SKOT-2AP), used only by Poland. Same as SKOT-2A but has new turret with same armament, curved top for higher elevation of +89.5o. Turret also fitted to OT-62C. Some vehicles have AT-3 Sagger ATGW mounted each side of turret.
OT-64C(1) with OT-62B turret. Morocco has a few of these local conversions.
DPT-64, is OT-64 modified for repair role.
OT-64 R-2M is command version.
OT-64 R-3MT and OT-64 R-4MT are radio versions.
WPT, armoured repair and maintenance vehicle.
Other versions include artillery resupply, minelayer, repair and

maintenance, OT-64 R-3Z, OT-64 R4 and OT-64 R6, all of
which are Polish.

Status
Production complete. In service with Cambodia, Czech
Republic, Hungary, India, Iraq, Libya, Morocco (status
uncertain), Poland, Slovakia, Sudan, Syria and Uganda (status
uncertain).

Manufacturer
Czechoslovak and Polish state factories.

Above: OT-62C(1) (SKOT2A) (8x8)

Above right: OT-62A (SKOT)

Right: OT-64C(1) 9SKOT-2A)

Thyssen Henschel Spähpanzer Luchs Reconnaissance Vehicle (Germany)

Key recognition features

● High hull with well sloped glacis plate on forward part of which is trim vane, horizontal hull top, turret slightly forward of vehicle centre, sloping hull rear

● Vertical hull sides sloping inward above wheels, access door in left hull side between second and third road wheels

● Four large road wheels each side with equal space between first/second and third/fourth road wheels, two propellers under hull rear

Specifications

Crew: 4
Configuration: 8x8
Armament: 1 x 20mm, 1 x 7.62mm MG (anti-aircraft), 2 x 4 smoke grenade dischargers
Ammunition: 375 x 20mm (turret), 100 x 7.62mm (turret)
Length: 7.743m
Width: 2.98m
Height: 2.905m (MG rail), 2.125m (hull top)
Ground clearance: 0.44m (hull), 0.58m (axles)
Wheelbase: 1.4m + 2.356m + 1.4m
Weight, combat: 19,500kg
Power-to-weight ratio: 20hp/tonne
Engine: Daimler-Benz OM 403 A 10-cylinder 90o V-4 stroke multifuel developing 390hp at 2,500rpm (diesel fuel)
Maximum road speed: 90km/hr
Maximum water speed: 9km/hr
Maximum range: 730km
Fuel capacity: 500 lit
Fording: Amphibious
Vertical obstacle: 0.6m
Trench: 1.9m
Gradient: 60%
Side slope: 30%
Armour: Classified
Armour type: Steel
NBC system: Yes
Night vision equipment: Yes (passive for commander, gunner and driver)

Luchs (8x8)

Development

In the mid-1960s the then West German Army issued a requirement for a new 8x8 armoured amphibious reconnaissance vehicle and after trials with two competing designs the Daimler-Benz model was selected. In December 1973 Rheinstahl Wehrtechnik (now Thyssen Henschel) was awarded a contract for 408 vehicles. First production vehicles, known officially as the Sp‰hpanzer Luchs, were delivered in 1975 and production continued until early 1978.

Driver sits front left, to his rear is the two-man turret, engine is rear on right side, second driver/radio operator is left side facing rear. Turret has full power traverse through 360°, weapon elevation from -15° to +69°. Manual controls provided for emergency use. The 7.62mm MG is mounted on a ring mount above commander's hatch on left side.

Luchs is fully amphibious, propelled by two propellers mounted rear. Steering is power-assisted and all eight wheels can be steered. When originally introduced into service Luchs had infra-red night vision equipment for all crew members, but this has now been replaced by thermal night vision equipment. Luchs has the same speed forwards and backwards.

Variants

No variants in service, although its chassis was proposed for a more mobile version of Euromissile Roland SAM.

As a private venture, Thyssen Henschel has developed a new family of 4x4 (TH200), 6x6 (TH400) and 8x8 (TH800) armoured vehicles but so far none of these has entered production. The APE amphibious engineer reconnaissance vehicle was designed at the same time as Luchs but never entered production.

Status

Production complete. In service with Germany Army only.

Manufacturer

Thyssen Henschel, Kassel, Germany.

Above left: Luchs (8x8) (Michael Jerchel)

Above: Luchs (8x8)

Consortium IVECO-OTOBREDA
Centauro B1 Tank Destroyer (Italy)

Key recognition features

● High hull with well sloped glacis plate, nose slopes back under hull. Horizontal hull roof with hull rear containing a door that opens to the right, hull rear slopes inwards

● Turret mounted towards rear of vehicle with distinctive external mantlet, turret sides slope slightly inwards with bank of four smoke grenade dischargers either side, 105mm gun extends over front of vehicle and has muzzle brake, thermal sleeve and fume extractor

● Four large road wheels either side with slightly larger gap between first and second road wheels. Upper part of hull slopes inwards with louvres in right side of hull above 1st/2nd road wheels

Specifications

Crew: 4
Configuration: 8x8
Armament: 1 x 105mm, 1 x 7.62mm MG (coaxial), 1 x 7.62mm MG (anti-aircrft), 2 x 4 smoke grenade dischargers
Ammunition: 40 x 105mm, 4,000 x 7.62mm
Length with gun: 8.555m
Length hull: 7.4m
Width: 3.05m
Height: 2.755m
Ground clearance: 0.417m
Wheelbase: 1.6m + 1.45m + 1.45m
Weight, combat: 24,000kg
Power-to-weight ratio: 21.66hp/tonne
Engine: IVECO FIAT MTCA V-6 turbocharged diesel developing 520hp at 2,300rpm
Maximum road speed: 100+km/hr
Range: 800km
Fuel capacity: 540 lit
Fording: 1.5m
Vertical obstacle: 0.55m
Trench: 1.2m
Gradient: 60%
Side slope: 30%
Armour: Classified
Armour type: Steel
NBC system: Yes
Night vision equipment: Yes (passive)

Development

The CEntauro B1 (8x8) tank destroyer is the first of a complete new family of armoured vehicles developed for the Italian Army to enter production. The others are the C1 Ariete MBT (qv), VCC-80 IFV (qv) and the Puma range of 4x4 and 6x6 vehicles (qv). OTOBREDA has responsibility for the tracked vehicles and armament aspects of all vehicles. IVECO is responsible for the wheeled vehicles and automotive aspects of all Tracked vehicles.

Following trials with a number of prototypes the Italian Army placed an order for the vehicle and the first production vehicles were completed in 1991. The original requirement was for some 450 vehicles but this has since been trimmed back to 400. IVECO at Bolzano build the chassis of the B1 and integrate this with the complete turret which is supplied by OTOBREDA at La Spezia.

The driver is seated on the left side of the vehicle at the front with the powerpack to his right and the power-operted turret at the rear. The commander and gunner are seated on the right with the loader being seated on the left. In addition to the two roof hatches there is also a hatch in the rear for crew escape and ammunition resupply. Turret traverse is a full 360° with weapon elevation from -6° to +15°, turret traverse and weapon elevation is powered with manual controls being provided for emergency use. The computerised fire control system is similar to that used in the C1 Ariete MBT and the VCC-80 IFV and includes a commander's stabilised sight and day/night sight for the gunner. Suspension system is of the hydropneumatic type with steering being power assisted on the front four wheels and standard equipment includes a central tyre pressure regulation system that allows the ground pressure to be adjusted to suit the type of terrain being crossed, winch located in the front of the hull and a fire detection and suppression system.

Variants
APC (prototype), ARV (projected) and 155mm SPG (prototype).

Status
In production. In service with the Italian Army.

Manufacturer
IVECO FIAT, Bolzano, Italy

Above: IVECO FIAT B1 Centauro

Right: IVECO FIAT B1 Centauro

TAB-77 APC (Romania)

Key recognition features

● Looks very similar to the Russian BTR-80 but has different turret with distinctive sight on left side and no smoke grenade launchers on the turret rear

● Four large road wheels each side, with door in lower part of hull between second and third road wheels, upper part of hull slopes inwards, trim vane folds back on to glassis

● Pointed front with commander and driver seated towards front and turret on roof in line with second road wheel, long exhaust pipe on either side of hull above last road wheel

Specifications

Crew: 3+9
Configuration: 8x8
Armament: 1 x 14.5mm MG (main), 1 x 7.62mm MG (coaxial)
Ammunition: 600 x 14.5mm, 2,500 x 7.62mm
Length: 7.4m
Width: 2.95m
Height: 1.92m (turret top)
Ground clearance: 0.525m
Wheelbase: 4.392m
Weight, combat: 13,350kg
Power-to-weight ratio: 19.77hp/tonne
Engine: 2 x Model 797-05M1 diesels, each developing 132 hp at 3000 rpm
Maximum road speed: 83km/hr
Maximum road range: 550km
Fuel capacity: 290 litres
Fording: Amphibious
Vertical obstacle: 0.5m
Trench: 2m
Gradient: 60%
Side slope: 30%
Armour: 8mm (estimate)
NBC system: Yes
Night vision equipment: Yes

Development

In the 1960s Romania developed the TAB-71 (see next entry):a version of the BTR-60PB. This was followed by the TAB-77, based on the BTR-70, but with minor differences. It has a new turret of local design and the original petrol engines are replaced by two locally manufactured diesel units. The commander and driver sit

Above:TAB-77 (8x8)   *Right: TAB-77 (8x8)*

at the front with one man manually operating the turret to their rear. The troop compartment extends almost to the rear where the engine compartment is located.

The turret traverses through 360 degrees and the turret armament elevates from -5 to +85 degrees. The TAB-77 is fully amphibious, being propelled in the water by a single waterjet mounted in the rear. Before entering the water, bilge pumps are switched on and the trim vane at the front is erected. Standard equipment includes a central tyre pressure regulation system, fire detection and suppression system, and a winch.

Variants

TAB-77 PCOMA, armoured artillery command post vehicle
TAB-77A, armoured command post vehicle
TERA-77L, maintenance and recovery vehicle

Status

Production complete. In service with Romania.

Manufacturers

Romanian state factories

TAB-71 APC (Romania)

Key recognition features

● Four equally spaced road wheels each side
● Hull sides slope slightly inwards with square door in each side above second/third road wheel, three firing ports each side
● Mounted on roof of vehicle, above the second road wheel, is the turret which is similar to that of the former Soviet BTR-60PB (8x8) APC (qv) but has a distinctive sight mounted externally to the left of the weapons

Specifications

Crew: 3+8
Configuration: 8x8
Armament: 1 x 14.5mm MG (main), 1 x 7.62mm MG (coaxial)
Ammunition: 500 x 14.5mm, 2,000 x 7.62mm
Length: 7.22m
Width: 2.83m
Height: 2.7m (turret top)
Ground clearance: 0.47m
Wheelbase: 4.21m
Weight, combat: 11,000kg
Power-to-weight ratio: 25.4hp/tonne
Engine: 2 x V-6 liquid cooled petrol developing 140hp each
Maximum road speed: 95km/hr
Maximum water speed: 10km/hr
Maximum road range: 500km
Fuel capacity: 290 lit
Fording: Amphibious
Vertical obstacle: 0.4m
Trench: 2m
Gradient: 60%
Side slope: 30%
Armour: 9mm (max turret), 7mm (max hull)
Armour type: Steel
NBC system: Yes
Night vision equipment: Yes (infra-red for driver)

Development

TAB-71 (8x8) was first seen in public during 1972 and is the Romanian equivalent of the former Soviet BTR-60PB (8x8) but with at least two major improvements: more powerful engines (2 x 140hp compared with 2 x 90hp of Soviet vehicle) and machine guns with higher elevation for use in the anti-aircraft role. TAB-71 is fully amphibious, propelled by a single waterjet at rear of hull. Central tyre pressure regulation system. Turret has manual traverse and MGs elevate manually from -5° to +85°.

Variants

TAB-71M, virtually same as standard TAB-71.
TAB-71AR, TAB-71 with turret removed and fitted with 81mm mortar.
TERA-71, TAB-71 modified for maintenance and recovery role.
TERA-71L, TAB-71 modified for maintenance and recovery role.
TAB-71A R1 450, TAB-71A R1 451, TAB-71A R1 452, TAB-71 modified for armoured command vehicle.
The TAB-71 was replaced in production by the TAB-77 for which there is a separate entry.
Note: TAB-79 (4x4) APC (qv)
TAB-71 (8x8) APC

Status

Production complete. In service with Romania and former Yugoslavia.

Manufacturer

Romanian state factories.

TAB-71 (8x8) APC

BTR-80 APC (Russia)

Key recognition features

● Similar in appearance to BTR-70 (8x8) APC (qv) but similar turret has a bank of six forward firing smoke grenade dischargers mounted on turret rear

● Between second and third road wheels is a new hatch/door arrangement, upper part opens to right and lower part opens downwards to form a ramp

● Hull rear is different from BTR-70/BTR-80 and has higher roof line with exhaust pipe almost horizontal

Specifications

Crew: 3+7
Configuration: 8x8
Armament: 1 x 14.5mm MG, 1 x 7.62mm MG (coaxial), 6 smoke grenade dischargers
Ammunition: 500 x 14.5mm, 2,000 x 7.62mm
Length: 7.65m
Width: 2.90m
Height: 2.35m
Ground clearance: 0.475m
Weight, combat: 13,600kg
Power-to-weight ratio: 19.11hp/tonne
Engine: 4-stroke V-8 water-cooled diesel developing 260hp
Maximum road speed: 90km/hr
Maximum water speed: 9.5km/hr
Road range: 600km
Fuel capacity: 290 lit
Fording: Amphibious
Vertical obstacle: 0.5m
Trench: 2m
Gradient: 60%
Side slope: 30%
Armour: 7mm (max turret), 9mm (max hull)
Armour type: Steel
NBC system: Yes
Night vision equipment: Yes (infra-red for commander and driver)

Development

BTR-70 (8x8) had a number of improvements over the original BTR-60 (8x8) family but still have disadvantages including two petrol engines and poor means of entry and exit. In the early 1980s the former Soviet Army took delivery of a new vehicle, BTR-80, which has the same layout as BTR-70 but a single V-8 diesel developing 260hp. The one-man manually operated turret is similar to BTR-70's but the 14.5mm KPVT MG elevates to +60° so it can be used against slow-flying aircraft and helicopters. The 7.62mm PKT MG is retained. Mounted on turret rear is a bank of six smoke grenade dischargers firing forwards. There are three firing ports in each side of troop compartment. Between second and third axles is a new hatch arrangement: upper part opens to front and lower part folds down to form step allowing infantry to leave more safely.

BTR-80 is fully amphibious, propelled by a single waterjet at rear, has central tyre pressure regulation system, steering on front four road wheels, front-mounted winch, NBC system and infra-red night vision equipment for driver and commander who sit at front of vehicle.

Variants

BTR-80 M1989/1, this is a command vehicle with additional communications equipment.
120mm 2S23 self-propelled gun, details of this vehicle, essentially a BTR-80 with the turret of the 2S9 are given in the Self-propelled Guns and Howitzers section.
RKhM-4 chemical and reconnaissance vehicle.
BREM-K armoured recovery vehicle.
BTR80A has new turret with externally mounted 30mm cannon and 7.62mm machine gun.

Status

Production. In service with Afghanistan, Russia, Finland, Hungary and Turkey.

BTR80A (8x8) APC

Manufacturer
Gorkiy Automobile Plant, Gorkiy, former USSR.

Left: BTR-80 (8x8) APC

Above right: BTR-80 (8x8) APC

Right: BTR-80 (8x8) APC

120mm 2S23 self-propelled mortar (Russia)

Key recognition features

● Based on BTR-80 (8x8) APC chassis with four road wheels each side with larger gap between second/third road wheel

● Large turret mounted in centre of hull roof, with 120mm ordnance mounted in sloping turret front, turret sides curve to rear with three smoke grenade dischargers either side

Specifications

Crew: 4
Configuration: (8x8)
Armament: 1 x 120mm mortar, 1 x 7.62mm MG (anti-aircraft), 2 x 3 smoke grenade dischargers
Ammunition: 30 x 120mm, 1,000 x 7.62mm
Length: 7.50m
Width: 2.90m
Height: 2.75m
Ground clearance: 0.475m
Weight, combat: 14,000kg
Power-to-weight ratio: 17.93hp/tonne
Engine: Four stroke V-8 water-cooled diesel developing 260hp
Maximum road speed: 80km/hr
Maximum water speed: 10km/hr
Maximum road range: 500km
Fuel capacity: 290 lit
Fording: Amphibious
Vertical obstacle: 0.5m
Trench: 2m
Gradient: 60%
Side slope: 30%
Armour: 15mm
Armour type: Steel
NBC system: Yes
Night vision equipment: Yes (infra-red for driver)

Development

The 120mm 2S23 (this being its industrial number) is essentially the BTR-80 armoured personnel carrier (qv) fitted with a 120mm breech loaded mortar in a turret. The mortar is related to the 120mm weapon of the 2B16 towed combination gun which is also known as the NONA-K. The 2S23 is also referred to as the NONA-SVK while the tracked 2S9 (qv) is referred to as the NONA-S.

The standard BTR-80 hull has been modified in a number of areas including removal of the firing ports and associated vision devices, modified door between second and third road wheels and modified roof hatches.

The turret is armed with a 120mm breech-loaded ordnance that firers a variety of projectiles to a maximum range of 8,000m, turret traverse is 35° left and right with weapon elevation from -4° to +80°. In addition to firing projectiles of Russian design, it can also fire French TDA 120mm mortar projectiles.

The 2S23 is fully amphibious being propelled in the water by a single waterjet at the hull rear. Before entering the water a trim vane is erected at the front of the hull.

Variants

There are no known variants of this system. Some 2S23 systems have however been observed fitted with thermal screens to the hulls and turrets.

Status

Production. In service with Russia.

Manufacturer

Russian state factories.

Above: 120mm 2S23 self-propelled howitzer/mortar system

Above right: 120mm 2S23 self-propelled howitzer/mortar system with thermal screens (Christopher F Foss)

Right: 120mm 2S23 self-propelled howitzer/mortar system with thermal screens (Christopher F Foss)

BTR-70 APC (Russia)

Key recognition features

● Similar in appearance to BTR-60B but with small door in lower part of hull between second and third road wheels, trim vane folds back onto glacis plate (on BTR-60 it folds under nose), commander's hatch front right is slightly domed, waterjet opening in hull rear has two-piece cover with hinge at top. BTR-80 also has different hull rear

● Commander and driver sit front, turret on roof in line with second road wheel, horizontal hull top which slopes down at far rear, exhaust pipe each side of hull at rear

● Four large rubber-tyred road wheels each side with slightly larger gap between second and third

Specifications

Crew: 2+9
Configuration: 8x8
Armament: 1 x 14.5mm MG, 1 x 7.62mm MG (coaxial)
Ammunition: 500 x 14.5mm, 2,000 x 7.62mm
Length: 7.535m
Width: 2.8m
Height top of turret: 2.235m
Ground clearance: 0.475m
Wheelbase: 4.4m
Weight, combat: 11,500kg
Power-to-weight ratio: 20.86hp/tonne
Engines: 2 x ZMZ-4905 6-cylinder petrol developing 120hp (each)
Maximum road speed: 80km/hr
Maximum water speed: 10km/hr
Maximum road range: 600km
Fuel capacity: 350 lit (estimate)
Fording: Amphibious
Vertical obstacle: 0.5m
Trench: 2m
Gradient: 60%
Side slope: 40%
Armour: 9mm (maximum) (estimate)
Armour type: Steel
NBC system: Yes
Night vision equipment: Yes (infra-red for driver and commander)

Development

BTR-70 is a further development of BTR-60 and was first shown in public during a Moscow parade in 1980. Main improvements over the BTR-60PB are slightly more powerful petrol engines which give improvement in power-to-weight ratio, improved vision for the troops with additional firing ports, and improved armour protection.

Commander and driver sit front with troop compartment extending towards rear, engines rear. Turret identical to BRDM-2 reconnaissance vehicle's, BTR-60PB's and armed with 14.5mm and a 7.62mm MG. Turret traverse is manual through 360°, weapons elevate from -5° to +30°. Steering is power-assisted on front four wheels, standard equipment includes front-mounted winch and central tyre pressure regulation system. BTR70 is fully amphibious, propelled by a single waterjet mounted at rear of hull. Before entering the water a trim vane is erected at front and bilge pumps switched on.

Variants

Some BTR-70s in Afghanistan were fitted with 30mm AGS-17 grenade launcher mounted on roof to rear of driver.
BTR-70MS is a turretless communications vehicle.
BTR-70KShM is a command/staff vehicle.
BREM is a turretless BTR-70 with bow-mounted jib crane and other equipment.
BTR-70Kh is chemical reconnaissance vehicle.
SPR-2 is a possible radar jamming variant.
Some BTR-70s have been fitted with complete turret of later BTR-80 (8x8) APC.

Status

Production complete. In service with Afghanistan and former USSR (Army and Naval Infantry). Also manufactured under licence in Romania as the TAB-77.

Manufacturer

Gorkiy Automobile Plant, Gorkiy, former USSR.

Above: BTR-70 (8x8)

Above right: BTR-70 (8x8) (C R Zwart)

Right: BTR-70 (8x8) Michael Jerchel)

Below: BTR-70 (8x8) (Steven Zacoga)

BTR-60PB APC (Russia)

Key recognition features

- Four road wheels each side with slightly larger gap between second and third
- Well sloped flat top turret on forward part of roof above second wheel station, square side door above second and third axle
- Blunt nose with engine at far rear and exhaust pipe on each side at 45o

Specifications

Crew: 2+14
Configuration: 8x8
Armament: 1 x 14.5mm MG (main), 1 x 7.62mm MG (coaxial)
Ammunition: 500 x 14.5mm, 2,000 x 7.62mm
Length: 7.56m
Width: 2.835m
Height: 2.31m (turret top), 2.055m (hull top)
Ground clearance: 0.475m
Wheelbase: 1.35m + 1.525m + 1.35m
Weight, combat: 10,300kg
Power-to-weight ratio: 17.47hp/tonne
Engines: 2 x GAZ-49B 6-cylinder in-line water-cooled petrol developing 90hp at 3,400rpm each
Maximum road speed: 80km/hr
Maximum water speed: 10km/hr
Maximum road range: 500km
Fuel capacity: 290 lit
Fording: Amphibious
Vertical obstacle: 0.4m
Trench: 2m
Gradient: 60%
Side slope: 40%
Armour: 7mm (max turret), 9mm (max hull)
Armour type: Steel
NBC system: Yes
Night vision equipment: Yes (infra-red for commander and driver)

Development

BTR-60P series 8x8s were developed in the late 1950s to replace BTR-152 (6x6) and were first seen in public in 1961. Throughout the 1960s it was continuously improved, final production model being BTR-60PB. It was replaced in production by the similar BTR-70 (8x8).

All members of BTR-60P series are fully amphibious, propelled by a single waterjet mounted at hull rear, have a 4,500kg capacity front-mounted winch, powered steering on front four wheels and central tyre pressure regulation system. BTR-60PB has fully enclosed troop compartment on top of which is a one-man turret almost identical to the BRDM-2 (4x4) amphibious scout car's. Turret has one 14.5mm KPVT MG with 7.62mm PKT MG mounted coaxial to right, both have manual elevation from -5° to +30°, turret traverse through 360°.

Variants

BTR-60P, first production model with open roof, has one to three 7.62mm MGs or 1 x 12.7mm and 2 x 7.62mm MGs.
BTR-60PA, second production model with fully enclosed troop compartment, first model with NBC system, roof-mounted 7.62mm MG.
BTR-60PB has 14.5mm/7.62mm turret of BRDM2 and OT-64C(1).
BTR-60PBK, command version of BTR-60PB.
BTR-60 1V18, artillery observation post vehicle.
BTR-60 1V19, fire direction centre vehicle.
BTR-60 communications are numerous and normally have an R or E designation, eg BTR-60-R-409BM.
BTR-60AVS, command post vehicle.
BTR-60PAU, artillery communications vehicle.
BTR-60PU-12M, air defence command post vehicle.
BTR-60 VVS, command post vehicle.
BTR-60P maintenance assist vehicle.
BTR-60 SPAAG, Cuba has some with twin 30mm AAG.

BTR-60 ACVR M1979(2), used by towed artillery units.
BTR-60PU command vehicle is BTR-60P with bows and
tarpaulin cover, additional communications equipment and
antenna. Also a command version of BTR-60PA with roof-
mounted generator and 10m high radio antenna.
BTR-60PU-12 command vehicle is BTR-60PA with large
stowage box on right side of hull, generator and telescopic
mast.
BTR-60 ACRV, artillery command and reconnaissance vehicle.
BTR-60MS radio vehicle has High Ball (NATO code name)
telescopic antenna.
BTR-60PB forward air control vehicle is BTR-60PB with
armament removed from turret and port covered by
plexiglass observation window. Additional communications
equipment, generator normally installed on roof.

Status

Production complete. In service with Afghanistan, Algeria,
Angola, Botswana, Bulgaria, Cambodia, China, Russia, Congo,
Cuba, Djibouti, Ethiopia, Finland, Guinea, Guinea-Bissau,
India, Iran, Iraq, North Korea, Libya, Mali, Mongolia,
Mozambique, Nicaragua, Romania (qv TAB-72), Somalia,
Syria, Turkey, Vietnam, Yemen, former Yugoslavia and Zambia.

Manufacturer

Gorkiy Automobile Plant, Gorkiy, Russia.

Above right: BTR-60PB (8x8)

Right: BTR-60PB (8x8) (Richard Stickland)

Reumech OMC Rooikat Armoured Car (South Africa)

Key recognition features

● Almost horizontal glacis plate with driver's hatch in upper part in centre, horizontal hull top with raised engine compartment at the rear, hull rear vertical

● Turret is centre of vehicle with flat front and sides that slope slightly inwards. Long barrelled 76mm gun has thermal sleeve and fume extractor and overhangs front of vehicle

● Four large road wheels either side with larger gap between 2nd/3rd road wheels, upper part of hull slopes slightly inwards, hull escape hatch in either side of hull side between 2nd/3rd road wheels

Specifications

Crew: 4
Configuration: 8x8
Armament: 1 x 76mm, 1 x 7.62mm MG (coaxial), 1 x 7.62mm MG (anti-aircraft), 2 x 4 smoke grenade dischargers
Ammunition: 48 x 76mm, 3,600 x 7.62mm
Length with gun: 8.2m
Length hull: 7.09m
Width: 2.9m
Height: 2.8m
Ground clearance: 0.4m
Wheelbase: 1.55m + 2.032m + 1.625m
Weight, combat: 28,000kg
Power-to-weight ratio: 20.11hp/tonne
Engine: V-10 water-cooled diesel developing 563hp
Maximum road speed: 120km/hr
Range: 1,000km
Fuel capacity: 540 lit
Fording: 1.5m
Vertical obstacle: 1m
Trench: 2m (crawl speed), 1m (60km/hr)
Gradient: 70%
Side slope: 30%
Armour: Classified
Armour type: Steel
NBC system: Yes (BC only)
Night vision equipment: Yes (passive)

Development

The first production vehicles were completed in 1989, and the first unit was equipped with Rooikats in 1990. The turret is made by Lyttleton Engineering Works (LIW), part of the Denel Group of companies while Reumech OMC is the overall prime contractor and responsible for the chassis and systems integration.

The driver is seated at the front of the hull, turret in the centre and the powerpack at the rear. The commander and gunner are seated on the right of the turret with the loader on the left. The commander is provided with a raised cupola for improved all-round observation.

The stabilised 76mm gun fires APFSDS-T and HE-T rounds and has an elevation of +20° and a depression of -10°, with turret traverse being a full 360°. Turret traverse and weapon elevation/depression is all-electric with manual controls for emergency use. The Rooikat has a computerised fire control system fitted as standard. The gunner's day/night sight incorporates a laser rangefinder and the commander has a roof-mounted periscopic day sight.

The driver can select 8 x 8 or 8 x 4 drive with steering being power assisted on the front four wheels and if required the vehicle can lay its own smoke screen by injecting diesel fuel into the exhaust. A fire detection suppression system is fitted as standard.

Variants

105mm, prototypes of a 105mm version firing NATO standard ammunition have been built.

ZA-35, this is a modified Rooikat chassis with a new two-man power-operated turret armed with a twin 35mm cannon, surveillance radar and electro-optical tracker. It is still at the prototype stage.

ZA-HVM, this is a modified Rooikat chassis with a new two-man power-operated chassis with four SAHV-3 surface-to-air missiles in the ready to launch position, surveillance radar and

electro-optical tracker. It is still at the prototype stage.
Rooikat 35 cavalry, 35mm model, proposal.
Rooikat 35/ZT-3, as above but with ZT-3 ATGWs, proposal.

Status

In production. In service with the South African Army.

Manufacturer

Reumech OMC, Boksburg, Transvaal, South Africa.

Below: 76mm Rooikat armoured car

*Right: 76mm Rooikat armoured car
(Christopher F Foss)*

*Below right: 76mm Rooikat armoured car
(Christopher F Foss)*

SELF-PROPELLED GUNS (TURRETLESS)

NORINCO Type 85 122 mm self-propelled gun (China)

Key recognition features

● Nose slopes back under hull with well sloped glacis plate leading up to horizontal hull top which extends to the rear. Hull rear vertical with single door and stowage box either side
● 122 mm howitzer mounted on top at rear with open roof, 122 mm ordnance extends just over front of hull and has distinctive multi-baffle muzzle brake
● Suspension either side consists of five road wheels, drive sprocket front, idler rear and track return rollers. Upper part of suspension covered by skirts. Upper part of hull slopes slightly inwards

Specifications

Crew: 6
Armament: 1 x 122 mm howitzer
Ammunition: 40 x 122 mm
Length gun forwards: 6.663 m
Length hull: 6.125 m
Width: 3.068 m
Height: 2.85 m (overall)
Ground clearance: 0.46 m
Weight, combat: 16 500 kg
Power-to-weight ratio: 19.4 hp/tonne
Ground pressure: 0.67 kg/cm
Engine: Type BF8L413F air cooled diesel developing 320 hp
Maximum road speed: 60 km/h
Range: 500 km
Fuel capacity: 450 l
Fording: amphibious
Vertical obstacle: 0.60 m
Trench: 2.2 m
Gradient: 53%
Side slope: 40%
Armour: Classified
Armour type: steel
NBC system: No
Night vision equipment: optional

Development

The NORINCO 122 mm self-propelled howitzer Type 85 is essentially the chassis of the Type 85 APC (or YW 531H as it is also referred to) fitted with the complete ordnance, elevating/traverse mechanism of the Chinese equivalent of the Russian 122 mm D-30 towed howitzer.

This 122 mm weapon has an elevation of +70 degrees, depression of -5 degrees with traverse being 22.5 degrees left and right. Firing a standard HE projectile a maximum range of 15 300 m can be achieved while firing an Extended Range Full Bore - Base Bleed projectile a maximum range of 21 000 m is achieved.

The driver and commander are seated front left with the powerpack to the right with the weapon mounted at the rear. For amphibious operations an inflatable pontoon is fitted either side of the hull and held in position by hoops, the vehicle is then propelled in the water by its tracks at a maximum speed of 6 km/h.

Variants

None. More recently this system has been offered mounted on the chassis of the latest Type 90 full tracked APC chassis.

Status

Production complete. In service with China.

Manufacturer

Chinese state factories.

OPPOSITE PAGE:
Above left: Type 85 122 mm SP gun

Above right: Type 85 122 mm SP gun

Below left: Type 85 122 mm SP gun

Below right: Type 85 122 mm SP gun

NORINCO Type 54-1 122mm self-propelled gun (China)

Key recognition features

● 122mm howitzer mounted rear of hull in open mount, can be fully enclosed by tarpaulin cover
● Chassis similar to Type 531 (YW 531) APC but with additional road wheel each side
● Suspension has five road wheels, drive sprocket front, idler rear, three track-return rollers, upper part of track covered by skirts

Specifications

Crew: 7 (maximum)
Armament: 1 x 122mm howitzer, 1 x 7.62mm MG
Ammunition: 40 x 122mm, 1,000 x 7.62mm
Length: 5.6m
Width: 3.07m
Height: 2.685m (top of gun), 1.976m (top of hull)
Ground clearance: 0.45m
Weight, combat: 15,300kg
Power-to-weight ratio: 17hp/tonne
Ground pressure: 0.6kg/cm2
Engine: Model 6150L 6-cylinder in-line water-cooled diesel developing 260hp at 2,000rpm
Maximum road speed: 56km/hr
Maximum road range: 450km
Fording: 1m
Vertical obstacle: 0.6m
Trench: 2.0m
Gradient: 60%
Side slope: 30%
Armour: 12mm (maximum)
Armour type: Steel
NBC system: None
Night vision equipment: Yes (driver only, infra-red)

Development

The first Type 54 122mm was essentially the standard Type 531 (YW 531) armoured personnel carrier with 122mm Type 54 towed howitzer with trails removed and mounted in troop compartment at rear. The more recent Type 54-1 has longer chassis with five instead of four road wheels and is more stable when firing.

The Type 54-1 is a copy of the Russian M1938 (M-30) and has short barrel with no muzzle brake and does not overhang front of vehicle. Type 54-1 retains its shield but has no protection to sides, rear or top for gun crew. 122mm howitzer has traverse of 22.5 degrees left and right with elevation -2.5 to +63 degrees.

The 122mm howitzer fires separate loading ammunition including high explosive, smoke and illuminating to maximum range of 11,800m. 7.62mm Type 67 MG, a copy of Soviet RP-46, is carried internally for both ground and anti-aircraft roles.

Variants

China is known to have built a new 122mm self-propelled howitzer (not the Type 85) which is very similar to the Soviet 122mm 2S1 system. The new Chinese system has six road wheels (similar to the Chinese Type 77 APC), drive sprocket at front, idler at rear, no track-return rollers. The fully enclosed turret is at the rear of the hull and is fitted with a roof mounted 12.7mm anti-aircraft machine gun. As far as it is known this system has yet to enter production.

Status

Production complete. In service with Chinese Army.

Manufacturer

Chinese state arsenals.

122mm Type 54-1 self-propelled gun with ordnance covered

Left: 122mm Type 54-1 self-propelled gun (Christopher F Foss)

GIAT 155mm Mk F3 self-propelled gun (France)

Key recognition features

● 155mm gun is fitted rear in unprotected mount and has barrel with double baffle muzzle brake that slightly overhangs front of vehicle. When travelling gun is locked 8 degrees to right of centre line
● Chassis has five road wheels with last acting as idler, drive sprocket front and three track-return rollers
● Two large spades at rear of hull

Specifications

Crew: 2 (on gun)
Armament: 1 x 155mm gun
Ammunition: None (on gun)
Length: 6.22m (excluding spades)
Width: 2.7m
Height, travelling: 2.085m
Ground clearance: 0.48m
Weight, combat: 17,400kg
Power-to-weight ratio: 14hp/tonne
Ground pressure: 0.84kg/cm2
Engine: SOFAM 8Gxb 8-cylinder water-cooled petrol developing 250hp at 3,200rpm (but see text)
Maximum road speed: 60km/hr
Maximum road range: 300km
Fuel capacity: 450 lit
Fording: 1m
Vertical obstacle: 0.6m (forwards), 0.4m (reverse)
Trench: 1.5m
Gradient: 40%
Side slope: 20%
Armour: 20mm (maximum)
Armour type: Steel
NBC system: No
Night vision equipment: Yes (driver only)

Development

The 155mm Mk F3 was developed in the 1950s based on AMX-13 light tank chassis. In French Army the system has now been replaced by 155mm GCT self-propelled gun. The 155mm gun is mounted at rear of chassis with no protection for crew from bad weather, NBC attack, small arms fire and shell splinters.

Before coming into action two spades at rear of hull have to be released manually. The 155mm gun elevates to a maximum of 67 degrees, with traverse 20° left and 300 right up to +50°, and 16° left and 300 right up to +67°. Elevation and traverse both manual. Firing a standard 155mm HE projectile maximum range is 20,047m. Other types of projectile include illumination, smoke and rocket-assisted.

Original production models were built with SOFAM petrol engine, but can have Detroit Diesel model 6V-53T 6-cylinder water-cooled diesel developing 280hp at 2,800rpm. This gives maximum road speed of 64km/hr with operating range increased from 300km to 400km. More recently Baudouin has offered its 6 F 11 SRY diesel developing 280hp at 3,200rpm for this and other members of AMX-13 family.

Other eight members of gun crew normally carried in 6x6 truck or AMX VCA tracked vehicle which carries 25 projectiles, 25 charges plus fuzes.

Variants

Apart from different engine options, there are no variants in service.

Status

Production complete. In service with Argentina, Chile, Cyprus, Ecuador, France, Kuwait, Morocco, Qatar, Sudan, United Arab Emirates and Venezuela.

Manufacturer

GIAT Industries, Roanne, France.

Top left: 155mm Mk F3 in travelling configuration

Above: 155mm Mk F3 in firing position (ECP Armees)

Centre left: 155mm Mk F3 from rear

Bottom left: 155mm Mk F3

Soltam L-33 155mm self-propelled gun (Israel)

Key recognition features

● High superstructure with vertical sides and rear. Glacis plate slopes at 45o then is vertical to roof
● 155mm howitzer has single baffle muzzle brake with fume extractor to rear, howitzer protrudes from gun compartment
● Superstructure overhangs chassis which has three bogies each with two road wheels, drive sprocket front, idler rear and three track-return rollers

Specifications

Crew: 8
Armament: 1 x 155mm howitzer, 1 x 7.62mm AA MG
Ammunition: 60 x 155mm, 1,000 x 7.62mm
Length gun forwards: 8.47m
Length hull: 6.47m
Width: 3.5m, 2.86m (over tracks)
Height: 3.45m
Ground clearance: 0.43m
Weight, combat: 41,500kg
Power-to-weight ratio: 10.08hp/tonne
Engine: Cummins VT 8-460-Bi diesel developing 460hp at 2,600rpm
Maximum road speed: 38km/hr
Maximum road range: 260km
Fuel capacity: 820 lit
Fording: 0.9m
Vertical obstacle: 0.91m
Trench: 2.3m
Gradient: 60%
Side slope: 30%
Armour: 12-64mm
Armour type: Steel
NBC system: No
Night vision equipment: Yes, driver only

Development

The L-33 was developed in the 1960s by Soltam to meet requirements of Israeli Army and is essentially a rebuilt Sherman tank chassis with original petrol engine replaced by a diesel and new fully enclosed superstructure. L-33 is same length as howitzer in calibres. It was first used operationally during 1973 Middle East conflict.

Soltam L-33 is fitted with a modified version of the standard Soltam 155mm M-68 gun/howitzer which is mounted well to rear. It has manual elevation from -4˚ to +52˚ and manual traverse of 30˚ left and right. When travelling, ordnance is held in travelling lock mounted on glacis plate.

The 155 mm gun fires separate loading type ammunition including high explosive, smoke and illuminating, with maximum range of 20,000m with unassisted projectiles. Out of 60 rounds of ammunition carried 16 are for ready use.

Variants

No known variants. Soltam is now offering a conversion package to replace the 33 calibre barrel by a 39 calibre barrel which will fire an HE projectile to 24,000m.

Status

Production/conversion complete. In service with Israeli Army.

Manufacturer

Conversions by Soltam, Haifa, Israel.

Right: Soltam L-33 155mm (Israeli Army)

240mm SPM M1975 (2S4) (Russia)

Key recognition features

● 240mm mortar is pivoted at rear of hull
● When travelling 240mm mortar barrel is in horizontal position above hull top pointing forwards with large spade at rear
● Suspension has six road wheels with drive sprocket front, idler at rear and four track-return rollers that support inside of track only, with gap between 1st/2nd, 2nd/3rd, 3rd/4th and 4th/5th road wheels

Specifications

Crew:4+5
Armament: 1 x 240mm mortar, 1 x 12.7mm MG (anti-aircraft)
Length: 7.94m
Width: 3.25m
Height: 0.4m
Ground clearance: 0.4m
Weight, combat: 27,500kg
Power-to-weight ratio: 18.9hp/tonne
Ground pressure: 0.6kg/cm²
Engine: V-59 V-12 diesel developing 520hp
Maximum road speed: 60km/hr
Maximum road range: 500km
Fuel capacity: 850 lit
Fording: 1m
Vertical obstacle: 0.7m
Trench: 2.79m
Gradient: 60%
Side slope: 30%
Armour: 20mm (max) (estimate)
Armour type: Steel
NBC system: Yes
Night vision equipment: Yes (IR for driver)

Development

This system was first identified in service with the then Soviet Army in 1975 and was therefore given the designation M1975 by NATO. Its correct designation is the SM-240 (2S4) and within the Russian Army it is commonly called the Tyulpan, or Tulip Tree. The system is normally accompanied by another vehicle that carries the remainder of the crew and additional ammunition. The chassis of the GMZ full tracked minelayer is used as the basis for the 2S4 system with the actual mortar being based on the towed 240mm M240 breech loaded mortar that was first fielded in the 1950s.

The powerpack is at the front of the vehicle on the right side with the commander and driver to the left and a crew/ammunition compartment at the rear. The 240mm mortar is mounted at the rear of the vehicle and fires an HE mortar bomb to a maximum range of 9650m. Other types of projectile include chemical and possibly concrete piercing. It is believed that an extended range mortar projectile with a maximum range of 18,000m is also available.

The mortar has an elevation of +50° to +80° with a limited traverse of 10° left and right with the mortar projectile being loaded with the aid of a crane that is positioned at the rear of the vehicle on the left side. The mortar is breech loaded.

Status

Production complete. In service with former Czechoslovakia, Iraq, and Russia.

Manufacturer

Russian state factories.

Right: 240mm SPM M1975 (Sm-240)(2S4)

152mm self-propelled gun (2S5) (Russia)

Key recognition features

● 152mm gun in unprotected mount at far rear of hull, pepperpot muzzle brake, no fume extractor

● Large spade at hull rear swings upwards when travelling

● Suspension has six road wheels, drive sprocket front, idler rear, track-return rollers, larger gap between first/second, second/third and third/fourth road wheels

Specifications

Crew: 5
Armament: 1 x 152mm gun
Ammunition: 30 x 152mm
Length gun forwards: 8.33m
Length hull: 7.3m
Width: 3.25m
Height: 2.76m
Ground clearance: 0.5m
Weight, combat: 28,200kg
Power-to-weight ratio: 19hp/tonne
Maximum road speed: 63km/hr
Maximum road range: 500km
Fuel capacity: 850 lit
Fording: 1.05m
Vertical obstacle: 0.7m
Trench: 2.5m
Gradient: 58%
Side slope: 47%
Armour: 15mm max (estimate)
Armour type: Steel
NBC system: Probable
Night vision equipment: Yes (IR for driver)

Development

The 152mm self-propelled gun 2S5 was developed in the 1970s and is believed to have entered service with the Russian army in 1980. It has the same ordnance as the 152mm 2A36 towed artillery system.

It is believed that the chassis of the 2S5 is also related to that of the GMZ full tracked minelaying system. The 152mm ordnance of the 2S5 is mounted at the rear of the hull with no protection provided for the crew. It has a traverse of 15° left and right and can be elevated from -2.5° to +57°. Maximum range using standard ammunition is 28,400m, or 40,000m with a rocket assisted projectile.

The layer is seated on the left side of the system at the rear with the ordnance being provided with a projectile and charge ramming system to enable a rate of fire of 15 rounds a minute to be attained.

A total of 30 projectiles and charges are carried with the projectiles being stowed vertically in a carousel device in the left side of the rear compartment. The 30 charges are stowed to the right in three rows of 10. Each row is on a conveyor belt that is under the floor of the vehicle.

Status

Production complete. In service with Finland and Russia.F

Manufacturer

Uraltransmash Work, Russia.

OPPOSITE PAGE:

Top left 152mm self-propelled gun 2S5 in travelling configuration (Ted Dyke)

Top right: 152mm self-propelled gun 2S5

Bottom right: 152mm self-propelled gun 2S5 in firing position

Bottom left: 152mm self-propelled gun 2S5 in firing position (Finnish Army)

203mm self-propelled gun M1975 (2S7) (Russia)

Key recognition features

● Fully enclosed cab at far front, well forward of front drive sprockets
● 203mm gun in unprotected mount at far rear, overhangs front of vehicle when in travelling lock
● Large spade at rear with ammunition handling system right

Specifications

Crew: 7
Armament: 1 x 203.2mm gun
Ammunition: 4 x 203.2mm
Length gun forwards: 13.12m
Length hull: 10.50m
Width: 3.38m
Height: 3.00m
Ground clearance: 0.40m
Weight, combat: 65,500kg
Weight, unloaded: 63,500kg
Power-to-weight ratio: 18.06hp/tonne
Ground pressure: 0.80kg/cm^2
Engine: V-12 liquid cooled diesel developing 840hp
Maximum road speed: 50km/hr
Maximum road range: 500km
Fuel capacity: Not available
Fording: 1.2m
Vertical obstacle: 0.70m
Trench: 2.6m
Gradient: 40%
Side slope: 20%
Armour: 10mm (max) (estimate)
Armour type: Steel
NBC system: Yes
Night vision equipment: Yes (driver)

Development

The 203mm self-propelled gun is designated M1975 by US Army although its correct Russian designation is SO-203 and industrial number is 2S7. It entered service with Russian Army in the late 1970s and is largest full tracked self-propelled gun in the world. Within the Russian Army it is also known as the Pion (Peony).

The chassis is a new design with fully enclosed armoured cab front, engine to immediate rear and 203mm gun mounted on top at far rear of hull. No protection for gun crew from small arms fire, shell splinters or NBC agents. When in firing position a large hydraulically operated spade is lowered at rear for more stable firing platform. Separate loading ammunition consisting of projectile and charge, load assist device on right side of chassis. In action it is accompanied by another vehicle carrying remainder of gun crew and ammunition.

The 203mm ordnance has a traverse of 15˚ left and right with elevation from 0˚ to +60˚. Maximum range firing an unassisted projectile is 37.5km while firing a rocket assisted projectile a maximum range of 47km can be achieved.

Variants

No known variants.

Status

Production complete. In service with Czech Republic, Poland, Russia and Slovakia.

Manufacturer

Russian state arsenals.

Above: 203mm self-propelled gun M1975 (SO-203) (2S7) in travelling configuration
Left: 203mm self-propelled gun M1975 (SO-203) (2S7) in travelling configuration

M110 203mm self-propelled gun (USA)

Key recognition features

● Short stubby barrel, no fume extractor or muzzle brake
● Howitzer is in unprotected mount towards rear of hull with large spade at far rear
● Chassis same as M107 175mm self-propelled gun (qv) with five large road wheels, front drive sprocket, no track-return roller

Specifications

Crew (on gun): 5
Armament: 1 x 203mm howitzer
Ammunition: 2 x 203mm
Length gun forwards: 7.467m (spade up)
Length hull: 5.72 (without gun or spade)
Width: 3.149m
Height: 2.93m (top of barrel travelling), 2.809m (top of mount), 1.475m (hull top)
Ground clearance: 0.44m
Weight, combat: 26,534kg
Weight, unloaded: 24,312kg
Power-to-weight ratio: 15.26hp/tonne
Ground pressure: 0.76kg/cm²
Engine: Detroit Diesel Model 8V-71T, turbocharged, 2-stroke liquid cooled, 8-cylinder diesel developing 405bhp at 2,300rpm
Maximum road speed: 56km/hr
Maximum road range: 725km
Fuel capacity: 1,137 lit
Fording: 1.066m
Vertical obstacle: 1.016m
Trench: 2.362m
Gradient: 60%
Side slope: 30%
Armour: Classified
Armour type: Steel
NBC system: No
Night vision equipment: Yes (driver only)

Development

The 203mm (8-inch) M110 was designed in the 1950s at the same time as M107 175mm which has identical chassis and mount. First production vehicles completed by Pacific Car and Foundry in 1962 with later production by FMC and finally BMY. The M110 was followed in production by the improved M110A1 and M110A2, some of which were conversions of the original vehicle.

The M110 has a total crew of 13 of whom five (commander, driver and three gunners) are carried on the actual M110 and remainder in the M548 tracked cargo carrier or truck which also carries projectiles, charges and fuzes.

The 203mm howitzer has powered elevation from -2° to +65°, powered traverse of 30° left and right. Maximum range is 21,300m with standard HE projectile, but other projectiles can be fired. When in firing position a large hydraulically operated spade is lowered at rear of hull to provide more stable firing platform. The gun crew has no protection from elements, NBC contamination, small arms fire or shell splinters.

The M110 series of self-propelled howitzers is now being phased out of service with a number of countries, for example United Kingdom and the United States, and replaced by the MLRS.

Variants

M110A1 is M110 with new, much longer barrel and therefore longer range.
M110A2 is same as M110A1 but barrel has muzzle brake.
M578 ARV used almost same chassis as M107/M110.

Status

Production complete. In service with Bahrain, Belgium, Germany, Greece, Iran, Israel, Italy, Japan (built under licence), Jordan, Pakistan, South Korea, Spain, Taiwan, Turkey. In most cases M110s have been converted to M110A2 standard.

Manufacturer

Pacific Car and Foundry Company, Renton, Washington; FMC Corporation, San José, California; and BMY, York, Pennsylvania, USA.

Above: M110 203mm self-propelled gun in travelling configuration

Above right: M110A2 203mm self-propelled gun in travelling configuration

Right: M110 203mm self-propelled gun in travelling configuration (US Army)

M107 175mm self-propelled gun (USA)

Key recognition features

● Long thin barrel, no fume extractor or muzzle brake
● Gun is in unprotected mount towards rear of hull with large spade at rear that is raised for travelling
● Chassis is same as M110 203mm self-propelled howitzer with five large road wheels, drive sprocket front, no track-return rollers

Specifications

Crew (on gun): 5
Armament: 1 x 175mm gun
Ammunition: 2 x 175mm
Length gun forwards: 11.256m (spade up)
Length hull: 5.72m (without gun or spade)
Width: 3.149m
Height: 3.679m (top of barrel travelling), 2.809m (top of mount), 1.475m (hull top)
Ground clearance: 0.46m
Weight, combat: 28,168kg
Weight, unloaded: 25,915kg
Power-to-weight ratio: 14.37hp/tonne
Ground pressure: 0.81kg/cm²
Engine: Detroit Diesel Model 8V-71T, turbocharged, 2-stroke liquid cooled, 8-cylinder diesel developing 405bhp at 2,300rpm
Maximum road speed: 56km/hr
Maximum road range: 725km
Fuel capacity: 1,137 lit
Fording: 1.066m
Vertical obstacle: 1.066m
Trench: 2.362m
Gradient: 60%
Side slope: 30%
Armour: Classified
Armour type: Steel
NBC system: No
Night vision equipment: Yes (driver only, passive)

Development

The 175mm M107 was designed in the 1950s at the same time as the M110 203mm (8-inch) self-propelled howitzer (qv) which has the same chassis and gun mount. First production vehicles were completed by Pacific Car and Foundry in 1962 with later production by FMC and finally BMY. A total of 524 M107s were built by BMY by the time production was completed in May 1980, but it has now been phased out of service with many armies including Germany, Italy, Netherlands, Spain, United Kingdom and the United States.

The M107 has a total crew of 13 of whom 5 (commander, driver and three gunners) are carried on the actual vehicle and the remainder in the M548 tracked cargo carrier (or truck) which also carries the projectiles, charges and fuzes.

The 175mm gun has powered elevation of -2° to +65°, powered traverse of 30° left and right. The 175mm gun is mounted at the rear of the hull with no protection being provided for the gun crew. A load assist device is mounted at the left rear to assist in loading projectiles into the breech of the weapon. In US Army service, the 175mm M107 only fired one combat projectile, the M437 high explosive which had a maximum range of 32,700m. In addition, the former Space Research Corporation developed a special projectile which could achieve a maximum range of around 40,000m. Israel was the only customer for this.

Variants

There are no variants of the M107 although the M110 self-propelled howitzer and M578 ARV use the same chassis.

Status

Production complete. In service with Greece, Iran, Israel, South Korea, and Turkey.

M107 175mm self-propelled gun in travelling configuration

Manufacturer

Pacific Car and Foundry Company, Renton, Washington; FMC Corporation, San José, California; and BMY, York, Pennsylvania, USA.

Above right: M107 175mm self-propelled gun in travelling configuration

Right: M107 self-propelled gun

M44 155mm self-propelled gun (USA)

Key recognition features

● 155mm howitzer with no muzzle brake or fume extractor is mounted in open-topped gun compartment rear and does not overhang front of vehicle

● Suspension has five road wheels, drive sprocket front, idler rear, four track-return rollers

● Chassis is almost identical to M52 105mm self-propelled howitzer's

Specifications

Crew: 5
Armament: 1 x 155mm howitzer, 1 x 12.7mm AA MG
Ammunition: 24 x 155mm, 900 x 12.7mm
Length: 6.159m (spade up)
Width: 3.238m
Height: 3.11m (with tarpaulin)
Ground clearance: 0.48m
Weight, combat: 28,350kg
Weight, empty: 26,308kg
Power-to-weight ratio: 17.63hp/tonne
Ground pressure: 0.66kg/cm^2
Engine: Continental AOS-895-3, 6-cylinder, air-cooled, supercharged petrol developing 500hp at 2,800rpm
Maximum road speed: 56km/hr
Maximum road range: 122km
Fuel capacity: 568 lit
Fording: 1.066m
Vertical obstacle: 0.762m
Trench: 1.828m
Gradient: 60%
Side slope: 30%
Armour: 12.7mm
Armour type: Steel
NBC system: No
Night vision equipment: None

Development

The M44 155mm was developed after the Second World War with production by Massey Harris. The M44 was followed in production by the M44A1 which has a Continental AOSI-895-5 engine with fuel injection. The M44 was replaced from 1962 in US Army by the 155mm M109 self-propelled howitzer.

The 155mm howitzer has manual elevation from -5o to +65o with traverse 30o left and right. It fires standard HE projectile to maximum range of 14,600m, although other types of projectile can be fired including agent, illuminating and smoke. When in firing position a large spade is lowered at rear to provide more stable firing platform. The open-topped gun compartment can be covered by tarpaulin and canvas. 12.7mm MG is mounted on ring mount at rear of gun compartment on left side, with driver seated to immediate front.

Variants

The M44T was developed by a German consortium to meet the requirements of Turkey. It has many improvements including the longer barrel of the 155mm FH-70 towed artillery system, new MTU diesel engine, new fuel tanks and new electrical system. It is in service with Turkish Army with conversions being carried out in Turkey.

Status

Production complete. In service with Greece, Jordan, Taiwan and Turkey (upgraded systems designated M44T).

Manufacturer

Massey Harris, USA.

Top: M44 155mm self-propelled howitzer (dotted line above roof shows position of tarpaulin cover when installed)
Above: M44 155mm self-propelled howitzer with ordnance in travelling lock (US Army)
Above right: M44 155mm self-propelled howitzer showing 12.7mm AA MG to rear of driver's position (US Army)
Right: One of the prototypes of the M44 showing spade at rear of hull and 12.7mm AA MG (US Army)

SELF-PROPELLED GUNS (WITH TURRETS)

ZVS Dana 152mm self-propelled gun (Former Czechoslovakia)

Key recognition features

● Cab front, turret centre, engine rear
● Eight road wheels, four front and four rear
● Turret higher than rest of vehicle with 152mm howitzer extending well over front of cab

Specifications

Crew: 5
Configuration: 8x8
Armament: 1 x 152mm howitzer, 1 x 12.7mm MG
Ammunition: 60 x 152mm
Length gun forward: 11.156m
Length hull: 8.87m
Width overall: 3.00m
Height: 2.85m (turret roof)
Wheelbase: 1.65m + 2.97m + 1.45m
Weight, combat: 29,250kg
Power-to-weight ratio: 11.79hp/tonne
Engine: Tatra 1-939-34 air-cooled diesel developing 345hp
Maximum road speed: 80km/hr
Maximum road range: 740km
Fording: 1.4m
Gradient: 60%
Side slope: 30%
Armour: 12.7mm maximum (estimated)
NBC system: Yes
Night vision equipment: Yes (driver only)

Development

The Dana 152mm was developed for the former Czechoslovak Army in the 1970s and was first seen in public in 1980. Its correct Czechoslovak designation is Vzor 77 self-propelled howitzer Dana. The chassis is based on a Tatra 815 (8 x 8) truck with extensive modifications including fully enclosed armoured cab at front, fully enclosed armoured turret in centre and engine moved to rear. Steering is power-assisted on front four wheels with central tyre pressure regulation system fitted as standard, for driver to adjust tyre pressure while travelling.

The 152mm howitzer elevates from -4° to +70°, turret traverses 225° left and right. Turret traverse and weapon elevation hydraulic with manual controls for emergency. Three hydraulic jacks are lowered to ground before firing, one at rear and one each side between second/third road wheels. Ordnance has single baffle muzzle brake but no fume extractor, with load assist device fitted as standard. The range of the 152mm howitzer is 18,700m using standard ammunition. Rate of fire is 3 rounds per minute for a period of 30 minutes. Ammunition includes APHE, HE, illuminating and smoke.

Variants

155mm Zuzana, latest model with many improvements including installation of 155mm/45 calibre ordnance which, when firing extended range full bore base bleed projectiles enables a range of 39,600m to be achieved.
Strop, twin 30mm self-propelled anti-aircraft gun system, also has fire and forget SAMs, prototype only.

Status

Production as required. In service with Russia, Czech Republic, Libya, Poland and Slovakia.

Manufacturer

ZVS Dubnica nad Vahom, Slovakia

Above: Dana 152mm in travelling configuration (Paul Beaver)

Above right: Dana 152mm in firing position

Right: Zuzana 155mm

NORINCO 152mm Type 83 self-propelled gun (China)

Key recognition features

● Well sloped glacis plate with driver left and louvres right, horizontal hull top with vertical hull rear and large door opening right

● Large turret mounted rear with vertical sides and rear, long 152mm ordnance with large double baffle muzzle brake and fume extractor, 12.7mm AA MG on right side of roof

● Suspension each side has six road wheels with distinct gap between first/second, third/fourth and fifth/sixth, drive sprocket front, idler rear, three track-return rollers, no skirts

Specifications

Crew: 5
Armament: 1 x 152mm, 1 x 12.7mm MG (AA)
Ammunition: 30 x 152mm, 500 x 12.7mm (estimate)
Length gun forwards: 7.33m
Length hull: 6.882m
Width: 3.236m
Height with AA MG: 3.502m
Height turret top: 2.686m
Ground clearance: 0.45m
Weight, combat: 30,000kg
Power-to-weight ratio: 17.33hp/tonne
Ground pressure: 0.68kg/cm²
Engine: Type 12150L diesel developing 520hp
Maximum road speed: 55km/hr
Maximum road range: 450km
Fuel capacity: 885 lit
Fording: 1.3m
Vertical obstacle: 0.7m
Trench: 2.7m
Gradient: 60%
Side slope: 40%
Armour: 10mm (maximum) (estimate)
Armour type: Steel
NBC system: Not known
Night vision equipment: Yes (infra-red for driver)

Development

The 152mm Type 83 was first seen in public in 1984 and is similar to Russian 152mm self-propelled gun/howitzer M-1973 (2S3) which entered service in the early 1970s.

Driver sits front left with engine to his right and whole of rear

152mm Type 83

occupied by large turret. Turret has hatches in roof and large forward-opening door in each side. The Type 83 ordnance is based on Type 66 152mm towed weapon and fires HE projectile to maximum range of 17,230m. Turret traverses 360° and ordnance elevates from -5° to +65°. Semi-automatic loading device achieves rate of fire of four rounds a minute. In addition to 12.7mm MG mounted on turret roof for air defence, 7.62mm MG and Type 40 rocket launcher are carried internally.

Variants

Trench digger, chassis of Type 83 is used as a basis for a trench digging machine.
425mm mine-clearing rocket launcher, based on Type 83 chassis, carries two Type 762 mine clearing rockets.
130mm self-propelled gun, for trials purposes a Type 83 has had its 155mm ordnance replaced by a 130mm gun used in the 130mm Type 59 towed artillery system.

Status

Production complete. In service with Chinese Army.

Manufacturer

Chinese state arsenals.

Above: 152mm Type 83

Right: 152mm Type 83

United Defense SP122 self-propelled gun (Egypt/USA)

Key recognition features

● Hull has vertical sides with glacis plate sloping up to horizontal hull top that extends to half way to rear. On this has been mounted a new superstructure with vertical sides and curved front
● Mounted in front of superstructure is 122 mm barrel with slotted muzzle brake, 12.7 mm machine gun on turret roof
● Suspension on either side conists of seven road wheels with drive sprocket front, idler rear, no return track rollers

Specifications

Crew: 5
Armament: 1 x 122 mm howitzer, 1 x 12.7 mm machine gun
Ammunition: 85 x 122 mm, 500 x 12.7 mm
Length gun forward: 6.957 m
Length hull: 6.957 m
Width: 3.15 m
Height: 3.28 m without AA machine gun
Ground clearance: 0.46 m
Weight, combat: 24 948 kg
Power-to-weight ratio: 16.23 ne
Engine: Detroit diesel model 8V-71T turbocharged 8-cylinder diesel developing 405 hp at 2350 rpm
Maximum road speed: 56.3 km/h
Maximum road range: 300 km
Fuel capacity: 484 l
Fording: 1.7 m
Vertical obstacle: 0.61 m
Trench: 2 m
Gradient: 60%
Side slope: 40%
Armour: classified
Armour type: aluminium
NBC system: no
Night vision equipment: no

Development

The SP122 was developed for the Egyptian army by the now United Defense LP (previously BMY Combat Systems) and, following trials with two competing designs, was selected for service. From 1994–5 a total of 76 US-built SP122s were shipped to Egypt.

The SP122 combines the chassis of the M109 SPG/M992 FAASV with a new, fully enclosed superstructure at the rear. In front of this is the Russian D-30 122mm gun/howitzer which has been manufactured under licence in Egypt for many years by the Abu Zaabal Engineering Industries Company.

The driver is seated front left, with the engine compartment to his right and the fighting compartment extending to the rear. The 122 mm D-30 has manual traverse of up to 30 degrees right or left and elevation from -5˚ to +70˚. Maximum range is 15,300 m firing standard HE. Longer ranges are obtainable with rocket-assisted projectiles.

Variants

None

Status

Production complete. In service with Eygptian army only.

Manufacturer

United Defense LP, York, Pennsylvania, USA

Right: SP122 self propelled gun

GIAT Industries 155mm GCT self-propelled gun

Key recognition features

● Large fully enclosed flat-sided turret mounted centre of chassis, 155mm gun with double baffle muzzle brake overhanging front of vehicle
● Chassis identical to AMX-30 MBT's with five road wheels, idler front, drive sprocket rear, four track-return rollers. The upper part of the suspension is sometimes covered by a skirt

Specifications

Crew: 4
Armament: 1 x 155mm gun, 1 x 7.62mm or 12.7mm AA MG, 2 x 2 smoke grenade dischargers
Ammunition: 42 x 155mm, 2,050 x 7.62mm or 800 x 12.7mm
Length gun forwards: 10.25m
Length hull: 6.7m
Width: 3.15m
Height: 3.25m (turret top)
Ground clearance: 0.42m
Weight, combat: 42,000kg
Weight, empty: 38,000kg
Power-to-weight ratio: 17.14hp/tonne
Engine: Hispano-Suiza HS 110 12-cylinder water-cooled supercharged multi-fuel developing 720hp at 2,000rpm
Maximum road speed: 60km/hr
Maximum road range: 450km
Fuel capacity: 970 lit
Fording: 2.1m
Vertical obstacle: 0.93m (forwards), 0.48m (reverse)
Trench: 1.9m
Gradient: 60%
Side slope: 30%
Armour: 20mm max (estimate)
Armour type: Steel
NBC system: Yes
Night vision equipment: Yes (driver only)

Development

The 155mm GCT (Grande Cadence de Tir) was developed from 1969 to replace the 105mm Mk 61 and 155mm Mk F3 self-propelled guns in service with French Army. Production commenced at GIAT facility, Roanne, in 1977 and first production vehicles completed in 1978 for Saudi Arabia. By 1995 over 400 had been built for the home and export markets.

The 155mm gun has powered elevation from -4° to +66° with turret traverse powered through 360°. 155mm gun is fed by fully automatic loader that enables rate of fire of eight rounds a minute although it can also be loaded manually, in which case rate of fire is reduced to three rounds a minute. Maximum range using standard 155mm ME M107 projectile is 18,000m although other types of projectile can be fired including illuminating, smoke, extended range and anti-tank (mine).

Variants

No variants although various options in fire-control system are available. For trials purposes the GCT turret has been fitted onto the chassis of the Russian T-72 MBT. A 155mm/52 calibre version is under development.

Status

In production. In service with France, Iraq, Kuwait and Saudi Arabia.

Manufacturer

GIAT Industries, Roanne, France.

Above: GT 155mm

Below: GCT 155mm turret on T-72 MBT chassis (Christopher F Foss)

Above right: GCT 155mm (Pierre Touzin)

Below right: GCT 155mm (GIAT)

Wegmann 155 mm PzH 2000 self-propelled gun (Germany)

Key recognition features

● Large chassis with well sloped glacis plate, vertical sides and rear. Turret mounted at rear with long barrel mounted in turret front that overhangs vehicle. Barrel is fitted with fume extractor two thirds back from the muzzle

● Turret overhangs rear, sides curve inwards to flat roof which is fitted with 7.62 mm MG

● Suspension consists of seven road wheels with drive sprocket front and idler rear, upper part of suspension covered by wavy skirt

Specifications
Crew: 5
Armament: 1 x 155 mm, 1 x 7.62 mm MG, 2 x 4 smoke grenades
Ammunition: 60 x 155 mm, 1000 x 7.62 mm
Length gun forward: 11.67 m
Length hull: 7.91 m
Width: 3.58 m
Height: 3.06 m
Ground clearance: 0.4 m
Weight, combat: 55 000 kg
Weight, empty: n/a
Power-to-weight ratio: 18 hp/tonne
Engine: MTU diesel developing 1000 hp
Maximum road speed: 60 km/h
Maximum road range: 420 km
Fuel capacity: n/a
Fording: n/a
Vertical obstacle: 1 m
Trench: 3 m
Gradient: 50%
Side slope: 25%
Armour: classified
Armour type: steel (see text)
NBC system: yes
Night vision equipment: yes

Development
A consortium led by Wegmann was selected to continue development of the Panzerhaubitze 2000 155 mm self-propelled artillery system for the German army. It was accepted for service in 1995 and the initial order was for 185 vehicles. Wegmann is the prime contractor, responsible for the turret and systems integration with MaK responsible for the complete chassis.

The driver is seated at the front right with the powerpack to his left and the fighting compartment to his rear. The 155 mm/52 calibre gun elevates from -2.5˚ to +65˚ and the turret can traverse through 360˚. An automatic loading system enables 8 rounds to be fired in 60 seconds. The charges are loaded manually. Maximum range is 40 km with assisted projectiles or 30 km with conventional munitions.

The PzH 2000 can be fitted with reactive armour on the upper hull and turret roof to protect it from top attack weapons.

Variants
None

Status
Entering production for the German army

Manufacturer
Wegmann & Co GmbH, Kassel, Germany

Above: PzH 2000

Above right: PzH 2000

Far right: PzH 2000

Right: PzH 2000

OTOBREDA Palmaria 155mm self-propelled gun (Italy)

Key recognition features

● Large flat-sided turret mounted centre of hull with 155mm howitzer and double baffle muzzle brake and fume extractor

● When travelling, turret is normally traversed to rear and 155mm howitzer held in position by travelling lock at hull rear

● Driver at front, turret centre, engine and transmission rear. Suspension has seven road wheels, idler front, drive sprocket rear, track-return rollers. Upper part of suspension covered by skirts

Specifications

Crew: 5
Armament: 1 x 155mm howitzer, 1 x 7.62mm AA MG, 2 x 4 smoke grenade dischargers
Ammunition: 30 x 155mm, 1000 x 7.62mm
Length gun forward: 11.474m
Length hull: 7.265m
Width: 3.35m
Height: 2.874m (without AA MG)
Ground clearance: 0.4m
Weight, combat: 46,000kg
Weight, empty: 43,000kg
Power-to-weight ratio: 16.3hp/tonne
Engine: MTU MB 837 Ea-500 4-stroke, turbocharged, 8-cylinder multi-fuel diesel developing 750hp
Maximum road speed: 60km/hr
Maximum road range cruising: 500km
Fuel capacity: 800 lit
Fording: 1.2m (without preparation), 4m (with preparation)
Vertical obstacle: 1m
Trench: 3m
Gradient: 60%
Side slope: 30%
Armour: Classified
Armour type: Hull steel, turret aluminium
NBC system: Optional
Night vision equipment: Optional

Development

The Palmaria 155mm was developed as a private venture by OTOBREDA specifically for export with first prototype completed in 1981 and first production vehicles the following year. It shares many automotive components with OTOBREDA Melara OF-40 MBT, also developed for export, and in service with United Arab Emirates.

Driver and auxiliary power unit are at front, turret centre, engine and transmission rear. 155mm howitzer has powered elevation from -5° to +70° with powered turret traverse through 360°. It fires HE projectile to maximum range of 24,700m, and other types including HE rocket-assisted, illuminating, and smoke. Palmaria fires one round per 15 seconds using automatic loader.

Variants

No variants in service but its chassis has been fitted with twin 35mm ATAK turret and could be fitted with OTOBREDA 76mm anti-aircraft/helicopter turret. Argentina ordered 25 turrets for installation on lengthened TAM tank chassis, with final deliveries during 1986/87.

Status

Production complete but can be resumed if required. In service with Libya and Nigeria, turret in service with Argentina on modified TAM chassis.

Manufacturer

OTOBREDA, La Spezia, Italy.

Above: Palmaria 155 mm

Right: Palmaria 155 mm

Below: Palmaria 155 mm

Below right: Palmaria 155 mm

435

Mitsubishi Type 75 155mm self-propelled gun (Japan)

Key recognition features

● Fully enclosed turret at far rear of hull with vertical sides and rear with chamfer between sides and turret roof
● 155mm howitzer has double baffle muzzle brake and fume extractor almost halfway down ordnance
● Suspension has six large road wheels with last road wheel acting as idler, drive sprocket front but no track-return rollers

Specifications

Crew: 6
Armament: 1 x 155mm howitzer, 1 x 12.7mm AA MG
Ammunition: 28 x 155mm, 1,000 x 12.7mm
Length gun forwards: 7.79m
Length hull: 6.64m
Width: 3.09m
Height to turret roof: 2.545m
Ground clearance: 0.4m
Weight, combat: 25,300kg
Power-to-weight ratio: 17.78hp/tonne
Ground pressure: 0.64kg/cm²
Engine: Mitsubishi 6ZF 2-cycle 6-cylinder air-cooled diesel developing 450hp at 2,200rpm
Maximum road speed: 47km/hr
Maximum road range: 300km
Fuel capacity: 650 lit
Fording: 1.3m
Vertical obstacle: 0.7m
Trench: 2.5m
Gradient: 60%
Side slope: 30%
Armour: Classified
Armour type: Aluminium
NBC system: Yes
Night vision equipment: Yes (driver only)

Development

Developed from 1969 to meet requirements of Japanese Ground Self Defence Force with first prototypes completed in 1971/72 and accepted for service as 155mm Type 75 self-propelled howitzer in October 1975. A total of 201 production systems was built for the Japanese Ground Self Defence Force with final deliveries taking place in 1968.

Layout and appearance is similar to US 155mm M109A1/M109A2 with driver and engine compartment front and fully enclosed turret rear. The 155mm howitzer has powered elevation from -5° to +65°, turret traverse through 360°, and fires US HE projectile to range of 15,000m or Japanese HE projectile to maximum range of 19,000m. Other types of projectile include illuminating and smoke. Semi-automatic loading system mounted in rear of turret allows 18 rounds to be fired in three minutes.

Variants

No variants but chassis may be used as basis for a new 155mm self-propelled howitzer using ordnance of towed FH-70 now being produced under licence in Japan.

Status

Production complete. In service with Japanese Ground Self Defence Force.

Manufacturer

Mitsubishi Heavy Industries (hull and final assembly), Japan Iron Works/Nihon Seiko Jyo (gun and turret), Japan.

Above: Type 75 155mm

Above right: Type 75 155mm showing roof-mounted 12.7mm (M2) HB AA MG (Paul Beaver)

Right: Type 75 155mm with ordnance in travelling lock

Model 89 122 mm SPH (Romania)

Key recognition features

- Low profile turret with curved front mounted at rear of long hull which has a pointed front
- Well sloped glacis plate, horizontal hull top, vertical hull rear with door
- Vertical hull sides with seven road wheels, drive sprocket front, idler rear and three track return rollers

Specifications

Crew: 5
Armament: 1 x 122 mm howitzer
Ammunition: 40 x 122 mm (estimate)
Length gun forwards: 7.305 m
Length hull: 7.305 m
Width: 3.15 m
Height: 2.665 m
Ground clearance: n/avail
Weight, combat: 17 500 kg
Weight, unloaded: 15 500 kg (estimate)
Power-to-weight ratio: 20.5 hp/t
Ground pressure: n/avail
Engine: 1240 V8DTS supercharged V-8 diesel developing 360 hp
Maximum road speed: 65 km/h
Maximum road range: 500 km
Fuel capacity: 600 l
Fording: amphibious
Vertical obstacle: 0.80 m
Trench: 2.50 m
Gradient: 60%
Side slope: 40%
Night vision equipment: yes
Armour: classified
Armour type: steel (see text)
NBC system: yes

Development

The Model 89 122 mm self-propelled howitzer was developed in the 1980s to meet the requirements of the Romanian Army and essentially consists of a locally designed chassis that incorporates some parts of the MLI-84 infantry combat vehicle which is in turn based on the Russian BMP-1 infantry combat vehicle.

The new chassis has been fitted with the complete turret of the Russian 122 mm 2S1 self-propelled howitzer which is covered in detail in the previous entry. The chassis has the driver and engine compartment at the front with the remainder of the space being taken up by the fighting compartment.

These turrets were imported from Russia and are armed with a 122 mm 2A31 howitzer which can be elevated from -3° to +70° with turret traverse a full 360°. Maximum range firing a standard HE projectile is 15 300 m or 21 900 m firing a rocket assisted projectile.

The vehicle is fully amphibious being propelled in the water by two waterjets mounted at the rear of the hull. The original Russian 2S1 is also fully amphibious but is propelled in the water by its tracks only.

Variants

There are no known variants.

Status

Production complete. In service only with Romania.

Manufacturer

Chassis, Romanian state factories. Turret, Russian state factories.

Main picture: *Model 89*

Inset: *Model 89*

152mm 2S19 self-propelled gun (Russia)

Key recognition features

● Well sloped glacis plate with turret in centre and powerpack at the rear

● Turret has vertical front, sides and rear with upper part curving inwards to flat roof on which a 12.7mm MG is mounted

● Chassis has six road wheels, idler front, drive sprocket at rear and track-return rollers, upper part of suspension is covered by skirt

Specifications

Crew: 5
Armament: 1 x 152mm, 1 x 12.7mm MG (AA)
Ammunition: 50 x 152mm, 300 x 12.7mm
Length overall: 11.917m
Width: 3.38m
Height to turret roof: 2.985m
Weight: 42,000kg
Power-to-weight ratio: 20hp/tonne
Engine: 840hp diesel
Maximum road speed: 60km/hr
Maximum road range: 500km
Fording: 1.2
Vertical obstacle: 0.5m
Trench: 2.8m
Gradient: 47%
Side slope: 36%
Armour: Classified
Armour type: Steel/advanced
NBC system: Yes
Night vision equipment: Yes (passive)

Development

The 152mm 2S19 was first revealed in 1990 and at that time was said to be in service in small numbers as the replacement for the older 152mm 2S3 self-propelled gun/howitzer. The 2S19 uses the same ordnance as the towed MSTA-A 2A65 152mm gun/howitzer which is referred to by NATO as the M1986, this being the year that it was first observed.

The 152mm 2S19 is based on a T-80 chassis that incorporates some components of the T-72 MBT, with the driver being seated at the front, fully enclosed turret in the centre and powerpack at the rear.

The 152mm ordnance is fitted with a muzzle brake and fume extractor and when travelling is held in position by a travel lock that is mounted on the glacis plate. The 152mm ordnance will fire a HE-FRAG projectile to a maximum range of 24,700m although using an extended range projectile a range of almost 40,000m can be achieved. Turret traverse is a full 360˚ with weapon elevation from -3˚ to +68˚. An automatic loading system is fitted which enables a maximum rate of fire of eight rounds a minute to be achieved. A bustle-mounted APU is fitted to the turret to allow it to be used with the main engine switched off.

Variants

As far as it is known there are no variants of the 152mm 2S19 self-propelled artillery system. Russian sources have stated that a 155mm version is under development for export market.

Status

Production. In service with Russia.

Manufacturer

Russian state factories.

Above: 152mm 2S19 self-propelled gun

Above right: 152mm 2S19 self-propelled gun (Christopher F Foss)

Right: 152mm 2S19 self-propelled gun (T J Gander)

152mm self-propelled gun M1973 (2S3) (Russia)

Key recognition features

● Large turret with curved front mounted rear of hull, commander's cupola offset to left
● 152mm barrel overhangs chassis and has double baffle muzzle brake and fume extractor
● Suspension has six road wheels, drive sprocket front, idler rear, four track-return rollers. Distinct gap between first/second and second/third road wheels

Specifications

Crew: 6 (4+2)
Armament: 1 x 152mm howitzer, 1 x 7.62mm AA MG
Ammunition: 46 x 152mm, 1500 x 7.62mm
Length gun forwards: 8.4m
Length hull: 7.765m
Width: 3.25m
Height: 3.05m
Ground clearance: 0.45m
Weight, combat: 27,500kg
Power-to-weight ratio: 17.33hp/tonne
Ground pressure: 0.59kg/cm²
Engine: V-59 V-12 water-cooled diesel developing 520hp
Maximum road speed: 60km/hr
Maximum road range: 500km
Fuel capacity: 830 lit
Fording: 1.0m
Vertical obstacle: 0.7m
Trench: 3.0m
Gradient: 60%
Side slope: 30%
Armour: 15mm (maximum turret), 20mm (maximum hull)
Armour type: Steel
NBC system: Yes
Night vision equipment: Yes (infra-red for driver and commander)

Development

The 152mm self-propelled gun/self-propelled gun M1973 (US Army designation) entered service with Russian Army in the early 1970s and is similar to US 155mm M109 self-propelled gun. Its correct Russian designation is SO-152 but in Russian Army it is commonly known as Akatsiya (Acacia); its industrial number is 2S3. M1973 is based on chassis of SA-4 Ganef SAM system but has six rather than seven road wheels. Driver's and engine compartment at front with fully enclosed power-operated turret at far rear. 152.4mm gun/howitzer is based on towed D-20 fun/howitzer and mounted in power-operated turret with traverse of 360°, elevation from -4° to +60°.

The 152.4mm howitzer fires HE-FRAG projectile to maximum range of 18,500m or rocket-assisted projectile to maximum range of 24,000m, other types of projectile including 2kT tactical nuclear, chemical, HEAT-FS, AP-T, illuminating and smoke. Of the six-man crew, two are normally deployed as ammunition handlers at hull rear when in firing position. They feed projectiles and charges to the turret crew via the two circular hatches in the hull rear.

Late production versions, with some modifications, are designated the 2S3M and 2S3M1.

Variants

No known variants although chassis shares a number of components with SA-4 Ganef, 240mm self-propelled mortar M1975, and 152mm self-propelled gun 2S5.

Status

Production complete. In service with Russia, Hungary, Iraq, Libya and Syria.

Manufacturer

Russian state arsenals.

152mm self-propelled gun/self-propelled gun M1973 (2S3)

Right: 152mm self-propelled gun/self-propelled gun M1973 (2S3) with ordnance in travelling lock

Below: 152mm self-propelled gun/self-propelled gun M1973 (2S3)

Below right: 152mm self-propelled gun/self-propelled gun M1973 (2S3) with ordnance in travelling lock

122mm self-propelled gun M1974 (2S1) (Russia)

Key recognition features

● Low profile turret mounted at rear of long hull
● Suspension has seven large road wheels, drive sprocket front, idler rear, no track-return rollers
● 122mm howitzer does not overhand front of chassis, has double baffle muzzle brake and fume extractor

Specifications

Crew: 4
Armament: 1 x 122mm howitzer
Ammunition: 40 x 122mm
Length: 7.26m
Width: 2.85m
Height: 2.732m
Ground clearance: 0.40m
Weight, combat: 15,700kg
Power-to-weight ratio: 19.1hp/tonne
Ground pressure: 0.49kg/cm²
Engine: YaMZ-238, V-8 water-cooled diesel developing 300hp at 2,100rpm
Maximum road speed: 60km/hr
Maximum water speed: 4.5km/hr
Maximum road range: 500km
Fuel capacity: 550 lit
Fording: Amphibious
Vertical obstacle: 0.70m
Trench: 2.75m
Gradient: 77%
Side slope: 55%
Armour: 20mm (max) (estimate)
Armour type: Steel
NBC system: Yes
Night vision equipment: Yes (infra-red for driver and commander)

Development

The 122mm self-propelled gun M1974 (US Army designation) entered service with Russian Army in the early 1970s and was first seen in public during Polish Army parade in 1974. Correct

Russian designation is SO-122 but in Russian Army is commonly known as Gvozdika (Carnation); its industrial number is 2S1. It uses many automotive components of MT-LB multi-purpose tracked armoured vehicle including engine and suspension.

Driver's and engine compartment is at front with fully enclosed power-operated turret towards rear. 122mm howitzer is modified version of ordnance used in D-30 towed howitzer and fires HE projectile to maximum range of 15,300m or HE rocket-assisted projectile to maximum range of 21,900m. Other 122mm projectiles fired by M1974 include HEAT-FS, illuminating and smoke. Turret traverses through 360° and 122mm howitzer elevates from -3° to +70°.

The M1974 is fully amphibious with very little preparation and once afloat is propelled by its tracks. An unusual feature is that its suspension can be adjusted to give different heights. Normal tracks are 400mm wide but 670mm wide tracks can be fitted for snow or swamp.

Variants

Artillery Command and Reconnaissance Vehicles. These are known as the MT-LBus (1V12 series) by the Russian Army and are based on the MT-LB chassis.
1V13 is called M1974-1 by NATO and is deputy battery commander's vehicle.
1V14 is called M1974-2A by NATO and is the battery commander's vehicle.
1V15 is called M1974-2B by NATO and is the battalion commander's vehicle.
1V16 is called the M1974-3 by NATO and is the deputy battalion commander's vehicle.
1V21/22/23/24 and 25 are air defence management vehicles.
MT-LBus is a jamming vehicle on M1974 chassis.

Above: 122mm M1974 (2S1)

Right: 122mm M1974 (2S1) (Finnish MoD)

Dog Ear radar vehicle used by air defence units is on M1974 series chassis.

M1979 mine-clearing vehicle has turret-like superstructure with three rockets fired across minefield towing hose filled with explosive which detonates on ground.

RKhM chemical reconnaissance vehicle has raised superstructure on which is mounted 7.62mm MG cupola with boxes for dispensing pennants showing path through contaminated areas.

Da1 NBC Reconnaissance Vehicle.

Zoopark-1 artillery locating radar system.

Status

In production. In service with Algeria, Angola, Bulgaria, Czech Republic, Ethiopia, Hungary, Iraq, Libya, Poland, Russia, Slovakia, Syria, Yemen and former Yugoslavia.

Manufacturer

Bulgarian, Polish and Russian state factories.

Right: 122mm M1974 (2S1) Christopher F Foss)

LIW G6 155mm self-propelled gun (South Africa)

Key recognition features

● Three large road wheels each side with distinctive gap between first and second road wheel, driver's compartment at very front of hull in centre with windscreens to his front and sides

● Large turret at rear with raised commander's cupola on right side, front and sides of turret slope slightly inwards, 155mm ordnance has long barrel with large single baffle muzzle brake and fume extractor. When travelling ordnance is horizontal and held in travel lock

● Hull front is pointed and hull rear vertical, louvres in upper sides of hull between first and second road wheel station

Specifications

Crew: 6
Configuration: 6x6
Armament: 1 x 155mm, 1 x 12.7mm MG (AA), 2 x 4 smoke grenade dischargers
Ammunition: 45 x 155mm, 1,000 x 12.7mm
Length gun forwards: 10.335m
Length hull: 9.2m
Width: 3.4m
Height: 3.8m (including MG), 3.3m (turret top)
Ground clearance: 0.45m
Weight, combat: 47,000kg
Weight, empty: 42,500kg
Power-to-weight ratio: 11.17hp/tonne
Engine: Air-cooled diesel developing 525hp
Maximum road speed: 90km/hr
Maximum road range: 700km
Fuel capacity: 700 lit
Fording: 1m
Vertical obstacle: 0.5m
Trench: 1m
Gradient: 40%
Side slope: 30%
Armour: 23mm (maximum)
Armour type: Steel
NBC system: Yes (BC only)
Night vision equipment: Yes (passive)

Development

The 155mm G6 self-propelled howitzer was developed by LIW to meet the requirements of the South African Artillery Corps for a highly mobile artillery system capable of operating over very rough terrain. The first prototype completed in 1981 was followed by a series of additional prototype and pre-production vehicles with the first production vehicles being completed in 1988. Prime contractor for the G6 is LIW, part of the Denel Group who also manufactures the 155mm G5 towed artillery system which has identical ballistic characteristics to the G6 as they both have a 155mm/45 calibre ordnance. Chassis of the G6 is manufactured by Reumech OMC.

The driver is seated at the very front of the vehicle in the centre, to his rear is the powerpack with the turret being mounted at the very rear. Turret traverse is 180°, although only 90o is used with weapon elevation being from -5° to +75°. Firing Extended Range Full Bore - Base Bleed (ERFB-BB) projectiles a maximum range of 39,000m can be achieved. A flick rammer is provided to obtain higher rates of fire. The G6 is normally supported in action by another vehicle which carries additional projectiles and charges. When deployed in the firing position, four stabilisers are lowered to the ground, one either side of the hull between the first and second road wheels and two at the rear.

Standard equipment includes an APU, air conditioning system, fire detection and suppression system, computerised fire control system, powered steering and a central tyre pressure regulation system.

Variants

Chassis has been proposed for other applications including being fitted with GEC-Marconi Marksman twin 35mm air defence turret. LIW have developed the T6 155mm/45 calibre turret from the G6 and this has been fitted to T-72 MBT for trials.

Status

In service with Oman, South Africa and the United Arab Emirates.

Manufacturer

LIW, Pretoria, South Africa (but see text).

Right: LIW 155mm G6

Far right: LIW 155mm G6

Below right: LIW 155mm G6 (Christopher F Foss)

Below: LIW 155mm G6

Bofors 155mm Bandkanon 1A self-propelled gun (Sweder

Key recognition features

● 155mm gun is mounted in fully enclosed turret at rear of hull with 14 round magazine and ammunition handling system protruding well to rear
● 155mm gun with pepperpot muzzle brake extends over front of vehicle, normally held in position by travelling lock
● Suspension each side has six large road wheels, last one acting as idler, drive sprocket front, no track-return rollers

Specifications

Crew: 5
Armament: 1 x 155mm gun, 1 x 7.62mm AA MG
Ammunition: 14 x 155mm
Length gun forwards: 11m
Length hull: 6.55m
Width: 3.37m
Height: 3.85m (with AA MG), 3.25m (turret top)
Ground clearance: 0.37m
Weight, combat: 53,000kg
Power-to-weight ratio: 10.18hp/tonne
Ground pressure: 0.9kg/cm2
Engine: Rolls-Royce K60 diesel developing 240hp at 3,750rpm and Boeing Model 502/10MA gas turbine developing 300shp at 38,000rpm
Maximum road speed: 28km/hr
Maximum road range: 230km
Fuel capacity: 1,445 lit
Fording: 1m
Vertical obstacle: 0.95m
Trench: 2m
Gradient: 60%
Side slope: 30%
Armour: 20mm (maximum)
Armour type: Steel
NBC system: No
Night vision equipment: Yes (driver only)

Development

The 155mm Bandkanon 1A was developed by Bofors in the late 1950s for the Swedish army and was produced in very limited numbers during 1967-68. It uses many automotive components of the Bofors S-tank also used by Swedish army. Engine and transmission are mounted at front of vehicle with fully enclosed four-man turret at rear. 155mm gun has manual elevation from -3˚ to +40˚ with powered elevation from +2˚ to +38˚. Traverse is manual 15˚ left and right at 0o elevation and above, and 15˚ left and 4˚ right below 0o depression. The 155mm gun is fully automatic, fed by magazine holding 14 rounds in two layers of seven at rear of turret, and fires HE projectile to maximum range of 25,600m.

More recently these systems have been upgraded with the Rolls-Royce diesel being replaced by a Detroit Diesel 6V-53T developing 290hp coupled to a new automatic transmission developed and produced by Bofors. The latest upgrade includes the installation of the Honeywell MAPS and gun interfaced with the new Swedish Army SKER fire control system.

Status

Production complete. In service with Swedish Army only.

Manufacturer

AB Bofors, Bofors, Sweden.

Left 155mm Bandkanon 1A in travelling configuration

Above: 155mm Bandkanon 1A in travelling configuration

Right: 155mm Bandkanon 1A in firing position

Vickers Shipbuilding and Engineering Limited 155mm AS90 self-propelled gun (UK)

Key recognition features

- well sloped glacis plate with driver on left and raised engine compartment to his right. Turret at very rear of chassis with sloped front, sloped sides and vertical rear
- 155mm ordnance has double baffle muzzle brake and when in travelling lock projects over front of hull. Travel lock is pivoted at very front of hull and lays back on glacis plate when not required
- Chassis has vertical sides and rear with each side having six dual rubber tyred road wheels, drive sprocket at front, idler at rear and three track-return rollers

Specifications

Crew: 5
Armament: 1 x 155mm, 1 x 12.7mm MG (AA), 2 x 5 smoke grenade dischargers
Ammunition: 48 x 155mm, 1,000 x 12.7mm
Length gun forwards: 9.90m
Length hull: 7.20m
Width: 3.40m
Height overall: 3m
Ground clearance: 0.41m
Weight, combat: 45,000kg
Power-to-weight ratio: 14.66hp/tonne
Ground pressure: 0.90kg/cm²
Engine: Cummins VTA 903T 660T-660 V-8 diesel developing 660bhp at 2,800rpm
Maximum road speed: 55km/hr
Maximum road range: 370km
Fuel capacity: 750 lit
Fording: 1.5m
Vertical obstacle: 0.88m
Trench: 2.8m
Gradient: 60%
Side slope: 25%
Armour: 17mm (max)
Armour type: Steel
NBC system: Yes
Night vision equipment: Yes (passive)

Development

In 1981 Vickers Shipbuilding and Engineering (VSEL) built the prototype of a 155mm artillery turret called the GBT 155. VSEL then started development work, as a private venture, on a brand new complete 155mm self-propelled artillery system which was called the AS90, the first of two prototypes of this were completed in 1986. The AS90 was subsequently entered in the British Army's Abbot Replacement Competition and in 1989 AS90 was selected and a contract placed for 179 systems, with final deliveries being made to the British Army early in 1995. AS90 has replaced all other self-propelled guns in the British Army.

The driver is seated at the front left with the powerpack to his right, and the turret at the rear. Access to the turret is via a large door in the chassis rear. Turret traverse is a full 360° with weapon elevation from -5° to +70°. The 155mm 39 calibre ordnance has a maximum range of 24,700m using standard ammunition or over 30,000m using extended range full bore ammunition. Of the 48 projectiles carried, 31 are stowed in the turret bustle magazine. A burst rate of three rounds in 10 seconds can be achieved with sustained rate of fire being 2 rounds a minute.

The suspension of the AS90 is of the hydropneumatic type and standard equipment on British Army systems includes muzzle velocity measuring equipment, land navigation system and a fully automatic gun laying capability.

Variants

There are no variants of the 155mm AS90 although Vickers Shipbuilding and Engineering has proposed the chassis for a wide range of other systems including recovery, maintenance and flatbed. Although British Army AS90s have a 39 calibre barrel, 45 and 52 calibre barrels have already been fitted for trials purposes. Some British Army AS90s will be fitted with a 155mm/52 calibre ordnance in future. AS90 turret has also been fitted onto T-72 MBT chassis for trials in India.

Status

Production complete but can be resumed. In service with British Army.

Manufacturer

Vickers Shipbuilding and Engineering Limited, Barrow-in-Furness, UK.

Right: AS90 155mm self-propelled gun

Below right: 155mm self-propelled gun

Below: 155mm self-propelled gun

United Defense, LP, M109A2 155mm self-propelled gun (USA)

Key recognition features

● Hull has vertical sides with glacis plate sloping up to horizontal hull top which extends to rear. Spade mounted each side of rear hull door

● Large turret-mounted rear with curved front, vertical sides and rear. Long barrel with fume extractor and double baffle muzzle brake that overhangs front of vehicle when travelling. Roof-mounted 12.7mm AA MG

● Suspension has seven small road wheels, drive sprocket front, idler rear, no track-return rollers

Specifications

Crew: 6
Armament: 1 x 155mm howitzer, 1 x 12.7mm MG
Ammunition: 36 x 155mm, 500 x 12.7mm
Length gun forwards: 9.12m
Length hull: 6.19m
Width: 3.15m
Height: 3.28m (including AA MG)
Height: 2.8m (reduced)
Ground clearance: 0.46m
Weight, combat: 24,948kg
Weight, empty: 21,110kg
Power-to-weight ratio: 16.23hp/tonne
Ground pressure: 0.85kg/cm²
Engine: Detroit Diesel Model 8V-71T, turbocharged, liquid-cooled 8-cylinder diesel developing 405bhp at 2,300rpm
Maximum road speed: 56.3km/hr
Maximum road range: 349km
Fuel capacity: 511 lit
Fording: 1.07m
Vertical obstacle: 0.53m
Trench: 1.83m
Gradient: 60%
Side slope: 40%
Armour: Classified
Armour type: Aluminium
NBC system: Optional
Night vision equipment: Optional (infra-red or passive for driver)

Development

M109 series was developed in the 1950s and shares common chassis with M108 105mm self-propelled howitzer. First production vehicles completed in 1962 and production of latest M109 continues with over 4000 built so far.

The driver sits front left, engine compartment to his right and large turret at hull rear. Turret traverses through 360° and 155mm howitzer elevates from -3° to +75°. Ammunition is separate loading type with 34 projectiles and charges carried, plus two Copperhead Cannon Launched Guided Projectiles. Following types of projectile fired by M109A2: HE (maximum range 18,100m), Improved Conventional Munition, Remote Anti-Armor Mine system (RAAMS), Area Denial Artillery Munition (ADAM), High Explosive Rocket Assist (HERA), illuminating, smoke, high explosive (grenade), and numerous other types.

Variants

M109, first model to enter service has very short barrel, double baffle muzzle brake and large fume extractor to immediate rear, maximum range 14,600m.
M109A1 is M109 with new and longer barrel and other improvements, maximum range (standard HE) 18,100m, as M109A2 which was built with these and other improvements.
M109A3 is an upgraded M109A1 with a number of modifications including new gun mount and improved RAM-D.
M109A4 is an upgraded M109A2 or M109A3 with improvements to NBC system etc.
M109A5 is upgraded M109A4.
M109A6 is the latest production model for US Army and is also

referred to as the Paladin with first production vehicles
completed in 1992. Many improvements including new turret
with longer barrel ordnance, automatic fire control system,
upgraded suspension and improved armour.

M109A3G is German Army M109G with many improvements
including new ordnance.

M109L, Italy has fitted its M109s with ordnance of FH-70,
these are known as M109L.

M109AL is Israeli version of M109.

M109 Taiwan uses M108/M109 chassis but without turret
and has 155mm weapon in open mount. Short barrel version
uses ordnance of towed M114 and more recent version has
new and much longer ordnance.

M992 Field Artillery Ammunition Support Vehicle, in service
with Saudi Arabia, Spain, Thailand and the United States is
M109 chassis with fully enclosed rear hull to carry 155mm
ammunition and feeds this to M109 self-propelled gun when
in firing position.

FDC, Fire Detection Centre or Fire Control Centre, uses same
chassis and hull as M992. Greece and Taiwan.

Status
In production. In service with Austria, Belgium, Canada,
Denmark, Egypt, Ethiopia, Germany, Greece, Iran, Israel, Italy,
Jordan, South Korea, Kuwait, Morocco, Netherlands, Norway,
Pakistan, Peru, Portugal, Saudi Arabia, Spain, Switzerland,
Taiwan, Tunisia, UK and USA.

Manufacturer
United Defense, LP, York, Pennsylvania, USA.

*Above:
M109A2 of
US Army
(US Army)*

*Right:
M109A1
(T Gander)*

453

M108 105mm self-propelled gun (USA)

Key recognition features

● Large turret with curved front mounted at rear of hull which is identical to M109 155mm self-propelled howitzer
● Very short barrel with fume extractor
● Chassis has seven small road wheels, drive sprocket front, idler rear, no track-return rollers

Specifications

Crew: 5
Armament: 1 x 105mm howitzer, 1 x 12.7mm AA MG
Ammunition: 87 x 105mm, 500 x 12.7mm
Length: 6.114m
Width: 3.295m, 3.149m (reduced)
Height: 3.155m (including AA MG), 2.794m (reduced)
Ground clearance: 0.451m
Weight, combat: 22,452kg
Weight, empty: 18,436kg
Power-to-weight ratio: 18.038bhp/tonne
Ground pressure: 0.71kg/cm²
Engine: Detroit Diesel Model 8V-71T, turbocharged, 2-stroke liquid-cooled, 8-cylinder diesel developing 405bhp at 2,300rpm
Maximum road speed: 56km/hr
Maximum water speed: 6.43km/hr
Maximum road range: 390km
Fuel capacity: 511 lit
Fording: 1.828m, amphibious with preparation
Vertical obstacle: 0.533m
Trench: 1.828m
Gradient: 60%
Side slope: 30%
Armour: Classified
Armour type: Aluminium
NBC system: No
Night vision equipment: Yes (driver only)

Development

The M108 105mm was developed in the 1950s at the same time as M109 155mm which has same chassis and turret with modifications. Production of M108 was by Cadillac Gage Motor Car Division of General Motors Corporation in 1962/63. In US Army it replaced M52 105mm self-propelled howitzer but M108 itself was soon replaced in US Army by M109.

The 105mm M103 howitzer has manual elevation from -4° to +74°, manual turret traverse through 360°. Maximum range firing HE round is 11,500m, other projectiles including rocket-assisted, illuminating and smoke.

Amphibious kit was developed for M108 which enabled vehicle to propel itself across rivers and streams by its tracks. As far as it is known this amphibious kit has not been deployed with any of the current unders of the M108 system.

Variants

Belgian Army has replaced its M108s with M109A2 155mm system and some M108s have been converted to command post vehicles designated VBCL.

Status

Production complete. In service with Brazil, Spain, Taiwan, Tunisia and Turkey.

Manufacturer

Cadillac Motor Car Division, General Motors, USA.

Top: M108 105mm
Above: M108 105mm with 12.7mm M2 HB anti-aircraft MG
Above right: M108 105mm (C R Zwart)
Right: M108 105mm (S Tunbridge)

SELF-PROPELLED ANTI-AIRCRAFT GUNS

M53/59 (Czech Republic/Slovakia)

Key recognition features

● 2 x 30mm cannon at rear in open mount with vertical magazines
● Engine front, crew compartment centre with plexiglass commander's cupola
● Six road wheels, two front and four rear

Specifications

Crew:
Armament: 2 x 30mm cannon
Ammunition: 600-800 x 30mm
Length: 6.92m
Width: 2.35
Height with magazines: 2.95m
Height without magazines: 2.585m
Firing height: 2.41m
Ground clearance: 0.4m
Weight, combat: 10,300kg
Power-to-weight ratio: 11.57hp/tonne
Engine: Tatra T 912-2 6-cylinder in-line air-cooled diesel developing 110hp at 2,200rpm
Maximum road speed: 60km/hr
Maximum road range: 500km
Fuel capacity: 120 lit
Fording: 0.8m
Vertical obstacle: 0.46m
Trench: 0.69m
Gradient: 60%
Side slope: 30%
Armour: 10mm (estimated)
Armour type: Steel
NBC system: No
Night vision equipment: No

Development

The M53/59 was developed to meet requirements of former Czechoslovak Army and entered service in the late 1950s. It consists of a much modified Praga V3S (6x6) truck chassis with removable version of standard M53 twin 30mm towed anti-aircraft gun system. The twin 30mm cannon have an effective anti-aircraft range of around 3,000m and types of ammunition fired include HE-T.

The open turret has powered traverse through 360° and cannon have powered elevation from -10° to +85°. Each gun is fed from vertical magazines holding 50 rounds of ammunition.

The M53/59 is a clear weather system only. Complete mount and guns can be removed for ground use. This is achieved by using two ramps that are stowed under the vehicle when not required. The weapons are winched back onto the vehicle using an onboard winch.

Variants

No variants.

Status

Production complete. In service with Czech Republic, Libya, Slovakia and former Yugoslavia.

Manufacturer

Avia Zavody Letnany, former Czechoslovakia (chassis), and former Czechoslovak state arsenals (armoured body, armament and final assembly).

Above left: M53/59 twin 30mm SPAAG in travelling position
Left: M53/59 twin 30mm SPAAG in travelling configuration showing vertical magazines
Top: M53/59 twin 30mm SPAAG in travelling configuration
Above: M53/59 twin 30mm SPAAG in firing position with guns to rear

Panhard M3 VDA (France)

Key recognition features

● Turret mounted on top of hull with two externally mounted 20mm cannon, radar scanner on turret rear
● When in firing position four hydraulic jacks normally deployed
● M3 APC hull has straight sides and rear with chamfer between side and top, glacis slopes at 45o to roof

Specifications

Crew: 3
Configuration: 4x4
Armament: 2 x 20mm cannon, 1 x 7.62mm MG, 2 x 2 smoke grenade dischargers
Ammunition: 600 x 20mm, 200 x 7.62mm
Length: 4.45m
Width: 2.4m
Height: 2.995m (without radar)
Ground clearance: 0.35m
Wheelbase: 2.7m
Weight, combat: 7,200kg
Power-to-weight ratio: 12.5hp/tonne
Engine: Panhard Model 4 HD 4-cylinder air-cooled petrol developing 90hp at 4,700rpm
Maximum road speed: 90km/hr
Maximum road range: 1,000km
Fuel capacity: 165 lit
Fording: Amphibious
Vertical obstacle: 0.3m
Trench: 0.8m (one channel), 3.1m (three channels)
Gradient: 60%
Side slope: 30%
Armour: 12mm (max)
Armour type: steel
NBC system: No
Night vision equipment: Infra-red or passive (driver)(optional)

Development

Developed as private venture specifically for export, design work on the M3 VDA commenced in 1972 with first prototype completed in 1972 and first production vehicles in 1975. The Panhard M3 VDA (Véhicule de Défense Antiaerienne) is modified Panhard M3 (4x4) APC with one-man power-operated turret designed and built by Dassault Electronique. It has surveillance radar on turret rear and two 20mm cannon, each of which has two cyclic rates of fire, 200 or 1,000 rounds per minute. Turret has powered traverse through 360°, 20mm cannon has powered elevation from -5° to +85°. Manual controls for emergency use. Clear weather system only.

Variants

The turret has been installed on wide range of other chassis including AMX VCI, VAB (6x6), ERC (6x6), SIBMAS (6x6) and Steyr (6x6), and is available with twin 23mm cannon. It was available without surveillance radar, and options include laser rangefinder, IFF system, TV tracker and NBC system.

This turret, armed with 23mm cannon and six Sakr Eye (reversed engineered SA-7) SAMs is used by Egypt mounted on a modified M113A1 series APC chassis.

Status

Production complete. In service with Ivory Coast, Niger and United Arab Emirates on M3 (4x4) chassis, and Oman on VAB (6x6) chassis (qv this entry APCs).

Manufacturer

Chassis: Société de Constructions, Mécaniques Panhard et Levassor, Paris; turret: Dassault Electronique, Saint Cloud, France.

436/A Above left: Panhard M3 VDA SPAAG in firing position with stabilisers lowered

436/B Above: Panhard M3 VDA SPAAG in firing position with stabilisers lowered

Gepard/CA 1 (Germany)

Key recognition features

● Based on Leopard 1 MBT chassis with much larger turret
● Surveillance radar above turret rear that retracts for travelling, tracking radar on turret front
● Twin 35mm cannon with muzzle velocity measuring equipment mounted externally on each side of turret

Specifications

Crew: 3
Armament: 2 x 35mm cannon, 2 x 4 smoke grenade dischargers
Ammunition: 620 (AA) and 40 (AP)
Length gun forwards: 7.73m
Length hull: 6.85m
Width overall: 3.37m
Width over tracks: 3.25m
Height radar up: 4.03m, 3.7m (Dutch version)
Height periscopes: 3.01m
Firing height: 2.37m
Ground clearance: 0.44m
Weight, combat: 47,300kg
Weight, empty: 44,800kg
Power-to-weight ratio: 17.54hp/tonne
Ground pressure: 0.95kg/cm²
Engine: MTU MB 838 Ca M500 10-cylinder multi-fuel developing 830hp at 2,200rpm
Maximum road speed: 65km/hr
Maximum road range: 550km
Fuel capacity: 985 lit
Fording: 2.5m
Vertical obstacle: 1.15m
Trench: 3m
Gradient: 60%
Side slope: 30%
Armour: 40mm max (estimate)
Armour type: Steel
NBC system: Yes
Night vision equipment: Yes (driver)

Development

The Gepard was developed in the late 1960s to meet requirements of German Army with prime contractor Contraves of Switzerland. Oerlikon-Bührle was responsible for turret and armament, Siemens for tracking radar, Hollandse Signaalapparaten for search radar and Krauss-Maffei/Porsche for chassis and power-supply system. After trials and modifications Gepard was adopted by German Army with 420 built between 1976 and 1980. Belgian Army took delivery of 55 Gepards from 1977 to 1980.

The turret has powered traverse through 360° and twin 35mm Oerlikon KDA cannon have power elevation from -10° to +85°. All-weather fire-control system includes computers, surveillance radar (turret rear) and tracking radar (turret front).

Variants

Netherlands Army version is called the CA 1 and has different tracking and surveillance radars and six smoke grenade dischargers each side of turret front, whereas German and Belgian Gepards have four. Total of 95 CA 1s delivered to Netherlands Army from 1977 to 1979.

To extend the operational life of part of their Gepard and CA 1 fleets into the next century, Germany and the Netherlands are carrying out a major improvement programme. The Gepards used by Belgium are to be phased out of service.

Status

Production complete. In service with Belgium, Germany and Netherlands.

Manufacturer

Krauss-Maffei, Munich, Germany assembled complete Gepard/CA 1; prime contractor Contraves, Zurich, Switzerland.

Gepard twin 35mm with dotted line to turret rear showing position of surveillance radar when retracted

Left: Gepard twin 35mm

Right: Gepard twin 35mm with surveillance and tracking radars erected

Above Right: Dutch CA 1 twin 35mm with different tracking and surveillance radars

OTOBREDA SIDAM (Italy)

Key recognition features

● Based on slightly modified M113A2 chassis with turret mounted centre of roof to rear of driver

● Armed with four 25mm cannon, two mounted externally one above the other on each side of turret

● Sights mounted in lower part of turret centre one above the other, gunner's hatch on turret roof that slopes upwards

Specifications

Crew: 3
Armament: 4 x 25mm cannon
Ammunition: 630 x 25mm
Length: 5.041m
Width: 2.686m
Height: 1.828m (hull top)
Ground clearance: 0.406m
Weight, combat: 15,100kg
Power-to-weight ratio: 17.54hp/tonne
Engine: Detroit Diesel 6V-53T 6-cylinder diesel developing 265hp
Maximum road speed: 64km/hr
Maximum road range: 550km
Vertical obstacle: 0.61m
Gradient: 60%
Side slope: 30%
Armour: 38mm (max)
Armour type: Aluminium
NBC system: Optional
Night vision equipment: Optional

Development

The SIDAM 25 quad 25mm was developed by OTOBREDA to meet requirements of Italian Army. Following trials with two prototype systems between 1983 and 1985 it was accepted for service with Italian Army. OTOBREDA build turrets for M113 chassis, upgraded to M113A2 standard by Astra Veicoli Industriali SpA.

Modifications to chassis include new Detroit Diesel 6V-53T developing 265hp, moving fuel tanks from inside hull to each side of rear ramp, uprated suspension and transmission and modified cooling system. Turret weighs about 3,000kg with total weight of modified M113A2 type vehicle with turret around 15,100kg. Turret is all-welded aluminium armour for protection from small arms fire and shell splinters. Turret is power-operated with manual controls for emergency use and traverses through 360° at 120° a second. Four 25mm cannon elevate from -5° to +87° at 90° a second.

Four 25mm Oerlikon-Contraves KBA cannon have cyclic rate of fire of 600 rounds per gun per minute, with 600 rounds of HEI-T ammunition carried for ready use (sufficient for eight two-second bursts) in addition to 30 APDS-T rounds for engaging ground targets. Gunner selects either single shots or bursts of 15 or 25 rounds. Two cannon are single fed and two dual feed (HEI-T and APDS-T). Turret has day clear weather and LLLTV camera sighting system which tracks targets automatically. Fire-control system includes laser rangefinder that feeds information to digital fire control computer. IFF system fitted as standard. Basic system is clear weather only but for night and all-weather operations a video-compatible thermal imager unit can be connected to optronic sight for use in haze and smoke conditions, together with passive IR night and day sight.

The SIDAM 25 can also receive target information from an external source through Target Alert Display Data Set (TADDS). Inertial navigation system optional. System has three men, commander seated in hull rear, gunner in turret and driver front left of hull, as in normal M113 series APC.

Variants

No variants but turret can be fitted to wide range of tracked and wheeled chassis.

Status
Production. In service with Italian Army.

Manufacturer
OTOBREDA, La Spezia, Italy.

Above: SIDAM 25 SPAAG on modified M113A1 series APC chassis

Top right: SIDAM 25 SPAAG on modified M113A1 series APC chassis

Right: SIDAM 25 SPAAG on modified M113A1 series APC chassis

Mitsubishi Type 87 (Japan)

Key recognition features

● Large turret with a 35mm cannon mounted externally on each side
● Tracking and surveillance radars mounted on turret roof at rear
● Chassis same as Type 74 MBT's with five road wheels, drive sprocket rear, idler front, no track-return rollers

Specifications

Crew: 3
Armament: 2 x 35mm cannon, 2 x 3 smoke grenade dischargers
Length gun forward: 7.62m
Length hull: 6.7m
Width overall: 3.2m
Height turret roof: 2.812m
Height radar up: 4.10m
Ground clearance: 0.2 to 0.65m
Weight, combat: 44,000kg
Power-to-weight ratio: 17hp/tonne
Engine: Mitsubishi 10ZF Type 22 WT 10-cylinder air-cooled diesel developing 750hp at 2,200rpm
Maximum road speed: 53km/hr
Maximum road range: 300km
Fuel capacity: 950 lit
Fording: 1m
Vertical obstacle: 1m
Trench: 2.7m
Gradient: 60%
Side slope: 30%
Armour: Classified
Armour type: Steel
NBC system: Yes
Night vision equipment: Yes (driver)

Development

To meet the requirements of the Japanese Ground Self Defence Force for a self-propelled all-weather anti-aircraft gun system, prototypes of a twin 35mm system based on a modified Type 74 MBT chassis were built under the designation of the AW-X. Following extensive trials this was accepted for service under the designation of the Type 87.

In concept the Type 87 is very similar to the German Gepard twin 35mm self-propelled anti-aircraft gun system and the Type 87 has a similar type of mounting system with the guns being mounted externally of the turret. Mounted on the turret roof at the rear are the tracking and surveillance radars which can be folded down to reduce the overall height of the system for travelling.

Variants

No variants.

Status

Production. In service with Japanese Ground Self Defence Force.

Manufacturer

Chassis by Mitsubishi Heavy Industries, Mitsubishi-Denki prime contractor for fire-control system, Nippon Seiko-Jyo for armament.

OPPOSITE PAGE:

Above left: Type 87 SPAAG

Above right: Type 87 SPAAG (Kensuke Ebata)

Right: Type 87 SPAAG (Kensuke Ebata)

2S6M Tunguska (Russia)

Key recognition features

● Almost vertical hull front with stepped glacis plate, turret in centre and powerpack at rear
● Large turret has surveillance radar at rear, tracking radar on lower front and armament mounted externally either side. Latter consists of two 30mm cannon and four SAM which can operate independent of each other
● Very high hull with vertical sides, suspension consists of six road wheels, idler front, drive sprocket rear and track-return rollers with upper part of track covered by skirt

Specifications

Crew: 6
Armament: 4 x 30mm, 8 x SA-19 SAM
Ammunition: 1,904 x 30mm, 8 x SA-19 SAM
Length: 7.93m
Width: 3.236m
Height: 4.021m (radar up), 3.356m (radar down)
Weight, combat: 34,000kg
Power-to-weight ratio: 15.29hp/tonne
Maximum road speed: 65km/hr
Maximum road range: 500km
Fuel capacity: Not available
Fording: 0.80m
Vertical obstacle: 1m
Trench: 2.0m
Gradient: 60%
Side slope: 30%
Armour: Classified
Armour type: Steel
NBC system: Yes
Night vision equipment: Yes

Development

The 2S6M (this being its industrial number) was developed in the early 1980s as the replacement for the ZSU-23-4 self-propelled anti-aircraft gun system and was first observed in 1986 and subsequently given the NATO designation of the M1986.

In overall layout the 2S6M is very similar to the German Gepard with the surveillance radar being mounted on the turret rear, which can be folded down for movement and the tracking radar being mounted on the front of the three-man turret.

Mounted either side of the turret are two twin 30mm cannon and four SA-19 surface-to-air missiles.

Typically the SA-19 would be used to engage targets at long range with the 30mm cannon being used to engage closer targets. The 30mm dual feed cannon has a maximum effective range of around 3,000m while the SA-19 SAMs have a maximum range of 8km.

The 2S6M has a computerised fire control system that includes a laser rangefinder and standard equipment includes an IFF system, land navigation system and an auxiliary power unit. Suspension is of the hydropneumatic type and is locked when the weapons are being fired to provide a more stable firing platform.

Variants

The first production model, which was only built in small numbers, is called the 2S6 and had a total of four missiles in the ready to launch position. The main production model, the 2S6M has eight missiles in the ready to launch position.

Status

Production. In service with Russia and India.

Manufacturer

Ulyanovsk Mechanical Plant, Russia.

Top: 2S6M SPAAG/SPAAM without missiles
(Christopher F Foss)
Top right: 2S6M SPAAG/SPAAM (Christopher F Foss)
Right: 2S6M SPAAG/SPAAM travelling (Ted Dyke)
Above: 2S6M (Christopher F Foss)

ZSU-57-2 (Russia)

Key recognition features

● Large open-topped turret with flat sides curved at top
● T-54 type chassis but only four road wheels
● Two long 57mm cannon with perforated muzzle brake

Specifications

Crew: 6
Armament: 2 x 57mm
Ammunition: 316 x 57mm
Length gun forwards: 8.46m
Length hull: 6.22m
Width overall: 3.27m
Height: 2.71m
Firing height: 2.05m
Ground clearance:0.425m
Weight, combat: 28,100kg
Power-to-weight ratio: 18.56hp/tonne
Ground pressure: 0.63kg/cm²
Engine: Model V-54, V-12 water-cooled diesel developing 520hp at 2,000rpm
Maximum road speed: 50km/hr
Maximum road range: 420km
Fuel capacity: 812 lit
Fording: 1.4m
Vertical obstacle: 0.8m
Trench: 2.7m
Gradient: 60%
Side slope: 30%
Armour: 15mm (max)
Armour type: Steel
NBC system: No
Night vision equipment: Yes (driver only)

ZSU-57-2 twin 57mm SPAAG

Development

The ZSU-57-2 twin 57mm was developed in the early 1950s: essentially a lightened T-54 chassis with four rather than five road wheels, thinner armour and new open-topped turret armed with twin version of towed 57mm S-60 anti-aircraft gun. Turret traverse is powered through 360° with powered weapon elevation from -5° to +85°. Ammunition is fed to 57mm guns in clips of four rounds with empty clips deposited in large basket at turret rear. The ZSU-57-2 is clear weather system only with no provision for all-weather fire control.

The maximum road range of the ZSU-57-2 can be increased from 420km to 595km using 595 litre auxiliary fuel tanks. Late production vehicles had a more sophisticated sighting system, this model is identified by two small ports in the upper portion of the turret front.

The ZSU-57-2 has been replaced in front-line Russian units by ZSU-23-4 self-propelled anti-aircraft gun system.

Variants

China produces similar system. Type 80 self-propelled anti-aircraft gun system, based on Type 69 MBT chassis.

Status

Production complete. In service with Algeria, China, Cuba, Egypt, Iran, Iraq, North Korea, Mozambique, Romania, Russia, Syria, Vietnam and former Yugoslavia.

Manufacturer

Russian state arsenals.

Right: ZSU-57-2 twin 57mm SPAAG

ZSU-23-4 (Russia)

Key recognition features

● Large square turret with four 23mm cannon in forward part and large dish-shaped radar antenna over turret rear
● Six large road wheels with idler front, drive sprocket rear, no return rollers
● Driver front, turret centre, engine rear

Specifications

Crew: 4
Armament: 4 x 23mm cannon
Ammunition: 2,000 x 23mm
Length: 6.54m
Width: 2.95m
Height including radar: 3.8m
Height excluding radar: 2.25m
Firing height: 1.83m (lower guns)
Ground clearance: 0.4m
Weight, combat: 20,500kg
Power-to-weight ratio: 20hp/tonne
Ground pressure: 0.68kg/cm2
Engine: Model V-6R, 6-cylinder in-line water-cooled diesel developing 280hp
Maximum road speed: 44km/hr
Maximum road range: 450km
Fuel capacity: 250 lit
Fording: 1.07m
Vertical obstacle: 1.1m
Trench: 2.8m
Gradient: 60%
Side slope: 30%
Armour: 15mm (max)
Armour type: Steel
NBC system: Yes
Night vision equipment: Yes (driver only)

Development

The ZSU-234 was developed in the early 1960s to replace ZSU-57-2 and in production from 1965 to 1983; it is often referred to as Shilka.

The turret has full powered traverse through 360° with elevation from -4° to +85°. Four 23mm cannon are water-cooled and have flash hiders. Mounted on turret rear is Gun Dish radar (NATO designation) for search and tracking functions in day and night conditions. Gun Dish radar can be folded down to turret rear to reduce overall height of system. Standard equipment includes vehicle navigation system.

The ZSU-23-4 has now started to be replaced by the 2S6 self-propelled air defence system that is armed with four 30mm cannon and eight surface-to-air missiles.

Variants

No variants but at least 19 differences between production models. Chassis and automotive components also used in PT-76 light amphibious tank and BTR-50 series armoured personnel carriers. SA-6 Gainful surface-to-air missile system has chassis very similar to ZSU-23-4's.

Status

Production complete. In service with Afghanistan, Algeria, Angola, Bulgaria, Congo, Cuba, Egypt, Ethiopia, Hungary, India, Iran, Israel, Iraq, Jordan, Laos, Libya, North Korea, Nigeria, Peru, Poland, Russia, Somalia, Syria, Vietnam and Yemen.

Manufacturer

Czechoslovak and Russian state arsenals.

ZSU-23-4 quad 23mm SPAAG

Right: Late production ZSU-23-4 quad 23mm SPAAG

Below: ZSU-23-4 quad 23mm SPAAG with radars retracted

M42 (USA)

Key recognition features

● Large open-topped turret mounted on forward part of hull with ammunition lockers above track guards

● Twin 40mm cannon have prominent flash suppressors which when turret is traversed to front overhang front of vehicle

● Suspension has five road wheels, idler front, drive sprocket rear, three track-return rollers

Specifications

Crew: 6
Armament: 2 x 40mm guns, 1 x 7.62mm MG
Ammunition: 480 x 40mm, 1,750 x 7.62mm
Length gun forwards: 6.356m
Length hull: 5.819m
Width: 3.225m
Height: 2.847m
Ground clearance: 0.438m
Weight, combat: 22,452kg
Weight, empty: 20,094kg
Power-to-weight ratio: 22.26hp/tonne
Ground pressure: 0.65kg/cm²
Engine: Continental or Lycoming AOS-895-3, 6-cylinder air-cooled supercharged petrol developing 500bhp at 2,800rpm
Maximum road speed: 72.4km/hr
Maximum road range: 161km
Fuel capacity: 530 lit
Fording: 1.016m
Vertical obstacle: 0.711m
Trench: 1.828m
Gradient: 60%
Side slope: 30%
Armour: 25.4mm (max)
Armour type: Steel
NBC system: No
Night vision equipment: Infra-red (driver only)

Development

The M42 was developed in the early 1950s under designation T141, with first production vehicles completed in late-1951. Many components are also used in M41 light tank, also produced by Cadillac Motor Car Division, General Motors Corporation, in the early 1950s. Production completed in June 1956, by which time over 3,700 had been completed. In regular US Army M42 has long since been replaced by M163 20mm Vulcan self-propelled anti-aircraft gun system.

The power-operated turret is the same as on the M19 twin 40mm self-propelled anti-aircraft gun system deployed during the Second World War. Turret traverses 360° and 40mm guns elevate from -3° to +85°, all under full power control. Practical rate of fire is 120 rounds per barrel per minute. Maximum anti-aircraft range is 5,000m and maximum range in ground fire role is 9,475m. M42 is a clear weather system with no provision for radar fire control.

Variants

Only variant in service is **M42A1** which has AOSI-895-5 engine with fuel injection, which is more fuel-efficient.

A number of companies have offered upgrade packages for the M42 system but as far as it is known none have so far entered service. Taiwan may have converted some vehicles into TOW ATGW carriers.

Status

Production complete. In service with Greece, Guatemala, Jordan, Lebanon, Taiwan, Thailand, Tunisia, Turkey and Venezuela.

Manufacturer

Cadillac Motor Car Division, General Motors Corporation, Cleveland Tank Plant; ACF Industries of Berwick, Pennsylvania, USA.

Top: M42 twin 40mm SPAAG without 7.62mm MG
Above: M42 twin 40mm SPAAG showing flash suppressors (US Army)
Above right: M42 twin 40mm SPAAG showing ammunition lockers above track guards (US Army)
Right: M42 twin 40mm SPAAG with turret to rear

M163 Vulcan (USA)

Key recognition features

● Open-topped turret mounted centre of hull roof with range-only radar on right side of turret
● Based on standard M113 chassis with additional buoyancy panels on glacis plate and hull sides
● Chassis has five road wheels, idler rear, drive sprocket front, no track-return rollers

Specifications

Crew: 4
Armament: 1 x 6-barrel 20mm cannon
Ammunition: 2,280 x 20mm
Length: 4.86m
Width: 2.85m (overall), 2.54m (reduced)
Height: 2.736m (overall), 1.83m (hull top)
Ground clearance: 0.406m
Weight, combat: 12,310kg
Power-to-weight ratio: 17.46bhp/tonne
Ground pressure: 0.61kg/cm²
Engine: Detroit Diesel Model 6V-53 6-cylinder water-cooled diesel developing 215bhp at 2,800rpm
Maximum road speed: 67.59km/hr
Maximum water speed: 5.6km/hr
Maximum road range: 483km
Fording: Amphibious
Vertical obstacle: 0.61m
Trench: 1.68m
Gradient: 60%
Side slope: 30%
Armour: 38mm (max)
Armour type: Aluminium
NBC system: No
Night vision equipment: Yes (driver only), infra-red or passive

Development

The M163 20mm Vulcan was developed in the early 1960s to replace the M42 twin 40mm system. First production systems completed by General Electric Company (now Lockheed Martin) in 1968 and a total of 671 systems was built before production was complete. The M163 self-propelled air defence system has now been phased out of US Army service as has its towed counterpart, the M167.

The M163 has four-man crew, one of whom mans power-operated turret with 20mm M61A1 Vulcan cannon and Navy Mk 20 Mod O lead-computing sight and range-only radar on right side of turret. Gunner selects one of two rates of fire, 1,000 or 3,000 rounds a minute (1,000 for ground role and 3,000 for air defence).

The turret has 360° traverse with weapon elevation from -5° to +80°. Gunner selects either 10, 30, 60 or 100 round bursts. 20mm cannon has maximum anti-aircraft range of 1,600rpm and maximum range in direct fire role of 3,000m. 1,180 rounds of ready-use ammunition carried with further 1,100 rounds in reserve. Main drawback is its short range and lack of all-weather fire-control system.

The South Korean Army has a similar system but fitted to the locally produced Korean Infantry Fighting Vehicle (KIFV) chassis.

Variants

From 1984 many US Army M163 systems were upgraded under Product Improved Vulcan Air Defense System (PIVADS) programme with initial order for 285 kits for both towed and self-propelled systems. Modifications include new sight and linking digital fire-control computer with range-only radar. Also fires new APDS round which increases effective range to 2,600m.

Status

Production completed. In service with Israel, Jordan, Morocco, Portugal, Sudan, Thailand, and Yemen.

Left: M163 20mm Vulcan

Right: M163 20mm Vulcan in firing configuration

Below right: M163 20mm Vulcan in travelling configuration (US Army)

Below left: M163 20mm Vulcan

Manufacturer

Armaments Systems Division, Lockheed Martin Defense Systems, Vermont (prime contractor), and United Defense, LP, San José, California, USA (chassis).

BOV (Former Yugoslavia)

Key recognition features

● Nose angled at 45o with slightly sloped glacis plate, hull top then horizontal, hull sides slope inwards from just above wheel arches

● Open-topped turret in centre of hull with angled front, sides and rear, three 20mm cannon in forward part with external circular magazines

● Each side of hull top, in line with turret sides, is a walk way, rectangular hatch in lower left side of hull only

Specifications

Crew: 4
Configuration: 4x4
Armament: 3 x 20mm cannon, 2 x 3 smoke grenade dischargers
Ammunition: 1,500 x 20mm
Length: 5.791m
Width: 2.525m
Height: 3.21m
Ground clearance: 0.325m
Wheelbase: 2.75m
Weight, combat: 9,400kg
Power-to-weight ratio: 15.74hp/tonne
Engine: Deutz type F 6L 413 F 6-cylinder diesel developing 148hp at 2,650rpm
Maximum road speed: 93.4km/hr
Maximum road range: 500km
Fuel capacity: Not available
Fording: 1.1m
Vertical obstacle: 0.54m
Trench: 0.64m
Gradient: 55%
Side slope: 30%
Armour: 8mm (maximum) (estimate)
NBC system: No
Night vision equipment: Yes (infra-red for driver)

Development

In the 1970s Yugoslavia developed BOV series 4x4 armoured vehicles, all of which share common hull modified to suit specialised applications such as BOV-1 (anti-tank), BOV-M armoured personnel carrier, BOV-3 with three 20mm cannon and BOV-30 with twin 30mm cannon. Hull is all-welded steel armour with commander and driver at front, turret on roof centre, engine and transmission rear.

The turret is based on standard 20/3mm gun M55 A4 B1 in service with former Yugoslav Army for some years. Each 20mm cannon has drum-type magazine each holding 60 rounds of ready-use ammunition. Each cannon has cyclic rate of fire of 750 rounds per minute, gunner selects single shots, bursts of 10 rounds, bursts of 10 to 20 rounds or sustained fire.

Turret traverse is powered through 360°and elevation is powered from -4.5° to +83°. Maximum anti-aircraft engagement altitude is quoted as 2,000m but effective range is between 1,000 and 1,500m. Cannon can also be used in direct fire support role against ground targets, when range is 2,000m. Ammunition includes HE-T, HEI-T, HEI, TP-T, TP, API, API-T and AP-T.

The BOV-3 is clear weather system only with no provision for external control. Standard equipment includes central tyre pressure regulation system and heater.

Variants

BOV-30 has different turret with two 30mm cannon with flash eliminators mounted one each side of turret, cyclic rate of fire of 600 rounds per gun per minute. Details of the BOV-VP (4x4) armoured personnel carrier are given in an earlier section.

Status

Production complete. In service with former Yugoslav Army and other countries in this area.

Manufacturer

Former Yugoslav state factories.

Above: BOV-3 triple 20mm SPAAG in travelling configuration

Above right: BOV-3 triple 20mm SPAAG in travelling configuration

Right: BOV-3 twin 30mm SPAAG in travelling configuration

SELF-PROPELLED SAMs

Oerlikon-Aerospace Air Defence/ Anti-tank System (ADATS) (Canada)

Key recognition features

● Depends on chassis but turret has four missiles in ready-to-launch position each side with electro-optic devices between and radar scanner on top of turret rear. Scanner folds for transportation

Specifications

Depends on chassis.

Development

In 1979 Oerlikon Contraves started private venture development of a modular missile system which could be mounted on a wide range of tracked and wheeled armoured vehicles and used to engage both aerial (aircraft and helicopters) and ground targets.

Today, Oerlikon-Aerospace of Canada is responsible for system integration and marketing while Oerlikon-Contraves of Switzerland, who originally designed the system, have built the actual missile. Lockheed Martin of the US was main sub-contractor with responsibility for the electro-optical module, Contraves Italiana for the roof mounted surveillance radar and Litton Systems Canada for some key electronics. First prototypes of the ADATS system, on a modified M113 series chassis, were completed in 1994.

After studying proposals from three consortia, the Canadian Armed Forces selected ADATS as part of the system to meet requirements for Low Level Air Defence (LLAD) system in April 1986. Other parts of system include Oerlikon-Contraves GDF-005 twin 35mm towed anti-aircraft gun and Contraves Skyguard fire-control system. By early 1994 the Canadian Armed Forces had taken delivery of all of the Skyguard radars and twin 35mm GDF series anti-aircraft guns and of the ADATS systems on the M113 chassis.

In addition to M113 series full tracked APC, ADATS can also be mounted on chassis such as MOWAG Armoured Combat Vehicle (10x10), and the United Defense Bradley chassis. So far the only production application is the M113 series chassis for the Canadian armed forces. Thailand has a few shelter mounted ADATS but without the surveillance radar.

ADATS consists of power-operated turret with surveillance radar, 8 to 12 micron wavelength forward-looking infra-red (FLIR) and TV trackers, neodymium-YAG laser rangefinder and carbon dioxide missile guidance laser. Each missile is sealed in a tube which is used for transport and launching. System is controlled by radar operator and gunner, who operates electro-optics, both of whom sit inside.

Typical aerial target is engaged as follows: target is first detected by surveillance radar and once designated as hostile, turret is traversed onto its bearing and search starts to bring it into field-of-view of FLIR or TV camera, latter mode depending on weather. Sensor then locks onto target and starts tracking. When within range, missile is launched and guided by 10.6 micron wavelength coded CO_2 laser to target.

ADATS engages aerial targets up to an altitude of 6,000m from ranges of 1km out to 10km; engagement of ground targets is from 500m to 8,000m. It is anticipated that each ADATS would be given a primary role of air defence or anti-tank. Missile penetrates 900mm of armour, anti-tank targets are acquired electro-optically and range determined by laser rangefinder.

Status

Production as required. In service in self-propelled configuration only with Canada.

Manufacturer

Oerlikon Aerospace, Inc, Canada.

Above: ADATS on M113 APC

Above right: ADATS on M113A2 APC

Right: ADATS on M113A2 APC (Christopher F Foss)

Thomson-CSF Shahine (France)

Key recognition features

● Chassis has high superstructure with straight top that extends almost to rear, glacis plate angled at about 70o, vertical sides with chamfer between sides and roof
● Mounted in centre of roof is turret with three missiles in launch containers each side and large circular tracking scanner between
● Suspension each side has five road wheels, drive sprocket rear, idler front, four track-return rollers, upper part normally covered by sand shields

Development

The Shahine low-altitude system was developed by Thomson-CSF for Saudi Arabia. Following trials with first battery consisting of two acquisition and four firing units, production commenced in 1979 and first production systems delivered in 1980. Final deliveries completed in 1982.

Main improvements over Thomson-CSF Crotale SAM, from which Shahine was developed, are greater cross-country mobility (based on tracked chassis rather than wheeled system), quicker into action times due to Inter-Vehicle Positioning and Data Link system, greater area of coverage due to more powerful radars, and greater distance between acquisition and firing units. In January 1984 Thomson-CSF was awarded a further contract by Saudi Arabia for improved Shahine SAM system as well as upgrade of original system to new standard. First deliveries of second order made in mid-1986. Second order includes standard tracked version mounted on modified AMX-30 MBT chassis and new Air-Transportable Towed System (ATTS), which is fully air-portable in C-130 Hercules transport aircraft.

Standard Shahine system has two main components, acquisition unit and firing unit, both of which are mounted on much modified AMX-30 MBT chassis with new all-welded steel superstructure. Automotive characteristics similar to basic MBT. The firing unit has six missiles in ready-to-launch position, three each side, no replacement missiles carried on vehicle (these brought forward by 6x6 truck with hydraulic crane). Mounted on forward part of turret is large circular tracking radar that guides one or two missiles to target.

Each missile is transported in sealed container which also acts as launcher. Missile has effective range against high speed Mach 1.2 manoeuvring low level targets of 500 to 11,500m at minimum and maximum engagement altitudes of 15 and 6,800m. Maximum missile range exceeds 15,000m.

Acquisition unit has almost identical chassis to firing unit and weighs 32,700kg. Mounted on roof is surveillance radar with range of 18.5km. Automatic information processing and threat evaluation system allows up to 40 targets to be registered and 18 targets handled simultaneously. Typically, acquisition unit would first detect target and once confirmed as hostile would allocate it to firing unit which would launch missile when in range and track it to target.

Variants

No variants except for Air-Transportable Towed System (ATTS).

Status

Production complete. In service only with Saudi Arabia which has taken delivery of 36 acquisition and 73 firing units on AMX-30 MBT chassis and 10 acquisition and 19 firing units in the ATTS shelter configuration. Used only by Saudi Arabia (Air Force and Army).

Manufacturer

Thomson-CSF, Bagneux, France. MATRA responsible for missiles and GIAT for chassis.

Above left: Shahine firing unit in operation

Above right: Shahine acquisition unit in travelling configuration

Below left: Shahine firing unit in travelling configuration

Euromissile Roland SAM (France)

Key recognition features

● Hull has vertical sides with glacis plate at about 70o, horizontal roof on which is mounted turret with single missile in launch position each side, vertical elliptical tracking radar between missiles and surveillance radar on turret top at rear

● Chassis based on AMX-30 MBT with five road wheels, drive sprocket rear, idler front, five track-return rollers, no track skirts

Specifications

Crew: 3
Armament: 1 launcher with two Roland SAMs, 1 x 4 smoke grenade dischargers
Ammunition: 10 Roland SAMs
(Automotive characteristics and physical dimensions are virtually identical to AMX-30 MBT with exception of height and weight)

Development

Roland was developed by Euromissile to meet requirements of French and German armies. France uses chassis of AMX-30 MBT and Germany uses Marder 1 ICV chassis. Two Roland missiles carried in ready-to-launch position with further eight missiles, four for each launcher arm, carried internally for automatic reloading. Roland 2 engages aircraft flying at maximum speed of Mach 1.3 up to maximum altitude of 3,000m with effective range of between 500 and 6,300m. System has two modes of operation, optical and radar.

Variants

Roland 2 on Marder 1 ICV chassis (qv this section).
Roland 3 has four missiles in ready-to-launch position (not yet in service).
Shelter Roland can be carried on truck such as MAN (8x8).
The Roland SAM system is now being improved in a number of key areas to enable it to remain effective through the 1990s. These improvements include replacement of the current optical sight by an optronic integrated infra-red sight assembly in order to provide a third operational mode for Roland, simplified man/machine interface, new computers and displays. The Crotale New Generation may also be integrated into Roland.

France has a special shelter mounted air-transportable version of Roland 2 for use by its Rapid Reaction Forces.

Status

Production of Roland 1 and 2 on AMX-30 chassis is complete but Roland system remains in production for export. In service/on order for Argentina (shelter), Brazil (Roland 2 on Marder 1 chassis), France (Roland 2 on AMX-30 chassis), Germany (Roland 2, Air Force uses MAN 8x8 chassis, Army uses Marder 1 chassis and Navy uses MAN 8x8 chassis), Iraq (Roland 2 on AMX-30 chassis), Qatar (Roland 2 on AMX-30 chassis and MAN 8x8 truck chassis), Spain (Roland on AMX-30 chassis) and Venezuela (Roland 2 in shelter configuration).

Manufacturer

Euromissile, Fontenay-Aux-Roses, France (joint company established by Aérospatiale of France and Daimler-Benz Aerospace of Germany). Systems integration of Roland on AMX30 by Aérospatiale.

OPPOSITE PAGE:

Main picture: Roland SAM missile being launched from AMX-30 chassis

Inset: Roland 2 SAM on AMX-30 chassis

Thomson-CSF Crotale (France)

Key recognition features

● Both acquisition and launch vehicles have same chassis with vertical sides, front and rear, which slope from hull roof to front and rear of launcher

● Four large rubber-tyred road wheels each end of vehicle. When deployed for action system is supported on three jacks with circular base plates, one each side and one at rear

● Acquisition unit has large elliptical radar scanner, firing unit has turret with two missiles in launch containers each side and circular radar antenna on front

Specifications

Vehicle type	Acquisition	Launch
Crew:	2	2
Configuration:	4x4	4x4
Armament:	nil	4 Crotale SAM
Length:	6.22m	6.22m
Width:	2.65m	2.65m
Height (reduced):	3.05m	3.41m
Ground clearance:		
(travelling)	0.45m	0.45m
(deployed)	0.156/0.656m	0.156/0.656m
Wheelbase:	3.6m	3.6m
Maximum road speed:	70km/hr	70km/hr
Maximum range:	600km	600km
Fording:	0.68m	0.68m
Vertical obstacle:	0.3m	0.3m
Gradient:	40%	40%
Armour: (max)	5mm	5mm
Armour type:	Steel	Steel
NBC system:	No	No

Development

Crotale low altitude SAM originally developed in the early 1960s to meet requirements of South Africa under the name Cactus. First production systems completed in 1971 since when it has been continuously developed to meet changing threat. Prime contractor for the complete system is Thomson-CSF with Matra being responsible for the actual missiles. System has two parts, each based on same 4x4 chassis: firing unit with four missiles in ready-to-launch position, and acquisition unit. One Crotale section or battery normally has one acquisition unit and three firing units.

Crotale has been designed to engage targets flying at maximum speed of Mach 1.2 at altitude from 15 to 5,000m. Acquisition unit carries out surveillance, identification and designation, then allocates target to firing unit which carries out engagement. Tracking radar on firing unit tracks one target and guides two missiles simultaneously. Once four missiles have been launched, new missiles in launch containers are brought up by truck and loaded with hydraulic crane.

Variants

Latest version is the 4000 series and has LIVH radio link, which not only enables system to be brought into action quicker but also allows it to be up to 3,000m apart.

For trials Crotale has been mounted on a MOWAG Shark (8x8) chassis. Also a shelter version. Further development of Crotale by Thomson-CSF resulted in Shahine (see separate entry).

The Crotale SAM system has been replaced in production by the Crotale New Generation, or Crotale NG as it is usually referred to. Whereas the older Crotale needed two vehicles, acquisition unit and firing unit, Crotale New Generation is a self-contained unit. The first production application is for Finland which uses a SISU XA-180 (6x6) APC as the platform (qv wheeled APC section). This has both tracking and surveillance radars and eight missiles in the ready-to-launch position. There is also a shelter-based system that is now in service with the French Air Force.

Status

Production complete. In service with Abu Dhabi, Chile, Egypt, France, Libya, Pakistan, Saudi Arabia and South Africa.

Manufacturer

Thomson-CSF, Bagneaux, France.

Above: Crotale SAM firing unit deployed

Right: Crotale SAM firing unit deployed

Below: Crotale SAM acquisition unit deployed with LIVH mast raised

Euromissile Roland (Germany)

Key recognition features

● Same chassis as Marder 1 mechanised infantry combat vehicle with turret slightly to rear
● Turret has two radar scanners, surveillance on top and tracking on front. One missile in ready-to-launch position on each side
● Chassis has six road wheels, idler rear, drive sprocket front, three track-return rollers. Upper part of suspension normally covered by wavy skirt

Specifications

Crew: 3
Armament: Launcher with two Roland SAMs, 1 x 7.62mm MG, 2 x 4 smoke grenade dischargers
Ammunition: 10 x Roland SAMs
Length: 6.915m
Width: 3.24m
Height: 2.92m (radar antenna lowered)
Ground clearance: 0.44m
Weight, combat: 32,500kg
Power-to-weight ratio: 18.5hp/tonne
Ground pressure: 0.93kg/cm²
Engine: MTU MB 833 Ea-500 6-cylinder liquid-cooled diesel developing 600hp at 2,200rpm
Maximum road speed: 70km/hr
Maximum road range: 520km
Fuel capacity: 652 lit
Fording: 1.5m (with preparation)
Vertical obstacle: 1.15m
Trench: 2.5m
Gradient: 60%
Side slope: 30%
Armour: Classified
Armour type: Steel
NBC system: Yes
Night vision equipment: Yes (driver)

Development

Roland was developed by Euromissile to meet requirements of French and German armies. France uses chassis of AMX-30 MBT, Germany uses chassis of Marder 1 ICV. German Army uses all-weather Roland 2 system, first of 140 systems delivered in June 1981.

Two Roland missiles carried in ready-to-launch position with further eight missiles, four for each launcher arm, carried internally for automatic reloading. Roland 2 engages aircraft flying at maximum speed of Mach 1.3 up to maximum altitude of 3,000m with effective range of between 500 and 6,300m. System has two modes of operation, optical and radar.

Variants

Roland 3 has four missiles in ready-to-launch position.
Shelter Roland which can be carried on truck chassis such as MAN 8x8.
France has taken delivery of some trailer mounted shelter Roland 2 SAMs for use by its rapid reaction forces.

Status

Production of Roland 2 on Marder chassis is complete but Roland remains in production for export. In service/on order for Argentina (shelter), Brazil (Roland 2 on Marder 1 chassis), France (Roland 2 on AMX-30 MBT chassis), Germany (Air Force - Roland 2 on 8x8 MAN truck chassis, Army - Roland 2 on Marder 1 chassis, and Navy - Roland 2 on 8x8 MAN truck chassis), Iraq (Roland 2 on AMX-30 chassis and on truck chassis), Nigeria (Roland 2 on AMX-30 MBT chassis), Qatar (Roland 2 on AMX-30 chassis and MAN 8x8 truck chassis), Spain (Roland 1 and Roland 2 on AMX-30 chassis, these were produced in Spain and known as AMX-30E), USA (Air Force has Roland 2 on MAN 8x8 truck chassis which are based in Europe and manned by Germans to protect US Air Force bases), and Venezuela (Roland 2 shelter versions on 8x8 truck chassis).

Manufacturer

Euromissile, Fontenay-Aux-Roses, France (joint company established by Aérospatiale of France and Daimler-Benz Aerospace of Germany). Systems integration of German Roland 2 by Daimler-Benz Aerospace at Thyssen Henschel facility, Kassel, Germany.

Above: Roland 2 on Marder 1 ICV chassis with missiles ready for action (Pierre Touzin)

Right: Roland 2 on Marder 1 ICV chassis (Pierre Touzin)

SA-4 Ganef (Russia)

Key recognition features

● Two large missiles on top of launcher which overhang front and side of chassis
● Cylindrical missiles each have four external boosters, four fins and four wings in two pairs
● Chassis has seven road wheels with drive sprocket front, idler rear, four return rollers

Specifications

Crew: 3-5
Armament: Launcher with two SA-4s
Ammunition: 2 x SA-4 SAM
Length: 9.46m (with missiles), 7.5m (launcher)
Width: 3.2m
Height: 4.472m (with missiles)
Ground clearance: 0.44m
Weight, combat: 30,000kg
Power-to-weight ratio: 17.33hp/tonne
Engine: Model V-59 V-12 water-cooled diesel developing 520hp
Maximum road speed: 45km/hr
Maximum road range: 450km
Fuel capacity: 850 lit
Fording: 1.5m
Vertical obstacle: 1m
Trench: 2.5m
Gradient: 60%
Side slope: 30%
Armour: 15mm (maximum)
NBC system: Yes
Night vision equipment: Infra-red (driver)

Development

SA-4 Ganef medium to high altitude SAM was developed in the mid-1950s but did not reach operational status until the late 1960s. NATO designation is SA-4 Ganef but in Russian Army is ZRD-SD (Zenitniy Raketniy Kompleks - Srednoye Deistive).

SA-4 Ganef is normally deployed in a brigade, each consisting of brigade headquarters and three battalions. Each battalion has eight ZSU-23-4 or ZU-23 23mm anti-aircraft guns, Long

SA-4 Ganef SAM in travelling configuration

Track surveillance radar and three SA-4 Ganef batteries.

In peacetime each SA-4 Ganef battery has one Pat Hand missile guidance station, three SA-4 launchers and four Ural-375 (6x6) reload vehicles each carrying one missile and an onboard loading system.

Missile range depends on version but maximum altitude 27,000m. Two missiles traverse through 360o on launcher and elevate up to about 45o, the left missile carried slightly higher than the right. Target is normally detected by Long Track radar which then passes target information to Pat Hand radar at battery level, which has similar chassis to SA-4 Ganef. Once within range an SA-4 Ganef missile is launched and guided to target by guidance beam of Pat Hand with semi-active terminal homing in final stages. It takes between 10 and 15 minutes to reload each launcher arm.

SA-4 Ganef is now being replaced in the Russian army by the

SA-11 Gadfly and SA-12 Gladiator SAM systems.

Variants

At least four sub-variants of the missile, designated 9M8, 9M8M, 9M81 and 9M82, last two versions being most common today. GMZ full tracked armoured minelayer uses components of SA-4 Ganef chassis.

Status

Production complete. In service with Bulgaria, Hungary, Poland, Russia and the Ukraine.

Manufacturer

Russian state arsenals.

Right: SA-4 Ganef SAM in travelling configuration

SA-6 Gainful (Russia)

Key recognition features

● Chassis similar to ZSU-23-4 SPAAG with six ribbed road wheels, drive sprocket rear, idler front, no track-return rollers
● Chassis has vertical sides and rear and sloping glacis plate with two rectangular hatches
● Launcher has three missiles in ready-to-launch position on forward part of roof, traversed to rear when travelling

Specifications

Crew: 3
Armament: Launcher with three SA-6 SAMs
Ammunition: 3 SA-6 SAM
Length: 7.389m (including missiles), 6.79m (hull)
Width: 3.18m
Height: 3.45m (with missiles), 1.8m (hull top
Ground clearance: 0.4m
Weight, combat: 14,000kg
Power-to-weight ratio: 17.14hp/tonne
Ground pressure: 0.48kg/cm^2
Engine: Model V-6R, 6-cylinder water-cooled diesel developing 240hp at 1,800rpm
Maximum road speed: 44km/hr
Maximum road range: 260km
Fuel capacity: 250 lit
Fording: 1.1m
Vertical obstacle: 1m
Trench: 2.5m
Gradient: 60%
Side slope: 30%
Armour: 9.4mm (maximum)
Armour type: Steel
NBC system: Yes
Night vision equipment: Infra-red (commander and driver)

Development

SA-6 Gainful (NATO designation) low to medium altitude SAM was developed in the 1950s and first seen in public during 1967. In Russian Army it is known as ZRK-SD Kub; export version is ZRK-SD Kvadrat. First operational use was during 1973 Middle East conflict when used by Egypt and Syria; since then it has also seen combat in Algeria, Angola, Iraq, Libya, Lebanon and Morocco.

Each SA-6 regiment has regimental headquarters with two Long Track and one Thin Skin-B radars and five SA-6 batteries. Each battery has one Straight Flush radar vehicle, four SA-6 SPU launchers and two ZIL-131 reload vehicles.

Effective missile range depends on version, but basic SA-6a has maximum of 24,000m and minimum of 3,700m, minimum effective altitude is 80 to 100m and maximum is 12,000m. Long Track radar used with system is on AT-T tracked chassis, Straight Flush radar is on similar chassis to SA-6's.

Variants

The SA-6b (NATO designation Gainful Mod 1) was an interim system based on the chassis of the SA-11 Gadfly and had three missiles in the ready-to-launch position and a Fire Dome radar mounted on the front of the launcher assembly.

Status

Production complete. In service with Algeria, Angola, Bulgaria, Cuba, Czech Republic, Egypt, Hungary, India, Iraq, Libya, Poland, Romania, Russia, Slovakia, Syria, Tanzania, Ukraine, Vietnam, Yemen and former Yugoslavia.

Manufacturer

Russian state arsenals.

Above: SA-6 Gainful SAM in travelling configuration

Above right: SA-6 Gainful SAM in travelling configuration

Right: SA-6 Gainful SAM in travelling configuration

SA-13 Gopher (Russia)

Key recognition features

● Based on standard MT-LB armoured multi-purpose tracked vehicle chassis with six road wheels, drive sprocket front and idler rear

● Mounted on roof is turret with four missiles in long box-shaped containers; when travelling they lay horizontally on top of hull

● Circular range-only radar antenna in centre between two twin launcher boxes, operator at turret base with large window at about 45o

Specifications

Crew: 3
Armament: Launcher with four SA-13 SAMs
Ammunition: 21 SA-13 SAM
Length: 6.6m
Width: 2.85m
Height: 3.8m (firing), 2.3m (travelling)
Ground clearance: 0.4m
Weight, combat: 12,300kg
Power-to-weight ratio: 19.52hp/tonne
Engine: YaMZ-238V diesel developing 240hp at 2,100rpm
Maximum road speed: 61.5km/hr
Maximum water speed: 5-6km/hr
Maximum road range: 500km
Fuel capacity: 450 lit
Fording: Amphibious
Vertical obstacle: 0.7m
Trench: 2.7m
Gradient: 60%
Side slope: 30%
Armour: 7mm (maximum)
Armour type: steel
NBC system: Yes
Night vision equipment: Infra-red (driver)

Development

SA-13 Gopher low altitude SAM was first seen in the mid-1970s and has now replaced SA-9 Gaskin (4x4) SAM system one-for-one. There are two versions of SA-13 designated TELAR 1 (transporter-erector-launcher-and-radar) and TELAR 2. TELAR 1 carries four Flat Box passive radar detection antenna units similar to those installed on one in four SA-9 Gaskins. One Flat

B is mounted on each corner of vehicle's rear deck, one facing aft and one between driver's vision ports at front.

NATO designation is SA-13 Gopher, Russian Army designation is ZREK-BD Strela 10. Four missiles are carried in ready-to-launch position with further eight carried in reserve in hull. Missile weighs 55kg and has estimated minimum range of 800m and maximum slant range of 5,000m. Altitude engagement range is 10 to 5,000m but at shorter ranges is reduced to about 4,000m. The SA-13 retains the amphibious characteristics of the MT-LB on which it is based.

Variants

Apart from TELAR 2 there are no variants, but some systems have been seen with 7.62mm MG for local defence and some with SA-9 Gaskin launcher boxes in place of SA-13, or a mixture of both.

Status

Production probably complete. In service with Afghanistan, Algeria, Angola, Bulgaria, Russia, Cuba, Czech Republic, Hungary, India, Iraq, Jordan, Libya, Poland, Slovakia, and Syria.

Manufacturer

Russian state arsenals.

Above left: SA-13 Gopher in travelling configuration (Christopher F Foss)

Above right: SA-13 Gopher in firing position (Christopher F Foss)

Right: SA-13 Gopher in firing position (Christopher F Foss)

Far right: SA-13 Gopher in travelling configuration (Michael Jerchel)

SA-9 Gaskin (Russia)

Key recognition features

● Hull identical to BRDM-2 (4x4) amphibious scout car but turret removed and replaced by new turret with four SA-9 missiles in ready to launch position
● Each missile in long square box which acts as transport container and launcher
● When travelling, launcher arms fold down each side of turret

Specifications

Crew: 3
Configuration: 4x4
Armament: Launcher with four SA-9 SAMs
Ammunition: 6 SA-9 SAM
Length: 5.9m
Width: 2.4m
Height: 2.3m (travelling)
Ground clearance: 0.43m
Wheelbase: 3.1m
Weight, combat: 7,000kg
Power-to-weight ratio: 20hp/tonne
Engine: GAZ-41 V-8 water-cooled petrol developing 140hp at 3,400rpm
Maximum road speed: 100km/hr
Maximum water speed: 10km/hr
Maximum road range: 750km
Fuel capacity: 290 lit
Fording: Amphibious
Vertical obstacle: 0.4m
Trench: 1.2m
Gradient: 60%
Side slope: 30%
Armour: 14mm (maximum)
Armour type: Steel
NBC system: Yes
Night vision equipment: Infra-red (driver)

Development

The SA-9 Gaskin low altitude SAM was developed in the 1960s with first systems operational in 1968. Used in combat Middle East (by Egypt, Iraq and Syria) and Angola but being replaced in

front-line Russian units by SA-13 Gopher full tracked SAM. SA-9 Gaskin normally employed in batteries of four systems, one with Flat Box passive detection system which provides target information to other three vehicles in battery.

SA-9 Gaskin is essentially standard BRDM-2 amphibious scout car with machine gun turret replaced by one-man manually operated turret with four infra-red fire-and-forget missiles in ready-to-launch position. Minimum range is 800m, maximum 6,500m, altitude limited from 15 to 5,200m. Once four missiles have been launched new missiles are loaded manually in five minutes, two reserve missiles normally carried externally. Missile itself is designated 9M31, later model being 9M31M with improved lock-on capability. The latter also has a minimum range of 560m and a maximum range of 8,000m with maximum altitude being 6,100m.

The system is fully amphibious, propelled by a single waterjet at rear of hull, has central tyre pressure regulation system for tyre pressure adjustment to suit ground being crossed, and front-mounted winch. Unlike BRDM-2 it does not have belly wheels.

Variants

Only known variant has Flat Box passive detection system consisting of four small radar antennas mounted one each side of hull above first road wheel station, one over rear engine deck and one under left wheel housing.

Status

Production complete. In service with Algeria, Angola, Benin, Bulgaria, Russia, Cuba, Croatia, Czech Republic, Egypt, Ethiopia, Hungary, India, Iraq, Libya, Mauritania, Mozambique, Nicaragua, Poland, Romania, Slovakia, Syria, Ukraine, Vietnam, Yemen and former Yugoslavia.

Manufacturer

Chassis: Molotov GAZ plant, Gorkiy, former USSR.

Above left: SA-9 Gaskin SAM in travelling configuration

Right: SA-9 Gaskin SAM with launcher raised

SA-8 Gecko (Russia)

Key recognition features

● Six-wheeled chassis with ribbed vertical sides, straight back and fully enclosed driver's cab front
● Launcher in centre of roof with tracking radar on front and surveillance radar on top at rear, which folds down to back for travelling
● SA-8a was initial version with two missiles each side, SA-8b has three missiles each side in transport/launch containers

Specifications

Crew: 5
Configuration: 6x6
Armament: Launcher with six SA-8 SAMs
Ammunition: 6 SA-8 SAM
Length: 9.14m
Width: 2.8m
Height: 4.2m (surveillance radar lowered), 1.845m (hull top)
Wheelbase: 3.075m + 2.788m
Weight, combat: 17,500kg
Power-to-weight ratio: 11.42hp/tonne
Engine: D20B-200 diesel developing 200hp at 2,000rpm
Maximum road speed: 60km/hr
Maximum water speed: 8km/hr
Maximum road range: 500km
Fuel capacity: 350 lit
Fording: Amphibious
Vertical obstacle: 0.5m
Trench: 1.2m
Gradient: 60%
Side slope: 30%
Armour: None
Armour type: Not applicable
NBC system: Yes
Night vision equipment: Infra-red (driver)

Development

The SA-8 Gecko (NATO designation) was developed in the late 1960s and first seen in public in 1975. In Russian Army it is known as ZRK-SD Romb or Strela 3. It was replacement for S-60 57mm towed anti-aircraft gun and fills gap between SA-9 Gaskin and manportable SA-7 Grail.

The SA-8 is based on 6x6 chassis named Transporter 5937, crew compartment at front and engine at rear. Vehicle is fully amphibious, propelled by two waterjets at rear of hull. Steering is power-assisted on front and rear axles with central tyre pressure regulation system fitted as standard. SA-8 is complete system with surveillance radar mounted on top at rear, tracking radar with missile guidance radar mounted each side at front. Missile has maximum speed of Mach 2 and engages targets from a minimum altitude of 25m up to maximum of 5,000m with minimum range 1,500m and maximum 12,000m. No reserve missiles carried, replacement missiles transported on specially modified Transporter 5937 chassis which carries 18 missiles which are loaded onto SAS-8 Gecko with onboard crane.

Variants

First version had two missiles each side of turret but SA-8b has three each side in combined transport/launcher containers. SA-8b has maximum range of 15,000m. The SA-8a is no longer believed to be in service.

Status

Production complete. In service with Algeria, Angola, Czech Republic, India, Iraq, Jordan, Libya, Poland, Russia, Syria, Ukraine and former Yugoslavia.

Manufacturer

Russian state arsenals.

Above: SA-8a Gecko SAM in travelling configuration

Right: TZM SA8 missile resupply vehicle

Below: SA-8b Gecko SAM with surveillance radar erected (Christopher F Foss)

Lvrbv 701 RBS-70 (Sweden)

Key recognition features

● Superstructure with glacis plate at about 70o, commander's and driver's cupolas front
● RBS-70 SAM launcher retracts into vehicle when not in action. When deployed, launcher with missile in launch tube is well above roof line with large IFF device above
● Suspension has six road wheels, idler front, drive sprocket rear, two track-return rollers. Front part of suspension covered by wavy skirt

Specifications

Crew: 4
Armament: 1 x RBS-70 SAM launcher
Length: 4.81m
Width: 2.54m
Height: 2.89m (including IFF), 2.46m (top of launcher), 2.07m (launcher and IFF stowed)
Ground clearance: 0.33m
Weight, combat: 9,700kg
Power-to-weight ratio: 14hp/tonne
Ground pressure: 0.4kg/cm^2
Engine: Ford Model 2658E V-6 petrol developing 136hp at 5,200rpm
Maximum road speed: 41km/hr
Maximum road range: 300km
Fuel capacity: 240 lit
Fording: 0.9m
Vertical obstacle: 0.61m
Trench: 1.5m
Gradient: 60%
Side slope: 30%
Armour: Classified
Armour type: Steel
NBC system: No
Night vision equipment: None

Development

The Lvrbv 701 low altitude SAM is old Ikv-102/Ikv-103 self-propelled infantry cannon extensively rebuilt, including new engine as fitted in unarmoured Bv 206 all-terrain vehicle. Conversion work undertaken by Hägglund and Söner (now Hägglunds Vehicle), production vehicles delivered to Swedish Army between 1984 and 1986.

In centre of hull roof is large two-part circular opening under which is Bofors RBS-70 surface-to-air missile launcher raised well above roof when in action. Reserve missiles are stowed in hull rear above engine compartment with access by elevating complete magazine to about 15˚. A bank of electrically operated smoke grenade dischargers is mounted on the front of the hull firing forwards.

Variants

Pvrbv 551 anti-tank missile carrier system has similar chassis to Lvrbv's with conversion work by Hägglund and Söner (now Hägglunds Vehicle) (details under TDs).

Status

Production complete. In service with Swedish Army only. RBS-70 can also be mounted on or in other armoured vehicles such as Panhard VCR (6x6) and M113. The latter version is used by the Pakistani Army which also mounts it in an armoured (4x2) tractor.

Manufacturer

AB Hägglund and Söner (now Hägglunds Vehicle), Ornsköldsvik, Sweden (conversion).

Right: Lvrbv 701

British Aerospace Tracked Rapier (UK)

Key recognition features

● Fully enclosed armoured cab at front with launcher mounted low down at rear, dome-shaped cover on top
● M548 type suspension with five road wheels, idler rear and drive sprocket front, no track-return rollers
● When in firing position tracking radar is raised above launcher and optical head is above cab roof

Specifications

Crew: 3
Armament: Launcher with eight Rapier SAMs, 2 x 6 smoke grenade dischargers (front), 2 x 4 smoke grenade dischargers (rear)
Length: 6.4m
Width: 2.8m
Height: 2.78m (optical tracker raised)
Ground clearance: 0.41m
Weight, combat: 14,010kg
Power-to-weight ratio: 14.89hp/tonne
Ground pressure: 0.63kg/cm^2
Engine: Detroit Diesel Model 6V-53 6-cylinder liquid-cooled diesel developing 210hp at 2,800rpm
Maximum road speed: 48km/hr
Maximum water speed: 5.6km/hr
Fuel capacity: 398 lit
Fording: Amphibious with preparation
Vertical obstacle: 0.609m
Trench: 1.68m
Gradient: 60%
Side slope: 30%
Armour: Classified
Armour type: Aluminium
NBC system: No
Night vision equipment: Optional (driver)

Development

Tracked Rapier was originally developed by British Aerospace Dynamics to meet requirements of Iranian Army, but order was cancelled by new Iranian Government in 1979. Following evaluation, British Army placed initial order for 50 and first was delivered in l1983. A further 20 systems were subsequently ordered bringing the total to 70.

Tracked Rapier is based on much modified US United Defense M548 Tracked Cargo carrier with fully enclosed three-man armoured cab at front, auxiliary generator immediately to cab rear and launcher at far rear. Launcher includes eight missiles in ready-to-launch position (four each side), surveillance and tracking radars. Rapier missile is identical to that used in Towed Rapier system, also used by British Army and many other countries. Missile has effective range of 227 to 6,858m and operates from very low levels up to over 3,00m.

Tracked Rapier is fully amphibious with flotation screen erected, propelled across rivers and streams by its tracks. The cab, which contains roof-mounted optical tracker and other electronic equipment, has no NBC system but Tracked Rapier crew can operate in NBC clothing.

Variants

Initial version of Tracked Rapier is known as **SP Mk 1A**. Fitted with tracker, optical, thermally enhanced (TOTE) it is **SP Mk 1B**.

In action Tracked Rapier is accompanied by M548 support vehicle with 20 Rapier missiles. Forward Area Support Team (FAST) vehicle carries spare parts.

Status

Production complete. In service only with the British Army, now being replaced by the Shorts Starstreak High Velocity Missile (HVM) on Stormer chassis.

Manufacturer

British Aerospace Dynamics, Filton, Bristol, UK. On modified chassis by United Defense, San José, California, USA.

Above: Tracked Rapier in travelling configuration

Above right: Tracked Rapier launching missile with surveillance antenna raised

Right: Rapier support vehicle (left) resupplies Tracked Rapier (right)

Loral Aeronutronic M48A1 Chaparral (USA)

Key recognition features

● Launcher on rear of flatbed cargo area with two missiles on each side in ready-to-launch position

● When ready for action anti-blase shield is fitted over cab and bows stowed on vehicle front

● Chassis is same as M548 cargo carrier with five road wheels, idler rear, drive sprocket front, no track-return rollers

Specifications

Crew: 5
Armament: Launcher with four Chaparral SAMs
Ammunition: 8 Chaparrals in reserve
Length: 6.06m
Width: 2.69m
Height: 2.68m (with bows)
Ground clearance: 0.4m
Weight, combat: 13,024kg
Weight, empty: 6,425kg (without launcher)
Power-to-weight ratio: 16.1bhp/tonne
Ground pressure: 0.61kg/cm²
Engine: Detroit Diesel Model 6V-53 6-cylinder water-cooled diesel developing 210bhp at 2,800rpm
Maximum road speed: 67.2km/hr
Maximum road range: 504km
Fuel capacity: 401 lit
Fording: Amphibious with preparation
Vertical obstacle: 0.62m
Trench: 1.68m
Gradient: 60%
Side slope: 30%
Armour: None
Armour type: Not applicable
NBC system: No
Night vision equipment: Yes (driver only)

Development

The M48A1 Chaparral low-altitude self-propelled SAM was developed in the early 1960s and consists of a modified M548 full tracked cargo carrier (itself a member of M113 family armoured personnel carriers) with powered one-man launcher on rear, two fire-and-forget surface-to-air missiles each side in ready-to-launch position. Launcher traverses through 360° and missiles elevate from -5° to +90°.

Chaparral has maximum effective range of 6,000m and effective altitude range from 50 to 3,000m. When not required for immediate action missiles are covered by bows and tarpaulin cover, and cab at front is also enclosed which makes system virtually indistinguishable from standard M548 tracked cargo carrier. When required for action bows and cover are removed and bows stowed on front of vehicle. The system is fully amphibious, propelled by its tracks. Power-operated winch at front of vehicle.

The system was originally made by Philco-Ford Corporation but this is now known as Loral Aeronutronic, and by early 1996 over 700 had been manufactured for home and export markets.

Variants

US Army Chaparral systems have been fitted with FLIR on left side of launcher for engaging targets at night. Automotive product improvement programme is under way, chassis designated M730A1. This has many improvements including the installation of a more powerful Detroit-Diesel Model 6V-53T engine developing 275bhp coupled to an X-200-4 automatic transmission.

Status

Production complete. In service with Egypt, Israel, Morocco, Portugal, Taiwan, Tunisia and USA.

Manufacturer

Loral Aeronutronic, Newport Beach, California, USA.

Above: Chaparral SAM in travelling order without bows or tarpaulin cover in position

Above right: M48A1 Chaparral SAM with FLIR pod on left side of mount

Right: Standard M48A1 Chaparral SAM (US Army)

Glossary

AA	anti-aircraft
AAAV	armored amphibious assault vehicle
ACRV	armored command and reconnaissance vehicle
ADAM	Area Denial Artillery Munition
ADATS	Air Defence Anti-tank System
AEV	armoured engineer vehicle
AFSV	Armoured Fire Support Vehicle
AIFV	Armoured Infantry Fighting Vehicle
AML	Automitrailleuse Legere (light armoured car)
AMX	Atelier de Construction d'Issy-les-Moulineaux
AP	armour piercing
APC	armoured personnel carrier
APC-T	armour-piercing capped - tracer
APDS	armour-piercing discarding sabot
APDS-T	armour-piercing discarding sabot - tracer
APERS-T	anti-personnel - tracer
APFSDS	armour-piercing fin-stabilised discarding sabot
APFSDS-T	armour-piercing fin-stabilised discarding sabot - tracer
APHE	armour-piercing high explosive
APSE-T	armour piercing secondary effect - tracer
API-T	armour piercing incendiary - tracer
AP-T	armour piercing - tracer
ARE	Atelier de Construction Roanne
ARRV	Armoured Repair and Recovery Vehicle
ATR	automotive test rig
ATGW	anti-tank guided weapon
ATTS	air-transportable towed system
AVGP	Armoured Vehicle General Purpose
AVLB	armoured vehicle launched bridge
AVRE	Armoured Vehicle Royal Engineers
BARV	Beach Armoured Recovery Vehicle
bhp	brake horsepower
BLR	Blindado Lingero de Ruedas
BMR	Blindado Medio de Ruedas
CAF	Canadian Armed Forces
CCV-L	Close Combat Vehicle - Light
CEV	combat engineer vehicle
CFE	Conventional Forces Europe
CFV	Cavalry Fighting Vehicle
CLGP	Cannon Launched Guided Projectile
COV	Counter Obstacle Vehicle
CVR(T)	Combat Vehicle Reconnaissance (Tracked)
CVR(W)	Combat Vehicle Reconnaissance (Wheeled)
DCA	Défense Contre Avions
EBG	Engin Blindé Genie
EBR	Engin Blindé de Reconnaissance
ERA	Explosive Reactive Armour
ERC	Engin de Reconnaissance Cannon
ESD	Electronique Serge Dassault
FAASV	Field Artillery Ammunition Support Vehicle
FCC	Fire Command Centre
FCS	Fire Control System
FDC	Fire Direction Centre
FISTV	Fire Support Team Vehicle
FLIR	Forward Looking Infra-red
FVRDE	Fighting Vehicles Research and Development Establishment
GIAT	Groupement Industriel des Armements Terrestres
GLLD	Ground Laser Locator Designator
HAV	heavy assault bridge

HB	heavy barrel		LAV	Light Armored Vehicle
HCT	HOT Compact Turret		lit	litres
HE	high explosive		LLLTV	low-light level television
HE-T	high explosive - tracer		LVT	landing vehicle tracked
HEAT	high explosive anti-tank		LVTC	landing vehicle tracked command
HEAT-FS	high explosive anti-tank fin-stabilised		LVTE	landing vehicle tracked engineer
HEAT-T-MP	high explosive anti-tank - tracer - multi-purpose		LVTH	landing vehicle tracked howitzer
HE-FS	high explosive - fin stabilised		LVTP	landing vehicle tracked personnel
HE-FRAG	high explosive fragmentation		LVTR	landing vehicle tracked recovery
HE-FRAG FS	high explosive fragmentation - fin stabilised		m	metre
HEI-T	high explosive incendiary - tracer		mm	millimetre
HESH	high explosive practice - tracer		MBT	main battle tank
HEP	high explosive plastic		MCT	MILAN Compact Turret
HE-T	high explosive - tracer		MEWS	mobile electronic warfare system
HERA	high explosive rocket assist		MG	machine gun
hp	horsepower		MICV	mechanised infantry combat vehicle
HVAP-DS-T	high velocity armour-piercing discarding sabot - tracer		MILAN	Missile d'Infanterie Léger Antichar
HVAP-T	high velocity armour-piercing tracer		MLRS	Multiple Launch Rocket System
IAFV	infantry armoured fighting vehicle		MVEE	Military Vehicles and Engineering Establishment
ICM	improved conventional munition		NBC	nuclear, biological, chemical
ICV	infantry combat vehicle		NVE	Night Vision Equipment
IDF	Israel Defence Forces		OHV	Over Head Valve
iff	identification friend or foe		RP	rocket propelled
IFV	infantry fighting vehicle		pto	power take-off
IR	infra-red		RAAMS	Remote Anti-armor Mine System
IS	internal security		RMG	ranging machine gun
ITV	Improved TOW Vehicle		ROBAT	Robotic Counter Obstacle Vehicle
KIFV	Korean Infantry Fighting Vehicle		ROKIT	Republic of Korea Indigenous Tank
kg/cm2	kilogram per centimetre square		RO	Royal Ordnance
km/hr	kilometre per hour		rpm	rounds per minute or revolutions per minute

GLOSSARY

SAM	Surface-to-Air Missile
SANTAL	Système Anti-aérien Léger
SATCP	Système Anti-aérien a Très Courtée
shp	shaft horse power
SPAAG	Self-propelled anti-aircraft gun
SPAAM	self-propelled anti-aircraft missile
SPATG	self-propelled anti-tank gun
SLEP	service life extension programme
SP	self-propelled
SPG	self-propelled gun
SPH	self-propelled howitzer
SPM	self-propelled mortar
TADDS	Target Alert Display Data Set
TAM	Tanque Argentino Mediano
TD	tank destroyer
TEL	transporter, erector, launcher
TELAR	transporter, erector, launcher and radar
TLS	Tank Laser Sight
TOGS	Thermal Observation and Gunnery System

TOW	Tube-launched, Optically-tracked, Wire-guided television
VARRV	Vickers Armoured Repair and Recovery Vehicle
VAB	Vehicule de l'Avant Blindé (front armoured car)
VAB	Vickers Armoured Bridgelayer
VBC	Véhicule Blindé Combat
VBL	Véhicule Blindé Léger
VCI	Véhicule de Combat d'Infanterie; Vehiculo combate infantria (infantry combat vehicle)
VCR	variable compression ratio
VCR	Véhicule de Combat à Roues
VCTP	Véhiculo de Combate Transporte de Personal
VCG	Véhicule de Combat du Génie
VDA	Véhicule de Defense Anti-aerienne
VEC	Véhiculo de Exploracion de Caballerie
VSEL	Vickers Shipbuilding and Engineering Ltd
WAPC	Wheeled Armoured Personnel Carrier
WFSV	Wheeled Fire Support Vehicle
WMRV	Wheeled Maintenance Recovery Vehicle